A KINGDOM NOT OF THIS WORLD

By the same author:

REVOLUTIONS AND CONSTITUTIONS:
Ideas, Power, and the Struggle for Moral Order

A KINGDOM NOT OF THIS WORLD

Religion, Politics, and the English Revolution

1640-1689

Thomas Ripley Myers

Telos Books

A Kingdom Not of This World: Rebellion, Pacifism, and the English Civil War

Telos Books
An Imprint of the Anacyclosis Group, LLC
St. Petersburg, Florida
tel-os-books.com
telosbooks.pub

Printed in the United States of America

ISBN: 979-8-9940412-0-8
Library of Congress Control Number: 2025925329

Cover: 1782 painting *Oliver Cromwell Dissolving the Long Parliament* by Benjamin West

Book design by author

DEDICATION

To Audrey, who makes me smile

CONTENTS

AKNOWLEDGEMENTS

This book began as a master's thesis, and my first debt is to Dr. Heather Thornton, whose guidance as my advisor shaped the foundation upon which everything else was built. Her patience with my arguments and her insistence on precision made this work possible.

Daryl Murphy deserves special recognition for providing both the advice and the motivation to transform a thesis into a book. Without that encouragement, this manuscript might still be gathering dust. Malcolm Tennant and Jean Carlos Dugrot graciously agreed to read the manuscript. Their willingness to engage seriously with this material improved it considerably. A note on method: lacking a human editor, I relied on artificial intelligence to assist with editing and revision. The interpretations, arguments, and errors remain entirely my own.

Finally, and most importantly, I want to thank my wife Rebecca, who allowed me to retreat into seventeenth-century England for far longer than any marriage should reasonably suffer. Her patience with a husband lost among Presbyterians, Independents, Anglicans, and Quakers—and her gentle reminders that the present century also required my attention—made the completion of this work possible. Whatever virtues this book possesses, none exceed hers.

Major Battles and Key Cities

DRAMATIS PERSONAE

Principal Actors in England's Religious and Political Crisis, 1640-1689

MONARCHS AND ROYALISTS

CHARLES I (1600-1649)

King of England, Scotland, and Ireland, 1625-1649. Defender of episcopal church government and divine right monarchy. His conflicts with Parliament over religion, taxation, and authority led to Civil War. Executed January 30, 1649. Royalists venerated him as martyr; opponents called him "that man of blood."

CHARLES II (1630-1685)

Son of Charles I; king in exile 1649-1660, restored to throne May 1660. Pragmatic ruler who sought stability after decades of upheaval. Initially promised "liberty to tender consciences" but signed the Clarendon Code persecuting Nonconformists. His Catholic sympathies troubled Protestant subjects.

JAMES II (1633-1701)

Brother of Charles II; openly Catholic king (1685-1688) whose attempts to advance Catholic interests provoked the Glorious Revolution. Fled to France in 1688, replaced by William and Mary. His reign tested Anglican doctrines of passive obedience.

WILLIAM LAUD (1573-1645)

Archbishop of Canterbury (1633-1645) under Charles I. His enforcement of ceremonial uniformity—moving altars, requiring vestments, prosecuting nonconformists—convinced many that England was sliding toward Catholicism. Imprisoned by Long Parliament 1641, executed 1645. His reforms' unpopularity helped trigger rebellion, but his supporters saw him as martyr for Anglican order.

THOMAS WENTWORTH, EARL OF STRAFFORD (1593-1641)

Charles I's chief minister and enforcer of royal authority. His "Thorough" policy centralized power and raised revenue but antagonized Parliament and gentry. Parliamentary leaders feared he would impose military rule. His trial and execution (1641) failed to appease Parliament's fears and convinced Charles that compromise was impossible.

EDWARD HYDE, EARL OF CLARENDON (1609-1674)

Royalist statesman and historian. Initially a parliamentary moderate who turned royalist over religious issues. Chief minister to Charles II (1660-1667). His *History of the Rebellion* shaped royalist interpretation of the Civil War. The "Clarendon Code" bears his name though he didn't write all its laws.

GILBERT SHELDON (1598-1677)

Archbishop of Canterbury (1663-1677). Confessor to Charles I, key architect of Restoration church settlement. His writings defended divine right monarchy and episcopal government. Refused comprehension of Presbyterians, insisting on strict uniformity.

PRINCE RUPERT OF THE RHINE (1619-1682)

Charles I's nephew; brilliant cavalry commander for royalist cause. His dashing charges won early victories but couldn't prevent ultimate defeat. Symbolized royalist military prowess and aristocratic honor.

THOMAS HOBBES (1588-1679)

Philosopher and royalist, though his religious views were suspect. *Leviathan* (1651) argued for absolute sovereign authority as bulwark against chaos. His materialist philosophy troubled orthodox Christians, but his political arguments supported Anglican order.

PARLIAMENT AND PRESBYTERIANS

JOHN PYM (1584-1643)

Parliamentary leader and master tactician. Presbyterian in religion, moderate in temperament. Held coalition of Presbyterians and Independents together against Charles I. His death in December 1643 removed Parliament's most skilled political manager, allowing more radical voices to dominate.

DENZIL HOLLES (1598-1680)

Presbyterian MP and leader of "peace party" that sought settlement with Charles I. Opposed Army's growing power and Independent religious radicalism. Purged from Parliament by Army in Pride's Purge (1648). After Restoration, briefly served Charles II but disagreed with persecution of Nonconformists.

RICHARD BAXTER (1615-1691)

Presbyterian minister at Kidderminster and Army chaplain. Prodigious writer whose works defended presbyterian discipline while opposing both episcopal compulsion and sectarian chaos. His *Holy Commonwealth* (1659) articulated vision of godly magistrate supporting reformed church. Refused bishopric at Restoration, ejected in 1662, imprisoned 1669 and 1685. His *Reformed Pastor* (1656) influenced generations of ministers.

PHILIP SKIPPON (c.1600-1660)

Professional soldier and Presbyterian sympathizer. Commander of London trained bands, later General of Foot in New Model Army. Deeply pious, he balanced religious conviction with military discipline. His denunciation of James Nayler at trial revealed Presbyterian fear of sectarian enthusiasm.

STEPHEN MARSHALL (1594-1655)

Presbyterian preacher whose sermons mobilized Parliament's cause. His "Meroz Cursed" (preached repeatedly to troops) transformed political conflict into holy war, arguing that those who didn't fight the King's "malignants" would suffer divine judgment.

INDEPENDENTS AND COMMONWEALTH MEN

OLIVER CROMWELL (1599-1658)

Parliamentary general who became Lord Protector (1653-1658). Rose from obscure gentry to reshape England through military genius and political skill. His Independent religious convictions led him to support liberty of conscience (within limits). Victor at Naseby (1645), he later struggled to create stable government. His Protectorate became increasingly authoritarian, disappointing those who hoped for freer commonwealth.

HENRY IRETON (1611-1651)

Cromwell's son-in-law and chief political theorist. At Putney Debates (1647) defended property qualifications for voting against Levellers' democratic demands. His intellect and devotion to "godly commonwealth" made him Cromwell's closest adviser. Died in Ireland while suppressing rebellion.

THOMAS RAINSBOROUGH (c.1610-1648)

Army colonel and highest-ranking officer to support Levellers. At Putney Debates spoke immortal words: "The poorest he that is in England hath a life to live, as the greatest he." Assassinated by royalists 1648—whether for his politics or military role remains debated.

EDWARD SEXBY (1616-1658)

Cavalry trooper turned agitator who represented common soldiers at Putney Debates. Later became disillusioned with Cromwell's rule, plotting (unsuccessfully) to assassinate him. His career embodied the radicalism unleashed by Civil War and the bitter divisions that followed.

JOHN MILTON (1608-1674)

Poet, pamphleteer, and Commonwealth's greatest intellectual defender. His *Areopagitica* (1644) remains the classic defense of free speech and unlicensed printing. Secretary for Foreign Tongues to Council of State, he wrote Latin defenses of regicide for European audiences. After Restoration, briefly imprisoned but spared execution. Spent final years writing *Paradise Lost* (1667), *Paradise Regained* (1671), and *Samson Agonistes* (1671).

JOHN BUNYAN (1628-1688)

Tinker turned Baptist preacher. Served in parliamentary army but saw no combat. His conversion experience led to powerful preaching that drew congregations in Bedford. Imprisoned 1660-1672 for unlicensed preaching; refused freedom in exchange for silence. Wrote *Grace Abounding to the Chief of Sinners* (1666) and *The Pilgrim's Progress* (1678), which became—after the Bible—the most-read book in English.

SIR HENRY VANE THE YOUNGER (1613-1662)

Republican idealist who opposed Cromwell's quasi-monarchical Protectorate. Former governor of Massachusetts Bay Colony where he defended Anne Hutchinson. In 1659 tried to build coalition with Quakers to preserve Commonwealth. His offer failed; Charles II executed him for treason despite promises of amnesty.

WILLIAM DELL (c.1607-1669)

Army chaplain and radical Independent. Preached that university education was unnecessary for ministry, that tithes should be abolished, and that gathered churches needed no state approval. His sermons to troops attacked clerical monopoly and encouraged soldiers' religious and political radicalism.

QUAKERS

GEORGE FOX (1624-1691)

Founder and guiding spirit of Quakerism. Son of weaver, apprenticed to shoemaker, left home at 19 seeking spiritual truth. His vision atop Pendle Hill (1647) launched movement teaching that Christ could teach his people directly through "inner light." Tireless traveler who preached, debated, and organized despite repeated imprisonments and beatings. His *Journal* (published posthumously 1694) became Quaker scripture. Married Margaret Fell 1669.

MARGARET FELL (1614-1702)

Called "Mother of Quakerism." Wealthy widow whose Swarthmoor Hall became movement's operational center. Managed vast correspondence network, coordinated traveling ministers, petitioned authorities for imprisoned Friends. Her *Women's Speaking Justified* (1666) defended women's preaching. Imprisoned 1664-1668 for allowing Quaker meetings at Swarthmoor. Married George Fox 1669.

JAMES NAYLER (1618-1660)

Gifted preacher and early Quaker leader who rivaled Fox's influence. Former parliamentary soldier turned evangelist. His 1656 entry into Bristol imitating Christ's entry to Jerusalem led to trial for blasphemy, brutal punishment, and imprisonment. The crisis forced Quakers to develop discipline and structure. Released 1659, he died shortly after. His writings on the "Lamb's War" shaped Quaker theology.

EDWARD BURROUGH (1634-1663)

Young, fiery Quaker controversialist and political spokesman. Prolific pamphleteer who debated Baptists, Presbyterians, and Anglicans. His exchanges with Richard Baxter and John Bunyan crystallized theological disputes between Quakers and others. Died in Newgate Prison at 29, victim of conditions during imprisonment.

GEORGE BISHOP (c.1620-1668)

Former parliamentary intelligence officer who became Bristol's Quaker organizer. His military networks helped coordinate movement under persecution. Pioneered "sufferings books"—detailed records of persecution used for appeals and solidarity. Though critical of Nayler's excess, he defended Quakers from charges of sedition.

WILLIAM PENN (1644-1718)

Son of Admiral Sir William Penn. His conversion to Quakerism scandalized his wealthy family but gave movement influential advocate. Eloquent defender of religious liberty who used connections to obtain charter for Pennsylvania (1681). His "Frame of Government" created colony as "holy experiment" in Quaker principles: religious toleration, peaceful Native American relations, humane criminal justice.

ROBERT BARCLAY (1648-1690)
Quaker theologian whose *Apology for the True Christian Divinity* (1676) provided systematic theology for movement. His work defended inner light, rejected outward sacraments, and explained Quaker positions in scholarly terms that gained respect even from critics.
MARY DYER (c.1611-1660)
Quaker martyr hanged in Boston for repeatedly returning to preach after banishment. Massachusetts Bay Colony made Quakerism capital offense, fearing it undermined godly order. Dyer's execution shocked England and embarrassed colonial authorities, helping turn opinion toward toleration.
ELIZABETH HOOTON (1600-1672)
Among first Quaker converts and first woman preacher. Traveled to America where Boston authorities beat her and left her in wilderness. Continued preaching until death in Jamaica. Her courage inspired countless Quaker women who faced mockery, beatings, and imprisonment for public ministry.

LEVELLERS

JOHN LILBURNE (1614–1657) "Freeborn John," the Leveller movement's most tireless agitator. Whipped through London streets 1638 for distributing unlicensed pamphlets; imprisoned by the Star Chamber, Parliament, and the Protectorate in turn. Rose to lieutenant-colonel in the parliamentary army before resigning over the Covenant. His pamphlets—*England's Birth-Right Justified* (1645), *The Free-Man's Freedom Vindicated* (1646)—articulated natural rights, jury trial, and constitutional limits on all governments. Tried for treason 1649 and 1653; juries acquitted him both times to London's jubilation. Converted to Quakerism 1655; died under house arrest 1657.

EDWARD SEXBY (1616–1658) Army agitator who rose from trooper to intelligence officer. Organized soldiers' grievances leading to Putney Debates 1647, where he challenged Cromwell and Ireton directly. Served as agent in France negotiating with Frondeurs. Grew disillusioned with Cromwell's quasi-monarchical rule; authored *Killing No Murder* (1657), a pamphlet justifying tyrannicide. Arrested in England while plotting Cromwell's assassination, he died in the Tower before trial—whether from illness or rougher treatment remains unclear.

WILLIAM WALWYN (1600–1681) Cloth merchant, Leveller theorist, and advocate for religious toleration. Unlike Lilburne, preferred reason to confrontation. His *The Compassionate Samaritane* (1644) argued that persecution created hypocrites, not believers. Accused of atheism by Presbyterian enemies who could not believe anyone genuinely tolerated all opinions. Imprisoned with Leveller leaders 1649; released after the movement's collapse. Spent remaining decades practicing medicine in obscurity, his radical years behind him.

THOMAS RAINSBOROUGH (1610–1648) Naval commander and army colonel; highest-ranking officer to support Leveller demands. At Putney

Debates spoke words that echoed through centuries: "the poorest he that is in England hath a life to live, as the greatest he." Advocated extending franchise to all freeborn Englishmen. Killed by royalist agents at Doncaster October 1648—whether assassination or botched kidnapping remains disputed. His London funeral became a mass Leveller demonstration, thousands wearing sea-green ribbons in mourning.

OTHER SIGNIFICANT FIGURES

THOMAS FAIRFAX (1612-1671)

Parliament's finest general and New Model Army's first commander. Led victory at Naseby (1645). Moderate Independent who opposed regicide—resigned command rather than invade Scotland under Cromwellian republic. His support for General Monck's 1660 march to restore Parliament helped make Restoration possible.

GEORGE MONCK (1608-1670)

Professional soldier who served both Charles I and Commonwealth. Governor of Scotland (1654-1660), he maintained order when England descended into chaos. His 1660 march to London, forcing Rump's dissolution and restoration of monarchy, was political masterstroke. Created Duke of Albemarle by grateful Charles II.

ROGER WILLIAMS (c.1603-1683)

English Puritan who fled to America, founded Rhode Island on principle of religious liberty and separation of church and state. His *The Bloody Tenent of Persecution* (1644) argued that state coercion in religion violated God's design and Christian charity. His ideas, too radical for England in his lifetime, influenced later toleration and American founding.

TIMELINE
Key Events 1640-1689

1640
April: Short Parliament meets; Charles I requests money; Parliament demands grievances addressed first; dissolved after three weeks.
November: Long Parliament convenes. Will sit (with interruptions) until 1660. Archbishop Laud imprisoned. Earl of Strafford arrested.

1641
May: Earl of Strafford executed after bill of attainder passed Parliament under pressure from London mobs.
October: Irish Rebellion erupts; rumors (exaggerated) of Catholic massacre of Protestants fuel English paranoia.
November: Grand Remonstrance passes House of Commons by narrow margin (159-148), listing grievances against Charles I. Debate nearly comes to swordplay; Presbyterian-Independent coalition begins to fracture.
December: Charles I attempts to arrest Five Members of Parliament including John Pym; they escape across Thames. Charles leaves London, never to return peacefully.

1642
January-March: Both sides prepare for war. Parliament issues Militia Ordinance claiming authority to raise troops; Charles issues Commission of Array calling loyal subjects to arms.
April: Sir John Hotham denies King entry to Hull's magazine—first act of military defiance.
June: Parliament sends Nineteen Propositions demanding control of military, appointments, and church reform. Charles rejects them as destruction of monarchy.
August 22: Charles raises royal standard at Nottingham—formal declaration of war. Strong winds blow it down; some take as evil omen.
October 23: Battle of Edgehill—first major engagement ends inconclusively. Both sides claim victory; both retreat to winter quarters.

1643
Spring-Summer: Various engagements favor neither side decisively. War settles into regional campaigns, sieges, and raids.
September: Solemn League and Covenant signed between English Parliament and Scottish Covenanters. Scots agree to send army south; Parliament agrees to reform English church along Presbyterian lines (though meaning of this remains contested).
December: John Pym dies of cancer. His death removes Parliament's most skilled coalition-builder; more radical voices gain influence.

1644

July: Battle of Marston Moor—Scots and Parliament decisively defeat royalists in North. Oliver Cromwell's cavalry discipline proves crucial. "God made them as stubble to our swords," he writes.
November: John Milton publishes *Areopagitica*, defending freedom of press and opposing Parliament's Licensing Order.

1645

January: Parliament authorizes New Model Army—professional, ideologically committed force led by Thomas Fairfax with Cromwell commanding cavalry.
April: Self-Denying Ordinance passes; MPs must resign military commands (making exception for Cromwell). Removes presbyterian Lords from command, allows Independent officers to dominate Army.
June 14: Battle of Naseby—New Model Army crushes royalist forces. Charles I's captured correspondence reveals he had negotiated for Irish Catholic and foreign troops, confirming Parliament's fears of "popish" plots.

1646

April-May: Charles I surrenders to Scottish army at Newark. Scots negotiate with Parliament over his fate and their payment for military service.
June-December: Parliament and Charles negotiate. Presbyterians seek settlement; Independents grow suspicious of both King and presbyterian peace party.

1647

January: Scots, unpaid and frustrated, hand Charles to Parliament and withdraw to Scotland.
March: Parliament votes to disband most of Army without full pay or indemnity for wartime actions. Army refuses.
June: Army seizes Charles from parliamentary control; refuses disbandment. General Council (officers and agitators) begins meeting to discuss Army's demands.
July-August: Army marches toward London. Presbyterian MPs flee or are intimidated. Independents gain control of Parliament.
October-November: Putney Debates in Army's General Council. Levellers present *Agreement of the People* demanding extended franchise and reserved rights. Debates reveal split between Cromwell/Ireton's moderate constitutionalism and Levellers' radical democracy.
November: Charles I escapes Army's custody; flees to Isle of Wight where he is imprisoned in Carisbrooke Castle. Resumes secret negotiations with various factions, playing them against each other.
December: Charles signs secret "Engagement" with Scots promising to establish Presbyterianism in exchange for military aid.

1648

Spring-Summer: Second Civil War—Scottish army invades; scattered royalist uprisings across England.

August: Cromwell crushes Scots at Battle of Preston. Second Civil War ends quickly but convinces Army radicals that Charles is incorrigibly treacherous—"that man of blood" who must be brought to justice.

December 6: Pride's Purge—Army colonel Thomas Pride bars moderate/presbyterian MPs from Parliament, leaving "Rump Parliament" of about 200 members, mostly Independents and Army sympathizers.

December: Rump Parliament prepares to try Charles I for treason. Most MPs want settlement; about 70 radicals drive prosecution.

1649

January 20-27: Trial of Charles I at Westminster Hall. King refuses to recognize court's authority: "I would know by what power I am called hither." Found guilty by 68 commissioners; 59 sign death warrant.

January 30: Charles I executed outside Banqueting House, Whitehall. Reportedly says "Remember" with his final breath. Large crowd witnesses; reactions mixed between horror and approval.

February: Monarchy and House of Lords abolished. England declared "Commonwealth and Free State."

March: *Eikon Basilike* ("The King's Image") published, purporting to be Charles's spiritual reflections. Becomes immediate bestseller, creating cult of "Charles the Martyr."

May: Levellers crushed at Burford. Their leaders captured; three troopers shot as examples. Commonwealth government's brief flirtation with radical democracy ends.

September: Cromwell invades Ireland to suppress rebellion and punish those he held responsible for 1641 "massacre." Sieges of Drogheda and Wexford result in mass slaughter that blackens Cromwell's reputation in Irish memory.

1650

June: Charles II (son of executed king) lands in Scotland; agrees to sign Covenant and establish Presbyterianism in exchange for Scottish support for his restoration.

September: Cromwell defeats Scots at Battle of Dunbar. Sees it as divine judgment vindicating Commonwealth.

George Fox's ministry expanding; early Quakers ("Children of the Light") begin traveling throughout North England preaching immediate revelation through "inner light."

1651

September 3: Battle of Worcester—Cromwell's "crowning mercy." Charles

II's Scottish army destroyed; he escapes to continent after adventures hiding in oak tree and disguised as servant. Will remain in exile nine years.

1652-1653
Quaker movement explodes: "Valiant Sixty" traveling ministers spread throughout England. George Fox, James Nayler, Edward Burrough, Margaret Fell and others preach, disrupt services, gather converts. Thousands join movement despite (or because of) persecution.
Gerrard Winstanley and Diggers attempt agrarian communism, occupying common land. Driven off by local authorities.
Various radical sects proliferate: Ranters (if they existed as organized group), Muggletonians, Fifth Monarchists. Presbyterian Thomas Edwards catalogs heresies in *Gangraena.*

1653
April 20: Cromwell dissolves Rump Parliament with soldiers: "You have sat too long for any good you have been doing. Depart, I say, and let us have done with you. In the name of God, go!"
July-December: "Barebone's Parliament" (Nominated Parliament)—140 "godly men" selected by Army officers and Independent churches. Debates radical reforms but splits between moderates and Fifth Monarchist radicals. Moderates dissolve it and hand power back to Cromwell.
December 16: Cromwell becomes Lord Protector under written constitution (*Instrument of Government*). Quasi-monarchical rule begins, disappointing republicans like Henry Vane.

1654-1658
Protectorate period: Cromwell rules through combination of Parliament (when cooperative) and military force (when necessary).
1655-1657: Rule of Major-Generals—England divided into military districts. Major-Generals enforce moral discipline: closing alehouses, prosecuting Sabbath-breaking. Deeply unpopular; abandoned after 18 months.
1657: Parliament offers Cromwell crown. He agonizes for weeks before refusing—cannot violate principles for which Civil War was fought. But accepts modified Protectorate with greater powers and quasi-monarchical trappings.
Quaker organization develops: Monthly and quarterly meetings established; traveling ministers recognized; discipline procedures developed. After Nayler's 1656 Bristol scandal and harsh punishment, Fox asserts leadership and guides movement toward greater structure.

1658
September 3: Oliver Cromwell dies on anniversary of Battles of Dunbar and Worcester—dates he considered divine favors. Succeeded by son Richard,

who lacks father's authority and military credibility.

1659

April: Richard Cromwell forced to recall Rump Parliament. Unable to control Army or Parliament; resigns Protectorate in May.
May-December: Political chaos. Rump restored, then expelled by Army officers (October), then restored again (December). Multiple factions compete for power: Commonwealthmen under Vane, Army grandees, Presbyterians seeking king's return.
Summer: George Fox's "time of darkness"—withdraws for ten weeks, emerges having decided Quakers must refuse political power and remain neutral.
Sir Henry Vane offers Quakers role in Commonwealth government; Fox declines. Many Quakers serve briefly on militia committees but withdraw by year's end.

1660

January-February: General George Monck marches from Scotland to London with disciplined army. Forces Rump to readmit excluded members (secluded members from Pride's Purge), making it Long Parliament again.
March: Long Parliament votes to dissolve itself; calls for Convention Parliament to negotiate settlement.
April: Charles II issues Declaration of Breda from Holland: promises amnesty (except regicides), property settlement by Parliament, payment of Army's arrears, and "liberty to tender consciences."
May 29: Charles II enters London to jubilant crowds. Restoration accomplished. Bells ring, bonfires blaze, fountains run with wine.
September: Rumors of Quaker uprising (false) lead to mass arrests of Friends.
January 1661: Quakers present Peace Declaration to Charles II: "We utterly deny all outward wars and strife, and fightings with outward weapons, for any end, or under any pretence whatsoever."

1661-1665: The Clarendon Code

1661: **Corporation Act**—requires municipal office-holders to take Anglican communion and renounce Solemn League and Covenant.
April-June 1661: **Savoy Conference**—Presbyterian and Anglican divines meet to revise Book of Common Prayer. Presbyterians propose hundreds of changes; bishops reject almost all. Comprehension fails.
1662: **Act of Uniformity** (effective August 24, St. Bartholomew's Day)—requires all clergy to accept Book of Common Prayer, receive episcopal ordination, renounce Covenant. **Great Ejection**: approximately 2,000 ministers refuse and are ejected from livings. Among them: Richard Baxter, Edmund Calamy, Thomas Watson.

1664: **Conventicle Act**—illegal to hold religious meetings of more than five people outside established church. Targets Nonconformist worship gatherings.
1665: **Five Mile Act**—ejected ministers banned from coming within five miles of incorporated towns or former parishes unless they swear not to seek "alteration of government in church or state."
1660-1672: John Bunyan imprisoned in Bedford jail for unlicensed preaching. Refuses freedom in exchange for silence. Writes *Grace Abounding* (1666).

1672
March: Charles II issues **Declaration of Indulgence**, suspending penal laws and allowing licensed Nonconformist worship. Many Quakers and other dissenters begin meeting openly.

1673
March: Parliament forces Charles to withdraw Declaration of Indulgence, asserting that king cannot suspend laws by prerogative.
Test Act passed—requires all office-holders to take Anglican communion, take oaths, and declare against Catholic doctrine of transubstantiation. Aimed primarily at Catholics but affects all Nonconformists.

1675-1677
Bunyan imprisoned again briefly; writes first part of *The Pilgrim's Progress.*

1678
***The Pilgrim's Progress* published**—becomes immediate bestseller, eventually second only to Bible in English homes.

1685
February: Charles II dies; succeeded by openly Catholic brother **James II**.
June: **Monmouth Rebellion**—Charles II's illegitimate Protestant son attempts to claim throne. Crushed at Battle of Sedgemoor. "Bloody Assizes" follow—Judge Jeffreys executes hundreds of rebels.
James II begins appointing Catholics to military commands, university positions, and government offices. Issues Declaration of Indulgence benefiting both Catholics and Nonconformists. Anglicans alarmed at Catholic advance under royal protection.
Richard Baxter tried for sedition, imprisoned, elderly and ill.

1688
June: James II's son born—ensuring Catholic succession troubles Protestant establishment.
November: William of Orange (James's Protestant son-in-law, married to James's daughter Mary) invades England at invitation of leading noblemen.

Glorious Revolution begins.
December: James II flees to France. Parliament declares throne "abdicated."

1689
February: **Convention Parliament** offers crown jointly to William and Mary. They accept, ruling as constitutional monarchs limited by Parliament.
May: **Toleration Act** passed—allows Protestant Nonconformists to worship openly if they subscribe to most Thirty-Nine Articles and register meeting places. Catholics and Unitarians still excluded. Act represents pragmatic accommodation rather than principled toleration, but grants legal existence to dissent.
October: **Bill of Rights** codifies limits on royal power established by Glorious Revolution.
Some Anglicans refuse oaths to William and Mary (having sworn allegiance to James), becoming **Non-Jurors**—schismatic group maintaining absolute passive obedience doctrine. Among them several bishops including Archbishop William Sancroft.

1691
January: George Fox dies in London, age 66, surrounded by Friends. His *Journal*, edited and published 1694, becomes foundational Quaker text.
December: Richard Baxter dies, age 76, after decades of ministry, persecution, and prolific writing. His works continue to influence Protestant spirituality across denominational lines.

PREFACE

This book began as a master's thesis examining why 17th-century English people fought and died over church government questions that seem remote today. What was at stake in disputes over bishops versus presbyteries, set prayers versus extemporary worship, or kneeling versus sitting for communion? And how did these theological conflicts produce the political innovations—limited monarchy, liberty of conscience, denominational pluralism—that shaped the modern world?

I have adapted that research for a broader audience while maintaining scholarly rigor, clarifying terminology, streamlining historiographical debates into endnotes, and expanding dramatic scenes that bring this world to life. The result serves multiple purposes: a scholarly contribution to understanding England's revolutionary century, an accessible narrative for general readers, and an invitation to think seriously about perennial questions of authority, conscience, and coexistence.

I first became interested in this subject while researching the American Revolution for a chapter of my book *Revolutions and Constitutions*. The English Revolution set the stage for the events in the colonies. In reading the demands of the Levellers—freedoms of assembly, free speech and religion, freedom from self-incrimination and quartering troops—students of the American Bill of Rights will recognize familiar ground. But deeper study revealed something unexpected: the religious and political factions of mid-seventeenth-century England mapped onto the classical forms of government that political philosophers had debated since Aristotle. Anglican monarchists defended royal supremacy in church and state alike. Presbyterian aristocrats sought rule by assemblies of qualified elders—in synods and in Parliament. Independent commonwealthmen advocated mixed government balancing the one, the few, and the many, mirrored in their gathered churches where congregations covenanted together yet deferred to godly magistrates. And Quaker anarchists rejected all human authority over conscience, acknowledging no ruler but the inner light of Christ.

That correspondence between ecclesiastical polity and political structure fascinated me. It revealed how theological convictions about authority, human nature, and divine order translated directly into competing visions of the commonwealth. Everywhere in mid-seventeenth-century England, people argued about whether truth came from institutions or individuals, how to balance order with liberty, whether the godly few or the consenting many should govern. These debates produced civil war, regicide, persecution, and finally—exhausted and pragmatic—toleration. The classical forms provided a framework for understanding why sincere Christians, reading the same Scriptures and serving the same God, reached such incompatible conclusions about how England should be governed. Understanding how these four visions competed, collided, and ultimately produced a settlement none fully intended became this book's driving question.

Approach and Argument

This book argues straightforwardly: **religion was central to England's 17th-century conflicts not secondary or epiphenomenal.** The Civil War was genuinely about religion—church government, worship, Scripture's authority, whether conscience could be coerced. Economic and political factors mattered enormously, but within religious frameworks that gave them meaning. A merchant opposed bishops because he believed episcopacy violated Scripture, not primarily because it threatened commercial interests.

The structure reflects this conviction. Part I (Chapters 1-2) provides chronological narrative from 1640 through 1646, establishing political and military context. Part II (Chapters 3-6) examine four religious visions—Presbyterian, Independent, Anglican, Quaker—that competed for England's soul, exploring each vision's theological foundations, institutional expressions, and political implications. Part III (Chapter 7) returns to chronology, tracing the path from regicide through Restoration to the 1689 Toleration Act.

This structure allows sustained attention to religious ideas while maintaining narrative thread, showing how theological commitments shaped political choices.

Intended Audience

For general readers: Accessible narrative showing how abstract principles were lived and fought over, requiring no specialized knowledge but engaging urgent questions about diverse communities, religious conviction, and pluralism.

For students: Comprehensive introduction combining chronological narrative with thematic analysis, explaining both what happened and why it mattered.

For scholars: Detailed analysis of how religious ideas shaped political developments, with notes engaging historiographical debates and documenting claims precisely.

I have tried writing for all audiences simultaneously meeting scholarly standards while remaining readable, including enough detail for specialists while explaining context for general readers, taking ideas seriously as genuine intellectual positions rather than curiosities.

Language, Dates, and Limitations

I have modernized spelling and lightly modernized punctuation in quotations for readability. Dates follow modern practice (year beginning January 1). Biblical quotations use the King James Version (1611) that 17th-century people used.

This book does not claim comprehensive coverage—excellent works exist on military history, Irish and Scottish dimensions, social and economic history, regional variations, and many topics I treat briefly. My focus is religious ideas and institutions and how they shaped political outcomes.

Nor does this book claim neutrality. I value religious liberty, limited government, and denominational pluralism—outcomes that emerged imperfectly from this period. I approach this history asking how we arrived at principles I find valuable while remaining aware of their costs and limitations.

Why This History Matters

Debates about religious liberty, church-state relations, and diverse communities coexisting remain urgent. The 17th century offers no simple answers—their problems differ from ours—but their struggles illuminate permanent tensions: between liberty and order, diversity and unity, conscience and authority, conviction and compromise.

They learned, painfully, that religious uniformity could not be enforced, that conscience could not be coerced, that diversity was fact. They learned that simple solutions all fail and that sustainable societies require balancing competing goods—work that is never finished.

The 17th century gives us no heroes without flaws, no visions without costs, no victories without compromise. It gives us something more valuable: perspective on how hard it is to build free societies, how fragile they are, and how much wisdom and humility they require.

I offer this book as contribution to understanding a crucial period whose struggles and partial solutions remain relevant to our time. May we learn from their failures as well as their achievements.

A NOTE ON NAMES, DATES, AND TERMINOLOGY

For Reader Orientation

Personal Names:

17th-century English people used naming conventions that can confuse modern readers:

- **Titles change**: Edward Hyde became Earl of Clarendon; Thomas Wentworth became Earl of Strafford. This book uses the name by which they're best known, with full titles in Dramatis Personae.
- **Women's names change at marriage**: Margaret Askew became Margaret Fell (first marriage), then Margaret Fox (second marriage). Usually called Margaret Fell in this book since that's her primary

identity in the movement.

- **Some have no surnames in records**: Early Quaker records often give only first names and locations ("Thomas of Lancaster"). This reflects Quaker testimony against worldly titles but creates historical ambiguity.

Dates:

England in this period used the Julian calendar, which was ten days behind the Gregorian calendar used on the Continent. Moreover, the English year began March 25, not January 1. This creates confusion:

- Charles I was executed January 30, 1648 (by English reckoning) or January 30, 1649 (by modern reckoning).

This book uses modern dating (year beginning January 1, dates adjusted to Gregorian calendar where necessary) for clarity. When quoting contemporary sources that use old-style dates, this is noted.

Terminology:

"Puritan": A slippery term. Originally an insult ("precisians" who wanted to "purify" the church), it was never a clear party label. This book uses "Puritan" for the general movement favoring further reformation, but prefers more specific terms (Presbyterian, Independent, etc.) where possible.

"Roundheads" and "Cavaliers": Popular nicknames for parliamentary and royalist soldiers. "Roundhead" referred to short haircuts (as opposed to long-haired courtiers); "Cavalier" was originally an insult suggesting papist Spanish cavalry. Both terms became badges of honor for their sides.

"Sectaries": Presbyterian term for Independents, Baptists, Quakers, and more radical groups. Meant dismissively but often embraced by those so labeled.

"Nonconformist": After the Restoration, legal term for Protestants who didn't conform to the Church of England. Includes Presbyterians, Independents, Baptists, Quakers—a political category more than a theological one.

"Dissent" and "Dissenters": Similar to Nonconformist but with more positive connotation, dissenting from establishment, not merely failing to conform.

"Levellers": Political movement centered in the New Model Army and London, 1647–1649. Led by John Lilburne, Richard Overton, and William Walwyn, they advocated expanded suffrage, written constitution, religious toleration, and natural rights. The name was an insult suggesting they would "level" property distinctions, a charge they denied. Their *Agreement of the People* anticipated later constitutional thought. Suppressed by Cromwell at Burford 1649; the movement collapsed but its ideas crossed the Atlantic.

"Quakers": Originally an insult—they "quaked" before the Lord—embraced by the movement itself. Formally the Religious Society of Friends and informally, simply as Friends. Founded by George Fox in the late 1640s, they rejected outward forms (clergy, sacraments, set prayers) for the "inner light" of Christ teaching each believer directly. Their refusal of oaths, hat-honor, and tithes brought persecution under every regime. After 1661, the Peace Testimony renounced all warfare.

"Seekers": Loose network of individuals who rejected all existing churches as corrupted, waiting for God to restore true apostolic ministry. Not an organized movement but a spiritual posture—seeking truth while refusing to settle for available options. Many early Quaker converts came from Seeker circles, including Francis Howgill and John Camm, who recognized in George Fox the authentic spiritual authority they had awaited. The term describes a transitional state more than a settled identity; most Seekers eventually found what they sought or tired of searching.

"Ranters": Label applied to antinomian radicals who allegedly believed the spiritually enlightened were free from moral law. Whether Ranters existed as an organized movement or were largely a Presbyterian invention to discredit religious liberty remains historically contested. The term was used promiscuously to tar Quakers, Seekers, and anyone whose enthusiasm seemed dangerous. This book treats "Ranter" as more accusation than description.

"Diggers": Small agrarian community led by Gerrard Winstanley, 1649–1650. They called themselves "True Levellers" and attempted to cultivate common land at St. George's Hill, Surrey, believing the earth was a "common treasury" for all. Local landowners destroyed their settlement within a year. Their writings—especially Winstanley's *The Law of Freedom*—influenced later socialist and communitarian thought far beyond their brief experiment.

Theological Terms:

"Visible saints": Independents' term for those showing credible evidence of God's saving grace. Only visible saints could join gathered churches.

"Inner light": Quakers' term for Christ's immediate teaching in each person's conscience. Not an inner divine spark (which would be heresy) but Christ's presence and instruction.

"Covenant theology": Presbyterian framework seeing God's relationship with humanity as covenantal—God promises grace; humans promise obedience. Applied to both church (covenant communities) and state (covenanted nations).

"Apostolic succession": Anglican claim that bishops descend in unbroken line from Christ's apostles, guaranteeing authority and valid sacraments.

"Antinomian": From Greek *anti* (against) and *nomos* (law). The belief that Christians under grace are freed from obligation to moral law. A serious accusation in seventeenth-century England, leveled against Quakers, Ranters, and anyone whose emphasis on inner experience seemed to discount outward conduct. Few claimed the label; most so accused denied it, insisting that true grace produced holy living without legal compulsion.

Places:

Modern readers may be unfamiliar with 17th-century English geography:

- **"The North"**: Lancashire, Yorkshire, Northumberland—distant from

London, less controlled by central authority

- **"The West Country"**: Devon, Cornwall, Somerset—traditionally royalist
- **"The Eastern Association"**: East Anglia, Norfolk, Suffolk, Essex, Cambridgeshire, Hertfordshire, and later Huntingdonshire and Lincolnshire—Parliament's most reliable heartland. Strongly Puritan, commercially prosperous, and geographically defensible. Oliver Cromwell organized his "Ironsides" cavalry here, and the Association's army became the nucleus of the New Model Army. Its relative security allowed Parliament to draw men, money, and supplies while royalist territory faced constant threat.
- **"The Midlands"**: Central England, contested throughout wars

Quotations:

17th-century English spelling and punctuation were inconsistent and can distract modern readers. This book:

- Modernizes spelling for readability (except in titles, which preserve original spelling)
- Lightly modernizes punctuation where it clarifies meaning
- Preserves original capitalization, which often signaled emphasis
- Indicates substantial editorial changes with [...] for omissions and [explanation] for clarifications

Where original spelling matters (showing dialect, emphasizing a point, etc.), it's preserved with explanatory notes.

READER'S NOTE: HOW TO USE THIS BOOK

This book can be read in several ways:

Straight Through (Recommended First Reading): The chapters build on each other, showing how four religious visions competed, collided, and ultimately produced a settlement none fully intended. Reading sequentially gives the narrative arc.

By Faction (For Those With Specific Interests): Each faction chapter (3-6) stands relatively independently:

- **Chapter 3 (Presbyterians)**: For those interested in discipline, order, godly magistracy
- **Chapter 4 (Independents)**: For those interested in liberty, consent, gathered churches
- **Chapter 5 (Anglicans)**: For those interested in tradition, authority, establishment
- **Chapter 6 (Quakers)**: For those interested in radical reformation, pacifism, spiritual immediacy

Thematically: Readers interested in specific themes can trace them across chapters:

- **Political thought**: Chapter 4 (Independents) and Chapter 5 (Anglicans) especially
- **Women's roles**: Throughout, but especially Chapters 3 and 6

- **Violence and peace**: Chapters 3, 4, and 6
- **Church-state relations**: All chapters, different angles

With Supplementary Materials:

- **Dramatis Personae**: Refer to this when encountering unfamiliar names
- **Timeline**: Use to orient yourself chronologically, especially if reading non-sequentially
- **Maps**: Consult to visualize geography, understand why location mattered
- **Notes**: Follow for primary source citations and deeper exploration

For Students and Teachers:

Each chapter includes:

- Opening dramatic scene (for engagement)
- Historical analysis (for understanding)
- Primary source integration (for evidence)
- Historiographical awareness (for critical thinking)

Discussion questions might include:

- What were each faction's core theological commitments, and how did these shape their politics?
- Could England's conflicts have been resolved without war and regicide?
- Were the Quakers' pacifism principled or pragmatic? Naive or prophetic?
- How did religious diversity become tolerable when it had seemed impossible?
- What did each faction contribute to modern Western political thought?
- What costs did religious conflict impose, and were they worth the gains?

For General Readers:

This is a book about ideas having consequences—theological debates producing political revolutions, religious convictions reshaping societies. The story matters because we still live with what these conflicts created: liberty of conscience, limited government, denominational pluralism, and ongoing tensions between order and freedom.

You need no specialized knowledge to read this book, but you'll emerge with understanding of how modern Western political culture was born in fire and forged through conflict.

INTRODUCTION — "THE KING IS COME!"

ENGLAND'S CRISIS OF AUTHORITY AND CONSCIENCE

The King Confronts Parliament, 4 January 1642

Charles Stuart, by the grace of God King of England, Scotland, and Ireland, walked through Westminster Hall with four hundred armed men behind him. It was just past three o'clock on a winter afternoon, the light already fading through the great hall's ancient windows. Members of Parliament, meeting in their chamber beyond, heard the clatter of boots and the metallic scrape of sword hilts against stone. Some thought it was a riot. Others suspected—correctly, as it turned out—that it was the King.[1]

Charles was forty-one years old, short in stature with a slight stammer that made public speaking an ordeal. He masked uncertainty with formality, maintaining the dignity he believed his office required. But today dignity had given way to desperation. Five members of the House of Commons—John Pym, John Hampden, Denzil Holles, Arthur Haselrig, and William Strode—had pushed him too far. They had accused his Catholic queen of treason, impeached his bishops, stripped him of control over the military, and now they were raising loans to arm forces against him. He would arrest them for treason, try them before the House of Lords, and restore order to a realm sliding toward chaos.[2]

The King reached the Commons chamber. The doorkeeper, a commoner named George Venn, stood aside—you did not bar a king's entry, no matter whose side you favored. Charles strode through the door, his guards remaining outside (even he recognized that armed men in the chamber would be too provocative). The Members fell silent. No reigning monarch had entered the Commons in memory. The Speaker, William Lenthall, rose from his chair. Charles waved him aside, the King would take the Speaker's chair, the symbol of parliamentary authority.[3]

"Mr. Speaker, I Must Borrow Your Chair a Little"

Charles stood where Speakers had stood for generations, looking down at the rows of benches where Members sat in shocked silence. He held a paper listing the five men he sought. His voice, when he spoke, betrayed neither the stammer that usually plagued him nor the fury that had driven him here: [4]

> *Gentlemen, I am sorry for this occasion of coming unto you. Yesterday I sent a serjeant-at-arms to apprehend some that by my command were accused of high treason. Instead of obeying my command, they have been warned, and I have just cause to believe that they are now within the House of Commons, whom I must desire you to deliver unto me, that they may answer the articles I have preferred against them.*

He paused, scanning the faces before him. The five men were not there. Someone—perhaps Pym's wife, perhaps a sympathetic Lord, or even the French Ambassador—had warned them. They had fled across the Thames to the City of London an hour before, where the King's writ ran weakly and the trained bands—citizen militia—were commanded by men loyal to Parliament.[5]

Charles realized his failure even as he asked: "Is Mr. Pym here?" Silence. His eyes moved across the chamber. "I do not see any of them. I think I should know them." More silence, tense and hostile. Then the King said the words that would be remembered and repeated for generations:[6]

> *Well, since I see all the birds are flown, I do expect that you will send them unto me as soon as they return. But I assure you, on the word of a king, I never did intend any force, but shall proceed against them in a legal and fair way.*

It was a lie, or at least a half-truth. He had come with four hundred armed men. That was force, whatever his intentions. And everyone in that chamber knew it.

The Speaker's Answer

Before leaving, Charles turned to Speaker Lenthall: "Mr. Speaker, do you know where these men are?" It was a direct question from the King, requiring an answer. Lenthall, a lawyer who had risen by balancing competing powers, knelt. His answer would become as famous as Charles's words:[7]

> *May it please Your Majesty, I have neither eyes to see nor tongue to speak in this place but as the House is pleased to direct me, whose servant I am here. And I humbly beg Your Majesty's pardon that I cannot give any other answer than this to what Your Majesty is pleased to demand of me.*

The response was perfect. Lenthall acknowledged the King's authority (kneeling, begging pardon) while refusing his command (claiming to speak only as Parliament directed). It was the constitutional crisis in miniature: two authorities, both claiming legitimacy, neither able to compel the other's obedience.

Charles left the chamber. As he walked back through Westminster Hall, he heard a voice from the crowd that had gathered: "Privilege! Privilege!" It was the cry of Parliament—the claim that its members were privileged against arrest, that the King could not seize them no matter what they had done. Other voices took up the cry: "Privilege! Privilege!" The sound followed Charles as he walked to his coach, past faces that no longer showed deference but defiance.[8]

The King Leaves London

Within a week, Charles had left London. He would not return except as prisoner. The five members emerged from hiding and were escorted back to Parliament in triumph by thousands of Londoners, armed and angry, showing where the City's loyalty lay. The trained bands, supposedly the King's militia, took orders from Parliament. Loans that should have filled the King's treasury went to Parliament's war chest instead. Control of London meant control of England's wealth, its government, its symbolic center. Charles had lost all three.[9]

In the months that followed, both sides prepared for war. Parliament issued the Militia Ordinance in March 1642, claiming authority to appoint military commanders—a power traditionally reserved to the Crown. Charles issued Commissions of Array in June, calling loyal subjects to arms. When the King tried to enter Hull in April to seize the arsenal there, Sir John Hotham, the parliamentary governor, refused him entry. It was the first act of military defiance—a subject, claiming Parliament's authority, denying the King access to a royal fortress.[10]

By August, both sides had armies in the field. On August 22, Charles raised his royal standard at Nottingham, formally declaring that his subjects were in rebellion and calling them to return to loyalty. A strong wind blew the standard down that night. Some took it as an omen; others said it was just wind. Either way, England was at war with itself.[11]

Two Authorities, One Realm

The confrontation in the Commons chamber revealed the impossible situation: England had two authorities, each claiming sovereignty, neither willing to yield its position.

The King's position: God anointed him; he ruled by divine right; subjects owed obedience; Parliament existed to advise and consent, not to command; to resist the King was to resist God's ordinance. "Shall I allow subjects to tell their King what he may and may not do?" Charles asked his advisors. "Then I am King in name only, a slave to Parliament's will. Better to fight and lose than to reign as a phantom."[12]

Parliament's position: The King existed to protect the realm and uphold its laws; when he became a tyrant, threatening subjects' liberties and their religion, Parliament—representing the community of the realm—had not just the right but the duty to resist; the King's person was sacred, but his office could be constrained; they fought not against the King but against his "evil counselors" who had led him astray. "We resist not His Majesty but those who have perverted his judgment," Parliamentary declarations insisted, "and we shall restore him to his proper authority once the malignants are removed."[13]

Each position was coherent within its own logic. Each was impossible to reconcile with the other. And underneath both positions lay deeper conflicts:

Religious: Should England's church be governed by bishops appointed by the King, by presbyteries elected by congregations, or by each gathered church independently? Should worship follow set liturgy or spontaneous prayer? Should ceremonies be prescribed or abolished? Was uniformity necessary for order, or did it violate conscience?

Political: Did sovereignty rest in the King alone, in the King-in-Parliament, or in Parliament alone? Could subjects ever justly resist their ruler? Who appointed military commanders, judges, and ministers of state? Where did authority ultimately reside?

Social: Were traditional hierarchies—king over subjects, nobles over commons, masters over servants, men over women—divinely ordained or merely customary? Could a tinker preach as validly as a university-trained minister? Could commoners judge their betters? Was social order natural or constructed?[14]

These questions, simmering for decades, boiled over in the 1640s. The King's failed attempt to arrest the five members was not the cause of civil war but its revelation, the moment when England's crisis of authority became undeniable and irreversible.

What This Book Is About

This book tells the story of how England answered—or failed to answer—these questions. It is a story of religious convictions producing political revolutions, of theological debates fought with swords as well as words, and of a nation trying to rebuild order after tearing down the old authorities.

Four religious visions competed for England's soul:

Presbyterians wanted a national church with reformed discipline—no bishops, but not chaos either. They sought godly order through presbyteries (councils of elders) that would enforce doctrine and morals, supported by a magistrate who would maintain the true faith and suppress heresy. Theirs was a vision of comprehensive reformation: one church, one doctrine, one discipline for all England.

Independents wanted gathered churches of visible saints—voluntary congregations that chose their own ministers and governed themselves. They sought liberty of conscience within the bounds of Protestant orthodoxy, a lean state that protected rights without enforcing uniformity, and trust that truth would emerge through free debate rather than coercion.

Anglicans wanted episcopacy restored—bishops in apostolic succession, liturgy from the Book of Common Prayer, and law enforcing attendance at the national church. They sought order through visible authority, unity through common worship, and stability through tradition tested by time. Liberty, they feared, led to chaos; only discipline maintained peace.

Quakers, and other sectarians, wanted something more radical than any of the others—no bishops, no presbyteries, no set liturgy, no ordained ministry, eventually no violence. They trusted the "inner light" of Christ teaching each person directly, gathered in meetings that waited in silence for the Spirit's leading, and they refused all deference to earthly authority. Theirs was the most radical challenge to the old order.[15]

None of these visions triumphed completely. Instead, England stumbled toward an unstable settlement that satisfied no one fully but allowed most to live with principled disagreements. This book traces how that happened—through war, regicide, military dictatorship, failed experiments, restoration, persecution, and finally grudging toleration.

Classical Political Theory and Ecclesiastical Polity

This book employs classical political philosophy and ecclesiastical polity as complementary frameworks for understanding these four factions. The correspondence is striking: each faction's preferred form of church government mirrors its preferred form of civil government. Anglicans favored episcopal rule—bishops governing the church from above—and monarchical rule in the state. Presbyterians favored rule by councils of elders in the church and by Parliament (an assembly of the propertied and educated) in the state. Independents favored congregational autonomy—each gathered church governing itself—and mixed government balancing the one, the few, and the many. Quakers, rejecting all outward forms of church government, acknowledged no human authority over conscience—a theological anarchism that translated into political radicalism.

These parallels were not accidental. Seventeenth-century English people understood church and state as interpenetrating realms. The same people who were subjects politically were also members ecclesiastically. How they organized their worship expressed and reinforced how they thought about political authority. Gilbert Sheldon could argue that episcopacy and monarchy "stood or fell together" precisely because both rested on the same assumptions about hierarchy, tradition, and divinely ordained order.

Polybius and the Theory of Anacyclosis

The classical tradition, stretching from Aristotle through Polybius to Machiavelli and beyond, identified three legitimate forms of government: monarchy (rule by one), aristocracy (rule by the few), and democracy (rule by the many). Each form had a corresponding corruption: tyranny, oligarchy, and mob rule. Polybius, a Greek intellectual who witnessed Rome's rise to greatness, developed the theory of *anacyclosis*—a cyclical revolution between these governmental forms. Monarchy degenerates into tyranny; tyranny is overthrown by aristocrats seeking the common good; aristocracy degenerates into oligarchy; oligarchy is overthrown by the people; democracy degenerates into mob rule; and from the chaos, a strong man emerges to restore monarchy.

Although "aristocracy" has become synonymous with hereditary nobility in modern usage, Polybius understood it as government "where power is wielded by the justest and wisest men selected on their merits." This book accordingly uses aristocracy to denote a politically powerful elite rather than traditional nobility alone. Wealthy merchants, landowning gentry, guildsmen, and members of Parliament exemplified such elites in seventeenth-century England.

Anacyclosis in Revolutionary England

England's revolutionary period compressed this classical cycle into a single generation. Charles I's monarchy, representing rule by one, became ineffective and tyrannical. Parliament, representing the few, gained power but grew increasingly radical in its efforts to appease the Army and the populace. As Parliament indulged democratic impulses—expressed most dramatically in the Putney Debates—the people became more unruly. Cromwell's Protectorate represented a return to rule by one, reasserting control through military force. Following Cromwell's death, Parliament attempted to maintain authority, but popular discontent threatened to descend into anarchy. Charles II's Restoration returned order to the nation. However, when his successor James II became tyrannical, Parliament summoned William and Mary and instituted constitutional government, establishing a new equilibrium between the one, the few, and the many.

Yet the cycle did not simply repeat. The Restoration settlement differed fundamentally from the Caroline regime it replaced. Parliament retained powers won during the Interregnum; religious dissent, though persecuted, was never entirely suppressed; and the foundations were laid for the Toleration Act of 1689 and the constitutional settlement following the Glorious Revolution. England emerged from its crisis not with a restored absolute monarchy but with a mixed constitution that balanced—imperfectly, contentiously—the claims of king, Parliament, and people.

Three Forms of Ecclesiastical Polity

Ecclesiastical polity—how churches are governed at both local and denominational levels—takes three principal forms that mirror the classical categories of secular government.

Episcopal polity derives from the Greek word *episkopos*, translated as "bishop" or "overseer." Authority flows from the top down; a bishop can ordain ministers and exercise jurisdiction over groups of local churches or an entire denomination. Bishops typically derive their authority from apostolic succession—the claim that they descend in unbroken line from Christ's original apostles. Episcopal churches emphasize tradition and the sacraments while enforcing discipline from above. Both the Catholic and Anglican churches exercised this form of government.

Presbyterian polity emphasizes plural leadership at both local and denominational levels. The Greek word for "elder," *presbuteros*, gives this form its name. The underlying principle holds that older, wiser men make better leaders than those younger and less experienced in the faith. Individual congregations connect through synods or general assemblies of representative elders. Presbyterians distinguish between teaching elders—often university educated and appointed by ruling elders with congregational consent—and ruling elders who exercise governance. Like episcopal polities, presbyterian churches emphasize tradition and the sacraments, though discipline is enforced through the plurality of elders rather than through bishops.

Congregational polity stresses two principles: autonomy and democracy.

This form of government recognizes that all believers have equal access to God, thereby diminishing emphasis on a clerical class. The entire congregation enforces discipline, and connection with other churches remains voluntary. Independent churches and Baptists number among those conforming to congregational polity. Unlike Presbyterians, Congregationalists hired and dismissed ministers rather than receiving appointments from a higher ruling body. They also placed less emphasis on formal educational credentials, particularly in the early years.

Religious Movements and Political Factions

Ecclesiastical polity remained highly fluid in seventeenth-century England. The established denominations of today had yet to be formalized; even the Anglican Church was not fully constituted before the Restoration. Given this institutional fluidity, the concept of a "religious movement" proves more useful than forcing analysis into the rigid categories of "church" and "sect." Movements differ from sects in that movements seek to change society while sects seek to escape it.

Three categories of religious movement can be distinguished. Endogenous movements strive for reform within existing religious institutions; Episcopalians and Presbyterians exemplify this type. Exogenous movements aim to change the society in which the religion exists; Puritans and congregational churches fall into this category. Generative movements create entirely new religious institutions; the Quakers represent this type.

These categories carry significant political implications. Endogenous movements tend toward political conservatism, seeking change while maintaining societal stability and working through existing governmental structures—enacting reform through acts of Parliament, for example. Exogenous movements pursue political power to alter society's fundamental character. Generative movements, as newly created outsiders, seek either political influence over or protection from existing institutional power. In the political realm, an endogenous movement would enact change through existing government, while a generative movement would seek to replace the governmental system and transform the social fabric.

Political theology articulates the religious justification for the political activities of these movements. While retaining the analytical value of "religious movement" as a concept, this book employs the term "religious political faction" to emphasize the inherently political character of these groups during the revolutionary period. The Monarchical Anglicans, Aristocratic Presbyterians, Commonwealth Independents, and Anarchist Quakers were not merely religious communities but political actors whose theological convictions shaped their constitutional vision.

Why This Framework Matters

The story matters beyond its immediate historical context. The questions England grappled with—how to balance order and liberty, authority and conscience, uniformity and diversity—remain our questions. The solutions

England developed—separation of church and state, liberty of conscience, limited government, denominational pluralism—shape our world. And the costs England paid—war, persecution, families divided, communities shattered—warn us what happens when religious and political conflicts become total.

The Structure of This Book

The chapters that follow trace England's crisis chronologically and thematically:

Chapter 1 sets the stage: the long fuse that led to explosion, from Elizabeth's settlement through James I's conflicts with Puritans to Charles I's disastrous policies of the 1630s. It shows how religious, political, and constitutional tensions accumulated until some spark—in this case, rebellion in Scotland and Ireland—would ignite them.

Chapter 2 examines the outbreak of civil war and the initial expectations: most thought the conflict would be brief, that one side would quickly prevail, that England would return to normalcy. Instead, war radicalized both sides, producing the New Model Army's military dominance and Parliament's fragmentation into competing factions.

Chapters 3-6 take each religious vision in turn, showing its theological foundation, political implications, institutional development, and ultimate fate:

- **Chapter 3 (Presbyterians):** The quest for godly order—aristocratic church government and parliamentary rule
- **Chapter 4 (Independents):** The case for gathered churches and free commonwealths—congregational autonomy and mixed government
- **Chapter 5 (Anglicans):** The defense of tradition and authority—episcopal hierarchy and monarchical rule
- **Chapter 6 (Quakers):** The radical witness of the Lamb's War and peace testimony—rejection of all human authority over conscience

Chapter 7 traces the path from Restoration persecution to Toleration Act, showing how exhaustion, pragmatism, and changed circumstances made religious diversity acceptable when it had seemed impossible.

The Conclusion weighs what England gained and lost, what these conflicts gave the wider world, and what questions remain for those who inherit this history.

A Word About Sources and Interpretation

This book draws on the extraordinary primary sources the period generated: parliamentary debates, trial transcripts, sermons, pamphlets, personal journals, correspondence, and the records of persecution that both sides kept meticulously. The 17th century was perhaps the first era when ordinary people's voices—soldiers, craftsmen, women, the poor—entered the historical record in significant numbers. We can hear Quaker women preaching, Army agitators debating franchise, Scottish Presbyterians negotiating with English Parliament, and Anglican divines defending tradition.

The challenge is making sense of the cacophony. Participants disagreed about basic facts (who started the war? who was truly loyal to England? what did Scripture command?). Modern historians disagree about interpretations (was this a Puritan revolution? a bourgeois revolution? a crisis of multiple kingdoms? a war of religion or a war for liberty?). This book takes a position: religion was primary, politics followed from religious convictions, and we cannot understand the period by reducing it to economic interests or class conflict—though those mattered too.[16]

The story is also tragic. Hundreds of thousands died (possibly 10% of England's population, higher percentages in Ireland and Scotland).[17] Families were divided, brother against brother, father against son.[18] Communities that had lived together for generations fractured. Property was destroyed, lives were ruined, and hopes were dashed. The victors, whether royalists in 1660 or whigs in 1689, paid steep prices for their victories. There were no clean hands, no pure motives, no easy judgments.

Yet from this tragedy emerged principles and practices that shaped the modern world: liberty of conscience, limited government, denominational pluralism, the marketplace of ideas, the separation of church and state, and the conviction that legitimate authority requires consent. These were not inevitable developments, they were fought for, bled for, argued over, and gradually, painfully institutionalized. Understanding how they emerged from England's crisis helps us appreciate their value and their fragility.[19]

To understand how Charles I came to walk into the Commons chamber with armed men behind him, how England's careful Tudor compromise unraveled into civil war, we must go back a generation—to the religious settlement that satisfied no one completely and the political tensions that accumulated through the reigns of Elizabeth, James, and Charles until they exploded.[20]

CHAPTER 1 — THE LONG FUSE

FROM ELIZABETH'S SETTLEMENT TO CHARLES'S DISASTERS, 1558-1640

The Hampton Court Conference, 14 January 1604

John Rainolds stood before the new king and felt his carefully prepared arguments scattering like leaves before wind. He had come to Hampton Court Conference expecting a theological debate, learned divines presenting cases, Scripture being examined, perhaps some modest reforms of the Church of England that would ease tender consciences without disrupting order. Instead, James Stuart, King of England for less than a year, was lecturing them about kingship, bishops, and Scottish presbyters as if they were schoolboys.[1]

Rainolds was fifty-two years old, President of Corpus Christi College, Oxford, one of England's finest biblical scholars. He was no radical, he wore the surplice without complaint, he opposed separatists, he wanted reformation within the established church, not destruction of it. He had come to Hampton Court with three other Puritan divines at the King's invitation to present their grievances about ceremonies, church government, and the Book of Common Prayer. Some changes would strengthen the church, they believed. Surely the King, himself a learned theologian who had written against papal authority, would listen.[2]

The conference had begun promisingly enough. On the first day (January 12), James had met privately with bishops to discuss church matters. On the second day (January 14), the King met with both bishops and the Puritan delegates. The bishops arrived dressed in their ecclesiastical finery—white rochets over black chimeres, the traditional garb of episcopal authority. The Puritan divines wore plain black Geneva gowns. The visual contrast spoke before anyone opened their mouths: hierarchy versus simplicity, tradition versus reform.[3]

The King's Opening

James VI of Scotland had become James I of England when Elizabeth died childless in March 1603. He was thirty-six years old, scholarly, pedantic, convinced of his own brilliance. He had ruled Scotland since infancy (crowned at thirteen months after his mother's forced abdication) and had survived plots, kidnappings, and the constant maneuvering of Scottish noble factions. He prided himself on being a survivor, a skilled politician, a theological expert, and—above all—a king by divine right who knew how to manage fractious subjects.[4]

He opened the conference with a speech about his vision for church and state: [5]

> *I will have one doctrine, one discipline, one religion in substance and in ceremony. I shall not be content that men should comply outwardly while dissenting inwardly. Those who will not conform may expect my severity, for I will make them conform or I will harry them out of the land.*

This was not the tone Rainolds and his colleagues had hoped for. But they proceeded anyway. Rainolds presented a written summary of Puritan grievances, carefully organized under four headings: church government, liturgy, church discipline, and translation of Scripture. He spoke with respect, acknowledging the King's learning and appealing to his judgment.[6]

The Presbyterian Trigger

Rainolds explained that many ministers found certain ceremonies troubling: signing with the cross at baptism (which seemed superstitious), wearing the surplice (which was associated with Catholic vestments), kneeling to receive communion (which might suggest adoration of the bread). These were "things indifferent" (*adiaphora*), he argued—neither commanded nor forbidden by Scripture—so why not make them optional for those whose consciences were troubled?

He also suggested reforms to church government. Some oversight of ministers was necessary, but perhaps bishops' power could be moderated by involving other clergy in decisions. He mentioned presbyteries—not as a demand for Scottish-style presbyterian government, but as one possible model for shared governance.[7]

James's reaction was explosive. At the word "presbytery," the King stood from his chair. His Scottish accent, usually masked by affected English pronunciation, became more pronounced as his anger rose:[8]

> *A Scottish presbytery agreeth as well with monarchy as God with the Devil! Then Jack and Tom and Will and Dick shall meet and at their pleasure censure me and my council and all our proceedings. If you aim at a Scottish presbytery, it agreeth as well with monarchy as God with the Devil! Then I must be subject to every Tom, Jack, and Will, who may meet and censure me. No bishop, no king!*

The bishops, arrayed behind the King, nodded approvingly. Richard Bancroft, Bishop of London (soon to be Archbishop of Canterbury), smiled—his enemy had walked into a trap. The King continued: [9]

I had experience of presbyteries in Scotland. They do nothing but contend against the King and his authority. I will have no such insolence here. I shall appoint bishops, and they shall govern the church by my authority. If you quarrel with this, you quarrel with monarchy itself.

Rainolds tried to clarify: he had not proposed abolishing bishops, only suggesting some accountability. But the King would not listen. James had survived Scottish presbyterian ministers who claimed they could excommunicate kings, who preached that subjects might resist tyrants, who insisted the Kirk (church) was independent of royal control. He would not allow such notions to infect England.[10]

The One Victory: A New Translation

The conference was not a total failure for the Puritans. Rainolds made one suggestion that bore fruit: England needed a new, authoritative translation of Scripture. The existing Geneva Bible, though excellent, had marginal notes with republican and presbyterian interpretations that troubled monarchs. The Bishops' Bible, commissioned by Elizabeth, was accurate but lacked literary grace. Could the King authorize a new translation?[11]

James liked this idea. A new Bible, translated by the best scholars from all perspectives, published under royal authority, with no divisive marginal notes—this would demonstrate his learning and provide England with Scripture that all could use. He appointed committees of translators and gave them clear instructions. The result, published in 1611, would be the King James Bible—the most influential English translation in history.[12]

But this single victory could not compensate for the conference's broader failure. James had made clear he would enforce conformity. The Book of Common Prayer would be used without modification. The ceremonies would be required. Ministers who refused would be deprived of their livings. "I will have one doctrine and one discipline," James repeated. "Conform or face my severity."[13]

After the Conference

In the months following Hampton Court, James issued new canons (church laws) that required ministers to:

- Use all ceremonies prescribed in the Book of Common Prayer
- Wear the surplice
- Make the sign of the cross at baptism
- Not preach against bishops or the established government
- Subscribe to the king's ecclesiastical supremacy and to the doctrine that the Book of Common Prayer contained nothing contrary to Scripture[14]

About ninety ministers—some 1% of England's clergy—refused to subscribe and were ejected from their livings. Most of these were not radicals but conscientious men who could not swear that ceremonies they thought unnecessary or even superstitious were fully agreeable to God's Word. They lost their incomes, their parsonages, their ability to preach and administer sacraments. Some went into exile. Others conformed under pressure, their consciences troubled. Still others were sheltered by sympathetic gentry who valued their preaching more than their ceremonial exactness.[15]

The Hampton Court Conference thus set the pattern for James's reign and his son Charles's after him: the crown would insist on uniformity, Puritans would seek accommodation, and when push came to shove, force—legal and eventually military—would be the final arbiter. The conference also revealed James's deepest political conviction: episcopacy and monarchy stood or fell together. "No bishop, no king" was not hyperbole but James's genuine belief. Any challenge to episcopal authority was, in his mind, a challenge to royal authority. This equation—church government equals political loyalty—would poison English politics for forty years.[16]

What Might Have Been

Historians still debate what might have happened if James had been more flexible at Hampton Court. The Puritan delegates were moderates, not separatists or radicals. They asked for modest accommodations—making some ceremonies optional, perhaps involving clergy in church courts, producing a new Bible translation. If James had granted these requests, might England have avoided civil war?[17]

Perhaps. Or perhaps not. The conflicts ran deeper than ceremonies and church government. They touched fundamental questions: Where did authority reside—in king, in law, in Scripture, in conscience? Who interpreted Scripture—bishops, presbyteries, individual believers? Could the state enforce religious conformity, or did conscience require liberty? These were not questions that compromise could easily resolve, because each side's position was coherent within its own framework and incompatible with the other's.[18]

But James's intransigence at Hampton Court certainly made conflict more likely. He turned potential allies into opponents, he equated modest reform proposals with sedition, and he convinced many Puritans that the established church would never accommodate their consciences. Some withdrew into private conventicles (small, illegal prayer meetings). Others emigrated to Holland or New England. Still others remained within the church but prepared for a day when circumstances might change and reformation might become possible.[19]

That day would come—but only after disaster, war, and the breakdown of the order James had worked so hard to preserve.

To understand why James reacted so explosively to any hint of presbyterian government, why he identified bishops with monarchy, and why English Puritans found his church settlement so troubling, we must go back further—to Elizabeth's reign and the religious settlement she crafted, which stabilized England after decades of violent religious oscillation but satisfied no one completely.

Elizabeth's Middle Way

The Inheritance of Chaos: Henry VIII's Break with Rome

England's religious turbulence began not with theology but with a king's marital troubles. Henry VIII (r. 1509-1547) wanted to annul his marriage to Catherine of Aragon, who had failed to produce a male heir. When Pope Clement VII refused (pressured by Catherine's nephew, the Holy Roman Emperor Charles V), Henry broke with Rome. The Acts of Supremacy (1534) declared the English monarch "Supreme Head" of the Church of England, rejecting papal authority. But Henry's church was Catholic without the Pope—same theology, same liturgy, same monks and monasteries, just with English rather than Roman oversight.[20]

The dissolution of the monasteries (1536-1540) was more revolutionary. Henry seized monastic lands—about a quarter of England's arable land—and sold or granted them to nobles and gentry. This created a propertied class with vested interest in preventing Catholic restoration (which might reclaim monastic lands). It also destroyed a social safety net: monasteries had provided charity, education, hospitality, and poor relief. Their dissolution left gaps that parishes and municipalities struggled to fill.[21]

Henry died in 1547, leaving England theologically ambiguous: Protestant in rejecting papal authority, Catholic in most doctrine and practice, and unstable because the settlement rested on royal will rather than popular consensus or theological clarity.

Edward VI's Protestant Revolution

Edward VI (r. 1547-1553) was nine years old at his accession. His regency council, dominated by Protestant reformers, moved England decisively Protestant. Thomas Cranmer, Archbishop of Canterbury, introduced the Book of Common Prayer (1549, revised 1552)—English liturgy replacing Latin Mass, reformed theology replacing transubstantiation, married clergy replacing celibate priesthood. Images were removed from churches, altars replaced with communion tables, and traditional vestments discouraged.[22]

These reforms pleased committed Protestants but alienated traditionalists. The Western Rebellion (1549) in Devon and Cornwall was a Catholic uprising demanding return to the Mass and rejection of the English prayer book. It was crushed with mercenary troops, leaving thousands dead. England was becoming Protestant by force, and traditional religious culture—processions, pilgrimages, prayers for the dead, veneration of saints—was being criminalized.[23]

Edward died at fifteen in 1553. His brief reign had been revolutionary but incomplete. Would England remain Protestant?

Mary's Catholic Restoration

Mary I (r. 1553-1558) was Henry's daughter by Catherine of Aragon, raised Catholic, and determined to restore England to Roman obedience. She repealed Edward's religious laws, restored the Mass, and reconciled with Rome. Then she began burning Protestants as heretics.[24]

The Marian martyrs—about 280 people burned between 1555 and 1558—included bishops (Thomas Cranmer, Hugh Latimer, Nicholas Ridley), ministers, and lay people. John Foxe's *Acts and Monuments* (1563), popularly known as Foxe's Book of Martyrs, chronicled their deaths in vivid detail, creating a Protestant martyrology that shaped English identity for generations. Cranmer's death was particularly dramatic: he recanted under pressure, then recanted his recantation, thrusting into the flames the hand that had signed his recantation. "This unworthy hand!" he cried as it burned.[25]

Mary's restoration failed. She died childless in 1558, her Protestant burnings having created martyrs and hatred. Her marriage to Philip II of Spain was unpopular—England wanted no foreign Catholic king. Her reign associated Catholicism with tyranny, foreign influence, and persecution. When Elizabeth succeeded her, England's religious character was still uncertain, but Catholic restoration by force had been discredited.

The Elizabethan Settlement: Ambiguity as Policy

Elizabeth I (r. 1558-1603) inherited a religiously divided realm. Perhaps half the population remained Catholic in sentiment, though few were willing to die for it. Perhaps a quarter were committed Protestants, including many who had fled to Geneva or German Protestant cities during Mary's reign and returned radicalized. The rest were conformists who would accept whatever settlement the crown imposed as long as it allowed them to live peacefully.[26]

Elizabeth herself was Protestant but pragmatic. She rejected papal authority (which had declared her illegitimate) but disliked zealous Protestantism with its emphasis on preaching and its contempt for ceremony. She reportedly said she didn't want to "make windows into men's souls"—an impossibility anyway, since religious conviction couldn't be controlled even if she wanted to.[27]

Her solution was the Elizabethan Settlement: a via media (middle way) that was Protestant in doctrine but traditional in ceremony, episcopal in government but Reformed in theology, legally enforced but with much practical flexibility. It was meant to include all but the most extreme: Catholics who rejected royal supremacy and Protestant radicals who rejected bishops could not conform, but most others could find accommodation within the settlement's breadth.[28]

The Settlement's Components

Act of Supremacy (1559): Restored royal supremacy over the church, though Elizabeth chose the less provocative title "Supreme Governor" rather than "Supreme Head." This asserted independence from Rome while acknowledging that Christ, not the monarch, headed the church in a spiritual sense.[29]

Act of Uniformity (1559): Required all churches to use the Book of Common Prayer (a moderate revision of Cranmer's 1552 version). Attendance at parish church on Sundays was compulsory; absence brought a fine of one shilling (a day's wage for a laborer)—enough to hurt but not enough to ruin. The prayer book was studied ambiguity: its communion service could be read as Catholic (Christ's real presence) or Reformed (spiritual presence), allowing consciences to interpret it variously.[30]

Thirty-Nine Articles (1563): Defined Church of England doctrine in broadly Protestant terms—justification by faith alone, Scripture's authority, rejection of purgatory and transubstantiation—but left room for disagreement on details. They were Protestant enough to be clearly not Catholic, but vague enough to allow high and low church interpretations.[31]

Episcopal Government: Elizabeth retained bishops, seeing them as useful tools for royal control. The Archbishop of Canterbury, appointed by the crown, oversaw lesser bishops who governed dioceses. Bishops ordained clergy, conducted visitations (inspections) of parishes, and enforced conformity through church courts. This hierarchy, rejected by most continental Protestants, became a flashpoint: were bishops required by Scripture (as Anglicans claimed) or merely useful traditions (as Elizabeth seemed to view them) or actually contrary to God's Word (as Presbyterians argued)?[32]

Ceremonial Ambiguity: The settlement required ministers to wear surplices, allowed (but didn't require) other traditional vestments, permitted church music and organs, and maintained the church calendar with its festivals. Many returning Marian exiles found these "popish rags" offensive, but Elizabeth insisted on them for decency and uniformity. When London clergy protested in 1566, Archbishop Parker enforced the "Advertisements"—requiring conformity or loss of livings. About forty ministers refused and were suspended. The Vestiarian Controversy (dispute over vestments) marked the first Protestant resistance to the settlement.[33]

The settlement worked as religious policy for several reasons:

First, enforcement was inconsistent. Bishops varied in zeal; some rigorously enforced conformity while others overlooked nonconformity if ministers were otherwise sound and effective. Similarly, gentry who controlled parish appointments (advowsons) protected ministers they valued even if those ministers were ceremonially lax.

Second, Elizabeth was flexible when pragmatism demanded. She didn't want zealous Protestantism, but she needed Protestant support against Catholic threats (assassination plots, Spanish Armada, Jesuit missions). When Presbyterian stirrings emerged in the 1570s-1580s, she suppressed them—but not brutally. Most Puritan leaders died in their beds, not on scaffolds.

Third, the settlement's breadth allowed most to participate. If you could tolerate bishops and use the prayer book, you were included. The only exclusions were Catholics (who rejected royal supremacy) and separatists (who rejected the very idea of a national church). These groups were tiny—most Catholics conformed outwardly, most Protestants worked for reform within the system.[34]

But the settlement left fundamental questions unresolved: Was England's church truly reformed or a compromise that needed further purification? Were bishops essential or obstacles? Did uniformity serve order or stifle truth? These questions would fester until they erupted under

Elizabeth's successors.

The Rise of Puritanism

"Puritan" was never a precise term. Coined as an insult (from "precisians"—those overly precise about religion), it covered a spectrum from moderate conformists who wanted better preaching and stricter Sabbath observance to radical separatists who rejected the national church entirely. What united Puritans was conviction that Elizabeth's settlement was incomplete—a good start, but needing further reformation.[35]

Most Puritans accepted episcopacy grudgingly, used the prayer book with reservations, wore the surplice under protest. They were not separatists—they worked within the established church while pushing for reform. They valued:

- **Preaching** over ceremony: the Word proclaimed, not rituals performed
- **Biblical authority** over tradition: Scripture alone determined doctrine and practice
- **Godly discipline** over lax morality: church and magistrate should enforce godly living
- **Sabbath holiness** over recreation: Sunday was for worship, not sports or alehouses
- **Plain worship** over ornate ceremony: simplicity honored God; elaborate ritual was "popish"[36]

The Presbyterian Impulse

In the 1570s-1580s, some Puritans proposed presbyterian church government: replace bishops with presbyteries (assemblies of ministers and elders), let congregations choose ministers, and create ascending courts (local, regional, national) to maintain doctrine and discipline. This was the Scottish and Genevan model, and it had theological appeal: presbyteries seemed more biblical than bishops, and they prevented the concentration of power in a few hands.[37]

Thomas Cartwright, Lady Margaret Professor of Divinity at Cambridge, lectured in 1570 that apostolic practice required presbyterian government. His lectures caused such controversy that he was deprived of his chair and eventually fled to the Continent. Walter Travers wrote *A Full and Plaine Declaration of Ecclesiastical Discipline* (1574, published 1580), arguing that presbyterian government was not merely preferable but commanded by Scripture. The Admonitions to Parliament (1572) called for root-and-branch reform: abolish bishops, establish presbyteries, purify worship of all ceremonies.[38]

Elizabeth responded through her bishops. John Whitgift, Archbishop of Canterbury from 1583, required subscription to three articles: accepting royal supremacy, accepting the Book of Common Prayer as lawful, and accepting the Thirty-Nine Articles. Those who refused were suspended from ministry. Whitgift also used the Court of High Commission—an ecclesiastical court with powers of fine and imprisonment—to prosecute nonconformity. His policies were harsh enough to alarm even moderate Puritans, who saw in them Catholic-style persecution.[39]

But the presbyterian movement never gained majority support even among Puritans. Most English Protestants were suspicious of clerical power—whether exercised by bishops or by presbyteries. They wanted a learned, godly ministry and freedom from "popish" ceremony, but they didn't want clergy dictating to laity. When the presbyterian leader John Field organized an underground "classis" movement (unofficial presbyterian assemblies) in the 1580s, it attracted only about 400 ministers—fewer than 5% of England's clergy—and collapsed after Field's death in 1588.[40]

Elizabeth thus bequeathed to her successors an unstable settlement: Protestant in doctrine, episcopal in government, and containing a significant minority who wanted further reformation. As long as threats (Catholic plots, Spanish invasion) made Protestant unity necessary, and as long as Elizabeth's political skill managed tensions, the settlement held. But remove those conditions, and the contradictions might explode.

James I and the Seeds of Conflict

Divine Right Meets Puritan Conscience

The Calvinist King and His Bishops

James's Scottish Experience

James VI of Scotland knew Presbyterian ministers well—too well for his comfort. The Scottish Kirk (church) was presbyterian in government, Calvinist in theology, and fiercely independent. Ministers like Andrew Melville insisted that the Kirk answered to Christ alone, not to the King. Melville once grabbed James by the sleeve and called him "God's sillie vassal"—a foolish servant who needed to remember his place. The Kirk claimed power to excommunicate even kings, and its General Assembly (governing body) acted as a rival power center to the crown.[41]

James spent his Scottish reign trying to control the Kirk. He gradually reintroduced bishops to Scotland, not because he loved episcopacy theologically but because he could control bishops (whom he appointed) more easily than presbyteries (which elected their own leaders). By the time he inherited England's throne in 1603, he had concluded that presbyterian government was incompatible with royal authority. "A Scottish presbytery agreeth as well with monarchy as God with the Devil," he would famously say.[42]

Yet James was also a committed Calvinist in theology. He had been tutored by George Buchanan, a fierce Presbyterian humanist. James's own theological writings defended predestination, attacked papal claims, and engaged seriously with Reformed theology. He was no crypto-Catholic, no ceremonialist who valued ritual over doctrine. He simply believed that bishops were the best governors for a Reformed church, and he insisted that religious uniformity was necessary for political stability.[43]

The Millenary Petition

Even before James reached London from Scotland in 1603, Puritan ministers presented him with the Millenary Petition—supposedly signed by a thousand ministers (though probably fewer actually signed). The petition was moderate in tone, asking not for presbyterian government but for relief from troubling ceremonies:[44]

- Abolish or make optional the sign of the cross at baptism
- Abolish or make optional the ring in marriage
- Discontinue use of terms like "priest" which suggested Catholic Mass rather than Protestant ministry
- Enforce strict Sabbath observance
- Improve clerical education and reduce pluralism (one minister holding multiple livings)

The petition promised that signers were "neither factious men affecting a popular parity in the Church, nor schismatics aiming at the dissolution of the State ecclesiastical"—in other words, they weren't presbyterian revolutionaries but loyal subjects seeking modest reforms. James agreed to a conference where bishops and Puritan divines could present their cases. The result was Hampton Court, and James's explosive reaction to any hint of presbyterian sentiment.[45]

The Jacobean Bishops

James chose his bishops carefully. He wanted learned men who would defend royal supremacy and episcopal government while also being sound Reformed theologians. His early appointments balanced these concerns reasonably:

George Abbot (Archbishop of Canterbury 1611-1633) was a convinced Calvinist who opposed Catholics vigorously but also enforced conformity against Puritans. He was competent but not brilliant, solid but not inspiring.

Lancelot Andrewes (Bishop of Winchester from 1619) was perhaps England's finest theologian and preacher. His sermons were masterpieces of learning and devotion. He defended episcopacy with historical and theological arguments that convinced even skeptics of bishops' utility if not their divine necessity.[46]

But James also promoted men whose ceremonialism troubled Puritans. He allowed elaborate ritual in the Chapel Royal (his personal chapel), arguing that beauty in worship honored God. He published his *Book of Sports* (1618), permitting Sunday recreations after church services—directly contradicting Puritan Sabbatarianism. These policies convinced many Puritans that James's church, despite its Reformed theology, was sliding toward Catholic practice.[47]

Parliament, Money, and Constitutional Friction

The Financial Problem

James's reign coincided with escalating costs of government and static royal revenues. Tudor monarchs had sold or granted away crown lands, reducing the monarchy's income. Inflation eroded the value of fixed revenues. Wars (England engaged in complex continental conflicts) required parliamentary subsidies. But Parliament controlled taxation, and MPs used their control to extract concessions.[48]

James believed in royal prerogative—the crown's inherent powers that Parliament couldn't constrain. He could conduct foreign policy, appoint officials, summon or dismiss Parliament, and govern the church through bishops. Parliament's role, in his view, was to grant taxes when needed and to pass laws the crown requested—not to dictate policy or attach conditions to supply.[49]

Parliament saw matters differently. MPs claimed ancient rights: freedom from arbitrary arrest, control over taxation, and the right to speak freely on any matter affecting the realm. They insisted that the crown couldn't levy taxes without Parliament's consent, that subsidies could be conditioned on grievances being addressed, and that Parliament's privileges were not gifts from the crown but inherent rights of free Englishmen.[50]

These claims collided in 1610 when James proposed the "Great Contract"—Parliament would grant him a fixed annual revenue of £200,000 in exchange for James surrendering certain unpopular feudal rights (wardship, purveyance). Negotiations dragged on for months before collapsing. Neither side could agree on the relationship between crown and Parliament, or on what rights each possessed. James dissolved Parliament in frustration.[51]

The Added Parliament and the Protestation

The "Added Parliament" of 1614 (so-called because it added no legislation) was summoned for money but immediately confronted James with grievances. MPs complained about impositions (customs duties James levied by prerogative), church appointments, and court favorites. James dissolved it after two months without receiving any taxation. He wouldn't call another Parliament until 1621.[52]

The 1621 Parliament was summoned to fund James's son-in-law (Frederick, Elector Palatine) whose lands had been seized by Catholic forces in the Thirty Years' War. MPs granted some money but also raised constitutional issues. They impeached Francis Bacon (Lord Chancellor) for corruption and demanded investigation of monopolies. When James tried to prevent Parliament from discussing foreign policy, MPs issued a Protestation asserting their rights:[53]

> *The liberties, franchises, privileges, and jurisdictions of Parliament are the ancient and undoubted birthright and inheritance of the subjects of England... and the arduous and urgent affairs concerning the King, State, and the defense of the realm and of the Church of England... are proper subjects and matter of counsel and debate in Parliament.*

James was furious. He tore the Protestation from the Commons Journal with his own hands and dissolved Parliament. The symbolic act—literally ripping out Parliament's record of its own rights—demonstrated the constitutional deadlock. James claimed absolute authority in certain spheres; Parliament claimed the right to discuss anything affecting the realm. The conflict was fundamental and unresolved.[54]

The Spanish Match and Protestant Paranoia

In 1623, James's son Charles (the heir after his brother Henry died in 1612) and the royal favorite George Villiers, Duke of Buckingham, undertook an extraordinary adventure. They traveled incognito to Madrid to woo the Spanish Infanta—Charles would marry her, cementing an alliance with Catholic Spain that James hoped would balance continental politics and avoid expensive war.[55]

Protestant England was horrified. Spain was the enemy—the power behind Catholic plots, the nation that had sent the Armada, the Inquisition's homeland. That the future king might marry a Catholic princess suggested betrayal of the Protestant cause. Rumors (exaggerated but believed) claimed James had promised Catholic toleration in England and that Jesuits would flood in once the Spanish match was secured.[56]

The mission failed. Spanish demands for Catholic toleration and concerns about Charles's Protestantism made negotiations collapse. Charles and Buckingham returned to England in October 1623 without a bride but with injured pride and newfound desire for war against Spain. Popular celebrations greeted their return—England rejoiced that the Spanish match had failed. Bonfires blazed, church bells rang, and preachers gave thanks that God had preserved England from popish marriage.[57]

The 1624 Parliament: War Fever

James reluctantly called Parliament in 1624, needing money to support Frederick in the Palatinate. But Charles and Buckingham, now advocating war against Spain, pushed for a naval campaign against Spanish treasure fleets. Parliament enthusiastically voted subsidies—not for James's defensive Continental policy, but for the aggressive anti-Spanish war Charles wanted.[58]

This Parliament also impeached Lionel Cranfield, Earl of Middlesex, the Lord Treasurer who had tried to impose fiscal discipline and opposed expensive wars. The impeachment was driven by Buckingham (who had personal grudges) and Charles (who wanted war and resented Cranfield's opposition). James protested that Parliament was attacking his ministers: "You are fools! You are making a rod with which you will be scourged yourselves!" His words proved prophetic—Charles would face parliamentary impeachment of his own favorites within years.[59]

The 1624 Parliament also passed bills against Catholics, tightening recusancy laws and banning Jesuits. Protestant paranoia about Catholic plots was at fever pitch. Rumors spread of secret treaties, of Charles promising to convert to Catholicism, of Buckingham being secretly Catholic. Most rumors were false, but they reflected genuine Protestant fears that the crown might compromise with the Counter-Reformation.[60]

James died in March 1625, exhausted and disappointed. His hopes for Protestant-Catholic balance in Europe had failed. His financial problems were unsolved. His relationship with Parliament was poisonous. And his son Charles—more rigid, less politically skilled, more trusting of favorites—

inherited all these problems along with the throne.[61]

Charles I and the Crisis Deepens

Arminianism, Arbitrary Government, and the Slide to War

The Arminian Turn in English Theology

What Arminianism Meant

"Arminianism" became a catchword for everything English Puritans feared. Strictly speaking, it referred to the theology of Jacobus Arminius (1560-1609), a Dutch theologian who questioned some Calvinist doctrines. Against Calvinist predestination (God chooses some for salvation, others for damnation, before creation), Arminius argued for conditional election (God chooses those who He foresees will believe). Against irresistible grace (God's saving grace cannot be resisted), Arminius argued that humans could resist or accept grace.[62]

These were real theological differences, debated at the Synod of Dort (1618-1619) where international Reformed churches condemned Arminian positions as heretical. The Dutch church expelled Arminians; some fled to England where they found sympathy from certain Anglican divines who disliked Calvinist rigor and valued human free will.[63]

But in English usage, "Arminian" came to mean more than theological position on predestination. It signified:[64]

- **Ceremonialism**: emphasis on ritual, vestments, and the sacraments as means of grace rather than preaching
- **High church ecclesiology**: exalting bishops' authority, claiming apostolic succession as essential
- **Clericalism**: insisting on clergy's special status and power, resisting lay control
- **Rejection of Calvinist "precision"**: mocking Puritan Sabbatarianism and strictness as excessive
- **Accommodation with Rome**: seeing Roman Catholics as erring brothers rather than agents of Antichrist

This package of positions alarmed Puritans because it seemed to be undoing the Reformation. If salvation depended on human will rather than divine grace, wasn't that semi-Pelagianism (the heresy that humans could earn salvation)? If ceremonies and sacraments were channels of grace, wasn't that Catholic sacramentalism? If bishops claimed divine right to govern, weren't they imitating papal tyranny?[65]

William Laud and the Beauty of Holiness

William Laud (1573-1645) became the face of English Arminianism, though he would have rejected the label. Born to a merchant family, educated at Oxford, Laud rose through church ranks by ability and determination. He became Bishop of London in 1628 and Archbishop of Canterbury in 1633, holding the latter position until his execution in 1645.[66]

Laud believed the Church of England had become slovenly. Churches were in disrepair, communion tables treated casually, services conducted carelessly, and preaching (especially Puritan preaching) elevated above sacrament. He wanted to restore "the beauty of holiness"—proper reverence in worship, churches maintained and beautified, clergy properly vested, rituals conducted decently and in order.[67]

His reforms included:[68]

- **Moving communion tables** to the east end of churches, railing them off, and treating them as altars (Puritans called them tables to emphasize communion as a meal, not a sacrifice; Laud's language and practice suggested sacrifice)
- **Requiring clergy to bow** at Jesus's name and toward the altar—gestures that seemed "popish" to Protestants
- **Enforcing clerical dress**: surplices mandatory, non-Protestant vestments encouraged
- **Decorating churches**: stained glass, ornate altar cloths, candles—beauty that Puritans saw as idolatry
- **Suppressing Puritan lectureships**: endowed sermon positions controlled by town corporations, allowing godly preaching outside bishops' control—Laud saw them as sources of sedition and worked to eliminate them

Laud also used church courts aggressively. He prosecuted Puritan ministers for ceremonial nonconformity, laypeople for Sabbath-breaking, and anyone who spoke against his policies. The most notorious cases involved physical punishments: William Prynne, Henry Burton, and John Bastwick (a lawyer, a minister, and a physician) had their ears cropped for writing pamphlets against bishops. They stood in the pillory at Westminster, were mutilated, and then imprisoned indefinitely.[69]

To Laud, he was restoring order and reverence. To Puritans, he was a crypto-Catholic tyrant destroying the Protestant church from within. John Pym would later denounce Laud's "innovations" as conspiracies to reconcile England with Rome. The charge was unfair—Laud was no Catholic, and he opposed papal supremacy as firmly as any Protestant—but his ceremonialism, his clericalism, and his persecution of Puritan nonconformity made him the most hated man in England.[70]

Charles's Support for Laud

Charles I fully supported Laud's program. Charles had married Henrietta Maria, a French Catholic princess, in 1625. The marriage treaty promised Catholic toleration, and Henrietta Maria maintained a chapel with Mass, French priests, and elaborate ceremony at court. Charles allowed this, and he attended occasionally (though he took Anglican communion, not Catholic sacrament). To Puritan observers, the court seemed increasingly Catholic in aesthetics if not doctrine.[71]

Charles also believed in order, ceremony, and hierarchy. He found Puritan preaching tedious and their emphasis on Scripture over liturgy troubling. When Laud proposed reforms, Charles backed him enthusiastically. This made Laud's program royal policy, not merely one bishop's preferences. To resist Laud was to resist the King.[72]

The Three Parliaments and Personal Rule

The 1625 Parliament: Buckingham and War

Charles's first Parliament, meeting in 1625 shortly after his accession, granted him taxes for one year only—not the customary grant of tonnage and poundage (customs duties) for life. MPs distrusted Buckingham, the favorite Charles had inherited from James, who now directed foreign and military policy. Buckingham's expedition to Cádiz (1625) was a disaster—English forces failed to capture the Spanish port, achieved nothing, and returned having lost thousands of men to disease and incompetence.[73]

When Parliament reconvened, MPs wanted to impeach Buckingham for corruption and military failure. Charles dissolved Parliament rather than allow his favorite to be attacked. He then collected tonnage and poundage anyway, without parliamentary grant, claiming it as necessary for government. This was legally dubious—customs duties required parliamentary consent—but Charles insisted that emergency and royal prerogative justified his action.[74]

The 1626 Parliament: Impeachment and Forced Loan

The 1626 Parliament immediately moved to impeach Buckingham. MPs catalogued his failures: military disasters, financial corruption, monopolizing royal favor, and giving bad counsel that endangered the realm. Charles tried to prevent the impeachment by removing parliamentary leaders from the Commons—making them sheriffs (which required residence in their counties during Parliament) or imprisoning them. When Parliament persisted, Charles dissolved it without receiving taxation.[75]

The Five Knights' Case (1627)

In 1627, Charles I demanded a forced loan from his subjects to fund an unpopular war against France. When five knights—Sir Thomas Darnel, Sir John Corbet, Sir Walter Earl, Sir John Heveningham, and Sir Edmund Hampden—refused to pay, they were imprisoned without charge. They petitioned for a writ of habeas corpus, demanding either release or formal charges they could answer.

The Crown's response alarmed Parliament and the legal community. The Attorney General argued that the King could imprison subjects "per speciale mandatum domini regis"—by special command of the King—without showing cause. The court declined to release the prisoners, accepting that royal prerogative permitted indefinite detention without stated charges.

The decision provoked a constitutional crisis. If the King could imprison subjects at will, without charge or trial, then no Englishman's liberty was secure. The case became a rallying point for parliamentary opposition and led directly to the Petition of Right (1628), which declared forced loans illegal and affirmed that no free man could be imprisoned without cause shown. Charles accepted the Petition—then ignored it. The unresolved tension between royal prerogative and subjects' liberties would fester for another decade before exploding into civil war.

The 1628 Parliament: Petition of Right

Charles needed Parliament again in 1628 to fund continuing wars (against France as well as Spain). MPs seized the opportunity to extract concessions. Led by Sir Edward Coke (the nation's foremost common lawyer) and John Pym, Parliament drafted the Petition of Right, listing grievances and demanding the King acknowledge subjects' rights:[78]

- No taxation without parliamentary consent
- No imprisonment without cause shown
- No billeting of soldiers in private homes
- No martial law in peacetime

Charles resisted, offering evasive responses. Parliament insisted on a clear answer. Finally, needing money desperately, Charles accepted the Petition of Right—though his acceptance was ambiguous about whether he was acknowledging pre-existing rights or merely granting a favor.[79]

But within months, Charles was violating the Petition's principles. He continued collecting tonnage and poundage without grant. When Parliament's 1629 session protested, Charles tried to adjourn the House. The Speaker, attempting to rise (which would end the session), was held in his chair by MPs who passed resolutions condemning religious innovations and illegal taxation. Charles dissolved Parliament in fury and arrested the leaders. He would not call Parliament again for eleven years.[80]

The Personal Rule, 1629-1640

Governing Without Parliament

Charles's "Personal Rule" (critics called it the "Eleven Years' Tyranny") demonstrated that England's monarchy could function without Parliament—barely. Charles avoided expensive wars, cut royal household costs, and exploited every legal (and quasi-legal) revenue source:[81]

Forest fines: Reviving medieval forest laws, Charles fined those who had encroached on ancient royal forests. Since forest boundaries hadn't been enforced for centuries, vast areas suddenly fell under forest law. The Earl of Salisbury was fined £20,000 for lands his family had held for generations.

Distraint of knighthood: An obsolete law required men with income over £40/year to take up knighthood. Charles fined those who hadn't—another anachronistic levy revived to raise money.

Ship Money: Traditionally, coastal counties paid for naval defense in wartime. Charles extended it to inland counties and collected it in peacetime (1634-1640), arguing that pirates threatened commerce and national defense required funding. Ship Money was legal under prerogative power, judges ruled, but it effectively created taxation without Parliament.[82]

John Hampden, a wealthy gentleman, refused Ship Money and became a test case (1637). His lawyers argued that taxation required parliamentary consent, that Ship Money was really a tax not a naval levy, and that the King was circumventing Parliament. Crown lawyers argued that emergency (pirates, foreign threats) justified prerogative taxation. The judges ruled 7-5 for the crown—Ship Money was legal. But the narrow margin and the widespread resentment showed that Charles's fiscal expedients were alienating the propertied classes whose support monarchy required.[83]

Laudian Enforcement

While Charles exploited prerogative for money, Laud exploited it for religious uniformity. He conducted metropolitical visitations (inspections) throughout England, requiring churches to:[84]

- Move communion tables to the east end and rail them as altars
- Bow at Jesus's name
- Use all prayer book ceremonies
- Suppress Puritan lecturers who preached without using full liturgy
- Maintain church buildings in good repair
- Ensure clergy wore proper vestments

Laud also enforced these requirements in Scotland—a catastrophic mistake. Charles had never understood Scotland. He assumed that as King of Scotland, he could govern its church as he governed England's. In 1637, he and Laud imposed a new prayer book on Scotland, modeled on England's but with even more ceremonial elaboration.[85]

The Scottish Revolt

When the new prayer book was first used at St. Giles Cathedral, Edinburgh (July 1637), riots erupted. Legend says Jenny Geddes, a market woman, threw her stool at the dean's head, shouting "Daur ye say Mass in my lug?" (How dare you say Mass in my ear?). Whether or not Jenny existed, the riot was real. Scots across the social spectrum—nobles, gentry, ministers, common people—rejected the prayer book as popish innovation.[86]

By early 1638, Scottish resistance had organized around the National Covenant—a document affirming Scotland's Presbyterian church government and rejecting Charles's innovations. Thousands signed, some in blood. The Covenanters (as they called themselves) weren't initially rebellious—they claimed loyalty to the King while resisting his religious policies. But when Charles refused compromise and prepared military force, Scotland prepared to resist.[87]

The Bishops' Wars and Financial Collapse

Charles's attempt to enforce conformity on Scotland militarily produced the Bishops' Wars (1639, 1640). England's army was poorly equipped, underpaid, and unmotivated—English soldiers had little desire to fight Scottish Protestants over bishops and prayer books. When the armies faced each other, Charles negotiated an inconclusive peace (1639).[88]

To raise money for a second campaign, Charles called the Short Parliament (April 1640). It lasted three weeks. MPs immediately raised eleven years of grievances: Ship Money, forest fines, Laudian innovations, imprisonment without trial. Charles demanded they vote taxation first, address grievances later. Parliament refused. Charles dissolved it.[89]

The second Bishops' War was even more disastrous. Scottish Covenanters invaded northern England, occupied Newcastle, and refused to leave until paid indemnity. Charles had no money, no army capable of dislodging them, and no choice but to call Parliament again. The Long Parliament, convening in November 1640, would sit (with interruptions) for twenty years and would destroy Charles's government, execute his ministers, try him for treason, and cut off his head.[90]

Why It Mattered

The Accumulated Tensions

By 1640, England had accumulated layers of conflict that made compromise nearly impossible:

Religious: Laudian Arminianism versus Puritan Calvinism; bishops versus potential presbyteries versus gathered churches; ceremony versus simplicity; uniformity versus liberty of conscience.

Constitutional: Royal prerogative versus parliamentary privilege; who controlled taxation, appointments, military; whether law constrained the King or the King was above law.

Financial: Crown's structural insolvency versus Parliament's control of taxation; subjects' resistance to novel levies versus monarchy's need for revenue.

Social: Traditional hierarchies challenged by commercial wealth, literacy, and religious conviction that valued godliness over birth; gentlemen and merchants wanting voice versus crown wanting deference.

Personality: Charles's rigidity, his conviction that any concession was weakness, his reliance on favorites (first Buckingham, then Laud and Strafford), his inability to compromise or read political situations accurately.[91]

The Irish and Scottish Dimensions

England's crisis cannot be understood in isolation. Charles ruled three kingdoms—England, Scotland, and Ireland—each with its own religious settlement, political culture, and relationship to the crown:

Scotland was presbyterian, proud of its independence, and fiercely Protestant. Charles's attempt to impose episcopal government and English liturgy violated the National Covenant (1638) and sparked resistance that Charles couldn't suppress militarily.

Ireland was majority Catholic, ruled by a Protestant minority (Anglican and Presbyterian), and deeply resented English conquest and settlement. Thomas Wentworth, Earl of Strafford, governed Ireland 1633-1640 with harsh efficiency, raising money and troops for Charles while alienating all factions. When rebellion erupted in Ireland (1641), it fed English fears of Catholic massacre and made compromise with Charles—who was suspected of planning to use Irish Catholic troops against English Protestants—impossible.[92]

Charles's inability to manage his multiple kingdoms, his insistence on religious uniformity across different cultures, and his provocation of the Scots created the crisis that forced him to call Parliament and set England on the path to civil war.

The Long Fuse Finally Lit

The "long fuse" of this chapter's title stretched from Elizabeth's incomplete settlement through James's conflicts with Puritans and Parliament to Charles's disasters of the 1630s. Each monarch kicked problems down the road, patched over contradictions, and hoped their successor would manage tensions they couldn't resolve.

But accumulated tensions don't disappear. They fester. And when crisis comes—in this case, Scottish invasion and Irish rebellion—the accumulated weight of unresolved conflicts produces not adjustment but explosion.

The Long Parliament, meeting in November 1640, began with apparent unity. MPs across the spectrum agreed: Laud's innovations must be reversed, Ship Money was illegal, forced loans were tyranny, Strafford must be punished. The question was how far reformation would go. Would Parliament stop at removing evil counselors and returning to Elizabethan norms? Or would it seize the opportunity for root-and-branch reform of church and state?[93]

That question would split Parliament into factions, produce civil war, and ultimately destroy the monarchy—temporarily. But before examining the war itself, we must understand the coalitions that fought it and the visions that motivated them. To that story—of how crisis produced opportunity, how reformation became revolution, and how England's civil wars began—we now turn.

When the Long Parliament convened in November 1640, Members came to Westminster with eleven years of grievances and high hopes for reformation. The King's minister Strafford and Archbishop Laud would be called to account. Illegal taxes would be abolished. The church would be purified. England would be set right. What no one expected was that within two years, England would be at war with itself, that within nine years the King would be beheaded, and that within twenty years the religious and political landscape would be transformed beyond recognition. To understand how it happened, we must see how unity in opposition gave way to division over what should replace the old order.

CHAPTER 2 — THE KING'S WAR

FROM PETITION TO SWORD, 1640-1646

Edge Hill, Warwickshire, 23 October 1642

The morning fog lifted slowly from the Warwickshire plain, revealing what no Englishman had seen in living memory: two English armies, banners flying and pikes bristling, preparing to kill each other. From his position on Edge Hill's summit, King Charles I surveyed the parliamentary forces assembling below. They had marched through the night to block his advance on London, and now they stood between him and his capital—perhaps 14,000 men, mostly infantry with cavalry on the flanks, commanded by the Earl of Essex who had once been Charles's own Lord Chamberlain.[1]

Charles's army numbered perhaps 13,000, arrayed along the ridge. Prince Rupert of the Rhine, the King's twenty-three-year-old nephew and cavalry commander, was eager to charge. The day was Sunday—some ministers with the royal army had suggested delaying battle until Monday, respecting the Sabbath. But military necessity trumped piety. If Essex's army escaped, it could fortify London's approaches and make the King's position impossible. The battle must be fought today.[2]

Neither side wanted this. For eighteen months since the Long Parliament convened, both King and Parliament had maneuvered, negotiated, and hoped to avoid war. They had executed the King's chief minister (Strafford), imprisoned his Archbishop (Laud), abolished his hated taxes (Ship Money), and dismantled eleven years of Personal Rule. They had argued over control of the militia, over church government, over who counseled the King and who would suppress the Irish Rebellion that had erupted in October 1641. They had issued declarations and counter-declarations, each claiming to defend England's ancient constitution while accusing the other of innovation and tyranny.[3]

But words had failed. In August 1642, Charles had raised his royal standard at Nottingham, declaring his subjects to be in rebellion and calling loyal men to arms. Parliament had claimed it fought not against the King but against his "evil counselors" who had misled him, a legal fiction that allowed Parliament to take up arms without committing treason. Now, on this October Sunday morning, the fiction was about to be tested with steel.[4]

The Armies Face Each Other

Robert Devereux, Earl of Essex, had not wanted this command. A nobleman of ancient lineage, he had served Charles loyally until the crisis forced him to choose sides. He chose Parliament because he believed Charles had fallen under evil counsel, because he feared popery and arbitrary government, and because his honor required him to defend the Protestant religion and English liberties. But he had no desire to kill the King or to destroy monarchy. He sought to bring Charles to reason, to restore him to his Parliament, to preserve what could be preserved of the old order.[5]

Essex's soldiers were a mixture: the trained bands from London and surrounding counties (citizen militia, shopkeepers and craftsmen in armor for the day), hastily raised regiments of volunteers, and some experienced officers who had fought in continental wars. Most had never seen battle. They carried pikes (eighteen-foot poles with steel points), muskets (heavy matchlock firearms that required rests to fire), and faith that God defended the righteous. Their banners proclaimed slogans: "For God, Parliament, and the Protestant Religion." Many wore orange scarves or ribbons, the color of Parliament's cause.[6]

On the ridge above, the royalist army was similarly mixed but included more cavalry—the aristocracy and gentry had horses and knew how to fight from horseback. Prince Rupert commanded three cavalry regiments on the right wing, his brother Prince Maurice commanded cavalry on the left. In the center stood infantry: pikemen in the front ranks, musketeers behind, and the King's Lifeguard of Foot—gentleman volunteers who had rallied to Charles at Nottingham. The royal banners displayed the King's arms and mottos proclaiming his sacred majesty. Royalists wore red scarves or ribbons—the King's color.[7]

Both armies included ministers to pray with the troops and assure them of God's favor. Dr. Henry Hammond preached to royalist soldiers that they defended lawful authority against rebellion—that to fight Parliament's unlawful army was to serve God by upholding the powers ordained by Him. On the parliamentary side, chaplains preached that they fought the Lord's battles against popish plotters and tyrannical counselors, that to preserve Parliament and Protestant religion was to do God's work though it meant drawing swords against the King's misguided forces.[8]

Each side believed God was with them. Both were about to discover that God permits men to kill each other regardless of how they justify their cause.

The Cavalry Charges

At one o'clock in the afternoon, Prince Rupert's cavalry charged down the hill at full gallop, three regiments of horse thundering toward the parliamentary left wing. The sound, hundreds of hooves pounding the earth, men shouting, trumpets blaring, was terrifying. The parliamentary cavalry, mostly inexperienced gentlemen and their servants, fired pistols ineffectually and then broke. Some stood and fought; most fled. Rupert's cavaliers pursued them for miles, cutting down stragglers and plundering the parliamentary baggage train.[9]

On the other flank, Prince Maurice's cavalry achieved similar success, routing the parliamentary right wing. Within thirty minutes, both of Essex's cavalry wings had disintegrated, leaving his infantry exposed. The royal cavalry had won the flanks decisively. If Rupert and Maurice had rallied and returned to attack Essex's infantry from behind, the battle might have ended in complete royalist victory.[10]

But cavalry that has charged successfully is hard to stop. Rupert's troopers, scattered across the countryside pursuing fleeing enemies and looting baggage, couldn't be quickly recalled. The cavalry that should have been delivering the killing blow to Essex's army was miles away, out of control, celebrating premature victory.

The Infantry Fight

In the center, the infantry closed. This was the brutal, grinding work of 17th-century warfare: pike blocks pushing against each other like rugby scrums, men shoving and stabbing with eighteen-foot poles; musketeers firing point-blank into enemy formations, then clubbing with musket butts when powder ran out; men falling with wounds from pike thrusts, musket balls, or sword cuts; screaming, cursing, praying.[11]

The King's infantry had the advantage of higher ground, but Essex's infantry were stubborn. The London trained bands, fighting for their homes and livelihoods, held their ground. For two hours the infantry battle swayed back and forth. Men who that morning had never killed found themselves stabbing neighbors—for these were not foreign enemies but fellow Englishmen, sometimes former friends or distant relatives, divided by politics and religion but speaking the same language and praying to the same God.[12]

Gradually, the royalist infantry pushed Essex's center back. Sir Edmund Verney, the King's standard-bearer, fell fighting. The royal standard, the sacred banner that represented the King's authority, was captured. If the royal standard fell, it was thought, the King's cause fell with it. Charles's men fought desperately to recapture it. In the melee, Verney's hand, still gripping the standard's pole, had to be cut off to retrieve it. The standard changed hands several times before royalists finally secured it.[13]

As afternoon turned to dusk, both armies were exhausted and disorganized. Rupert's cavalry finally returned but too late to affect the outcome. Essex's army had been badly mauled but hadn't broken. Both sides held parts of the field. As darkness fell, soldiers from both armies lay mixed together on the cold ground, wounded, dying, calling for water or for mothers. The living built fires and tried to sleep, knowing that morning would bring either renewed battle or acknowledgment that neither side had won.[14]

The Morning After

Dawn revealed the horror. Bodies lay scattered across the field and along the roads where Rupert's cavalry had pursued. Perhaps 1,500 men were dead; another 2,000 to 3,000 were wounded, many mortally. Soldiers from both sides picked through the corpses, looking for friends or relatives, stripping the dead of anything valuable (bodies were stripped naked, armor, clothes, shoes, and weapons were all too valuable to waste on the dead).[15]

Neither commander wanted to resume fighting. Essex's army had been badly shaken, but it still existed and blocked the road to London. Charles's army had failed to destroy Essex's force, and the King lacked the resources for a siege of London even if he could reach it. By unspoken consent, both armies disengaged. Essex marched toward London; Charles moved to Oxford, which would become his headquarters for the rest of the war.[16]

The battle of Edgehill was a draw in military terms but a strategic victory for Parliament. The King had failed to destroy the parliamentary army or to march triumphantly into London. The war would continue—not the swift, decisive campaign both sides had expected, but a long, grinding conflict that would last four more years and cost hundreds of thousands of lives.

What Both Sides Learned

The battle taught hard lessons:

First, this would not be a short war. Both sides had assumed that one battle would decide the matter—the righteous side would win, the other would collapse, and England would return to peace. Edgehill proved that assumption wrong. Men would fight and die for both causes. Victory would require not one battle but years of campaigning.

Second, enthusiasm was not enough. Both armies had discovered that inexperienced troops—no matter how motivated—could not stand against determined opposition without training and discipline. Parliament would eventually build the New Model Army with professional training and meritocratic promotion. The King would struggle to match it, relying on aristocratic leadership and regional levies that could seldom be fully integrated.

Third, the war was truly civil. These were not foreign invaders or religious crusaders from abroad but Englishmen killing Englishmen. Families were divided, sons fought fathers, brothers fought brothers. The Verney family exemplified this: Sir Edmund Verney (who died carrying the King's standard at Edgehill) had a son, Ralph, who fought for Parliament. Neither wanted to fight the other; circumstance and conscience forced them to opposite sides. Such divisions ran throughout England.[17]

Fourth, God's will was ambiguous. Both sides had expected divine intervention, that God would show by victory which cause was righteous. The battle's inconclusiveness troubled both. Royalist preachers claimed that God was testing their faithfulness; parliamentary preachers claimed that God was teaching them to trust in discipline rather than righteousness alone. Both interpretations allowed the war to continue while preserving belief in divine providence.[18]

As soldiers buried the dead in mass graves near Radway village, they could hear church bells from nearby parishes. It was Sunday evening, and some churches still held services despite the battle. The bells rang as they always had, marking the hours of worship, calling the living to prayer. But the world those bells rang in had changed forever. England was at war with itself, and no one knew how or when it would end.

To understand how England reached Edgehill, how the unity of November 1640 fractured into civil war by October 1642, we must trace the Long Parliament's first two years: from the initial consensus that Strafford and Laud must fall, through the constitutional innovations of 1641, to the breakdown over church government and control of the militia that made war inevitable.

The Long Parliament's First Year

From Unity to Fracture, November 1640-December 1641

The Fall of Strafford and Laud

Strafford's Return and Arrest

When the Long Parliament convened on 3 November 1640, Thomas Wentworth, Earl of Strafford, was Charles's most powerful minister. As Lord Lieutenant of Ireland (1633-1640), he had governed with efficiency and ruthlessness, raising money and troops for the King while alienating all Irish factions, Catholic Old English, Protestant New English, and Gaelic Irish alike. His policy of royal authority overriding local privileges had succeeded in Ireland, and Charles had recalled him to apply the same methods in England.[19]

But Strafford's effectiveness made him dangerous. Parliamentary leaders, especially John Pym, feared he would use the Irish army he had raised to suppress English liberties. Rumors spread that Strafford had advised Charles to bring Irish Catholic troops to England to crush Parliament. The rumors were exaggerated, Strafford had discussed using the Irish army against the Scots, not against England, but plausibility mattered more than accuracy.[20]

On 11 November, just eight days into the Parliament, Pym rose in the House of Commons to impeach Strafford for treason. The charges were comprehensive: subverting laws, raising arbitrary taxes in Ireland, counseling the use of Irish army against English subjects, and conspiring to alter the fundamental government. Strafford was arrested and imprisoned in the Tower of London. Charles protested but lacked the power to protect his minister.[21]

The impeachment trial began in March 1641 in Westminster Hall. Strafford defended himself brilliantly, arguing that his actions in Ireland were legal under Irish law, that he had never counseled using the Irish army against England, and that even if he had given bad advice (which he denied), bad counsel was not treason. The impeachment appeared to be failing, the House of Lords seemed likely to acquit or at least to impose a lesser punishment than execution.[22]

The Bill of Attainder

Pym changed tactics. He introduced a Bill of Attainder, a legislative act declaring Strafford guilty without trial. This was constitutionally questionable but politically effective. The Commons passed it quickly. The Lords, under pressure from London mobs that surrounded Westminster shouting for Strafford's death, passed it narrowly.[23]

Charles faced an agonizing choice. Strafford was his loyal servant who had sacrificed everything for royal authority. To sign the bill was betrayal. But Charles also feared for his family's safety, mobs surrounded the palace, and he had no military force to protect his wife and children. On 10 May 1641, Charles signed the bill of attainder, condemning Strafford to death. He would later call it the greatest sin of his life and claim that God punished him with execution for having executed Strafford.[24]

Strafford was beheaded on Tower Hill on 12 May 1641, before a crowd estimated at 100,000. He died with dignity, forgiving his enemies and proclaiming his loyalty to the King. His execution satisfied Parliament's demand for vengeance but solved nothing. Charles never forgave those who had forced him to sacrifice his minister, and he never trusted Parliament again.[25]

Laud Imprisoned

Archbishop William Laud had been impeached in December 1640 and imprisoned in the Tower. Unlike Strafford, Laud was not immediately executed, he had no army behind him, and he posed no military threat. But his religious policies made him almost as hated as Strafford. MPs cataloged his "innovations": moving communion tables, bowing toward altars, persecuting Puritan ministers, attempting to impose the prayer book on Scotland.[26]

Laud's imprisonment effectively ended his authority over the church. Bishops' power collapsed as Parliament dismantled the ecclesiastical courts that had enforced conformity. The Court of High Commission, Laud's tool for prosecuting nonconformity, was abolished by statute in 1641. Church discipline, which had depended on episcopal authority backed by courts, simply ceased in many areas. This created both opportunity (for Presbyterian and Independent experiments) and anxiety (about religious chaos).[27]

Laud would remain in the Tower until 1645, when Parliament finally executed him—not for what he had done but for what he represented: the episcopal system and ceremonial religion that Parliament was determined to uproot.

Constitutional Revolution, 1641

The Triennial Act

In February 1641, Parliament passed and Charles reluctantly signed the Triennial Act: Parliament must meet at least once every three years, whether the King summoned it or not. If the King failed to summon Parliament within three years, officials (and eventually the peers themselves) were empowered to do so. This addressed Charles's eleven-year Personal Rule by ensuring Parliament would exist regardless of royal preference.[28]

The act was revolutionary. For centuries, summoning Parliament had been the King's prerogative. Now, statute required it. Charles signed because he needed Parliament's money and support against the Scots, but the act fundamentally altered the constitutional balance. The crown could no longer govern without Parliament indefinitely.

Abolition of Prerogative Courts

Parliament also abolished the courts that had enforced royal prerogative: the Court of Star Chamber (which had prosecuted cases involving the King's interests), the Court of High Commission (ecclesiastical court), the regional Councils of the North and Wales (which had extended royal authority into the peripheries), and various smaller prerogative courts.[29]

These courts had been useful tools of royal governance but also sources of abuse. Star Chamber had imposed savage punishments (cropping ears, branding faces) on the King's critics. The High Commission had prosecuted religious nonconformity. The regional councils had overridden local privileges. Their abolition was popular even among royalists who had suffered from arbitrary punishment or excessive fines.[30]

But abolishing these courts created a problem: how would the crown enforce its will? The remaining common law courts followed established precedents and procedures that limited royal discretion. Without prerogative courts, the King's ability to respond to emergencies or to bypass local obstruction was severely limited. Parliament was dismantling the machinery of Personal Rule without replacing it with anything except parliamentary oversight, which required Parliament to be in session continuously, something unprecedented in English history.

Taxation and Fiscal Reform

Parliament also addressed Charles's fiscal expedients:

- **Ship Money** declared illegal
- **Forest fines** abolished
- **Distraint of knighthood** ended
- **Monopolies** abolished (again—they had been declared illegal in James I's reign but revived under Charles)
- **Tonnage and poundage** required parliamentary grant[31]

These reforms were popular and largely uncontroversial. Even royalists admitted that Ship Money and forest fines had been oppressive. But eliminating these revenue sources left the crown financially dependent on Parliament—unable to govern independently even if Parliament allowed it.

Parliament granted some taxation but conditioned it on reforms. Charles signed bills abolishing his revenue sources because he desperately needed Scotland's army out of northern England (they still occupied Newcastle and demanded payment before withdrawing) and he needed Parliament's help to suppress the Irish Rebellion that erupted in October 1641.[32]

By summer 1641, Charles had lost almost all his independent governing capacity. He could not summon or dissolve Parliament at will (Triennial Act), he could not enforce his will through prerogative courts (abolished), he could not raise money independently (illegal taxation abolished), and he had to accept Parliament's choice of counselors (Strafford and Laud gone, replaced by men

Parliament trusted). Constitutional monarchy, in the sense of a king limited by law and Parliament, had emerged, though neither Charles nor Parliament fully recognized what had happened.

The Irish Rebellion and Its Consequences

October 1641: Ireland Erupts

The Irish Rebellion that began in October 1641 was England's worst nightmare made real. Irish Catholics, frustrated by decades of English Protestant settlement, discrimination, and Strafford's oppressive government, rose to expel English and Scottish planters from Ulster and reclaim confiscated lands.[33]

The rebellion's violence was real but exaggerated in English reports. Some thousands of Protestants died, killed in attacks, driven from homes in winter to die of exposure, or caught in the breakdown of order. But English pamphlets claimed tens of thousands or even hundreds of thousands murdered, with lurid details of Catholic atrocities: priests leading massacres, women and children killed, Protestant Bibles burned, and victims forced to choose between death and conversion to Catholicism.[34]

The exaggerations served political purposes. Puritans in Parliament used reports of Irish Catholic massacres to argue that popery was inherently murderous, that England faced similar danger if Catholics gained influence, and that the Queen's Catholic chapel at court was a fifth column waiting to strike. Charles's alleged sympathy for Catholics (based on his Catholic wife, his ceremonial church policies, and Laud's seeming accommodation with Rome) became evidence that he might be complicit in Catholic conspiracy against Protestant England.[35]

The Militia Ordinance Crisis

The Irish Rebellion required military response, an army must be raised and sent to suppress the revolt. But who would control that army? Parliament feared that if Charles commanded an army raised to fight Irish Catholics, he might instead turn it against Parliament. Charles insisted that command of military forces was the crown's prerogative—to deny it was to deny his kingship.[36]

In February-March 1642, Parliament passed the Militia Ordinance, claiming authority to appoint military commanders without royal assent. Charles refused to accept it. Parliament insisted that emergency (the Irish Rebellion, threats to the realm) justified this extraordinary measure. The King countered that Parliament's claim to control the militia was rebellion disguised as law.[37]

The militia question revealed the fundamental constitutional impasse: In cases where King and Parliament disagreed about what the realm's safety required, whose judgment prevailed? The old answer, the King's, was precisely what Parliament now rejected. But the new answer, Parliament's, required accepting that subjects could override the King, which royalists saw as destroying monarchy itself.[38]

Alongside the militia question came the church question: How should England's church be governed and reformed? This would prove even more divisive, splitting Parliament's own coalition and making civil war inevitable. To that question, and to the factions it produced, we now turn.

The Religious Crisis and Parliamentary Factions

Bishops, Presbyteries, and the Fracturing of Unity

The Root and Branch Petition

December 1640: London's Demand

On 11 December 1640, just weeks after Parliament convened, London citizens presented a petition with 15,000 signatures demanding "root and branch" reform of the church. The petition called for abolition of episcopacy itself, not merely reform of bishops' powers but elimination of the office. In its place, the petitioners wanted some other form of church government (implicitly presbyterian, though the petition didn't specify).[39]

The Root and Branch Petition reflected years of accumulated resentment against Laud's innovations, episcopal arrogance, and church courts' oppression. It argued that bishops were: [40]

- Unscriptural (the New Testament prescribed elders, not bishops with coercive power)
- Corrupt (wealthy, worldly, more concerned with power than piety)
- Tyrants (using church courts to persecute godly ministers and laity)
- Obstacles to reform (blocking efforts to purify worship and improve ministry)
- Causes of the current crisis (Laud's policies had provoked Scottish rebellion)

The petition demanded that Parliament abolish episcopacy and establish a new church government "according to God's Word"—a vague phrase that allowed both moderate reformers and radical Puritans to support it while meaning different things.

Parliamentary Division

The Root and Branch Petition divided Parliament. Some MPs enthusiastically supported it, abolishing bishops would complete the Protestant Reformation and establish godly discipline. Others, including many who had opposed Charles's policies, thought abolishing episcopacy too radical, reform bishops' powers, limit their wealth, make them accountable to clergy councils, but don't destroy an ancient office that provided order and continuity.[41]

The division wasn't simply between pro- and anti-bishop factions. It reflected deeper questions:[42]

- Could the church be reformed gradually, or did it require wholesale reconstruction?
- Were bishops' problems due to bad bishops (like Laud) or to episcopacy itself?
- What would replace bishops? Would presbyteries be better or worse?
- Was religious uniformity necessary, or could England tolerate some diversity?

Edward Dering's Speech (exemplifying moderate position) argued:[43]

I desire as much as any man the reformation of the church, but I desire we may not destroy what is good while we are removing what is bad. Bishops have been abused; let us reform the abuse. But to pull down an ancient order because recent bishops misused it is like burning the house to roast the pig.

Edmund Calamy's Sermon (exemplifying radical position) preached to the Commons:[44]

God commands not that we reform episcopacy but that we establish His own order. The question is not whether these bishops or better bishops, but whether bishops at all are according to God's Word. If Scripture prescribes presbyteries, human tradition cannot justify diocesans.

The debate revealed that the parliamentary coalition which had united against Strafford and Laud was fracturing over what should replace them. Constitutional reforms were relatively easy to agree on, no one defended the Star Chamber or Ship Money. But religious reform cut deeper, touching theology, ecclesiology, and social order itself.

The Grand Remonstrance

November 1641: Pym's Gambit

By November 1641, John Pym feared the parliamentary coalition was dissolving. Some MPs thought enough had been achieved, Strafford was dead, Laud was imprisoned, prerogative courts and illegal taxes were abolished, Parliament's existence was secured. Time to reach accommodation with the King and restore normal government.[45]

Pym disagreed. He believed Charles was unreformed, that evil counselors still influenced him (especially the Queen and her Catholic circle), and that the King was plotting to use the army being raised for Ireland against Parliament instead. To maintain parliamentary unity and popular support, Pym pushed through the Grand Remonstrance, a massive document (over 200 clauses) cataloging all Charles's misgovernment since 1625 and demanding further reforms.[46]

The Remonstrance was both history and manifesto. It listed:[47]

- Charles's promotion of Arminians (as if they were crypto-Catholics)
- Laud's ceremonial innovations (as if they were steps toward Rome)
- Ship Money and other illegal taxes (as tyranny)
- Dissolution of Parliaments (as violation of subjects' rights)
- Attempt to impose prayer book on Scotland (as cause of rebellion)
- Irish Rebellion (as result of Charles's Catholic sympathies and bad government)

The Remonstrance demanded that Charles employ only counselors Parliament approved, that church reform proceed toward abolishing episcopacy and establishing presbyterian government, and that Parliament control the militia. These demands went far beyond what many MPs had envisioned in 1640.

The All-Night Debate

The Grand Remonstrance was debated on 22 November 1641, from early afternoon until past midnight. The House was packed, the atmosphere tense, the debate passionate. Some speeches defended the Remonstrance as necessary to preserve liberties and religion. Others attacked it as inflammatory, unprecedented, and likely to provoke rather than prevent conflict.[48]

Sir Edward Dering (who had earlier expressed ambivalence about bishops) opposed the Remonstrance: "When I first heard of a Remonstrance, I presently imagined that like faithful counselors we should hold up a glass unto his Majesty... I did not dream that we should remonstrate downward, tell stories to the people, and talk of the King as of a third person." Publishing grievances to the people, Dering argued, would inflame popular passions and undermine the King's authority.[49]

Oliver Cromwell, sitting in his first Parliament at age forty-one, defended the Remonstrance. He argued that the King's continued promotion of Arminians and toleration of popery around the Queen required Parliament to take extraordinary measures. "If the Remonstrance had been rejected," Cromwell reportedly said later, "I would have sold all I had the next morning and never seen England more." He saw the Remonstrance as a test of Parliament's resolve.[50]

The vote, taken after midnight, was extremely close: 159 for, 148 against. Eleven votes decided it. Some MPs tried to block having the division (vote count) recorded, they didn't want the King to know how narrowly the Remonstrance passed or who had voted against it. This led to shouting, threats, and hands on sword hilts. Members nearly came to blows in the chamber. The Speaker had to restore order by threatening to leave his chair (which would end the session).[51]

The Grand Remonstrance's passage and narrow margin revealed that Parliament was dividing. About half thought it had gone far enough; the other half wanted further reformation. The division roughly tracked religious views: those wanting presbyterian reform supported the Remonstrance; those wanting moderate episcopal reform opposed it. But it wasn't perfectly aligned—some moderates supported Pym from fear of Catholic plots, while some radicals opposed the Remonstrance as not going far enough.[52]

The Five Members and the Slide to War

January 1642: Charles's Coup Attempt

We opened this book with Charles's attempt to arrest five members of Parliament in January 1642 (the scene that opens the Introduction). Here we see it in context: Charles acted because he believed Pym and his allies were conspiring with the Scots, preparing to impeach the Queen, and planning to seize control of government entirely. The Grand Remonstrance, published and distributed to the people, seemed to Charles an attempt to turn his subjects against him. The five members—Pym, Hampden, Holles, Haselrig, and Strode, were the core of parliamentary opposition, and Charles thought removing them would restore his authority.[53]

The attempt failed catastrophically. The five members were warned and escaped. Charles's entry into the Commons with armed men violated parliamentary privilege and confirmed parliamentary fears that the King would use force against them. Within days, Charles left London, which he would not reenter except as prisoner.[54]

The five members' return to Parliament in triumph (escorted by thousands of armed Londoners) showed where the capital's loyalty lay. London's trained bands, its militia, its financial resources, and its symbolic importance all favored Parliament. Charles had lost his capital, and with it much of his ability to govern or to wage war effectively.

The Nineteen Propositions and Final Break

In June 1642, Parliament sent Charles the Nineteen Propositions—demands that would have reduced him to a figurehead:[55]

- Parliament to approve all privy counselors and major officials
- Parliament to control military forces
- Parliament to control the education and marriages of the King's children
- Episcopal church government to be "reformed" by Parliament (implicitly abolishing bishops)
- Catholic clergy to be expelled, including the Queen's priests
- Parliament's legislation to be valid even without royal assent

Charles's answer was defiant. In *His Majesty's Answer to the Nineteen Propositions*, Charles (or his advisors) articulated a theory of mixed government: England's constitution balanced monarchy (the King), aristocracy (the House of Lords), and democracy (the House of Commons). Each checked the others' excesses. The Nineteen Propositions would destroy this balance, making Parliament supreme and reducing the King to nothing. "This would be a total subversion of the fundamental laws and that excellent constitution of this kingdom," Charles wrote.[56]

The Answer was actually too sophisticated, it admitted that England's government was "mixed" rather than purely monarchical, which contradicted Charles's own claims to absolute prerogative. But it crystallized the issue: Parliament wanted to control the King; Charles insisted that monarchy required independent executive power. Neither would yield.

By August 1642, both sides were raising armies. Charles issued Commissions of Array, calling subjects to arms in defense of lawful authority. Parliament issued the Militia Ordinance, claiming authority to appoint commanders and raise forces. Local communities divided, some supported the King, others Parliament, many tried to remain neutral but were forced by circumstance to choose. England's civil war had begun, and it would not end until either King or Parliament was destroyed.

The First Civil War, 1642-1646

From Stalemate to the New Model Army

The Geography and Sociology of Division

Which Regions Supported Which Side?

England's division in 1642 followed rough patterns, though no region was uniformly royalist or parliamentarian:

Royalist Strength:[57]

- **The North and West**: Yorkshire (except Hull and Bradford), Lancashire (except Manchester), Cheshire, Cornwall, Devon—regions with traditional social structures, strong gentry leadership, and distance from London's commercial culture
- **Rural areas**: Agricultural regions where gentry influence was strong and traditional deference persisted
- **Cathedral cities**: Oxford, Chester, York—places where bishops and cathedral clergy influenced opinion and where ceremonial worship had adherents
- **The royal household and court**: Aristocracy with personal ties to Charles, those who had benefited from royal patronage, and those who believed in divine right monarchy

Parliamentary Strength:[58]

- **London and the Southeast**: The capital, Home Counties, East Anglia—commercially developed, Puritan-influenced, suspicious of court culture
- **Port cities and market towns**: Bristol (contested), Hull, Plymouth—places engaged in trade, with merchant classes sympathetic to Parliament's defense of commercial rights
- **The cloth-producing regions**: East Anglia, parts of the West Country—areas with proto-industrial development and Puritan preaching
- **Scotland**: The Covenanters allied with Parliament in 1643, seeing Charles as a threat to Presbyterian church government

Neutralism: Many, perhaps most, ordinary English people wanted neither side to win if it meant their side losing—they wanted peace, normal harvests, and freedom from plundering armies. "Clubmen" movements emerged in various regions, armed bands of locals who tried to keep both armies out of their areas. They were usually suppressed by whichever army was stronger in their region.[59]

Social and Economic Divisions

The conflict also tracked social and economic lines, though imperfectly:

Royalists tended to be:

- Aristocracy and greater gentry (titled nobility, large landowners)
- Those whose status came from traditional sources (birth, royal favor, land)
- Anglicans who valued liturgical worship and episcopal order
- Those suspicious of commerce and hostile to social mobility
- Rural populations following their social superiors

Parliamentarians tended to be:[60]

- Middling gentry, merchants, professionals (lawyers), and substantial yeomen
- Those whose wealth came from trade, industry, or professional services
- Puritans who valued preaching, godly discipline, and Reformed theology
- Urban populations with commercial interests and literacy
- Those who saw opportunity in social mobility and resented aristocratic privilege

But these patterns had many exceptions. Some great nobles supported Parliament (Essex, Manchester, Warwick). Some lesser gentry supported the King. Some commercial towns (Newcastle) were royalist. Some agricultural regions (East Anglia) were parliamentarian. Family, religion, personal grudges, and accident all influenced choices.

The Verney family again exemplifies the complexity. Sir Edmund Verney fought and died for the King at Edgehill despite privately doubting Charles's wisdom. His son Ralph fought for Parliament despite personal affection for his father. Ralph's brother Mun fought for the King. Their choices reflected genuine conscience, family pressure, and the impossibility of remaining neutral once war began.[61]

The War's Course, 1642-1644

Initial Stalemate, 1642-1643

After Edgehill's indecisive result (October 1642), the war settled into regional campaigns, sieges, and skirmishes. Neither side could deliver a knockout blow:

Royalist advantages:[62]

- Better cavalry: aristocrats and gentry knew horsemanship; Prince Rupert was a brilliant cavalry commander
- Interior lines: Oxford as headquarters allowed Charles to shift forces to threatened regions more easily than Parliament
- Welsh support: Wales was predominantly royalist, providing recruits and safe territory

Parliamentary advantages:[63]

- London: control of the capital meant money (customs revenues, loans from merchants), supplies, and symbolic legitimacy
- Navy: the fleet sided with Parliament, controlling coasts and preventing foreign aid to royalists
- Scotland: potential alliance with Covenanters would bring a large, experienced army

The year 1643 saw mixed fortunes. Royalists won significant victories:

- **Roundway Down (July 1643)**: Royalist cavalry crushed a parliamentary army in Wiltshire
- **Bristol captured (July 1643)**: Prince Rupert took England's second

city, giving royalists a major port

- **First Battle of Newbury (September 1643)**: Though technically inconclusive, it prevented Parliament from threatening Oxford[64]

But Parliament held London and the economically crucial Southeast. More importantly, Parliament opened negotiations with Scotland that would change the war's balance.

The Solemn League and Covenant, 1643

In September 1643, English Parliament and Scottish Covenanters signed the Solemn League and Covenant. Scotland agreed to send an army to fight alongside Parliament. Parliament agreed to reform England's church "according to the Word of God and the example of the best reformed churches"—language that Scots understood to mean presbyterian government but that English Independents interpreted more flexibly.[65]

The Covenant required subscribers to swear to:[66]

- Preserve the Reformed religion in Scotland
- Reform religion in England and Ireland "according to the Word of God"
- Extirpate (root out) popery and prelacy (bishops)
- Preserve Parliament's and King's authority (in proper balance)
- Preserve peace between the kingdoms

The religious clauses were deliberately ambiguous. Scottish commissioners wanted explicit commitment to presbyterian government; English Independents wanted flexibility for gathered churches. The compromise wording allowed both to sign while meaning different things, a formula that would create problems later.

Militarily, the Covenant was crucial. In January 1644, a Scottish army of about 20,000 men crossed into northern England under the Earl of Leven. They besieged Newcastle (capturing it in October 1644), tying down royalist forces that might otherwise have reinforced Charles's main armies. The Scottish intervention essentially made the war unwinnable for Charles unless he could defeat both Parliament and Scotland simultaneously.[67]

The Covenant also had religious consequences: Parliament established the Westminster Assembly of Divines (July 1643) to advise on church reform. The Assembly, meeting in Westminster Abbey's Jerusalem Chamber, included about 120 ministers plus parliamentary commissioners. Its task was to replace the Thirty-Nine Articles and Book of Common Prayer with new standards reflecting Reformed theology and (presumably) presbyterian government. The Assembly would meet for five years, producing the Westminster Confession (Presbyterian creedal statement), catechisms, and a proposed church government. But its implementation would be overtaken by events—by the time the Assembly finished its work, the Independent Army had become too powerful to accept presbyterian uniformity.[68]

Marston Moor and the Changing War

July 1644: The Decisive Battle

On 2 July 1644, the largest battle of the civil war was fought on Marston Moor, near York. A combined Scottish-parliamentary army (about 27,000 men) faced a royalist army under Prince Rupert (about 18,000 men). The stakes were control of northern England, if the royalists won, they could drive the Scots back and possibly threaten Parliament's eastern strongholds. If Parliament and the Scots won, royalist power in the north would be broken.[69]

The battle began late in the evening. The allied army attacked just as royalists were standing down for the night, achieving surprise. Rupert's cavalry, usually devastating, found themselves disorganized. On the allied left wing, Oliver Cromwell commanded cavalry regiments from the Eastern Association (Parliament's forces in East Anglia). These troops were different from the usual parliamentary cavalry, they were disciplined, trained to rally after charging, and led by godly officers who maintained order.[70]

Cromwell's cavalry broke the royalist right wing, then rallied and wheeled to attack the royalist center from behind—something cavalry rarely managed to do. The combination of discipline and tactical flexibility was revolutionary. Meanwhile, Scottish infantry pushed forward in the center, and though they took heavy casualties, they held together while royalist infantry broke.[71]

The battle was a crushing royalist defeat. Prince Rupert fled the field (leading to his lifelong nickname "Rupert the Devil"). York surrendered within weeks. The Marquess of Newcastle, who had commanded royalist forces in the north, went into exile on the Continent. Royalist power north of the Midlands was destroyed. Parliament and the Scots now controlled the north, and Charles's strategic position had deteriorated decisively.[72]

Cromwell's Emergence

Oliver Cromwell came to national attention at Marston Moor. He had been a minor gentleman (though related to Thomas Cromwell, Henry VIII's minister), a relatively obscure MP in the Long Parliament, and a cavalry commander in the Eastern Association. But his performance at Marston Moor—his cavalry's discipline, their ability to rally and return to battle, their decisive charge—marked him as an exceptional military leader.[73]

Cromwell had strong views about military organization. He believed:[74]

- **Godliness mattered**: Officers should be chosen for piety and ability, not birth or wealth. "I had rather have a plain russet-coated captain that knows what he fights for and loves what he knows, than that which you call a gentleman and is nothing else."
- **Discipline was essential**: Cavalry must be trained to rally after charging, to obey orders, to function as units rather than as individual glory-seekers
- **Meritocracy produced results**: Promoting men based on performance, not social status, created effective armies
- **Religious motivation**: Soldiers who believed they fought for God's cause, who prayed together and discussed Scripture, would endure hardships that mercenaries or pressed men would not

These principles informed the New Model Army, which Parliament would create in 1645. Cromwell didn't solely create the New Model—Sir Thomas Fairfax was its commander, and many officers contributed to its organization—but Cromwell's vision of godly, disciplined, meritocratic military force shaped it profoundly.[75]

Marston Moor also revealed that the war was not ending quickly. Despite the decisive victory, Parliament still faced royalist forces in the south and west. Charles's main army remained intact. Oxford was secure. The war would continue for two more years, but the trajectory had shifted decisively toward Parliament.

The New Model Army and Victory

Creating the Army That Would Reshape England

The Self-Denying Ordinance and Army Reform

The Crisis of 1644-1645

Despite Marston Moor's victory, Parliament's war effort was faltering by late 1644. Three separate armies, the Eastern Association under Manchester, Essex's army in the south, Waller's army in the west, operated independently, coordinated poorly, and competed for resources. Their commanders were aristocrats (Earl of Essex, Earl of Manchester) who had social status but varied military ability.[76]

Moreover, some parliamentary generals didn't want to win too completely. The Earl of Manchester, though a committed parliamentarian, feared that total victory over the King would produce chaos. "If we beat the King ninety-nine times," Manchester reportedly said, "he would still be King. But if he beat us once, we would all be hanged." Manchester favored fighting to a negotiated settlement, not to unconditional victory.[77]

Oliver Cromwell and others disagreed. They wanted decisive victory, believing that God would not bless half-measures. Cromwell attacked Manchester in Parliament (December 1644), accusing him of military incompetence and lack of will to win. The accusation was politically dangerous—Cromwell was a commoner attacking a peer, but it reflected genuine frustration with the war's conduct.[78]

The Self-Denying Ordinance

The solution was radical: remove all MPs and peers from military command. The Self-Denying Ordinance (April 1645) required all members of Parliament to resign their military commissions. This meant that the Earl of Essex, the Earl of Manchester, and Oliver Cromwell (who was an MP) would all lose their commands.[79]

The ordinance served multiple purposes:

- **Military**: It allowed competent officers (regardless of birth) to command
- **Political**: It removed aristocratic generals who might negotiate with the King rather than defeat him

- **Factional**: It weakened the presbyterian peace party (Essex, Manchester) and strengthened the Independent war party

In practice, the ordinance was applied selectively. Essex and Manchester resigned and retired from military life. But Sir Thomas Fairfax, though a peer, was appointed commander of the new army (he wasn't an MP, so the ordinance didn't technically apply). And Cromwell, though required to resign, was repeatedly granted temporary commissions to continue commanding cavalry, these "temporary" commissions became permanent in practice.[80]

The Self-Denying Ordinance thus produced meritocratic military leadership without explicitly saying so. It removed commanders based on social status and replaced them with commanders based on ability—a revolutionary change in a society that valued birth above competence.

The New Model Army: Organization and Ideology

Structure and Training

The New Model Army, authorized by Parliament in February 1645, was England's first national standing army. It consisted of:[81]

- **22,000 men**: 11 regiments of cavalry, 12 regiments of infantry, 1 regiment of dragoons (mounted infantry)
- **Unified command**: Sir Thomas Fairfax as Lord General, Oliver Cromwell (eventually) as Lieutenant-General commanding cavalry
- **Standardized pay and supply**: Soldiers were paid regularly (in theory—arrears would become a huge problem) and supplied uniformly
- **Professional training**: Officers drilled troops in standard tactics; discipline was enforced through military courts
- **Red coats**: Infantry wore red coats (thus "redcoats"), cavalry wore various colors, creating visual identity

The army was recruited from existing parliamentary forces, volunteers, and (when necessary) impressment (conscription). Officers were chosen by Fairfax and his council of war based on ability and loyalty to the cause. Many were "mere" gentlemen or even commoners—men who would never have commanded under the old system of aristocratic leadership.[82]

Training emphasized discipline and coordination. Infantry practiced pike and musket drill, learning to form defensive squares, to fire in volleys, and to advance in formation. Cavalry practiced the charge-rally-charge sequence that Cromwell had pioneered. Dragoons practiced dismounting to fight as infantry, providing flexibility. The result was an army that functioned as an integrated fighting force rather than as a collection of individual regiments.[83]

Religious Culture

What made the New Model Army revolutionary wasn't just its organization but its religious culture. The army became a mobile community of godly believers, a church on horseback:

Preaching and prayer: Army chaplains preached regularly. Soldiers held prayer meetings where they discussed Scripture, shared religious experiences, and discerned God's will. Some meetings allowed common soldiers to speak, a radical leveling where a trooper might prophesy while officers listened.[84]

Godly discipline: Officers enforced moral standards: swearing was punished, drunkenness was discouraged, plunder was (sometimes) prevented, Sabbath observance was required. The army prayed before battles, sang psalms after victories, and attributed success to God's favor. When they won, they gave glory to God; when they suffered setbacks, they searched for sins that had provoked divine disfavor.[85]

Religious diversity: The army included Presbyterians, Independents, Baptists, and (eventually) Quakers. Cromwell's policy of tolerating "godly" men regardless of denominational differences meant the army was more religiously diverse than Parliament or the nation. This tolerance would later produce conflict with Presbyterian MPs who wanted uniformity, but during the war it created unity—soldiers who might disagree about church government agreed about fighting for God's cause against popery and tyranny.[86]

Political radicalization: The army's religious culture fostered political radicalism. If common soldiers could pray and prophesy, why couldn't they discuss politics? If God called a tinker to preach, why couldn't He call a trooper to judge political matters? The leveling implicit in radical Protestantism, all believers equal before God, encouraged political leveling. This would explode in 1647 when soldiers elected "agitators" to represent them and demanded political reforms. But even during the war, the army's religious culture made it different from traditional hierarchical military forces.[87]

Naseby and the War's End

14 June 1645: The Decisive Victory

On 14 June 1645, near the village of Naseby in Northamptonshire, the New Model Army fought its first major battle. Charles's main army (about 9,000 men) faced Fairfax and Cromwell's forces (about 13,500 men). The royalists were outnumbered but confident, they had Prince Rupert commanding cavalry, veteran infantry, and the King himself present to inspire loyalty.[88]

The battle followed a now-familiar pattern: Rupert's cavalry charged and broke Parliament's right wing, then pursued too far. Cromwell's cavalry on the left wing broke the royalist left, then rallied and wheeled to attack the royalist infantry from behind. The New Model Army's infantry, though pushed back initially, held together and counterattacked. By mid-afternoon, the royalist army was destroyed.[89]

Charles tried to rally his forces personally, but his guards pulled him away, losing the battle was acceptable; losing the King was not. The royal army fled, leaving behind all its artillery, baggage train, and, most damaging, the King's personal correspondence. Parliament published Charles's captured letters, which revealed he had been negotiating with Irish Catholics, with the Pope's representative, and with foreign Catholic powers. The letters confirmed everything Parliament had claimed: Charles was conspiring with papists, he couldn't be trusted, and his word meant nothing.[90]

Naseby broke royalist power in the midlands. Within a year, the war was effectively over. Royalist strongholds fell one by one: Bristol (September 1645), the West Country (early 1646), finally Oxford (June 1646). Charles, seeing that further resistance was futile, surrendered to the Scottish army at Newark in May 1646. The First Civil War was over. Parliament and the New Model Army had won.[91]

What Victory Meant

But what had they won? Parliament now controlled England, but it was deeply divided:[92]

- **Presbyterians** wanted to establish presbyterian church government, disband most of the army (keeping only forces needed to suppress Ireland), and negotiate with Charles to restore him to limited monarchy
- **Independents** wanted gathered churches with liberty of conscience, a settlement that secured parliamentary and religious gains, and retention of the army until terms were secure
- **The Army** had its own views, having won the war, soldiers expected to shape the peace

Charles, imprisoned but undefeated in spirit, would play these factions against each other, refusing settlement terms that might have preserved him while hoping that divisions among his enemies would restore his power. He miscalculated catastrophically, his intransigence and his attempts at manipulation would ultimately cost him his life.

From Edgehill to Naseby

We began this chapter on the field at Edgehill, where on a cold October morning in 1642 two English armies discovered that they could and would kill each other. We end with Naseby, where the King's cause was destroyed by an army of shopkeepers, farmers, and godly believers who had been forged into a military instrument unlike anything England had seen.

The transformation between these two battles was profound:

Military: From amateur enthusiasm to professional discipline, from aristocratic cavalry charges to coordinated infantry-cavalry tactics, from regional levies to a national army. The New Model Army was a revolutionary instrument, and it would soon become a revolutionary political force.[93]

Political: From near-unanimous opposition to Charles's Personal Rule to deep divisions over what should replace it. The parliamentary coalition that had united to execute Strafford and abolish Ship Money had fractured over religion, over war aims, over whether to negotiate with Charles or defeat him utterly.[94]

Religious: From broad agreement that Laud's innovations must be reversed to bitter conflict over whether bishops should be reformed or abolished, whether presbyterian discipline or gathered churches should replace episcopacy, and whether uniformity or liberty should govern England's religious life.[95]

Social: From deference to traditional hierarchies to the emergence of a godly meritocracy in the army, from assuming that birth determined authority to promoting men based on ability and grace, from the gentry monopolizing leadership to tinkers preaching and troopers prophesying.[96]

The Cost

The war's human cost was staggering. Modern estimates suggest:[97]

- **England**: 85,000 combat deaths, perhaps 100,000 additional deaths from disease and hardship in a population of about 5 million—roughly 3.7% mortality
- **Scotland**: Perhaps 28,000 deaths in a population of 1 million—2.8% mortality
- **Ireland**: Perhaps 200,000 deaths in a population of 1.5 million—over 13% mortality, most in Cromwell's brutal suppression

These percentages exceed England's losses in World War I. Almost every English family lost someone, a father, son, brother, husband. Property was destroyed, livestock slaughtered, fields left unplanted. Plague spread through armies and into civilian populations. The economic disruption lasted years beyond the war's end.

And for what? By 1646, Parliament had won, but it had no clear vision for what should replace the monarchy it had defeated. The King was in custody but unrepentant. The army that had won the war was owed massive arrears of pay and increasingly had its own political agenda. Scotland expected England to establish presbyterian government in fulfillment of the Solemn League and Covenant. Parliament was divided between Presbyterians who wanted settlement with Charles and Independents who didn't trust him. None of these factions could impose its will on the others.[98]

The War That Didn't End

The First Civil War concluded with military victory but not political settlement. The question that had driven men to fight, where authority resided, how church and state should be ordered, what England's constitution required, remained unanswered. Charles's surrender merely moved these questions from battlefield to negotiating table, where they proved even harder to resolve.[99]

The years 1646-1649 would see:[100]

- Negotiations between Charles, Parliament, and Army, with none trusting the others
- Charles playing factions against each other while secretly plotting restoration by force
- The Army politicizing, demanding not just pay but political and religious reforms
- Presbyterian and Independent factions in Parliament irreconcilably divided
- A Second Civil War as Charles escaped and renewed fighting
- Finally, the Army's decision that Charles was irredeemable and must be executed

These developments would be shaped by the religious visions we've examined: Presbyterian demands for discipline, Independent insistence on liberty, Anglican hopes for restoration, and disruptive Quaker conscience. Each vision had been strengthened by the war, Presbyterians now had Scottish backing and parliamentary support, Independents had the Army, Anglicans had the King's martyrdom-in-waiting, and Quakers would soon emerge as a radical alternative to all established positions.

To understand how these religious visions shaped the attempts at settlement and the ultimate failure to restore England's old order, we must examine each vision in detail. We begin with the Presbyterians, who thought the war had won them the opportunity to build the godly commonwealth they had long desired, a national church with reformed discipline, a magistrate who would maintain true religion, and uniformity that would finally complete England's Reformation.

PART II — INTRODUCTION

The Classical Forms and England's Crisis

The four chapters that follow examine England's religious and political factions through the lens of classical political theory. This approach illuminates connections that confessional or purely economic analyses often obscure. When we see Presbyterians as aristocrats, Anglicans as monarchists, Independents as mixed-government theorists, and Quakers as anarchists, we recognize patterns that transcend the seventeenth century and touch the permanent questions of political philosophy: Who should rule? By what authority? Within what limits?

The classical tradition, stretching from Aristotle through Polybius to Machiavelli and beyond, identified three pure forms of government: monarchy (rule by one), aristocracy (rule by the few), and democracy (rule by the many). Each form had a corresponding corruption: tyranny, oligarchy, and mob rule. The cycle between these forms—what Polybius called *anacyclosis*—described how governments rise and fall in predictable sequence. Monarchy degenerates into tyranny; tyranny is overthrown by aristocrats seeking the common good; aristocracy degenerates into oligarchy; oligarchy is overthrown by the people; democracy degenerates into mob rule; and from the chaos, a strong man emerges to restore monarchy.

Anacyclosis in England

England's revolutionary period compressed this cycle into a single generation. Charles I's perceived tyranny—his eleven years of personal rule, his religious innovations, his attempts to govern without Parliament—provoked resistance from an aristocratic Parliament claiming to defend the ancient constitution. Parliament's victory in the First Civil War did not restore equilibrium; instead, the Army's democratic impulses—expressed in the Putney Debates and the Leveller movement—threatened to carry reform far beyond what the parliamentary gentry had intended. The chaos of the late 1640s produced Cromwell's quasi-monarchical Protectorate, a military dictatorship dressed in constitutional forms. Cromwell's death left no stable succession; the brief restoration of republican government in 1659 collapsed into near-anarchy; and from that chaos emerged the restored monarchy of Charles II.

Yet the cycle did not simply repeat. The Restoration settlement differed fundamentally from the Caroline regime it replaced. Parliament retained powers won during the Interregnum; religious dissent, though persecuted, was never entirely suppressed; and the foundations were laid for the Toleration Act of 1689 and the constitutional settlement following the Glorious Revolution. England emerged from its crisis not with a restored absolute monarchy but with a mixed constitution that balanced, imperfectly, the claims of king, Parliament, and people.

The Transformation of 'Commonwealth'

To understand the ideological stakes, we must also grasp what James Hankins has called 'exclusive republicanism.' In the classical tradition, *respublica* meant simply the 'common good' or 'public thing,' any government that served the welfare of its people, whether monarchical, aristocratic, or democratic. A king who ruled justly presided over a *respublica* no less than an elected senate. But during the Renaissance, a transformation occurred. Increasingly, 'republic' came to mean non-monarchical government, popular sovereignty exercised through representative institutions, explicitly opposed to the rule of kings.

The English word 'Commonwealth' underwent precisely this transformation during the 1640s. When Parliament abolished the monarchy in 1649 and declared England a 'Commonwealth and Free State,' the word took on revolutionary significance. Commonwealth was no longer compatible with kingship; it was kingship's opposite. Milton would argue in *The Readie and Easie Way* that republican government was spiritually superior to monarchy—that Israel under judges had been a 'commonwealth of God's own ordaining,' and that the demand for a human king represented disobedience inviting divine wrath.

Ecclesiastical Polity and Political Structure

Most remarkable is the parallel between each faction's preferred church government and its preferred civil government. This was not accidental. Seventeenth-century English people understood church and state as interpenetrating realms, the same people who were subjects politically were also members ecclesiastically. How they organized their worship expressed and reinforced how they thought about political authority.

Anglicans favored episcopal church government, rule by bishops claiming apostolic succession, and monarchical civil government, rule by a king claiming divine appointment. Both structures were hierarchical, both claimed ancient legitimacy, and both reinforced each other. Gilbert Sheldon would argue that episcopacy and monarchy 'stood or fell together.'

Presbyterians favored presbyterian church government, rule by assemblies of elders (presbyteries and synods), and aristocratic civil government—rule by Parliament representing the propertied and educated. Both structures gave power to qualified elites rather than to individuals (whether kings or commoners); both claimed to mediate between God's will and human society through representative institutions.

Independents favored congregational church government, each gathered church autonomous, covenanting together, choosing its own officers, and mixed civil government, balancing the one, the few, and the many in a constitution that prevented any single element from dominating. Both structures emphasized consent, covenant, and the distribution of power.

Quakers favored no outward church government at all, only the inner light of Christ teaching each believer directly, and no human authority over matters of faith. This was anarchism in its etymological sense: *an-archos*, without rulers. Early Quakers did not withdraw from political engagement; they challenged magistrates, refused oaths, disrupted services, and demanded liberty of conscience. But they denied that any human authority, king, Parliament, synod, or congregation, had legitimate power over the individual's relationship with God.

Four Areas of Comparison

The chapters that follow compare these four factions across four theological and political areas:

First, the nature of man, which touches on original sin, the possibility of perfection, heaven and hell, the person and work of Christ, the Holy Spirit's indwelling, the authority of Scripture, election and free will, and the equality or inequality of human beings. What one believes about human nature shapes what one expects from government and church.

Second, the Kingdom of God, which includes the tension between spiritual and temporal authority, the relationship between church and state, individual rights and civic duties, and the difference between subjects (who obey) and citizens (who participate). How one understands God's sovereignty shapes how one understands human sovereignty.

Third, liberty of conscience, including questions of taxes, tithes, toleration, and oaths. May the magistrate compel religious conformity? Must believers support a church they reject? Can one refuse oaths without being suspected of disloyalty? These practical questions revealed fundamental differences about the limits of authority.

Fourth, justice, blood guilt, and divine wrath, the conviction that unpunished sin brought divine judgment on the nation. All factions shared this belief; they differed on who bore guilt. Was Charles I a 'man of blood' whose execution satisfied divine justice? Or were the regicides themselves guilty of murder and sacrilege? Was the nation's guilt in tolerating blasphemers—or in persecuting the saints?

By examining each faction's position on these four areas, we can see how theological convictions produced political conclusions, and how political circumstances shaped theological emphasis. The chapters proceed in roughly chronological order of each faction's rise to prominence: Presbyterians first (leading resistance to Charles I), then Independents (dominating through the Army), then Anglicans (returning with the Restoration), and finally Quakers (emerging from the chaos to develop a distinctive alternative).

CHAPTER 3 — THE HOLY COMMONWEALTH

PRESBYTERIAN ARISTOCRACY

Jerusalem Chamber, Westminster Abbey, 1 July 1643

One hundred and twenty-one ministers filed into Westminster Abbey's Jerusalem Chamber on a warm summer morning, summoned by Parliament to rebuild England's church from its foundations. The chamber was historic—Henry IV had died there, and medieval abbots had met in it for centuries. Now it would witness something unprecedented: a divinely-appointed assembly of learned men who would craft the confession, catechisms, and church government that would (they hoped) finally complete England's Reformation and establish godly discipline throughout the realm.

Dr. William Twisse, rector of Newbury and one of England's most learned theologians, took the Prolocutor's chair (moderator). At sixty-eight, his white hair and beard gave him the appearance of an Old Testament prophet, which suited the assembly's self-understanding. They were not merely ecclesiastical bureaucrats revising church policies but instruments of providence, called by God through Parliament to build His house correctly after decades of episcopal corruption.[1]

Stephen Marshall, the fiery Presbyterian preacher who had mobilized Parliament's cause from hundreds of pulpits, rose to preach the opening sermon. His text was from Haggai 2:7-9: "I will shake all nations, and the desire of all nations shall come: and I will fill this house with glory, saith the Lord of hosts." Marshall's voice filled the chamber as he applied the prophecy to their present task:

> *Brethren, the Lord has shaken England—shaken it from its bishops, from its ceremonies, from its complacent slumber in half-reformed religion. And why? That He might fill His house with glory. We are called to build that house—not with wood and stone but with true doctrine, pure worship, and godly discipline. The nations watch us. Scotland has already built according to God's pattern. We must do no less. The glory of this latter house shall be greater than the former, if we build faithfully.*[2]

The assembled divines, mostly Presbyterians, but with a minority of Episcopalians (who would attend only briefly before being excluded) and Independents (who would remain to argue for gathered churches), listened with varying degrees of enthusiasm. They agreed on much: Reformed theology, rejection of Laudian ceremonialism, commitment to godly discipline. But they would discover, in the months and years ahead, that their agreements masked profound disagreements about church government, toleration, and the relationship between spiritual and civil authority.[3]

The Westminster Assembly represented Presbyterianism's bid to remake England according to its vision: a godly commonwealth governed by learned elites, a national church disciplined by assemblies of ministers and elders, a society where true religion was established by law and error suppressed by magistrate and minister working in concert. It was a vision of order—but whose order, and at what cost to liberty?[4]

The Assembly's Composition and Mandate

Parliament had summoned the Westminster Assembly through ordinance (not requiring royal assent, which Charles would never have given). The Assembly's stated purpose was to advise Parliament on settling "the government and liturgy of the Church of England, and for vindicating and clearing of the doctrine of the said Church from false aspersions and interpretations." It was advisory only, Parliament retained final authority, but the divines understood they were drafting documents that would shape English Christianity for generations.[5]

But everyone understood the real task: to replace episcopacy with Presbyterianism, to abolish the Book of Common Prayer and substitute a simpler directory for worship, and to establish a system of church courts that would discipline England into godliness. The Assembly would meet for nearly ten years (1643-1652), producing the Westminster Confession of Faith, the Larger and Shorter Catechisms, the Directory for Public Worship, and the Form of Presbyterian Church Government—documents that would outlast the political circumstances that produced them and shape Reformed Christianity worldwide.

The Assembly's Composition and Conflicts

The membership reflected Parliament's vision of godly reformation. **The Presbyterian Majority** (perhaps 80-90 of the divines): These were ministers who had chafed under Laud's episcopal tyranny, who valued learning and order, who believed Scripture prescribed a specific form of church government (presbyterian), and who wanted a comprehensive national church that would include all English people under godly discipline. Key figures included:[6]

- **William Twisse** (1578-1646): The Prolocutor, a brilliant Supralapsarian Calvinist (believing God's decree of election preceded the Fall) whose theological works were respected across Reformed Europe.
- **Stephen Marshall** (1594-1655): Perhaps Parliament's most influential

preacher, whose sermon "Meroz Cursed" had mobilized troops and whose speaking style combined learning with populist fire.

- **Edmund Calamy** (1600-1666): London minister who had preached the Root and Branch sermon, defender of presbyterian government against both episcopacy and independency.
- **Thomas Goodwin** (1600-1680): Initially Presbyterian but increasingly Independent, his presence showed the spectrum within Reformed thought.
- **Cornelius Burges** (1589-1665): Assessor (assistant moderator), learned divine and skilled debater.

The Independent Minority (perhaps 5-7 voting members, with supporters among parliamentary commissioners): These men accepted Reformed theology but rejected presbyterian church government. They argued for gathered churches of "visible saints," voluntary congregations that chose their own ministers and governed themselves. Though few in number, they were disproportionately influential because they had allies in the Army and among powerful MPs. The "Five Dissenting Brethren" would delay and complicate presbyterian implementation:[7]

- **Thomas Goodwin** (1600-1680): Former president of Magdalen College, Oxford, he had fled to Holland where he encountered gathered church practices.
- **Philip Nye** (1595-1672): Had ministered in Holland, experienced with Independent congregations, skilled controversialist.
- **Jeremiah Burroughes** (1599-1646): Gentle and irenic, he sought to maintain unity while defending congregational government.
- **William Bridge** (1600-1670): Had pastored English church in Rotterdam, known for devotional works.
- **Sidrach Simpson** (1600-1655): Radical Independent who pushed for widest possible toleration.

The Episcopalian Remnant (perhaps 8-10 initially): These were moderate bishops and episcopal divines who wanted to retain episcopacy but reform its abuses. They attended early sessions but found themselves marginalized as Parliament's anti-episcopal sentiment hardened:[8]

- **James Ussher** (1581-1656): Archbishop of Armagh, famous for his biblical chronology, he proposed "reduced episcopacy" (bishops with limited power, sharing authority with presbyters).
- **Daniel Featley** (1582-1645): Scholar who had debated Catholics and Puritans, he tried to defend episcopacy as ancient and scriptural but was arrested for royalist correspondence and excluded.

The Episcopalians' exclusion came quickly. By late 1643, most had either stopped attending or been excluded for royalist sympathies. The Assembly became a Presbyterian-Independent debate, with Presbyterians holding numerical superiority but Independents exercising influence through delay, argument, and external allies.

The Scottish Commissioners

Critically, the Assembly included Scottish commissioners, ministers sent by the Kirk to ensure that England's reformation aligned with Scotland's. They couldn't vote but could speak, and their presence shaped every debate. Scotland had already achieved what English Presbyterians wanted: a national church governed by presbyteries and General Assembly, independent of royal control. The Scots came as advisors, examples, and (they hoped) partners in creating a unified British Protestantism:[9]

- **Alexander Henderson** (1583-1646): Moderator of the Kirk's General Assembly, architect of the National Covenant, Scotland's most influential churchman.
- **Samuel Rutherford** (1600-1661): Fierce polemicist and theologian whose *Lex, Rex* (1644) would argue for popular sovereignty and limited monarchy.
- **George Gillespie** (1613-1648): Young but brilliant, his arguments against Erastian control of the church (state dominating church) shaped Assembly debates.
- **Robert Baillie** (1602-1662): Chronicler whose letters provide invaluable record of Assembly proceedings and frustrations.

The Scots came expecting England to adopt presbyterian government like Scotland's—a national church with ascending church courts (kirk session, presbytery, synod, General Assembly) independent of state control. They would be disappointed. English circumstances were different: Parliament wanted to control the church, not liberate it; English Presbyterians were more cautious than Scottish; and the Independent minority, backed by the Army, would prevent full presbyterian implementation.[10]

The First Debates: Where to Begin?

The Assembly's opening debates revealed divisions that would persist throughout:[11]

Should they revise the Thirty-Nine Articles or write a new confession? Conservatives wanted revision; reformers wanted complete rewriting. They eventually chose to write new standards (the Westminster Confession and Catechisms) while also producing a revision of the Articles that was never implemented.

Presbyterians wanted to establish government first (settling the constitutional question); Independents wanted to clarify doctrine first (avoiding premature decisions on contested polity). They eventually did both simultaneously, with different committees working on different documents.

How should Scripture inform church government? This was the central hermeneutical question:[12]

Presbyterian view: Scripture provided a clear pattern for church government (presbyters/elders ruling in ascending courts), which could be derived from Acts, the Pastoral Epistles, and apostolic practice. This pattern was *jure divino* (by divine right), not merely convenient but commanded by God.

Independent view: Scripture provided principles (churches should have elders, discipline should be exercised) but not detailed organizational structures. Gathered churches implementing these principles in various ways were all legitimate. The specific form of church government was a matter of prudence, not divine command.

Erastian view (held by some in Parliament): Scripture provided spiritual guidance, but church organization was a matter of civil prudence, and Parliament could order the church as it saw fit for the realm's peace.

These hermeneutical differences were not merely academic, they determined whether England would have a national presbyterian church (with clergy power), gathered independent churches (with congregational autonomy), or an Erastian settlement (with parliamentary supremacy). The Assembly debated; Parliament decided; and the Army, eventually, overruled them all.

Robert Baillie's Frustration

Robert Baillie, the Scottish commissioner, kept detailed letters chronicling the Assembly's proceedings. As early as August 1643, he was writing to colleagues in Scotland with mounting frustration:[13]

> *We have been detained these many weeks, and are like to be longer detained, upon the first Article of the Creed. The Independents, though they are but five, yet they are so able and so tenacious, and the [English] Presbyterians so fearful of engaging them, that we are in great danger to be laid aside all our days upon such preliminaries... The Independents here are a very subtle and active party, and they have too much favour, both in the Parliament and in the Army.*

Baillie's lament captured the Assembly's predicament: The Presbyterian majority could win every debate but couldn't implement their conclusions if the Independent minority had military and political power outside the Assembly. Theological correctness would prove no match for armed force and parliamentary politics.

As the summer heat intensified in the Jerusalem Chamber, the divines settled into their work, drafting confessions, parsing Greek texts, debating the fine points of covenant theology and church government. They believed they were building God's house. They didn't yet realize they were building a beautiful edifice that would never be completed because the ground beneath them was shifting. The New Model Army, forming even as they debated, would have its own ideas about England's religious future, ideas shaped more by battlefield experience and gathered church practices than by the Westminster Assembly's learned deliberations.

To understand what the Presbyterian divines at Westminster wanted to build, what 'godly discipline' meant in their vision, and why they believed it essential not merely for church order but for social stability—we must examine the Presbyterian system itself: its courts, its discipline, and its theology of order.

The Presbyterian System

Courts, Discipline, and the Rule of Elders

The Ascending Courts: From Kirk Session to General Assembly

The Fourfold Structure

Presbyterian church government rested on a system of ascending courts; each level with defined authority, each providing oversight and appeal for the level below. The system was modeled on Scotland's Kirk (itself influenced by Geneva and France) and was presented as biblical, derived from Acts 15 (the Jerusalem Council) and the organization of elders in New Testament churches.[14]

The Kirk Session (or Consistory): The local church court consisting of the minister(s) and ruling elders elected by the congregation. The kirk session:[15]

- Examined candidates for church membership (in Reformed churches that required conversion testimony)
- Administered discipline to members who sinned (from admonishing to excommunicating)
- Oversaw poor relief, visiting the sick, ensuring children were catechized
- Met weekly, keeping detailed records of proceedings (Scottish session records are treasure troves for social historians)

The kirk session was where discipline happened concretely: When someone committed fornication, drunkenness, Sabbath-breaking, or other public sins, they were summoned before the session, examined, and assigned appropriate penance—typically public confession before the congregation, wearing sackcloth on the 'stool of repentance,' or (for serious sins) exclusion from communion until repentance was evident.[16]

The Presbytery: A regional court consisting of all ministers and ruling elder representatives from kirk sessions within a geographical area (perhaps 10-20 churches). The presbytery:[17]

- Ordained and installed ministers after examining their doctrine and life
- Resolved disputes between kirk sessions or involving ministers
- Provided oversight and counsel to weaker churches
- Served as first court of appeal from kirk session decisions
- Met monthly or quarterly

The Provincial Synod: A larger regional court covering several presbyteries, meeting perhaps twice yearly. In practice, synods handled fewer matters than presbyteries or General Assemblies, but they provided another layer of oversight and appeal, ensuring that no presbytery became a law unto itself.[18]

The General Assembly: The national church court, consisting of ministers and ruling elders from all presbyteries, plus ruling elders elected by local sessions. In Scotland, the General Assembly met annually and claimed authority to:[19]

- Define doctrine and resolve theological controversies
- Legislate for the whole church (subject to no earthly authority—this was the point that troubled monarchs)

- Judge cases appealed from lower courts
- Communicate with civil government and with Reformed churches abroad

The genius of the system was its combination of local immediacy (kirk sessions knew their members personally) with broader oversight (presbyteries prevented local tyranny or error). No single person, no bishop, no king, no minister, could dominate. Power was distributed through assemblies of ministers and elders, all theoretically equal (though in practice, prominent divines influenced decisions more than obscure rural ministers). Decisions were made by assemblies deliberating together, accountable to one another and ultimately to Christ, whom Presbyterians called the only Head of the church.

The Problem of Authority

But the system had a fundamental problem when transplanted to England: **Who had final authority—church courts or Parliament?**[20]

In Scotland, the Kirk claimed independence from crown and Parliament. The General Assembly could excommunicate anyone, even the King (which happened to James VI). The Kirk insisted that Christ alone was Head of the church and that civil magistrates had no authority over spiritual matters. This 'Two Kingdoms' theology distinguished sharply between the spiritual realm (where Christ ruled through church courts) and the temporal realm (where magistrates ruled through civil law).

But English Presbyterians faced different circumstances. They were trying to establish presbyterian government through parliamentary legislation. Parliament was creating presbyteries by law, defining their jurisdictions, determining their membership. This meant Parliament, not the General Assembly, would be the final authority. English presbyterian government would be Erastian (state-controlled) from the start.[21]

Scottish commissioners at Westminster were horrified. Samuel Rutherford and George Gillespie argued passionately that church courts must be independent:[22]

> *Christ is the King of His church. No earthly power, not even Parliament, can bind Christ's conscience. If Parliament can overrule church courts, then Parliament, not Christ, governs the church. This is Erastianism—the civil magistrate usurping Christ's throne. We did not fight bishops to install Parliament as a new pope.*

But English politicians and some English Presbyterians disagreed. Thomas Coleman, an English divine, argued for parliamentary oversight:[23]

> *We do not question that Christ governs His church. But Christ governs through means—through magistrates as well as ministers. The godly magistrate has responsibility for the commonwealth's peace, which includes religious peace. Therefore, Parliament must have oversight of church courts, else we have created a new clergy tyranny replacing the episcopal tyranny we destroyed.*

This debate, church independence versus state control, was never resolved at Westminster. The documents the Assembly produced (especially the *Form of Presbyterian Church Government*) assumed church court independence. But

Parliament's implementing ordinances assumed parliamentary supremacy. The ambiguity would cripple English presbyterian implementation.[24]

Without clear authority, presbyteries couldn't discipline effectively. Without civil enforcement, excommunication meant little in practice. The Presbyterian system required either church independence (Scottish model) or wholehearted state support (Genevan model). England provided neither.

Discipline as the Third Mark of the Church

The Theological Foundation

Reformed Protestants traditionally identified two marks of the true church: right preaching of the Word and right administration of the sacraments. Where these existed, there was a true church, however imperfect. But Reformed Christians in Geneva, Scotland, and Holland added a third mark: **godly discipline**. A church that did not discipline its members—that tolerated open sin without correction—was not merely imperfect but defective, perhaps not a true church at all.[25]

The logic was theological:[26]

First, church membership should be limited to believers. Unlike the Catholic or episcopal view (where everyone in the parish was in the church through infant baptism), Reformed thought emphasized that the church was a covenant community of professing believers and their children. Discipline maintained this boundary, distinguishing the church from the world.

Second, discipline was pastoral care, not punishment. The goal was restoration, not condemnation. Matthew 18:15-17 provided the pattern: private admonition first, then witnesses, then church involvement, finally excommunication, but always aiming at the sinner's repentance and return.[27]

Third, discipline maintained the church's witness. A church that tolerated open sin among members dishonored Christ before the watching world. Discipline showed that Christians took holiness seriously, that the church was genuinely different from unregenerate society.[28]

Fourth, discipline protected the congregation. Paul's image of leaven (1 Corinthians 5:6-7) warned that tolerating sin would corrupt the whole community. One unrepentant adulterer or heretic could infect others. Discipline removed the leaven before it spread.

Richard Baxter, the Presbyterian pastor of Kidderminster, expressed this perfectly in his *The Reformed Pastor* (1656):[29]

> *If discipline does not reform the sinner, it yet protects the church. If the excommunicated person will not be saved, at least his leaven will not corrupt the congregation. And it shows watching unbelievers that we are serious about holiness, that we do not merely talk about Christ but truly follow Him.*

The Practice: Richard Baxter's Kidderminster

Nowhere did Presbyterian discipline function better in England than in Richard Baxter's Kidderminster parish (1641-1660). Baxter arrived to find a population of perhaps 2,000, mostly weavers and craftspeople in the cloth trade, with (he claimed) minimal religious knowledge and widespread irreligion. When he left nearly twenty years later, he claimed transformation: crowded churches, eager learners, a town where godliness had become the norm rather than the exception.[30]

Baxter's method combined rigorous catechizing with personal discipline:[31]

Catechizing: Every family in the parish had to send members for systematic religious instruction. Baxter and his assistant(s) met with fifteen to sixteen families per week, examining them on doctrine using his catechism, answering questions, pressing for personal application. This wasn't perfunctory; sessions could last an hour per family, probing understanding and pressing for genuine faith.

Public preaching: Baxter preached twice on Sundays (morning and afternoon) and often on weekdays. His sermons combined doctrinal instruction with passionate application. He preached for conversion (not assuming his hearers were Christians), for sanctification (not assuming converts would grow automatically), and for preparation for death (not assuming anyone had time to spare).[32]

Discipline: Baxter worked with elected elders to exercise discipline. When someone committed public sin, the elders investigated. If the person was guilty, they were called before the session (Baxter preferred the term 'eldership'). If they repented, they were restored after appropriate acknowledgment. If they refused, they were excluded from communion—though Baxter tried to avoid excommunication, preferring suspension with continued pastoral care.[33]

The result, Baxter later claimed, was transformation: "When I came thither first, there was about one Family in a Street that worshipped God and called on his Name, and when I came away, there were some Streets where there was not past one Family in the side of a Street that did not so." This may be exaggeration, pastors tend to overstate their success, but contemporary accounts confirm that Kidderminster became unusually godly by 17th-century standards. People walked miles to hear Baxter preach. Other ministers visited to learn his methods. And Kidderminster became the Presbyterian answer to Independent claims that only gathered churches could maintain purity.[34]

Baxter's success depended on circumstances that couldn't be replicated everywhere: a relatively small, concentrated population; a minister of enormous ability and energy; a supportive gentry family (the Foleys) who protected Baxter from episcopal interference; and a community engaged in textile work that produced both modest prosperity and literacy. But it proved that Presbyterian discipline could function in English contexts, if implemented by gifted ministers with congregational cooperation.

The Westminster Documents

The Confession of Faith

The Westminster Confession, completed in 1646, is one of Reformed Christianity's most influential creedal statements. It covered:[35]

God and Scripture (Chapters 1-2): Scripture's authority and sufficiency, God's being and decrees, predestination (supralapsarian—God's decree preceded the Fall)

Covenant Theology (Chapter 7): The covenant of works with Adam (obey and live), the covenant of grace through Christ (believe and be saved)—this framework structured Reformed soteriology

Christ and Salvation (Chapters 8-18): Christ's person and work, effectual calling, justification by faith alone, sanctification, assurance, perseverance of the saints

The Church and Sacraments (Chapters 25-29): The visible and invisible church, communion of saints, baptism and the Lord's Supper (affirming infant baptism, denying transubstantiation)

Church Government (Chapters 30-31): Presbyterian courts, church discipline, the relationship between church and magistrate

Last Things (Chapters 32-33): Death, resurrection, judgment

The Confession was thoroughly Reformed, affirming predestination, covenant theology, and the sovereignty of God's grace. It was also carefully political, especially in Chapter 23 on the civil magistrate: affirming the magistrate's duty to maintain true religion while carefully avoiding claims that would offend either Parliament or the Scottish Kirk.[36]

The Confession became the doctrinal standard for presbyterian churches in Scotland, England (briefly), and later America. It remains the creedal foundation for many Presbyterian and Reformed denominations worldwide; a testament to the Westminster divines' theological rigor even though their church government vision was never fully realized in England.

The Catechisms

The Assembly produced two catechisms for religious instruction:[37]

The Larger Catechism (196 questions): For ministers, elders, and educated laity, it provided detailed exposition of Reformed doctrine, organized around the Apostles' Creed, the Ten Commandments, the Lord's Prayer, and the sacraments. Its treatment of the Decalogue was especially comprehensive, deriving duties and sins from each commandment with scholastic precision.

The Shorter Catechism (107 questions): For children and common people, it condensed essential doctrine into memorable questions and answers. Its opening is famous:

Q. 1. What is the chief end of man?

A. Man's chief end is to glorify God, and to enjoy him forever.

The Shorter Catechism became one of the most widely memorized religious texts in the English-speaking world. Presbyterian children learned it by rote; ministers used it for instructing the ignorant; missionaries carried it across oceans. Its concise summaries of Reformed doctrine shaped millions of minds for generations.

The Directory for Public Worship

The Directory for Public Worship (1645) replaced the Book of Common Prayer, which Parliament had officially banned in January 1645. Unlike the prayer book, which provided set liturgies, the Directory offered guidelines: it told ministers *what* should happen in worship and in *what order*, but not the exact words to use. This reflected Presbyterian liturgical theology:[38]

- Scripture reading and exposition (sermons) were central
- Prayers were extemporaneous but following prescribed topics and order
- Psalms were sung (but not hymns—those were human compositions, not Scripture)
- Sacraments were administered with dignity but without elaborate ceremony
- The liturgical calendar was abolished—no Christmas, Easter, or saints' days (these were considered popish inventions)

The Directory represented Presbyterian liturgical philosophy: structured but not scripted, orderly but not ceremonial, focused on the Word preached and the sacraments simply administered. It avoided both the elaborate ceremony of Laudian worship and the complete freedom of some Independents and Baptists.

But the Directory was never widely implemented outside Scottish-influenced areas. Many English parishes continued using the prayer book (illegally), others developed their own practices, and Independents rejected any imposed liturgy. Like presbyterian government itself, the Directory remained more aspirational than actual, Presbyterian liturgical ideals without means of enforcement.

Man's Nature and the Need for Discipline

The Presbyterian Doctrine of Human Depravity

The Westminster Confession articulated a rigorous doctrine of original sin. Adam's fall had corrupted the entire human race. All humans inherited not merely a tendency toward sin but a corrupted nature that was "utterly indisposed, disabled, and made opposite to all good, and wholly inclined to all evil." Even the regenerate, those whom God had elected and effectually called, retained "remnants of corruption" that would not be fully purged until death.[39]

This anthropology was not merely theoretical. It shaped Presbyterian politics profoundly. If human beings were radically corrupted, they could not be trusted to govern themselves without external discipline. The multitude, especially, needed guidance from the learned and godly. Democratic government was dangerous precisely because it trusted fallen human judgment. Wisdom required education, experience, and the sanctifying work of the Spirit; even the wisest retained sinful tendencies that required checking.

Richard Baxter developed this point extensively in his debates with Quakers. When Quakers disrupted services at Kidderminster in 1654, claiming immediate guidance from the inner light, Baxter was appalled. He published *The Quakers' Catechism* (1655), challenging their optimistic anthropology. The heart of his argument concerned whether perfection was possible in this life.[40]

The Baxter-Nayler Debate on Perfection

James Nayler, the Quaker preacher who would later suffer Parliament's punishment for blasphemy, responded to Baxter's attack. The exchange illuminated the fundamental anthropological divide between Presbyterian and Quaker thought.[41]

Baxter argued that the church was a "hospital" for the sick, not a community of the perfect:

> *Christ's kingdom is a hospital; he hath no subjects but diseased ones. The whole need not a physician, but they that are sick. While we are in this body of flesh, we shall carry about with us the remnants of corruption... Only when we part with flesh shall we be presented faultless before his glorious presence.*

Nayler countered that Baxter underestimated the power of Christ's indwelling Spirit. The inner light was not a mere faculty of conscience but Christ himself, present in the believer. If Christ dwelt within, why should the believer remain in bondage to sin? The gospel promised victory, not perpetual struggle. "Art thou not ashamed to say sin shall never be destroyed while we are on earth?" Nayler demanded. "Is the blood of Christ of so little value that it cannot cleanse from all sin?"

The stakes extended far beyond academic theology. If Baxter was right—if sin remained ineradicable until death—then human beings needed external discipline throughout their lives. They needed ministers to preach God's law, elders to exercise discipline, and magistrates to punish transgression. The apparatus of church and state existed because human nature required it. But if Nayler was right—if the inner light could perfect the believer in this life—then the entire Presbyterian system was unnecessary at best, a hindrance to spiritual freedom at worst.

Scripture as External Authority

The Presbyterian insistence on human depravity also shaped their understanding of Scripture's role. Because the human heart was deceitful above all things, private judgment could not be trusted. Individuals needed an external authority—objective, unchanging, available to all—against which to test their impressions and experiences. Scripture provided that authority.[42]

The Westminster Confession declared Scripture "the only rule of faith and life." This was not merely a statement about inspiration or truthfulness; it was a statement about epistemological method. Religious truth was not discovered by introspection, private revelation, or mystical experience. It was discovered by studying the Bible, comparing scripture with scripture, and submitting one's conclusions to the judgment of the learned. The individual Christian read Scripture in the context of the church's teaching, tested by centuries of interpretation, guided by ministers trained in the original languages.

This created a conservative hermeneutic. Innovation was suspect; tradition was a check on private enthusiasm. When Quakers or other radicals claimed new revelation, Presbyterians responded that the canon was closed. What the Spirit had revealed to prophets and apostles was sufficient. Any "new light" must be tested by the old light of Scripture—and the testing was done not by individuals but by assemblies of the learned.

Election, Free Will, and Human Inequality

Presbyterian Calvinism held to double predestination: God had elected some to salvation and passed over others, leaving them in their sins to face just condemnation. This was not arbitrary but reflected God's sovereign wisdom, inscrutable to human understanding. The elect were chosen "not for any foreseen faith or good works" but purely by God's good pleasure. Human free will, after the Fall, was bondage to sin; only divine grace could liberate the will to choose the good.[43]

This theology had political implications. If God had distinguished the elect from the reprobate, human inequality was built into the cosmic order. Some people, the elect, were destined for glory; others were destined for destruction. While no one could know with certainty who was elect, there were probable signs: profession of faith, godly living, response to preaching and discipline. Those who showed such signs were more likely elect and thus more qualified to govern.

The Quaker doctrine of the inner light in every person challenged this directly. If every human being possessed the light of Christ, the ground of election seemed to shift from divine choice to human response. And if every person possessed the same light, the basis for hierarchy seemed to disappear. Presbyterians and Quakers were not merely arguing about salvation; they were arguing about the structure of society.

The Godly Magistrate and the Holy Commonwealth

Church and State in Presbyterian Political Theology

The Two Kingdoms in Harmony

Presbyterian political theology rested on a specific understanding of church and state as distinct but cooperative institutions, each with its own sphere but both responsible for establishing God's kingdom on earth. This was neither theocracy (church ruling state) nor Erastianism (state ruling church) but coordination—two kingdoms serving one King.[44]

The church's kingdom was spiritual: It exercised authority through Word, sacraments, and discipline. It taught doctrine, administered baptism and communion, excommunicated the impenitent, and provided pastoral care. Its weapons were persuasion, instruction, and censure—not physical force. Ministers could not imprison or execute; they could only preach and discipline.

The magistrate's kingdom was temporal: Civil government maintained order, punished crime, defended the realm, and promoted the common good. The magistrate wielded the sword—literal power to imprison, fine, and execute. Unlike the church, the state could coerce bodies, though it could not (Presbyterians insisted) coerce consciences.

But these kingdoms were not separate, they overlapped in the godly commonwealth. The magistrate had duties regarding religion:[45]

Maintain true worship: Provide for ministers' support (through tithes), build and maintain churches, ensure public worship could occur safely

Suppress heresy and blasphemy: Punish those who denied fundamental doctrines or publicly blasphemed, protecting the church and society from false teaching

Enforce the First Table of the Law (commandments 1-4, dealing with duties to God): Prohibit idolatry, blasphemy, and Sabbath-breaking

Support church discipline: Give civil effect to church censures, ensuring that excommunicated persons faced social and legal consequences

This vision required a godly magistrate—a civil ruler who was himself a Christian, who understood his duty to maintain true religion, and who would cooperate with church courts without trying to control them. It was a vision of harmony—but harmony required both parties to agree on their boundaries, which they rarely did.[46]

The Two Kingdoms Adapted

Presbyterian political theology adapted Martin Luther's Two Kingdoms doctrine in distinctive ways. Luther had distinguished the spiritual kingdom (where Christ rules through the Gospel) from the temporal kingdom (where the magistrate maintains order through law). Both kingdoms were ordained by God but operated differently: the spiritual kingdom persuaded consciences; the temporal kingdom coerced bodies. Christians lived in both kingdoms simultaneously.[47]

Presbyterians accepted this basic framework but insisted on closer coordination between the kingdoms. The magistrate was not merely to maintain civil order but to "nurse" the church, supporting true religion, suppressing false religion, and giving civil effect to church discipline. The minister, in turn, was to preach the magistrate's duties and hold rulers accountable to God's law. Baxter put it memorably: "The magistrate rules the pastor by the sword; the pastor rules the magistrate by the word."

This created a delicate balance, or a recipe for conflict. Who decided when the magistrate had crossed into spiritual matters reserved for the church? Who decided when the minister had crossed into civil matters reserved for the magistrate? In Scotland, the Kirk maintained considerable independence from crown and Parliament. In England, Parliament showed no intention of allowing an independent church to discipline its members. The result was Erastianism—state control of the church—which Presbyterians deplored in theory but often accepted in practice.

Samuel Rutherford's Lex, Rex

The most radical Presbyterian political theory came from Samuel Rutherford's *Lex, Rex* (1644), written to justify Scottish resistance to Charles I. The title meant "Law is King"; law, not the monarch's will, was the ultimate authority. Rutherford systematically demolished divine right theory:[48]

Rutherford built his argument on covenant theology. God had established a threefold covenant: between God and the king, between God and the people, and between the king and the people. The king's authority derived from this covenantal structure. He was not, as royalists claimed, God's direct appointee answerable only to heaven. He was the people's choice, confirmed by God, bound by law, and subject to correction if he violated his trust. "A king," Rutherford wrote, "is a living law, and a law a dumb king; and the king, in regard of his office, is the law's creature."[49]

This did not mean democracy. Rutherford was clear that the people delegated their authority to the "estates", Parliament and the nobility, not to the multitude. The estates, composed of the wise and propertied, represented the people and could act on their behalf. When the king became a tyrant, the estates, not the mob, had authority to resist. This was aristocratic constitutionalism: rule by the few on behalf of the many, constrained by law, accountable to God.

First, all authority comes from God but is mediated through the people. God gives power to communities, which then establish rulers by consent. Rulers receive their power from below (through popular choice) as well as from above (through divine approval). The people can withdraw what they gave if the ruler proves unworthy.

Second, rulers are under law, not above it. The king is not *legibus solutus* (absolved from laws) but bound by the laws of God, nature, and the realm. If the king violates these laws, he ceases to be a lawful king and becomes a tyrant, and tyrants have no right to obedience.

Third, tyrants may be resisted. Lesser magistrates (nobles, Parliament) have a duty to resist tyrants on behalf of the people. In extreme cases, even private individuals may resist, though Rutherford was cautious about this. Resistance is not rebellion against God's order but defense of God's order against the one who violated it.

Fourth, the people retain ultimate sovereignty. If all lesser magistrates fail to resist tyranny, the people as a body politic retain the right to depose tyrants and establish new government. This was revolutionary doctrine, it placed ultimate authority not in the king but in the community.[50]

Lex, Rex was revolutionary for its time and would be burned as seditious after the Restoration. But it expressed Presbyterian political convictions: authority required consent, rulers were accountable to law, and the people, through their representatives, could resist tyranny.[51]

Rutherford's work also revealed a tension in Presbyterian thought: they wanted strong magistrates to support the church and suppress heresy, but they also wanted limited magistrates who couldn't interfere with church independence. This tension was never fully resolved, it depended on whether the magistrate was godly (then give him power) or ungodly (then limit him).

The Solemn League and Covenant Revisited

September 1643: The Terms

The Solemn League and Covenant, signed between the English Parliament and Scottish Covenanters in September 1643, was the hinge document of Presbyterian hopes. Militarily, it brought Scottish armies south to fight for Parliament, crucial support that helped turn the war. Religiously, it committed both nations to reformation "according to the Word of God and the example of the best reformed churches", language the Scots understood as Presbyterian, but the English interpreted more flexibly.[52]

The key religious clauses bound signers to:[53]

"Preservation of the reformed religion in the Church of Scotland, in doctrine, worship, discipline, and government," this was clear; Scotland's presbyterian system was to be preserved.

"Reformation of religion in the kingdoms of England and Ireland, in doctrine, worship, discipline, and government, according to the Word of God, and the example of the best reformed churches"—this was ambiguous. What were the "best reformed churches"? Scotland said its Kirk; Independents said Reformed churches with more congregational autonomy.

"Extirpation [rooting out] of popery, prelacy [episcopacy]... superstition, heresy, schism, profaneness," Presbyterians and Independents agreed on eliminating popery and prelacy. But what counted as "heresy" and "schism"? Presbyterians thought Independency was schism; Independents thought Presbyterian uniformity was tyranny. "Preservation of the rights and privileges of the Parliaments, and the liberties of the kingdoms, and... preservation and defense of the King's Majesty's person and authority" this tried to balance parliamentary liberty with royal authority, a balance that would collapse when Parliament tried the King.

The Covenant was sworn publicly with solemn ceremony. MPs and ministers took it in St. Margaret's Westminster. Citizens took it in parishes throughout parliamentary-controlled England. Refusing the Covenant became grounds for exclusion from office and (later) for suspicion of royalism.

The Covenant's Failure

But the Covenant never achieved its aims:[54]

Scotland sent its army, which helped win the war, but Scotland never got England's Presbyterianism. The Westminster Assembly drafted Presbyterian documents, but Parliament never fully implemented them. England remained religiously diverse, with Independents, Baptists, and eventually Quakers flourishing alongside the nominal presbyterian establishment.

England got military help but not religious uniformity. Parliament established nominal presbyterian structures in London and some other areas (1646-1648), but they were Erastian, Parliament-controlled, not independent church courts as Scotland expected. And after Pride's Purge and the King's execution, even these structures crumbled.

Ireland remained chaotic, with Catholic rebellion, Protestant plantation communities, and complex ethnic-religious divisions that neither English Parliament nor Scottish Kirk could resolve. Cromwell's brutal campaign (1649-1650) brought military subjugation, not religious settlement. The King was never "preserved" in any meaningful sense—his "person and authority" were violated by trial and execution in 1649, making the Covenant's pledge to protect him moot.

Robert Baillie, the Scottish commissioner, watched with growing dismay as

English political realities frustrated Scottish religious hopes. By 1645, he was writing bitterly:[55]

> *The Independents, by their faction in the Army and in the House, have so prevailed, that we are in great hazard to get nothing done of all our intentions in ecclesiastical matters... Our brethren here are so full of fears that they dare not adventure upon any bold conclusions.*

The Solemn League and Covenant thus became a symbol of failed Presbyterian hopes—military alliance that won the war but couldn't establish the godly commonwealth Presbyterians envisioned. It bound England and Scotland together religiously in theory while they drifted apart in practice, the Scots maintaining their Kirk while England descended into religious diversity.

Richard Baxter's Vision: The Holy Commonwealth

The Book and Its Reception

Richard Baxter's *A Holy Commonwealth* (1659) was his attempt to articulate the Presbyterian political vision comprehensively, what a truly godly magistrate would do, how church and state would cooperate, what "reformation" would look like in practice. It was published as the Protectorate collapsed and the Restoration loomed, both the culmination of Presbyterian political thought and its epitaph.[56]

Baxter defined commonwealth as "a society of God's subjects ordered for common good." Note the key terms: society (not isolated individuals), God's subjects (all human authority derives from and answers to God), ordered (not chaotic or democratic), common good (not private interest or factional advantage).

Baxter rejected democracy as the worst form of government. He cited the recurring refrain in Judges: "In those days there was no king in Israel; every man did that which was right in his own eyes." This was not praise but condemnation—without proper authority, Israel fell into chaos, idolatry, and civil war. The same would happen in England if authority were given to the uneducated multitude. "The major vote of the people," Baxter wrote, "is ordinarily the worst; and the lesser number, the wiser."[57]

The book argued for:

Mixed government: Not pure monarchy, aristocracy, or democracy, but a balance of the one (a chief magistrate, perhaps a king, perhaps a protector), the few (a senate or House of Lords), and the many (a House of Commons representing the people). Each element would check the others, preventing tyranny from any quarter.[58]

Godly magistracy: The chief magistrate and other officials must be Christians who acknowledged Christ's kingship and Scripture's authority. Not that unbelievers couldn't hold office (Baxter was no theocrat in the strict sense), but that the government's overall direction must be Christian, supporting true religion, suppressing false religion, and promoting godliness among the people.

Religious establishment with toleration: The magistrate should maintain and fund a national church teaching Reformed doctrine and practicing presbyterian government. But within broad orthodox bounds, diversity might be tolerated. Those who held fundamental Christian doctrines (Trinity, Scripture's authority, justification by faith) should not be persecuted, even if they differed on church government or minor points.[59]

Limited popular participation: Baxter feared both tyranny and democracy. He wanted representation (a strong Parliament) but not universal suffrage—only property-holders and the educated should vote. The masses were too easily deceived, too prone to follow demagogues, too lacking in judgment to be trusted with the commonwealth's direction.[60]

The book was published in 1659 but suppressed after the Restoration. Royalists hated it for justifying resistance to Charles I. Republicans hated it for defending magisterial power over religion. It pleased no one except moderate Presbyterians, a dwindling constituency as England polarized between episcopalian royalism and sectarian radicalism.

Baxter's Moderate Presbyterian Vision

What made Baxter's vision "moderate" Presbyterian was his willingness to compromise:[61]

On church government: Unlike strict Presbyterians who insisted on classical presbyterian courts with independence from state control, Baxter accepted "reduced episcopacy," bishops with limited power sharing authority with presbyters. He thought the presbyterian-episcopal dispute was about form, not essence, and that cooperation was possible.

On ceremonies: Unlike Puritans who wanted to abolish all ceremonies not explicitly commanded in Scripture, Baxter accepted many traditional practices as "things indifferent" (adiaphora). Kneeling at communion, wearing surplices, using set prayers—these might be continued where people valued them, abolished where people found them offensive.

On toleration: Unlike Presbyterians who wanted uniformity enforced by both church courts and magistrates, Baxter advocated limited toleration. Peaceable dissenters who held fundamental Christian doctrines shouldn't be persecuted, even if they wouldn't conform to the national church. Coercing conscience was both impractical and unchristian.

On the magistrate: Unlike Erastians who wanted Parliament to control the church, and unlike high Presbyterians who wanted church independence, Baxter advocated cooperation. The magistrate should support the church but not dictate to it; the church should advise the magistrate but not claim civil power.

These moderate positions made Baxter influential as a pastor and devotional writer but ineffective as a political leader. His willingness to compromise meant neither Presbyterian hardliners nor Independent radicals trusted him fully. He spent the Restoration years trying to negotiate comprehension—a broad national church that could include moderate Presbyterians—but failed repeatedly.

Yet Baxter's moderation represented a strand of Presbyterian thought that would survive: the conviction that godly discipline was essential, that magistrates had duties regarding religion, but that persecution was counterproductive and liberty of conscience, within limits, was both Christian and prudent.

Subjects, Citizens, and the Common Good

Presbyterian political thought distinguished between subjects and citizens, a distinction with profound implications. Subjects were those who lived under a government's authority, bound to obey its laws, protected by its power, but having no formal voice in its direction. Citizens were those who participated in governance, voting, holding office, shaping policy. In Presbyterian thought, most people were subjects; only some were citizens.[62]

This was not arbitrary discrimination but principled limitation. To participate in governance required qualifications: property (which gave one a stake in the commonwealth), education (which enabled informed judgment), and godliness (which ensured right motivation). The unpropertied, the ignorant, and the ungodly had no business directing affairs of state. They should obey lawful authority, pursue their callings, and trust their betters to govern wisely.

The common good, the purpose for which government existed, was not determined by counting heads. Popular opinion could be wrong; the masses could be manipulated; passion could overcome reason. The common good was determined by wisdom—by those qualified to judge what would truly benefit the commonwealth. This was aristocratic thinking applied to politics; just as the sick consult physicians rather than voting on their treatment, so the commonwealth consulted its wisest members rather than polling the ignorant.

The Church as Political Formation

Presbyterian ecclesiology had indirect but powerful political effects. The system of ascending courts, session, presbytery, synod, General Assembly, trained members in representative governance. Elders were elected by congregations; representatives were sent to higher courts; debates followed procedures; decisions bound the whole. This was parliamentary politics in ecclesiastical form.[63]

When Scottish Presbyterians sent commissioners to the Westminster Assembly, they brought experience of this system. When English Presbyterians implemented provincial assemblies in 1646-1648, they created similar structures. The experience of church governance, debating, voting, submitting to majority decisions, appealing to higher courts, formed habits that transferred to civil governance. Presbyterianism was a school of aristocratic politics.

But the education was limited. Lay elders participated, but ministers dominated. The uneducated had no voice in synods. And the whole system remained hierarchical, local courts submitted to regional courts, regional courts to national. This was not democracy but layered aristocracy, each layer representing a wider circle but still composed of the qualified few.

Liberty of Conscience, Tithes, and Toleration

The Presbyterian Limits on Religious Freedom

The Defense of Compulsory Tithes

Presbyterians consistently defended compulsory tithes, the tenth of agricultural produce and other income that supported the parish ministry. Critics (Quakers, Baptists, Levellers) demanded voluntary support for religion. If the church was a gathered community of believers, why should unbelievers be forced to support it? If ministers were servants of God, why did they sue parishioners for tithes?[64]

Presbyterians responded on multiple grounds. First, the principle was biblical: Levitical priests had received tithes; Christian ministers were their successors. Second, the practice was ancient: tithes had supported the English church for centuries. Third, the need was practical: without compulsory support, ministers would be dependent on wealthy patrons or popular whim, compromising their prophetic freedom. Fourth, the benefit was universal: even those who did not attend parish worship benefited from the social order that a supported ministry maintained.

Baxter added a characteristically moderate argument. While he preferred voluntary contributions in principle, the sinfulness of human nature made compulsion necessary in practice. If tithes were abolished, most people, being unregenerate, would contribute nothing. The godly minority could not support the ministry alone. Better to maintain an imperfect system than to see the gospel die for lack of funding.

The Limits of Toleration

Presbyterian attitudes toward toleration varied, but most held a position between two extremes. On one side, strict uniformists wanted all English people to worship identically, with severe penalties for nonconformity. On the other side, radical separatists wanted complete religious freedom, with the magistrate having no role in spiritual matters.[65]

Most Presbyterians sought middle ground: substantial uniformity in essentials, liberty in circumstances. The "fundamentals" of Christian faith, Trinity, Incarnation, Atonement, Scripture's authority, must be maintained by law. Those who denied these fundamentals (Socinians denying Christ's divinity, for instance) could not be tolerated because they undermined the foundations of Christian society. But on "circumstantials," exact forms of worship, specific ceremonies, details of church government, diversity might be permitted.

Baxter developed this distinction carefully. He distinguished "intolerable errors" (those that destroy salvation or social order) from "tolerable errors" (those that, while wrong, do not damn or destabilize). The former must be suppressed; the latter might be permitted for the sake of peace. Catholics were intolerable because they owed allegiance to a foreign power (the pope) and had proven willing to use violence for their ends. Quakers were borderline: their disruption of services, refusal to pay tithes, and apparent denial of Scripture's authority threatened order, but their peaceable members might be tolerated with restrictions.

Oaths and Civil Loyalty

The question of oaths, solemn promises calling God as witness, revealed tensions in Presbyterian thought. Oaths were everywhere in seventeenth-century society: oaths of allegiance to the crown, oaths of supremacy acknowledging the monarch's ecclesiastical authority, oaths in courts of law, oaths of office. Presbyterians had no theological objection to oaths; they considered them lawful when properly administered and sincerely taken.[66]

The problem was content. Could a Presbyterian swear allegiance to Charles I while believing Charles had violated his coronation oath? Could one swear the Solemn League and Covenant (binding oneself to presbyterian reformation) and later swear the Engagement (accepting the Commonwealth that had killed the king)? These were not abstract questions; they determined who could hold office, who could vote, who could practice law.

When Quakers refused oaths entirely, citing Jesus's command "Swear not at all," Presbyterians responded that Quakers were confusing moral prohibition of false or frivolous oaths with blanket prohibition of all oaths. The Old Testament commanded oaths in God's name; the New Testament recorded apostles taking oaths; the practice of the church through centuries assumed oaths were lawful. Quaker refusal was another example of enthusiasm overriding sober interpretation of Scripture.

Justice, Blood Guilt, and Divine Wrath

The Presbyterian Response to Regicide

The Concept of National Blood Guilt

All seventeenth-century English factions shared the conviction that unpunished sin brought divine judgment on the nation. This was not metaphor but practical politics: plague, famine, military defeat, and social chaos were God's punishments for collective guilt. The question was: guilty of what?[67]

The biblical concept of "blood guilt" was central. Numbers 35:33 declared: "Blood defiles the land, and the land cannot be cleansed of the blood that is shed in it, except by the blood of the one who shed it." Unpunished murder polluted the entire community, inviting divine wrath until justice was done. The execution of criminals was not merely punishment but purification, removing the pollution that endangered everyone.

Applied to politics, this meant that national sins required national repentance and punishment. When Parliament accused Charles I of being a "man of blood," one whose wars had shed innocent blood, they invoked this framework. The continued chaos of the late 1640s, in this view, resulted from failure to punish the king. Only his execution could cleanse the land and restore divine favor.

The Presbyterian Dilemma over Regicide

Presbyterians found themselves in an agonizing position when the Army pushed for the king's trial and execution. On one hand, Presbyterian resistance theory, Rutherford's *Lex, Rex* and the covenanting tradition, justified resistance to tyranny. Charles had violated his covenant with God and people; he bore responsibility for the blood shed in civil war. On the other hand, Presbyterian constitutionalism insisted that resistance must come through proper channels, the estates, Parliament, not through the Army's arbitrary action.[68]

The majority of Presbyterian ministers opposed the king's execution. They acknowledged his guilt but denied that the Army and rump Parliament had authority to try and execute him. The trial was not constitutional; it was revolutionary violence dressed in legal forms. The Army's purge of Parliament (Pride's Purge) had removed Presbyterian members who would have opposed the trial. What remained was not the true Parliament but a faction ruling by force.

Moreover, many Presbyterians feared the consequences. If the king could be executed by military force, what protected any other institution? Today the king; tomorrow the nobility; the day after, the ministry. The logic of revolution, once unleashed, consumed all in its path. Presbyterian order required stability—legitimate authority, established procedures, predictable hierarchies. Regicide threatened all of these.

Philip Skippon and the Warning Against Toleration

Seven years after the regicide, the question of blood guilt took a different form. When James Nayler was brought before Parliament in 1656, charged with blasphemy for his theatrical entry into Bristol, Philip Skippon articulated the Presbyterian fear clearly:[69]

> *It has been always my opinion that the growth of these things is more dangerous than the most intestine or foreign enemies. Their principles strike both at ministry and magistracy... Nayler's sin will prove a national sin, and consequently a national judgment, if suffered to go unpunished.*

Skippon, the Presbyterian major-general who had commanded infantry at Naseby, now sat in judgment over a Quaker whose followers sang "Holy, holy, holy" while he rode a horse through the mud. The threat had shifted from royal tyranny to sectarian chaos. But the theological framework remained the same: national sin brought national judgment. If Parliament tolerated blasphemy, allowed the inner light to claim equality with Christ, God would punish the entire nation.

This was not hypocrisy but consistency. Presbyterian thought insisted on order: proper authorities enforcing proper standards, the wise and godly governing for the common good, sin punished and virtue rewarded. Whether the threat came from above (royal tyranny) or below (popular enthusiasm), the Presbyterian response was the same, restore order through legitimate means, maintain discipline, and trust that God would bless a godly commonwealth.

The Failure of Presbyterian Establishment

Why England Never Became Scotland

The London Presbyterian Experiment, 1646-1648

Parliament passed a series of ordinances between 1645 and 1648 attempting to establish presbyterian government:[70]

March 1646: An ordinance created the basic structure, twelve provincial assemblies, each subdivided into "classical presbyteries" (roughly equivalent to dioceses), under which individual congregations would function. London was divided into twelve classes with about 108 parishes.

August 1646: An ordinance established provincial assemblies (synods) with authority over multiple classes. These would handle appeals from presbyteries and coordinate regional church affairs.

June 1647: An ordinance created a parliamentary committee to hear appeals from provincial assemblies, effectively making Parliament the final court of appeal, which horrified Scots who saw this as Erastianism in action.[71]

The system looked impressive on paper: ascending courts, defined jurisdictions, mechanisms for discipline and appeal. But implementation was chaotic:[72]

Not all congregations participated. Many parishes simply ignored the ordinances, continuing with their existing practices (whether episcopal-leaning, Independent, or just traditional). The ordinances required compliance but provided no effective means of enforcement.

Elders were hard to find. The system required godly, able laymen willing to serve as ruling elders, examining converts, exercising discipline, attending presbytery meetings. In some parishes, such men existed; in others, they couldn't be found or wouldn't serve.[73]

Money was a problem. Parliament had abolished tithes collected by the episcopal system but hadn't replaced them with a functioning alternative. Ministers' salaries were uncertain, coming from various sources (parliamentary grants, sequestered royalist estates, voluntary contributions) that were often inadequate or unreliable.

The London Experiment: Modest Success

London's twelve classes came closest to functioning Presbyterianism. The capital had concentrated population, many learned ministers, and parliamentary oversight (the physical presence of Parliament in Westminster gave its ordinances more weight in London than elsewhere).[74]

The London provincial assembly met regularly, handled discipline cases, ordained ministers, and attempted to coordinate the classes. Some discipline was exercised: Edmund Rosier, a minister in Tower Hamlets, was suspended for scandalous behavior; Thomas Lambe, a Baptist, was censured for heterodox views; various laypeople were excommunicated for adultery, drunkenness, or attending Independent meetings.[75]

But even in London, the system struggled:[76]

Independents defied it openly. John Goodwin, minister at St. Stephen's Coleman Street, refused to acknowledge the presbytery's authority and continued operating his gathered church. William Greenhill and other Independent ministers simply ignored presbyterian structures. The presbytery could censure them but couldn't enforce compliance, these men had congregational support, often had parliamentary or Army backing, and could safely defy presbyterian authority.[77]

Disputes with Parliament persisted. When presbyteries tried to excommunicate without parliamentary approval, Parliament asserted its right to review all excommunications. When presbyteries claimed power to ordain without parliamentary consent, Parliament insisted on its authority to approve candidates. The Erastian structure Parliament had created meant presbyteries couldn't function as independent church courts.[78]

Popular resistance occurred. Some of those excommunicated simply attended other parishes or Independent meetings. Excommunication meant exclusion from communion in one's parish church, but if multiple options existed, determined sinners could find worship elsewhere.

By 1648, London's presbyterian experiment was struggling. It existed, it functioned after a fashion, but it was neither the independent church courts Scots envisioned nor an effective national church that Presbyterians wanted.

The Army as Independent Power

The Politicization of the New Model Army

The New Model Army's religious culture, as we saw in Chapter 2, was Independent rather than Presbyterian. Cromwell's toleration policy allowed Baptists, Independents, and eventually even Quakers to serve as officers and soldiers. Prayer meetings became political discussions. Army chaplains preached religious and political radicalism. The Army was becoming a gathered church in arms—and gathered churches didn't submit to presbyteries.[79]

By 1647, the Army had become a political force that Presbyterians couldn't control:[80]

The Army refused disbandment (spring 1647): Presbyterian MPs, wanting to negotiate settlement with Charles and having no more use for the Army, voted to disband most of it without full back pay and without indemnity for actions during the war. The Army refused, electing 'agitators' to represent common soldiers and presenting demands that mixed grievances (pay, indemnity) with political demands (no persecution of tender consciences).

Pride's Purge (December 1648): When Presbyterian MPs tried to continue negotiating with Charles after he had resumed war (the Second Civil War, summer 1648), the Army decided Parliament itself needed purging. Colonel Thomas Pride, with soldiers, physically blocked Presbyterian MPs from entering the Commons. About 140 members were excluded, 45 arrested. The remaining 'Rump Parliament' (perhaps 200 members, predominantly Independent) then proceeded to try the King.[81]

The Army's actions demonstrated that military power trumped parliamentary legitimacy. Presbyterians had won parliamentary majorities and passed ordinances establishing their system. But the Army, representing Independent and sectarian religion, simply overrode parliamentary decisions when they conflicted with Army interests. The godly commonwealth required godly force, and the force was on the Independents' side.

The Presbyterian Response: Accommodation or Resistance?

Presbyterians divided over how to respond to Army power:[82]

Accommodationists (including Baxter and many ministers): These accepted the Purge as fait accompli, tried to work with whatever government existed, and hoped to influence it toward moderation. They wouldn't endorse the King's execution but wouldn't resist it either. They continued ministering, hoping for better times.

Resisters (including hardline Presbyterians and those with royalist sympathies): These saw Pride's Purge and the King's execution as rebellion against God's order. Some fled to the Continent or to Scotland. Others stayed but refused cooperation with the Commonwealth government, waiting for restoration of legitimate authority.

Neutralists (probably the majority of Presbyterian laity): These simply tried to survive, attending whatever church services were available, avoiding political involvement, and hoping the chaos would eventually end.

The Army's triumph effectively ended Presbyterian hopes for establishing their system in England. The Commonwealth period (1649-1653) and Cromwell's Protectorate (1653-1658) were Independent-friendly regimes that tolerated diversity rather than enforcing uniformity. Presbyterians survived as one denomination among several, not as the national church they had hoped to build.

The Restoration: Presbyterian Hopes and Disappointments

1660: The Brief Moment

When Charles II returned in May 1660, many Presbyterians hoped for comprehensive settlement. They had opposed Charles I's policies but not monarchy itself. They had fought for parliamentary liberties and reformed religion, not for regicide and sectarian chaos. Now they hoped Charles II would accept constitutional monarchy, reformed (but not abolished) episcopacy, and a broad national church that could include moderate Presbyterians.[83]

Initial signs were promising:[84]

The Declaration of Breda (April 1660): Charles promised "liberty to tender consciences," suggesting religious toleration or at least comprehension within a broad national church.

The Worcester House Declaration (October 1660): Charles proposed modified episcopal government—bishops would govern with presbyterian-style councils of clergy, there would be latitude on ceremonies, and conscientious dissenters would not be persecuted.

Personal assurances: Charles met with Presbyterian leaders including Baxter, Calamy, and Reynolds. He spoke sympathetically, promised moderation, and appointed some Presbyterians to positions (Edward Reynolds was made Bishop of Norwich, a Presbyterian bishop!).

But Anglican royalists wanted no compromise. They had suffered under the Interregnum, had seen bishops imprisoned and the prayer book banned, had hidden their theological convictions and worshiped secretly or in exile. Now they wanted full restoration of the episcopal church with its ceremonies, its discipline, and its legal monopoly. They controlled Parliament (the Cavalier Parliament, elected in 1661, was overwhelmingly royalist and episcopalian) and increasingly controlled the King's ear.

The Savoy Conference, 1661

Charles called the Savoy Conference (April-July 1661) to revise the Book of Common Prayer in ways that might accommodate Presbyterian concerns. Twelve bishops met with twelve Presbyterian divines to discuss revisions. The Presbyterians proposed hundreds of changes:[85]

• Remove or make optional ceremonies that seemed popish

• Add more Scripture to the liturgy

• Provide alternative forms for those troubled by set prayers

• Moderate language that suggested Catholic doctrine

• Reform church government to include presbyterian elements

The bishops, led by Gilbert Sheldon (soon to be Archbishop of Canterbury), rejected nearly everything. They made minor verbal changes but no substantive alterations. The revised Book of Common Prayer (1662) was essentially the 1604 book with small adjustments, no accommodation of Presbyterian scruples.[86]

The Savoy Conference thus became, like Hampton Court in 1604, a missed opportunity for comprehension. Had bishops been more flexible, moderate Presbyterians like Baxter might have conformed and brought their congregations into the national church. Instead, the bishops' intransigence created Nonconformity, a permanent body of Protestant dissenters outside the Church of England.

The Great Ejection, 1662

The Act of Uniformity (1662) required all ministers to:[87]

• Use the Book of Common Prayer exclusively

• Receive episcopal ordination or reordination

• Renounce the Solemn League and Covenant

• Swear they would not "endeavor any alteration of government in church or state"

The deadline was August 24, 1662, St. Bartholomew's Day. About 2,000 ministers refused and were ejected from their livings. This "Great Ejection" included:[88]

• Edmund Calamy, who had preached for Parliament and sat in the Westminster Assembly

• Thomas Manton, whose sermons had been published and widely read

• Thomas Watson, renowned for practical theology

• Richard Baxter, though technically he wasn't ejected since he had no living at the time, was prohibited from ministry

• Hundreds of others, obscure country ministers and prominent London divines alike

The ejected ministers formed the core of English Nonconformity. Some preached illegally, risking fine and imprisonment. Others emigrated to New England or Holland. Still others found employment as chaplains to sympathetic gentry or as schoolteachers. But they were united in refusing to conform—in maintaining their presbyterian or independent convictions against legal establishment.

The Presbyterian Legacy

What Discipline Left Behind

Scottish Presbyterianism's Triumph[89]

If English Presbyterianism failed, Scottish Presbyterianism succeeded—not immediately or smoothly, but ultimately. The Restoration brought bishops back to Scotland (Charles II and his brother James tried to impose episcopacy), triggering the "Killing Times" when Covenanters were hunted and executed. But the Glorious Revolution (1688-1689) permanently established presbyterian government in Scotland. The claim of Right (1689) abolished episcopacy and restored the Kirk's independence.

The Church of Scotland, Presbyterian in government and Reformed in theology, became one of Scotland's defining institutions. It maintained:[90]

The Kirk Session, Presbytery, Synod, General Assembly structure: These courts governed Scottish religious life, exercised discipline, and maintained doctrinal standards. The General Assembly met annually, claiming authority directly from Christ without needing royal permission.

Independence from state control: Unlike England's established church (subordinate to crown and Parliament), Scotland's Kirk claimed Christ as its only head and insisted on freedom from civil dictation in spiritual matters. This "spiritual independence" remained contentious but foundational.

Educational and cultural influence: The Kirk's emphasis on literacy (so everyone could read Scripture) and on catechizing created a highly educated Scottish populace. Scottish universities (St. Andrews, Glasgow, Edinburgh, Aberdeen) trained ministers and educated professionals. Scottish Enlightenment thinkers, such as Hume, Smith, and Reid, grew in soil prepared by Presbyterian education.[91]

American Presbyterianism

Scottish and Scotch-Irish immigration to America carried presbyterian polity across the Atlantic. The Presbyterian Church in America, founded in 1706, adopted the Westminster Confession and Catechisms as its doctrinal standards. American Presbyterianism showed both the polity's strengths and its tensions:[92]

Strengths: The connecting structure of presbyteries and synods created institutional coherence across vast geography. Presbyterian emphasis on education produced a learned clergy and founded colleges (Princeton, 1746, was established to train Presbyterian ministers). The tradition of church courts debating and deciding created habits of democratic governance.[93]

Tensions: American conditions challenged Presbyterian assumptions about uniformity and magisterial support. Religious diversity was fact, not choice, Presbyterians were one denomination among many. Voluntary religion replaced establishment. The "Old Side-New Side" split (1741-1758) revealed tensions between confessional orthodoxy and revivalist enthusiasm that would recur throughout Presbyterian history.[94]

The Westminster Confession remained the American Presbyterian standard, revised in 1788 to remove references to magistrate's duty to suppress heresy (impossible in an American church-state separation context). American Presbyterianism thus embodied Westminster theology without Westminster's establishment assumptions.

Nonconformist Contributions to English Life

The Dissenting Academies

Excluded from Oxford and Cambridge (which required Anglican subscription), Nonconformists founded "dissenting academies," schools that trained ministers and educated middle-class youth. These academies became centers of educational innovation:[95]

Curriculum: Unlike the classics-focused Oxford and Cambridge, dissenting academies taught modern subjects, natural philosophy (science), modern languages, mathematics, history, logic. They combined traditional learning with practical education for commerce and professions.

Quality: Some academies rivaled or exceeded universities in quality. Tutors included brilliant scholars excluded from universities for conscience's sake. Students received rigorous education that prepared them for business, law, medicine, and ministry.

Influence: Dissenting academy graduates included prominent merchants, scientists, and writers. Joseph Priestley (chemist who discovered oxygen), Daniel Defoe (novelist), Samuel Johnson's teacher and other influential figures passed through dissenting academies.

The academies transmitted Presbyterian values, emphasis on education, disciplined study, moral seriousness, intellectual rigor, beyond Presbyterian communities, shaping English middle-class culture and contributing to the intellectual ferment that produced the Industrial Revolution.

The Nonconformist Conscience

"Nonconformist conscience" became shorthand for a cluster of moral and political commitments shaped by Presbyterian and other dissenting traditions:[96]

Social reform: Nonconformists disproportionately supported abolition of slavery, prison reform, factory legislation protecting workers, temperance (restricting alcohol), and opposition to gambling. These causes combined religious conviction (human dignity, moral discipline) with political activism.

Political liberalism: Excluded from full political participation until the 19th century (Test and Corporation Acts not repealed until 1828), Nonconformists supported expanding suffrage, limiting aristocratic privilege, and reforming institutions that excluded them. Their experience of persecution made them defenders of civil liberties.

Educational emphasis: Nonconformist support for public education, literacy campaigns, and Sunday schools reflected Presbyterian conviction that reading Scripture and understanding doctrine were essential for salvation and civilization. Education was religious duty.

Economic ethics: Presbyterian emphasis on discipline, hard work, honesty, and stewardship produced the "Protestant work ethic" Max Weber famously analyzed. Nonconformist businessmen built reputations for reliability; both Quaker and Presbyterian firms (Cadbury, Rowntree, etc.) became bywords for ethical commerce.[97]

The Nonconformist conscience shaped Victorian England profoundly, even though Nonconformists remained minorities. Their moral seriousness, their activism, and their conviction that religion should shape public life influenced British politics, social reform, and cultural values well into the twentieth century.

What Presbyterian Discipline Taught the World

Contributions and Costs

Presbyterian discipline's legacy is mixed, genuine contributions alongside real costs:[98]

Contributions:

Corporate discernment over individual or hierarchical authority: Presbyterianism showed that neither papal authority nor individual conscience alone was adequate, communities of believers could collectively discern truth and exercise discipline. This model of deliberative decision-making influenced democratic practices beyond religious contexts.

Education as religious duty: Presbyterian insistence that all believers must read Scripture and be catechized produced emphasis on literacy, education, and intellectual rigor. Scottish and American Presbyterian communities became centers of learning.[99]

Accountability structures: Presbyterian discipline demonstrated that liberty required responsibility. Freedom of conscience didn't mean freedom from oversight. The system provided mechanisms for addressing misconduct, maintaining standards, and preserving community integrity.[100]

Federal theology: Presbyterian covenant theology, understanding God's relationship with humanity as covenantal, with mutual obligations and federal representation (Adam representing humanity, Christ representing the elect), influenced political thought about social contracts and limited government.[101]

Costs:

Rigidity: Presbyterian discipline could become oppressive. Session records from Scotland show people summoned for minor infractions, subjected to humiliating public penance, and sometimes driven from communities. The system that aimed at restoration sometimes crushed those it sought to help.[102]

Intolerance: Presbyterian confidence that Scripture provided one correct pattern of church government produced intolerance of variation. Baptists,

Quakers, and Independents were "schismatics" who should be corrected or suppressed. Presbyterian establishment, where achieved, meant persecution of dissenters.[103]

Legalism: Emphasis on discipline and moral standards sometimes overshadowed grace. Presbyterian preaching could emphasize duty more than gospel, producing guilt-driven religion rather than grace-transformed lives.[104]

Social control: Presbyterian discipline served social control functions, especially in Scotland where kirk sessions regulated sexual behavior, economic relations, and social conformity. This maintained order but also enforced patriarchal hierarchies and limited individual freedom.[105]

The Presbyterian legacy thus includes both gifts and warnings. Its emphasis on education, accountability, and corporate discernment enriched Reformed Christianity and influenced broader culture. But its tendencies toward rigidity, intolerance, and social control remind us that even good structures can become oppressive when applied without wisdom and grace.

From Jerusalem Chamber to the World

We began this chapter in Westminster Abbey's Jerusalem Chamber, watching divines gather to build God's house through theological precision and disciplined order. We end by recognizing that, while the house they built never fully stood in England, it nevertheless shaped Reformed Christianity worldwide.

The Presbyterian Wager

Presbyterians made a specific wager about human nature and divine grace: that regenerate persons, organized in ascending courts, could maintain doctrinal purity and moral standards through corporate discipline guided by Scripture. The wager assumed that Scripture provided clear guidance, that godly elders could interpret it correctly, and that discipline would produce holiness rather than hypocrisy.[106]

The wager succeeded in Scotland, where circumstances, national covenant identity, independence from England, broad elite support, allowed presbyterian government to function as designed. It succeeded in American Presbyterianism, adapted to voluntary religion and denominational competition. It succeeded wherever Presbyterian churches maintained their distinctive polity and theological commitments.

But it failed in England for reasons both circumstantial and structural:

Circumstantial failures:

Timing: Presbyterians had momentum in 1646 but lost it as the Army became Independent and as Cromwell's tolerationist policies encouraged diversity rather than uniformity

Political competition: The need to work through Parliament made presbyterian structures Erastian, which alienated Scots and satisfied no one fully

Lack of enforcement: Without magisterial power to back church discipline, presbyteries couldn't compel conformity or prevent Independent defiance

Structural problems:

The church-state question: Presbyterians never resolved whether church courts should be independent (Scottish model) or subordinate to Parliament (Erastian model). This ambiguity crippled implementation because no one knew who had final authority.

Diversity of conviction: English Puritanism was broader than Presbyterianism alone. Many who opposed bishops didn't necessarily want classical presbyterian government. The coalition that fought Charles I dissolved when it came time to build a new church order.

The impossibility of uniformity: England by the 1640s was too diverse, too commercially developed, too influenced by print culture and religious debate to accept imposed uniformity. Presbyterian assumption that one right form existed and should be enforced collided with English reality of multiple competing convictions.[107]

What Remained

Though English Presbyterianism failed as national establishment, it survived and influenced:

As dissenting tradition: English Presbyterians became Nonconformists after 1662, maintaining their convictions through persecution, eventually gaining toleration (1689), and contributing to English intellectual, commercial, and political life for centuries.

As theological heritage: The Westminster Confession and Catechisms became foundational documents for Reformed Christianity worldwide. Their theological precision, pastoral wisdom, and comprehensive scope influenced Protestant theology far beyond presbyterian churches.

As model of ordered liberty: Presbyterian polity demonstrated that liberty and order weren't opposites but complements. Ascending courts provided structure without hierarchy, accountability without tyranny. This model influenced democratic thought and practice beyond religious contexts.

The Discipline That Couldn't Be

English Presbyterianism's failure reflected the impossibility of restoring a comprehensive religious establishment in the post-Reformation world. Once religious diversity existed, once people had tasted liberty of conscience uniformity could not be reimposed without coercion that most were unwilling to apply. Presbyterians wanted order, but the order they wanted required consensus that no longer existed.

The future belonged not to a unified national church but to denominations: particular traditions maintaining their identities while coexisting with others in competitive religious marketplaces. This wasn't what Presbyterians wanted. But it was what England got and eventually accepted as normal, even valuable.

The Putney debates revealed the challenge that would confront Presbyterian aristocracy: the Levellers' insistence that "the poorest he that is in England hath a life to live, as the greatest he." If consent was the foundation of legitimate government, why shouldn't every man consent? The next chapter follows that question into the gathered churches and the Free Commonwealth.

If Presbyterians sought order through discipline and ascending courts, the Independents we meet next sought liberty through gathered churches and voluntary covenants. Both were Calvinist in theology, both wanted godly reformation, both opposed episcopal tyranny. But their visions of the godly commonwealth differed fundamentally, and their conflict would shape England's revolutionary decades.

CHAPTER 4 — THE FREE COMMONWEALTH

INDEPENDENTS AND COMMONWEALTH MEN

The Putney Debates, 28 October 1647

By the Thames, candles guttered over a table crowded with soldiers' papers. The autumn evening had settled over Putney, and inside St. Mary's Church, the Army's General Council assembled for what would become the most extraordinary political debate in English history. Ministers, captains, and agitators, elected representatives from the common soldiers—argued past midnight about conscience, about the franchise, about how to keep a hard-won peace without rebuilding the old chains. Outside, sentries stamped their feet against the cold; inside, the air sparked with a new claim: that gathered churches and a freer state might stand together.[1]

Oliver Cromwell sat at the head of the table, his son-in-law Henry Ireton beside him. These were the Army's political leaders, architects of victory at Naseby, negotiators with the King. They had summoned this council to address a crisis: the New Model Army's rank and file, having defeated the King, now demanded a say in England's future. And their demands, set forth in a document called *The Agreement of the People*, went far beyond what Cromwell and Ireton had imagined.[2]

The Leveller Challenge

Across the table sat the agitators and their allies. Edward Sexby, cavalry trooper and sometime preacher, had a voice that carried weight among the common soldiers. Beside him sat Colonel Thomas Rainsborough, highest-ranking officer to support the Levellers' cause. And on the benches behind them, though not officially part of the council, sat John Wildman and Maximilian Petty, civilian Levellers who had helped draft the *Agreement*.[3]

The *Agreement of the People* proposed revolutionary changes:

- Dissolve the current Parliament and call new elections
- Redistribute constituencies to reflect population (not ancient custom)

- Extend the franchise to all men who were not servants or recipients of alms
- Reserve certain rights as beyond Parliament's power: liberty of conscience, freedom from military conscription, equality before the law
- Establish that government derives from the people's consent, not from ancient constitution or divine right[4]

Cromwell opened the meeting with prayer, long, searching, asking God to guide them to truth. When he finished, Ireton spoke, his lawyer's mind organizing the issues. "We must consider," he said, "whether we are bound by our engagements to the King, whether we have authority to remodel the government, and whether the proposals before us will preserve property and prevent anarchy."[5]

"The Poorest He That Is in England"

But it was Thomas Rainsborough who spoke the words that would echo through centuries. The debate had turned to the franchise, who should vote in the new England they were trying to build. Ireton argued that only men with property should vote, for they alone had a "fixed interest" in the kingdom. To give voting rights to the propertyless would endanger property itself, they might vote to redistribute wealth, and England would descend into chaos.[6]

Rainsborough stood, his voice carrying both passion and precision:[7]

> *For really I think that the poorest he that is in England hath a life to live, as the greatest he; and therefore truly, sir, I think it's clear, that every man that is to live under a government ought first by his own consent to put himself under that government; and I do think that the poorest man in England is not at all bound in a strict sense to that government that he hath not had a voice to put himself under.*

The room stirred. Here was the logic of consent taken to its radical conclusion: not just that kings required consent, but that every commoner who must obey law deserved a voice in making it. Ireton responded immediately, sensing the danger. If men without property could vote, he argued, they would vote to abolish property. "No man hath a right to an interest or share in the disposing of the affairs of the kingdom... that hath not a permanent fixed interest in this kingdom."[8]

The debate continued for days. The chaplain William Dell preached that God was no respecter of persons—rich and poor stood equal before Him. How then could civil law give voice only to the wealthy? John Wildman argued from first principles: men were born free, not born into subjection. Government was a social compact, and every man party to that compact deserved representation.[9]

Cromwell's Dilemma

Cromwell listened, increasingly troubled. He sympathized with the agitators' religious arguments—God did regard the poor as well as the rich. But he feared the political consequences. The New Model Army had become a school of radical religion and politics. Chaplains preached liberty of conscience; prayer meetings became political debates; ordinary soldiers claimed the right to speak on affairs of state. This was exhilarating and dangerous.[10]

Moreover, Cromwell needed to negotiate with the King. Charles I, imprisoned but not deposed, still commanded loyalty from much of the nation. Any settlement required his cooperation, or at least his neutrality. But if the Army adopted the *Agreement of the People*, negotiations would collapse. The King would never accept a government based on popular sovereignty and extended franchise.[11]

On the third day of debates, Cromwell made his move. He proposed they adjourn to consider the *Agreement* more carefully, that the officers return to their regiments, that they seek God's guidance through prayer and fasting. It was a delaying tactic, and the Levellers knew it. But Cromwell's authority, military, political, spiritual, was too great to openly defy. The council agreed to adjourn.[12]

November 1647: The Rendezvous and the End

Two weeks later, Cromwell orchestrated the Army's rendezvous at three different locations, dividing potential Leveller support. At Corkbush Field, some regiments appeared with copies of the *Agreement* stuck in their hats, shouting "England's freedom, soldiers' rights!" Cromwell rode among them, tore the papers from their hats, and arrested the ringleaders. Three were court-martialed; one, Private Richard Arnold, was shot as an example.[13]

The Leveller moment in the Army was broken. The movement would continue, Leveller pamphlets would flood London for another two years , but they had lost their military base. The New Model Army would remain under the control of its officers, and those officers would make England's future without consulting the common soldiers who had won the war.[14]

Inside the Church: Two Visions

But the Putney debates revealed something permanent: two visions of the Independent commonwealth, both claiming to follow Christ, both opposed to king and bishop, but differing on fundamental questions.

Cromwell's Vision (ordered liberty): A godly commonwealth led by godly men, not by birth or wealth alone, but by visible grace and proven capacity. Liberty of conscience for sincere Protestants, but within bounds set by magistrates who served God. Property protected, but regulated for common good. A mixed constitution balancing the one, the few, and the many—perhaps with Cromwell himself as the one.[15]

The Levellers' Vision (radical democracy): A commonwealth based on natural rights and popular sovereignty. Every man equal before the law, regardless of wealth or birth. Liberty of conscience absolute , the magistrate punishes crimes but not opinions. Property protected but not privileged—no man's vote worth more than another's. No single ruler, no House of Lords, just a Parliament elected by the many and answerable to them.[16]

Both visions were Independent in church government, gathered congregations, voluntary covenants, local choice of ministers. Both opposed compulsory religion. Both drew on the same Scriptures and prayed to the same

God. Yet they could not be reconciled. One required hierarchy and deference; the other insisted on equality. One feared anarchy more than tyranny; the other feared tyranny more than anarchy.

The Putney debates lead to defeat for the Levellers, but their arguments entered England's political bloodstream. The questions they posed, Who should vote? What rights are inalienable? Where does legitimate authority come from?, would be asked again and again, in England and across the Atlantic. To understand how those questions emerged from Independent religion, we must see how gathered churches cultivated habits of consent, debate, and conscience that scaled from the congregation to the commonwealth.

Gathered Churches and the Practice of Consent

Covenant, Discipline, and Voluntary Community

What "Independent" Meant in Practice

The Congregational Principle

"Independent" was a slippery term in 17th-century England, sometimes a self-description, often an insult hurled by Presbyterians who saw it as code for anarchy. But at its core, Independence meant congregational autonomy: each local church was complete in itself, choosing its own minister, governing its own affairs, and answerable to no bishop, presbytery, or synod.[17]

The model came partly from New England. John Cotton's *The Way of the Churches of Christ in New England* (1645) circulated widely among English Independents, describing how Plymouth and Massachusetts churches operated. Cotton explained the gathered church: believers who had experienced God's grace examined one another's conversions, covenanted together to walk in Christian fellowship, and elected their own officers (pastor, teacher, ruling elders, deacons). The congregation, not any external authority, held the keys of the kingdom—the power to admit members, administer discipline, and interpret Scripture.[18]

English Independents adapted this model. In the 1640s, as censorship collapsed and religious experimentation flourished, Independent congregations sprang up in London and provincial cities. Some met openly; others, fearing Presbyterian or Anglican persecution, met in homes or at odd hours. They varied in practice, some more structured, others more spontaneous, but shared core commitments: voluntary membership, congregational governance, liberty of conscience.[19]

The Covenant: Bedford Church, 1650

The church covenant was the founding document, the social compact that created the congregation. When Independents in Bedford gathered to form a church in 1650, they drafted a covenant that John Bunyan (who joined soon after) would later describe:

"We whose names are underwritten do, in the fear and reverence of Almighty God, and in the sense of our own unworthiness, covenant and agree together to walk in all God's ways and ordinances as He has revealed or shall reveal them to us out of His holy word, promising by His assistance to cleave to Him and to one another, and to watch over one another's souls and conversations."[20]

The language was deliberate. "We... covenant and agree" indicating voluntary action and mutual consent. "Walk in all God's ways... as He has revealed or shall reveal," openness to "new light," refusal to be bound by human traditions. "Watch over one another," corporate responsibility, not just individual piety. "Promising by His assistance," acknowledging dependence on God's grace, not their own strength.

The covenant created the church. No bishop's approval was needed, no presbytery's permission. The gathered saints, convinced of one another's grace and committed to mutual edification, constituted themselves as Christ's body in that place. It was a radical democratization of church authority, though Independents would have said it was simply returning to New Testament practice.[21]

Membership and the "Visible Saints"

Not everyone who attended could join. Independent churches examined prospective members carefully, requiring testimony of conversion—a credible account of how God had brought them from sin to grace. This examination served multiple purposes:[22]

- **Theological**: To ensure members understood the gospel and had experienced it personally
- **Social**: To create a community of the committed, not the merely nominal
- **Disciplinary**: To establish grounds for later discipline—those who joined voluntarily could be held accountable

The Bedford church, like others, examined candidates before the congregation. Bunyan described his own examination: "I was put to it to give an account of the work of grace upon my soul; and I had spoken what I could, and they were satisfied." His testimony convinced the church he was genuinely converted, and they admitted him to membership and eventually to preaching.[23]

This practice, requiring conversion testimony, was foreign to presbyterian and episcopal churches, where parish membership came by geography and infant baptism. Independents insisted on regenerate membership: only visible saints, those showing evidence of God's work in their lives, could join the covenant. This didn't guarantee perfect churches, Independents acknowledged that hypocrites might deceive and genuine converts might fall, but it aimed for communities of faith, not geographic parishes of mixed believers and unbelievers.[24]

Discipline Without Coercion

The Process of Church Discipline

Independent churches took discipline seriously but eschewed coercion. The pattern came from Matthew 18:15-17: if a brother sins, speak to him privately;

if he won't hear, take witnesses; if he still won't hear, tell the church; if he rejects the church's judgment, treat him as an outsider.[25]

This process played out regularly in Independent congregations. When a Bedford church member, John Child, was accused of drunkenness in 1653, the church appointed two brothers to speak with him privately. Child initially denied the charge, then admitted he had been drinking but insisted he wasn't drunk. The two brothers reported back to the church, which appointed them to speak with witnesses who had seen Child that night.[26]

The investigation took weeks. Finally, with witnesses' testimony confirmed, the church called Child to answer. He appeared, was confronted with evidence, and broke down in tears. "I have sinned against God and His people," he confessed. The church then debated: Was his repentance genuine? Some thought it was; others suspected he was only sorry he'd been caught. After prayer and discussion, the church decided to accept his repentance but suspend him from the Lord's Supper for three months, a time of testing to see if his amendment was real.[27]

Three months later, Child's behavior had indeed changed. The church restored him to full fellowship. The discipline had worked as intended: not punishment but restoration, not coercion but corporate discernment and pastoral care.

Excommunication as Last Resort

If a member persistently refused discipline, the church could excommunicate, remove them from fellowship. But this wasn't the presbyterian or Catholic excommunication, with civil penalties attached. It was purely ecclesial: the person could no longer take communion or vote in church meetings, but they remained free to attend services, and they faced no civil punishment.[28]

More importantly, excommunication was reversible. If the person repented, even years later, the church could restore them. The goal was always restoration, not permanent exclusion. As one Independent divine put it: "We cast out that Satan might not utterly devour; we exclude from the table that the person might hunger and thirst for righteousness; we treat as a heathen that they might see themselves outside Christ's fold and desire to return."[29]

The contrast with magisterial churches was stark. Presbyterians excommunicated but expected magistrates to punish heresy and schism with fines and imprisonment. Anglicans excommunicated and could bring the force of law against dissenters. Independents excommunicated but had no civil sword to wield, their only power was the congregation's collective judgment and the hope that the Holy Spirit would use that judgment to convict conscience.[30]

This made Independent discipline dependent on voluntary submission. A person who didn't care about the church's opinion could simply leave. This seemed like weakness to Presbyterians, but Independents saw it as strength. True repentance came from conviction, not coercion. A person forced to conform outwardly but unchanged inwardly was worse than useless, they were a hypocrite who dishonored God and corrupted the church.

Democracy in the Congregation

Who Decides? The Congregational Meeting

Independent churches made major decisions corporately. Should they call a new minister? The congregation voted. Should they buy property for a meetinghouse? The congregation decided. Should they excommunicate a persistent sinner? The congregation judged, after hearing the case.[31]

This was startling to contemporaries used to hierarchical churches. A weaver and a merchant had equal votes in an Independent congregation. A woman who could testify to her conversion could speak in church business meetings (though practices varied, some churches restricted women's speech more than others). Education and wealth mattered less than spiritual maturity and the congregation's confidence in a member's judgment.[32]

Bunyan, who had been a tinker (a traveling mender of pots and pans) before his conversion, became pastor of the Bedford church in 1672. His lack of university education was a scandal to educated clergy. Bunyan didn't care: "I have received my commission from heaven," he said, "and not from men, though I be never so much frowned upon by the world." The congregation had examined him, found him gifted in preaching and pastoral care, and called him as their minister. No bishop's ordination, no presbytery's approval, just the church's recognition of God's gifts in him.[33]

Limits on Democracy

But Independent democracy had limits. Not every opinion was equal. When doctrinal questions arose—Is Christ truly divine? Can believers lose their salvation?—churches didn't simply vote. They examined Scripture together, consulted writings of learned divines, and sought the Spirit's guidance. Some voices carried more weight: the minister (usually educated), elders (recognized for spiritual maturity), and members known for biblical knowledge.[34]

Moreover, Independents distinguished between essentials and circumstantials. On essentials—the Trinity, Christ's incarnation, justification by faith—there could be no compromise. A church member who denied these was excluded, not by democratic vote but by the nature of Christian orthodoxy. On circumstantials—singing psalms or not, allowing baptized children to take communion or not, governance details—churches could differ and still be in fellowship.[35]

This distinction was crucial. It meant Independents could be tolerant on many matters while still insisting on core doctrines. They could allow liberty of conscience without descending into the "anything goes" that critics feared. But the line between essentials and circumstantials was contested. What one person called essential, another called circumstantial. This tension would produce both creativity and conflict.

The congregational practice of debate, voting, and decision-making taught political habits. Members learned to:[36]

- **Articulate reasons publicly**: You couldn't just assert your opinion;

you had to defend it with Scripture and reason.

- **Listen to contrary views**: The congregation heard all sides before deciding.
- **Accept corporate decisions**: Even if you disagreed, once the church decided, you submitted (or left).
- **Hold leaders accountable**: Ministers and elders served at the congregation's pleasure and could be removed if they failed in their duties.

These were habits that transferred to politics. Independents who practiced congregational democracy found it natural to demand representative government, freedom of debate, and accountability of rulers. The gathered church was a school of citizenship.

If Independent churches taught democratic habits through covenant and congregational discipline, the New Model Army taught them on a larger scale. When the Army became, in effect, a political party in arms, it carried Independent religious culture into the heart of England's revolution. To see how religion and politics intertwined, we turn to the Army and its extraordinary chaplains.

Army Religion and the School of Liberty

How Military Discipline Produced Political Radicalism

The New Model Army as Religious Community

Cromwell's Recruitment Strategy

When Parliament authorized the New Model Army in early 1645, Oliver Cromwell saw an opportunity. The old armies had been local militias, commanded by noblemen, recruited by traditional loyalties. They were undisciplined, prone to plunder, and not particularly ideological. Cromwell wanted something different: an army of believers, motivated by conviction rather than pay or feudal duty.[37]

He recruited for godliness as much as military skill. "I had rather have a plain russet-coated captain that knows what he fights for, and loves what he knows," Cromwell famously said, "than that which you call a gentleman and is nothing else." This was revolutionary: valuing religious commitment over social status, promoting common soldiers to officer ranks based on ability and piety rather than birth.[38]

The result was an army unlike any England had seen. Troopers debated theology around campfires. Officers led prayer meetings before battles. Chaplains preached not just obedience but the righteousness of the cause. When the New Model Army crushed the King's forces at Naseby (June 1645), they sang Psalms as they charged and credited God with the victory.[39]

The Chaplains: Dell, Peters, Saltmarsh

The Army's chaplains were not moderates. Parliament had appointed presbyterian chaplains initially, but many regiments replaced them with Independents and more radical preachers who better reflected the soldiers' religious convictions.

William Dell (c.1607-1669) was perhaps the most influential. A Cambridge-educated minister who rejected the idea of a learned clergy, Dell preached that the Holy Spirit could teach anyone, regardless of education. "The universities are the forge where the fetters are made," he said, attacking clerical monopoly on ministry. Dell argued that tithes should be abolished, that every believer was a priest, and that gathered churches needed no state approval or support.[40]

His sermons electrified the troops. In *The Building and Glory of the Truly Christian and Spiritual Church* (1646), preached to Fairfax's regiment, Dell proclaimed:

"The saints are called out of the world to be a peculiar people... They are not to be regulated by the world's laws nor by the world's wisdom, but by the Spirit of Christ dwelling in them. The magistrate may govern men's outward actions, but he cannot rule their consciences. The sword of steel may cut the body, but it cannot touch the soul."[41]

This was Independent ecclesiology turned into political theory: the separation of spiritual and temporal authority, the limitation of magisterial power, the inviolability of conscience.

Hugh Peters (1598-1660) was more militant. An energetic preacher who had spent years in New England before returning to fight for Parliament, Peters believed God was raising up the Army to defeat Antichrist and prepare for Christ's kingdom. He preached at executions of royalist spies, urged soldiers forward in battle, and celebrated victories as divine judgments against the wicked.[42]

Peters saw no tension between Christianity and warfare—not this warfare, at least. The Army fought for God's cause against a tyrannical king allied with papists. To kill in such a cause was righteous. "The sword of the Lord and of Gideon!" Peters would cry, and soldiers would answer with cheers. His sermons assumed that godly men could wield the sword without spiritual compromise—a position most Quakers would eventually reject.[43]

John Saltmarsh (d.1647) represented the Army's radical wing. An antinomian (one who believed grace freed believers from the moral law), Saltmarsh preached universal salvation, opposed compulsory tithes, and defended the Levellers' political program. His *Smoke in the Temple* (1646) attacked the presbyterian establishment as a new tyranny replacing the old episcopal one.[44]

Saltmarsh died young, in 1647, but his influence outlasted him. He had articulated a vision of radical liberty: free grace leading to free churches leading to free government. No coercion in religion, no privilege by birth, no deference to clergy or gentry. Christ had freed His people, and they should live as free.

These chaplains—Dell, Peters, Saltmarsh, and others—made the New Model Army a seminary of radical religion. Soldiers heard sermons questioning traditional authority, exalting individual conscience, and imagining new political possibilities. When those soldiers became agitators demanding a say in

England's future, they were putting into practice what Army religion had taught them.

Prayer Meetings as Political Assemblies

The Blurring of Worship and Politics

New Model Army regiments held regular prayer meetings—gatherings where soldiers prayed, sang psalms, heard sermons, and discussed matters of conscience. These meetings were supposed to be devotional, but they inevitably became political. How could they not? The Army's mission was political: defeat the King, secure Parliament, reform the church. Every prayer for victory was a political act; every sermon on righteousness touched on public affairs.[45]

As the war wound down (1646-1647) and questions about England's future became urgent, the prayer meetings intensified. Soldiers debated: Should they disband as Parliament ordered, or stay together until their demands were met? Should they negotiate with the King, or try him for blood-guilt? Should they support the presbyterian peace party or demand broader reforms?[46]

Officers couldn't control these discussions. The gathered church model, where every member had voice, transferred to military prayer meetings. A cavalry trooper who could testify to God's grace felt empowered to speak on political matters too. After all, if the Spirit taught all believers, why should common soldiers defer to officers on questions of justice and liberty?[47]

The Agitators Emerge

In spring 1647, as Parliament moved to disband much of the Army without paying arrears or providing indemnity for wartime actions, the soldiers organized. Each regiment elected "agitators," representatives to speak for the men. These agitators were often the same soldiers who led prayer meetings and spoke most boldly about conscience and rights.[48]

The agitators brought Leveller ideas into the Army. Many had been reading Leveller pamphlets circulating from London, John Lilburne's attacks on tyranny, Richard Overton's arguments for natural rights, William Walwyn's pleas for toleration. The language of these pamphlets resonated with Army religion: both spoke of freedom, of conscience, of rights that no earthly power could justly violate.[49]

In June 1647, the Army refused disbandment and marched toward London. The officers, including Cromwell and Ireton, tried to maintain control by creating the General Council—a body including officers and agitators to discuss the Army's demands. This was the council that would meet at Putney in October.[50]

The General Council meetings often began with prayer. Cromwell would pray for an hour or more, seeking God's guidance. But then the debate would turn intensely political: What form should England's government take? Who should have the franchise? What rights are inalienable? The participants moved seamlessly between theological and political language, seeing no sharp division between them.[51]

This fusion of religion and politics produced the Putney debates' extraordinary character. When Rainsborough argued that "the poorest he" deserved a vote, he grounded it in theology: all men were created in God's image, all were equally fallen, all were equally redeemed by Christ's blood. How then could civil law privilege the rich over the poor? When Ireton defended property qualifications for voting, he too used theological language: God had ordained degrees of wealth and status; to overturn these would be to rebel against providence.[52]

The prayer meetings had created a space where religious authority and political power were equally contestable. A soldier who could challenge a minister's interpretation of Scripture felt empowered to challenge an officer's political judgment. This was explosive, and ultimately, Cromwell would contain it by force. But the genie couldn't be fully returned to the bottle. Army religion had taught thousands of ordinary Englishmen that their consciences mattered, their voices deserved hearing, and their consent was necessary for legitimate government.

Liberty of Conscience as Military Necessity

Cromwell's Pragmatic Toleration

Oliver Cromwell was not a systematic political thinker. He was a practical soldier who solved problems as they arose. One problem was religious diversity in the Army. His regiments included presbyterian-leaning Independents, Baptists who rejected infant baptism, antinomians who troubled traditional Calvinism, and (by the late 1640s) early Quakers who rejected all formal ministry.[53]

Cromwell could have imposed uniformity, required all soldiers to conform to a standard confession, expelled dissenters, and maintained discipline through religious conformity. Many presbyterian MPs urged him to do exactly that. But Cromwell refused. He believed in liberty of conscience for "godly" men, and he valued military effectiveness over religious uniformity.[54]

His famous letter to the Westminster Assembly (March 1644) after the siege of Lincoln made his position clear:

"I had rather have a plain, russet-coated Captain that knows what he fights for, and loves what he knows, than that which you call a gentleman and is nothing else... Presbyterians, Independents, all had here the same spirit of faith and prayer... they agree here, know no names of difference: pity it is it should be otherwise anywhere. All that believe have the real unity."[55]

This was not principled toleration of the sort Roger Williams advocated (Williams wanted liberty even for Catholics, Jews, and Muslims). Cromwell's toleration extended only to those he judged "godly," sincere Protestants who walked uprightly, even if they held eccentric views. He would not tolerate Catholics (whom he saw as idolaters serving a foreign power) or Anglicans (whom he saw as crypto-papists). But within the bounds of Reformed Protestantism, he allowed remarkable diversity.[56]

The Practical Results

Cromwell's toleration policy had practical benefits. The New Model Army could recruit from a wider pool, drawing godly men regardless of denominational affiliation. It avoided the sectarian conflicts that plagued other armies, the Army rarely saw the kind of religious violence common in the Thirty Years' War, where Catholic and Protestant soldiers massacred one another.[57]

But it also had radical implications. If Baptists and Independents could fight side by side, why should the state enforce uniformity? If antinomians and Calvinists could cooperate in military affairs, why not in civil life? If conscience could be free in the Army, why not in the nation?[58]

John Milton would make exactly this argument in *Areopagitica* (1644) and later works. Truth, he argued, emerged through free contest of ideas. To suppress opinions was to assume infallibility, to claim you already possessed all truth and needed hear no more. But history showed that new light often came from unexpected sources. Better to allow free debate and trust that truth would prevail.[59]

The Army's experience seemed to prove Milton right. Diverse religious beliefs hadn't produced chaos or military ineffectiveness. On the contrary, the New Model Army was the most disciplined and successful force England had fielded. Perhaps religious diversity, rather than uniformity, was compatible with social order. Perhaps liberty of conscience, rather than being dangerous, was actually beneficial.

This was a revolutionary conclusion, and it terrified Presbyterians who saw in it the dissolution of all authority. If the state couldn't enforce religious conformity, what could it enforce? If conscience was free, who would obey unjust laws? The Presbyterians' fears weren't unfounded, liberty of conscience did undermine traditional authority. But Independents wagered that voluntary consent, not coerced conformity, could sustain a free commonwealth.

If the Army was a school of liberty, its most brilliant student was not a soldier but a poet. John Milton, watching from his study in London, absorbed the lessons of Independent religion and Army politics and transformed them into the most eloquent defense of free speech and free conscience that England had yet produced. To understand the Independent vision at its fullest, we turn to Milton.

John Milton and the Case for Openness

Speech, Print, and the Marketplace of Ideas

The Man and His Moment

Milton's Formation

John Milton (1608-1674) was born into London's commercial class, son of a scrivener (a legal document writer) who had become prosperous enough to give his son an excellent education. Milton studied at Cambridge, considered entering the ministry, but chose instead a life of scholarship and poetry. By his thirties, he had written some of England's finest lyric poetry but remained largely unknown outside literary circles.[60]

The Civil War transformed him. Milton became convinced that England was entering a kairos moment, a time when history turned and new possibilities opened. The defeat of the King, the collapse of censorship, the flowering of religious and political debate, all seemed to herald a new age. Milton threw himself into controversy, writing pamphlets on divorce (he had personal experience of an unhappy marriage), education, church government, and freedom of the press.[61]

His prose was not the plain style favored by many Puritans. Milton wrote in elaborate, Latinate sentences, dense with classical allusions and biblical imagery. His arguments demanded educated readers. Yet his influence was profound. He articulated the Independent vision with a philosophical rigor and rhetorical power that no one else matched.[62]

The Presbyterian Threat, 1643-1644

By 1643, Parliament was winning the military war but losing the ideological peace. Presbyterians dominated Parliament and the Westminster Assembly. They were preparing to replace episcopal tyranny with presbyterian discipline, a national church with compulsory attendance, mandatory tithes, and suppression of schism and heresy.[63]

They also moved to reimpose press censorship. The Licensing Order of June 1643 required all books to be approved by official licensers before publication. This was the old episcopal censorship with new enforcers. The order aimed to stop the flood of radical pamphlets, Baptist, Independent, antinomian, and worse, that poured from London's underground presses.[64]

Milton had recently published pamphlets arguing that unhappy marriages should be dissolvable, a radical position that scandalized Presbyterians. When his *Doctrine and Discipline of Divorce* (1643) appeared without license, Presbyterian divines denounced it from pulpits and in print. Herbert Palmer, preaching to Parliament, didn't name Milton but clearly targeted him: "A wicked booke is abroad and uncensored, though deserving to be burnt, whose Author hath been so impudent as to set his Name to it and dedicate it to your selves!"[65]

Milton realized the Presbyterian establishment intended to silence dissent as thoroughly as the bishops had. He responded with *Areopagitica* (November 1644), the most famous defense of free speech in English literature, though it was not titled as such and was itself unlicensed, violating the very order it protested.[66]

***Areopagitica*: The Argument**

Truth Needs Contest

Milton's central argument was that truth emerges through free debate, not through censorship. In a famous passage, he wrote:[67]

> *And though all the winds of doctrine were let loose to play upon the earth, so Truth be in the field, we do injuriously by licensing and prohibiting to misdoubt her strength. Let her and Falsehood grapple; who ever knew Truth put to the worse, in a free and open encounter?*

This was a revolutionary claim. Most 17th-century thinkers assumed error was more attractive than truth—falsehood glittered while truth was plain.

Therefore, magistrates must suppress error to protect the weak-minded masses from deception. Milton inverted this logic: truth was stronger than falsehood and would prevail if given fair contest. Censorship didn't protect truth; it weakened it by preventing the testing that would demonstrate its superiority.[68]

Milton used a commercial metaphor that would become central to liberal thought: the "marketplace of ideas." Just as free trade allowed good products to outcompete bad ones (assuming honest weights and measures), free debate allowed true ideas to outcompete false ones (assuming good-faith argument and rational listeners). To license printing was like granting monopolies, it protected inferior products (ideas) from competition.[69]

Reading as Moral Exercise

Milton also argued that encountering error was necessary for moral development. He wrote:[70]

> *I cannot praise a fugitive and cloistered virtue, unexercised and unbreathed, that never sallies out and sees her adversary, but slinks out of the race where that immortal garland is to be run for, not without dust and heat. Assuredly we bring not innocence into the world, we bring impurity much rather: that which purifies us is trial, and trial is by what is contrary.*

The metaphor was athletic: virtue must be exercised like a muscle, tested in combat, proven through struggle. A person who had never encountered temptation or error wasn't virtuous but merely inexperienced. True virtue came from choosing good after having seen evil, from embracing truth after having considered falsehood.[71]

This argument assumed a high view of human capacity, or at least of sanctified human capacity. Believers indwelt by the Holy Spirit could discern truth from error if given the tools: Scripture, reason, and free debate. This was more optimistic than the Calvinist anthropology that dominated Reformed thought. Calvin emphasized human depravity and the need for external authority (church, magistrate) to restrain error. Milton emphasized human potential under grace and the need for liberty to cultivate discernment.[72]

Censorship Breeds Tyranny and Hypocrisy

Milton warned that licensing would produce two evils: tyranny and hypocrisy.

Tyranny because licensers inevitably abused power. Who guards the guardians? If licensers could suppress what they judged false or dangerous, they could suppress anything that challenged their authority. "This is the greatest censorship," Milton wrote, "that can befall learning and Truth." He pointed to the Spanish Inquisition and papal Index of Forbidden Books as warnings of where licensing led, not to protection of truth but to protection of corrupt power.[73]

Hypocrisy because licensing made people hide true beliefs. "You must learn to practise hypocrisy," Milton warned, if licensing continued. Writers would say what licensers allowed, not what they believed. Readers would nod publicly while thinking privately. The result: a nation of liars, conforming outwardly while seething inwardly, a pressure cooker that would eventually explode.[74]

Better honest error openly expressed than secret dissent festering. At least with open debate, truth and error could be distinguished, arguments tested, and minds changed. Under censorship, everything went underground, and genuine persuasion became impossible.

Milton concluded with an appeal to Parliament's better angels. They had fought against arbitrary power; would they now impose it themselves? They had demanded liberty; would they deny it to others? "Give me the liberty to know, to utter, and to argue freely according to conscience, above all liberties."[75]

Milton's Limits and Blindspots

Who Deserves Liberty?

Milton's *Areopagitica*, for all its eloquence, was not a defense of universal toleration. He explicitly excluded Catholics ("I mean not tolerated Popery, and open superstition") because he saw Catholicism as both false religion and political conspiracy serving a foreign power (the Pope). He also excluded "that also which is impious or evil absolutely either against faith or manners"—leaving magistrates broad power to censor what they deemed immoral.[76]

Milton's toleration extended to sincere Protestants who might disagree on church government, sacraments, or points of theology. It did not extend to those he judged idolaters (Catholics), blasphemers, or the openly immoral. This was broader than Presbyterian toleration (which barely tolerated Independents) but narrower than the radical toleration Roger Williams advocated.[77]

The Problem of Class

Areopagitica also assumed an educated readership. Milton's argument worked for those who could read Latin, follow complex reasoning, and had time for study and debate. It was less clear how it applied to the illiterate masses or those too busy with manual labor to engage in theological disputation.[78]

This wasn't unique to Milton, most 17th-century political thought assumed politics was for the educated and propertied. But it created tension with the radical democratic impulses of Army agitators and Levellers who insisted ordinary people could judge political and religious truth for themselves. Milton sympathized with the Levellers (to a point) but never fully embraced their vision of universal political participation.[79]

Nevertheless, *Areopagitica* became foundational. Its arguments would be recycled by John Locke, John Stuart Mill, and 20th-century free speech advocates. The "marketplace of ideas," "truth emerging through contest," "censorship breeding hypocrisy," these became commonplaces of liberal political thought. And they originated in Independent ecclesiology: if gathered churches could judge truth without bishops or synods, why couldn't the nation judge truth without licensers?

Milton's Commonwealth and Its Failure

The Republic's Defender

When Parliament executed Charles I in 1649 and declared England a

Commonwealth, Milton became the new regime's chief propagandist. Appointed Secretary for Foreign Tongues to the Council of State, he wrote defenses of the regicide in Latin for European audiences. His *Tenure of Kings and Magistrates* (1649) argued that tyrants could justly be deposed and punished. His *Defence of the English People* (1651) answered Royalist attacks on the Commonwealth.[80]

Milton genuinely believed England was attempting something glorious: a republic based on virtue, guided by godly men, and offering liberty of conscience within the bounds of Protestant orthodoxy. He saw Cromwell as the providential leader who would complete the work of reformation that the Long Parliament had begun.[81]

The Collapse and Its Lessons

But the Commonwealth failed. Cromwell's Protectorate became increasingly authoritarian. Liberty of conscience narrowed. The Major-Generals' rule (1655-1657) was petty tyranny justified as godly discipline. When Cromwell died in 1658, the whole structure collapsed within two years. The Restoration brought back king, bishops, and censorship, everything Milton had fought against.[82]

Milton's final political pamphlet, *The Readie and Easie Way to Establish a Free Commonwealth* (1660), was a desperate plea to prevent the Restoration. It proposed a perpetual Parliament, religious toleration, and decentralized government. It was ignored. When Charles II returned, Milton went into hiding, expecting execution. He was spared but politically silenced. He spent his remaining years writing poetry, producing *Paradise Lost* (1667), *Paradise Regained* (1671), and *Samson Agonistes* (1671), works that processed his disappointment and maintained hope that God's purposes transcended political failure.[83]

Milton articulated the Independent vision's intellectual heights: truth discovered through free debate, virtue cultivated through trial, tyranny resisted by free citizens. But visions require institutions to sustain them. The Independents' attempt to build such institutions, a lean state that protected liberty without enforcing uniformity, occupies our next section.

Commonwealth Men and the Lean State

Governing Without Compulsion

The Theory of Limited Magistracy

What the State Should Not Do

Independents agreed on what the magistrate should not do more easily than on what he should do. The magistrate should not:[84]

- Compel conscience in matters of worship
- Enforce attendance at a national church
- Collect mandatory tithes for clergy
- Require oaths that violated conscience
- Punish heresy or schism (unless accompanied by civil disorder)
- Dictate church government or doctrine

This represented a radical contraction of magisterial authority. For centuries,

English magistrates had done all these things. The parish church was the center of civic life; attendance was required; the church courts handled moral offenses; heresy was a civil crime. To remove all this from magisterial competence was to reimagine the relationship between church and state.[85]

The theological grounding was the Two Kingdoms doctrine, inherited from Luther but radicalized. Luther had distinguished the spiritual kingdom (ruled by Word and Spirit) from the temporal kingdom (ruled by sword and law). But Luther still gave magistrates broad authority over church matters for the sake of order. Independents narrowed magisterial authority dramatically: the magistrate ruled only temporal matters (property, contracts, violence), while the church ruled spiritual matters (doctrine, worship, discipline).[86]

Roger Williams, the most radical Independent, argued for a "wall of separation" between church and state. In *The Bloody Tenent of Persecution* (1644), he wrote:[87]

> *The civil magistrate, being a civil officer, has his civil sword, his civil realm, his civil subjects, his civil peace, his civil justice. But what can these things do in matters spiritual? The spiritual sword is God's Word preached, not the magistrate's weapon. To use civil force in religion is like using a sword to heal a wound—it only makes things worse.*

Williams went further than most Independents, but his direction was theirs: minimize state involvement in religion, maximize liberty of conscience, trust the Spirit rather than the sword to maintain true faith.

What the State Should Do

The positive case was harder. If the magistrate couldn't enforce religious conformity, what could he do?

Protect rights and punish harms: The magistrate should protect life, property, and contracts. He should punish murder, theft, fraud, and violence. This was uncontroversial, everyone agreed magistrates must maintain civil order.[88]

Defend the realm: The magistrate should protect the nation from invasion and maintain military forces for defense. Most Independents (pre-Quaker) accepted this without question, though they debated whether defensive war could become offensive and whether Christians could serve in military roles.[89]

Maintain justice: The magistrate should provide courts, judges, and means of resolving disputes. Again, uncontroversial in principle, though Independents wanted legal reform, simpler procedures, cheaper justice, and elimination of corruption.[90]

Enable (but not compel) religion: Here controversy emerged. Should the magistrate fund ministers' salaries from taxes? Independents split. Some said yes, ministers need support, and tax funding ensured they weren't dependent on wealthy patrons. Others said no, voluntary support kept ministers accountable to congregations and prevented corruption.[91]

Should the magistrate protect churches from disruption? Yes, if Quakers interrupt worship, the magistrate can remove them for disturbing the peace.

But should the magistrate punish Quakers for holding their own meetings? Independents debated. Some said no, let them worship as conscience dictates. Others worried that unlimited toleration would produce chaos.[92]

The practical reality was messier than the theory. During the 1650s, England tried various experiments: Cromwell's Protectorate offered broad (but not unlimited) toleration; local magistrates exercised varying degrees of enforcement; gathered churches met openly in some places, secretly in others. No coherent system emerged before the Restoration ended the experiments.[93]

The Experiment of the 1650s

The Nominated Parliament (Barebone's Parliament), 1653

After Cromwell expelled the Rump Parliament in April 1653, he faced a dilemma: how to provide legitimate government without king or parliament? His solution was the Nominated Parliament, 140 men selected by Army officers and Independent churches for their godliness and commitment to reform.[94]

The assembly included Fifth Monarchists (who believed Christ's return was imminent and wanted to prepare by imposing biblical law), moderate Independents, and a few crypto-Presbyterians. For five months they debated radical reforms:[95]

- Abolish tithes
- Codify and simplify law
- Create civil marriage (so people needn't use Anglican rites)
- Reform the legal system to reduce costs and delays
- Establish religious toleration

The moderates and radicals clashed constantly. Fifth Monarchists wanted thorough biblical reformation; moderates feared alienating property owners and gentry. When the Fifth Monarchists proposed abolishing tithes immediately, moderates panicked—this would impoverish parish ministers and alienate conservative supporters. In December 1653, the moderates dissolved the assembly and handed power back to Cromwell.[96]

The Nominated Parliament's failure taught Independents a hard lesson: godly intentions weren't enough. Governance required coalition-building, compromise, and attention to practical consequences. Pure principle couldn't sustain a government.

The Protectorate and Its Compromises (1653-1658)

Cromwell accepted the title Lord Protector and governed through a written constitution (the *Instrument of Government*) that balanced executive and legislative power. The Protectorate was not the free commonwealth Milton wanted, it was closer to constitutional monarchy without a king.[97]

But it did provide significant religious liberty. The *Instrument* declared: "That to the public profession of the Christian religion, liberty be given to all who profess faith in God by Jesus Christ, though differing in judgment from the doctrine, worship, or discipline publicly held forth." The exception: "provided this liberty be not extended to Popery or Prelacy, nor to such as, under the profession of Christ, hold forth and practise licentiousness."[98]

This was broader toleration than England had ever known. Independents, Baptists, and even Quakers could meet openly (though Quakers were sometimes prosecuted for disturbing the peace). But it wasn't unlimited, Catholics and Anglicans remained under restrictions, and "licentiousness" (however defined) could be punished.[99]

Cromwell also experimented with funding. He maintained some parish ministers on state salaries but allowed gathered churches to operate without state support. Tithes continued in modified form, causing ongoing conflict. The system satisfied no one fully but worked tolerably—better than the chaos some predicted, worse than the godly commonwealth true believers wanted.[100]

The Major-Generals' rule (1655-1657) showed the Protectorate's authoritarian side. After a Royalist uprising, Cromwell divided England into military districts, each governed by a Major-General who enforced moral discipline: closing alehouses, prosecuting Sabbath-breaking, suppressing "immoral" entertainments. This was presbyterian-style moral regulation imposed by military force, the opposite of the voluntary, congregational discipline Independents preferred. The experiment was deeply unpopular and abandoned after eighteen months.[101]

The Protectorate's contradictions revealed a fundamental tension: Could Independents govern? Their ecclesiology emphasized voluntary consent, limited authority, and congregational autonomy. But government required coercion, taxes must be collected, laws enforced, order maintained. The attempt to build a state on Independent principles produced an unstable hybrid that collapsed when Cromwell died.

Why the Commonwealth Failed

The Coalition Fractures

The parliamentary coalition that defeated the King was always fragile: Presbyterians wanted national church with reformed discipline; Independents wanted congregational liberty; Army radicals wanted political and economic reform; Levellers wanted democracy. These groups cooperated against the King but had incompatible visions for England's future.[102]

By 1649, with the King dead and the Royalists defeated, the coalition fractured. Cromwell purged Presbyterians in Pride's Purge (December 1648), then suppressed Levellers at Burford (May 1649). The Rump Parliament, theoretically sovereign, was actually controlled by the Army. When the Rump proved too conservative, Cromwell expelled it (April 1653).[103]

Each purge narrowed the regime's base. By the late 1650s, the Commonwealth rested on Army pikes and Cromwell's personal authority. When he died, there was nothing left. His son Richard lacked military credibility; the generals competed for power; civilian leaders saw opportunity for restoration. Within two years, England invited the King back.[104]

The Public Was Exhausted

Twenty years of war, revolution, and experimentation had exhausted the nation. People wanted normalcy: familiar liturgy, settled law, predictable government. The Commonwealth offered liberty but at the cost of instability. The King offered order, even if it meant less freedom.[105]

Moreover, the Commonwealth's godly discipline alienated ordinary people. Closing alehouses, prosecuting Sabbath sports, banning Christmas celebrations (as papist superstition), these measures were unpopular. The Major-Generals' enforcement felt like military occupation, not godly government. When the Restoration came, many celebrated not because they loved the King but because they hated the killjoys who had ruled in Parliament's name.[106]

The Theological Problem

Finally, there was a theological problem: Could sinful humans govern without coercion? Presbyterians said no, you need discipline, authority, hierarchy to restrain sin. Independents hoped yes, given liberty of conscience and spiritual transformation, people would live uprightly.

The 1650s suggested Presbyterians were right, at least partially. Liberty did produce disorder, not the apocalyptic chaos critics predicted, but enough instability to frighten the propertied and powerful. Sects multiplied, each claiming divine authority. Quakers disrupted services and refused deference. To conservatives, this looked like religion's dissolution; to worried Independents, it looked like liberty becoming license.[107]

The question lingered: How much diversity can a society tolerate? How much liberty can a people handle? The Independents' answer, quite a lot, was ahead of its time. But it would require another generation, and migration across the Atlantic, before societies fully tested their wager.

The Independent commonwealth failed in England but succeeded elsewhere. In New England, gathered churches created communities that lasted centuries. In the Middle Colonies, experiments with toleration produced surprising stability. And in England itself, the Independents' defeat proved temporary. Their arguments for liberty of conscience, limited government, and voluntary religion would resurface in the Toleration Act of 1689 and, eventually, in the American founding. To measure that legacy, we turn to the afterlives.

Afterlives

From Commonwealth to Congregationalism

Survival in Restoration England

The Ejection and Its Aftermath

The Act of Uniformity (1662) ejected about 2,000 ministers who couldn't accept the Book of Common Prayer, episcopal ordination, and the oaths it required. Many were Presbyterians, but Independents were heavily represented. John Owen, the leading Independent divine, refused a bishopric and left Oxford. Thomas Goodwin, another prominent Independent, was ejected from his church. John Bunyan, not yet famous, was imprisoned for unlicensed preaching and would spend twelve years in Bedford jail.[108]

These ejected ministers formed the core of English Nonconformity. They preached in homes, barns, and fields, risking fine and imprisonment. Their congregations met secretly, maintaining gathered church practices under persecution. The Clarendon Code laws (Corporation Act, Act of Uniformity, Conventicle Act, Five Mile Act) made Nonconformist life difficult but didn't destroy the movement.[109]

Bunyan's Witness

John Bunyan's experience typified Independent resilience. Imprisoned in 1660 for preaching without license, he remained in Bedford jail until 1672 (with a brief release in 1666). He refused offers of freedom in exchange for ceasing to preach. "If I were out of prison today," he told magistrates, "I would preach the gospel again tomorrow, by the help of God."[110]

In prison, Bunyan wrote. *Grace Abounding to the Chief of Sinners* (1666) told his conversion story, showing how God's grace worked in a tinker's life. *The Pilgrim's Progress* (1678, written during a second brief imprisonment) became one of English literature's greatest works, an allegory of Christian life as journey from the City of Destruction to the Celestial City.[111]

Pilgrim's Progress encoded Independent theology: Christian's conversion was individual (not through infant baptism), his pilgrimage was aided by fellow believers but ultimately personal, his destination was assured by God's grace but required perseverance. The book was accessible to common readers, no Latin, no complex theology, just vivid narrative. It became a bestseller, second only to the Bible in English homes, and spread Independent piety far beyond gathered churches.[112]

New England's Covenanted Communities

The Massachusetts Model

While England's Commonwealth collapsed, New England's covenanted communities thrived. Massachusetts Bay, Connecticut, and New Haven colonies were founded by Independents (though they called themselves Congregationalists) who sought to build ideal Christian societies.[113]

The New England Way combined gathered church principles with territorial establishment. Each town had a Congregational church with rigorous membership requirements, conversion testimony, examination by existing members, covenant commitment. Only church members could vote in town meetings (initially, though this was relaxed over time). The result was an oligarchy of visible saints—hardly the democracy Levellers wanted, but more participatory than England's hierarchy.[114]

New England churches were independent in government but connected through ministerial associations and synods that advised (but didn't command). The Cambridge Platform (1648) codified New England practice: congregational autonomy, elder oversight, and the principle that errors should be corrected by persuasion and the Spirit's work, not by civil coercion—though in practice, Massachusetts magistrates did punish heresy, most notoriously in the execution of Quakers (1659-1661).[115]

The Halfway Covenant and Its Tensions

By the 1660s, New England faced a problem: the founding generation's children. Many had been baptized as infants (New England Congregationalists practiced infant baptism, unlike Baptists) but hadn't experienced conversion. They couldn't give testimony that satisfied membership requirements, so they remained outside the covenant. But what about their children, could grandchildren of members be baptized even if parents weren't full members?[116]

The Halfway Covenant (1662) said yes: baptized but unconverted adults could have their children baptized, creating "halfway" membership. This preserved the gathered church principle (only converted adults took communion and voted) while recognizing the reality of covenant families. Critics attacked it as compromise—opening church membership to the unconverted. Defenders argued it maintained standards while showing pastoral care.[117]

The debate revealed tensions in the Independent model: Could gathered churches sustain themselves across generations? If each generation must convert anew, would the churches shrink? If they relaxed standards to maintain numbers, would they become the mixed parishes they'd rejected? New England never fully resolved these questions, but their experiment showed that covenanted communities could create durable, ordered societies without bishops or presbyteries.[118]

The Toleration Act and Beyond

1689: Legal Recognition

The Glorious Revolution (1688-1689) finally brought legal toleration. When Protestant William and Mary replaced Catholic James II, Parliament passed the Toleration Act (1689), allowing Nonconformists to worship openly if they subscribed to most of the Thirty-Nine Articles (Anglican doctrine) and took oaths of allegiance. Independents, Presbyterians, and Baptists could now build meetinghouses, call ministers, and worship without fear of prosecution.[119]

Toleration was limited, Catholics remained under restrictions, officeholding required Anglican communion, universities admitted only Anglicans. But it was real. Nonconformist communities flourished. By 1700, hundreds of Independent and Baptist congregations existed openly in England. The gathered church model, suppressed in the 1660s, reemerged stronger.[120]

The Dissenting Academies

Excluded from universities, Nonconformists founded dissenting academies, schools that trained ministers and educated the middle class. These academies often offered better, more modern education than Oxford or Cambridge: natural philosophy (science), modern languages, practical subjects alongside classics and theology. Graduates included prominent merchants, scientists, and writers.[121]

The academies transmitted Independent principles to new generations: liberty of conscience, congregational autonomy, resistance to arbitrary authority, confidence in reason and debate. Through them, Independent habits shaped English culture beyond religious boundaries. The "Nonconformist conscience," socially engaged, morally serious, politically liberal, became a force in 18th and 19th century Britain, driving abolition, prison reform, and democratic movements.[122]

The Independents lost the battle for England in 1660 but won a longer war for liberty of conscience, limited government, and voluntary religion. Their defeat in the Commonwealth taught valuable lessons: coercion was incompatible with their principles, purity was less important than persistence, and institutional survival mattered more than political triumph. When we measure what the four factions gave England and the wider world, the Independents' gift of structured liberty, less orderly than Presbyterians wanted, less anarchic than critics feared, proved remarkably durable. To the last of our four factions, the Quakers who combined Independents' liberty with radical disruption, we have already turned. But first, we meet those who thought the whole revolutionary project was a mistake—the Anglicans who defended king, bishops, and the long habit of law.

From Putney to Pennsylvania

We began this chapter at Putney, watching soldiers and officers debate franchise and freedom by candlelight. We end with a movement that never held power securely but shaped the Anglo-American political tradition profoundly. The Independents' gathered churches taught habits that became civic virtues: voluntary association, corporate decision-making, acceptance of diversity within bounds, and trust that truth emerged through debate rather than coercion.[123]

What Made Them Different

The Independents differed from other factions not primarily in theology (they shared much with Presbyterians) but in their wager about authority and persuasion. Where Presbyterians trusted discipline, Independents trusted consent. Where Anglicans trusted tradition, Independents trusted Scripture and Spirit. Where everyone else thought uniformity necessary for order, Independents thought diversity compatible with stability, if governance was light enough and conscience free enough.[124]

This made them simultaneously radical and conservative: radical in rejecting coercion, conservative in maintaining orthodox doctrine; radical in trusting common believers, conservative in requiring conversion testimony; radical in political implications, conservative in refusing to spell those implications out fully. The tensions produced creativity and frustration in equal measure.[125]

The Legacy

When Americans wrote the First Amendment, "Congress shall make no law respecting an establishment of religion, or prohibiting the free exercise thereof," they drew on Independent principles more than Anglican or Presbyterian ones. When they created denominations with local autonomy and voluntary support, they built Independent ecclesiology into national life. When they trusted that social order could be maintained without religious coercion, they took the Independent wager.[126]

The wager has costs: fragmentation, relativism, and the challenge of maintaining shared values in diverse communities. But the Independents thought those costs worth paying for liberty of conscience and voluntary faith. They believed, against most of human history, that people could govern themselves, that truth didn't need state enforcement, and that God's kingdom advanced through persuasion rather than compulsion.[127]

Yet the most articulate opposition to this vision came not from Presbyterians who wanted more discipline, but from Anglicans who thought the whole project of gathered churches and free commonwealths was built on sand. Better, they said, a visible church with ancient orders, a king by divine appointment, and the tried wisdom of tradition than experiments that ended in chaos. To that case, made after twenty years of civil war proved, to many, the wisdom of stability, we now turn.

CHAPTER 5 — THE KING'S PEACE

ANGLICAN MONARCHISTS AND THE RETURN TO ORDER

The Great Ejection, 24 August 1662

The bell rang again, this time in 1662, and the parish filed into a church made familiar by the Book of Common Prayer. The psalms were chanted in their ancient cadences, the collect read from the prayer book's elegant prose, the creed confessed in unison. Outside, in the vicarage next door, a minister packed his books into crates. Inside, the congregation breathed relief and loss in equal measure. Anglican order had returned with the King.[1]

William Bates, who had served St. Giles for seventeen years, would preach his final sermon this morning. He was one of nearly 2,000 ministers who faced a choice: accept everything in the Book of Common Prayer, renounce the Solemn League and Covenant, receive episcopal ordination (or reordination if their previous ordination was deemed irregular), and swear canonical obedience to bishops—or leave their pulpits forever. The Act of Uniformity, which came into force tomorrow on St. Bartholomew's Day, allowed no middle ground.[2]

Bates was a moderate Presbyterian, the kind who had hoped for comprehension, a settlement that would include godly ministers like him within a reformed episcopal church. He had attended the Savoy Conference in 1661, where Presbyterian and Anglican divines had met to revise the prayer book. The Presbyterians had proposed hundreds of changes to accommodate tender consciences: make controversial ceremonies optional, remove prayers that sounded Catholic, add more Scripture to the liturgy. The bishops had rejected nearly everything.[3]

The Final Sermon

Bates climbed the pulpit stairs slowly. He was fifty years old, his health declining from years of study and preaching. The congregation, merchants, craftsmen, their wives and children, looked up expectantly. Many had known no other minister. He had baptized their children, married their young people, buried their dead, preached comfort during plague years and political turmoil.[4]

"Beloved," he began, his voice carrying the weariness of defeat, "this is the last time I shall speak to you from this place. Tomorrow the Act of Uniformity comes into force, and I cannot in conscience subscribe to all it requires. I leave not because I despise this church or its people, but because I must obey God rather than men."[5]

He preached from Acts 20:32: "And now, brethren, I commend you to God, and to the word of his grace, which is able to build you up, and to give you an inheritance among all them which are sanctified." His text was Paul's farewell to the Ephesian elders, knowing he would see them no more. The parallel was obvious and painful.[6]

Bates did not attack the bishops or the King. He expressed no bitterness, no prophecy of divine judgment on the persecutors. He simply explained his conscience: he believed some ceremonies were superstitious, some prayers ambiguous, some requirements unnecessary. He could not swear that everything in the prayer book was lawful and good. To do so would be to lie before God.[7]

"I do not judge those who can subscribe," he continued. "Perhaps they see more clearly than I. Perhaps I am overly scrupulous. But conscience is God's throne in the soul, and I dare not violate it. If I err, I pray God will show me my error. But until He does, I must follow conscience."[8]

The congregation wept. Some, those who had become convinced Presbyterians during the 1640s, wept for the loss of their pastor and the triumph of bishops they despised. Others, those who had always preferred the prayer book and episcopal order, wept from sympathy for a good man caught in impossible circumstances. A few, the most convinced Anglicans, wept from relief that the chaos of the Interregnum was truly ending, even at this cost.[9]

Outside: The New Vicar Waits

In the churchyard, the newly appointed vicar waited. Thomas Manton had been chosen by the patron and approved by the bishop. He was young, orthodox, and willing to use every ceremony the prayer book prescribed. He would read morning and evening prayer daily, wear the surplice, use the sign of the cross in baptism, require kneeling for communion, and observe all holy days. He would make St. Giles an exemplary Anglican parish.[10]

Manton was not cruel or power-hungry. He genuinely believed the Church of England represented the best and most ancient form of Christianity: episcopal in government, reformed in doctrine, beautiful in worship, and comprehensive enough to include all but the most factious dissenters. He thought the Interregnum's experiments had proven that liberty of conscience led to chaos. Better the discipline of common prayer, the authority of bishops, and the unity that came from settled forms.[11]

When Bates finished and descended from the pulpit, the congregation sang a final psalm. Then Bates walked down the aisle, stopped at the church door, and turned for a last look at the place where he had ministered for nearly two decades. Manton stood aside respectfully. The two men nodded to each other—acknowledgment, not friendship. Bates stepped into the summer sunlight and did not look back.[12]

The Broader Scene: England's Choice

What happened at St. Giles that August Sunday happened in nearly 2,000 parishes across England. Some departing ministers were angry; some were resigned; some were defiant. Some congregations followed their ministers into Nonconformity; others stayed in the parish church, glad to have the old liturgy back; many were divided, families split over whether to conform or separate.[13]

The Great Ejection was the Restoration settlement's definitive act. Charles II had promised in the Declaration of Breda (1660) to respect "liberty to tender consciences." But once restored, the King found he needed the bishops' support and couldn't afford to alienate the Anglican gentry who controlled Parliament. Liberty gave way to uniformity, and uniformity came at the cost of driving godly ministers from their pulpits.[14]

The question the Ejection posed was the question that had driven England's conflicts for twenty years: Can a nation be united by force, or only by persuasion? The Anglicans who crafted the Restoration settlement believed force was necessary. They had seen what persuasion and liberty produced: sectarian chaos, social leveling, regicide, and military dictatorship. Better to impose order, they thought, even if it cost some conscientious men their livings.[15]

Two Visions of the Same Scene

An Anglican watching Bates's departure might have thought: *Here is a man who preferred his own judgment to the church's wisdom. He claims conscience, but conscience must be formed by authority, not private opinion. If every man follows his own conscience, we return to the anarchy of the 1650s. Bates is a good man led astray by Presbyterian errors. In time, perhaps, he will see his mistake and return. Until then, the church must maintain standards.*[16]

A Presbyterian watching might have thought: *Here is tyranny dressed in surplice and stole. Bates harms no one, teaches sound doctrine, lives godly—yet he is cast out for refusing ceremonies that Scripture never commanded. The bishops care more for power than piety, more for uniformity than truth. This is persecution, and God will judge it.*[17]

An Independent might have thought: *Both sides are wrong. Bates should not have depended on a state church in the first place. Gathered churches need no bishops' permission. And the bishops should not force conscience. But both Presbyterians and Anglicans want national uniformity—they differ only on the form. The real solution is separation: let each congregation worship as it sees fit, and let the state keep out of religion entirely.*[18]

A Quaker might have thought: *All these hireling priests with their steeples and set prayers and debate over ceremonies—they have missed the point entirely. Christ teaches his people directly. Neither prayer book nor presbytery can replace the inner light. When will they learn that the kingdom of God is within?*[19]

The Great Ejection completed what the Restoration began: the reassertion of Anglican order after twenty years of experiment and upheaval. To understand why the bishops acted as they did, why they refused to compromise and insisted on uniformity, we must see the Anglican case from within: their theology of visible authority, their fear of faction, and their conviction that only the church's ancient order could heal England's wounds. We must also see what that order cost and what it preserved.

Bishops, Prayer Book, and the Law

The Anglican Defense of Visible Authority

Richard Hooker and the Laws of Ecclesiastical Polity

The Elizabethan Settlement and Its Defender[20]

The theological foundation of Anglican order was laid not in the Restoration but sixty years earlier, in Richard Hooker's massive *Of the Lawes of Ecclesiastical Politie* (1593-1597). Hooker wrote to defend the Elizabethan church settlement against Puritan attacks. His arguments, sophisticated and learned, shaped Anglican thinking for generations.[21]

Hooker began with a principle: law governs all creation. God governs the universe by eternal law; nature operates by natural law; human society requires human law. The church, being both divine and human, the mystical body of Christ organized in visible communities, operates under both divine law (Scripture) and human law (church tradition and civil legislation).[22]

Puritans insisted Scripture alone should govern the church: *sola scriptura* meant nothing could be required in worship or government unless explicitly commanded in Scripture. Hooker replied that Scripture provided principles, not exhaustive rules. Many matters were "things indifferent" (*adiaphora*), neither commanded nor forbidden. In such matters, the church could legislate according to reason, tradition, and circumstances.[23]

For example: Should ministers wear vestments? Scripture doesn't command it or forbid it. Therefore, it's a matter of order, not doctrine. The church, exercising its God-given authority, may require vestments for the sake of decency and uniformity. To refuse is to exalt private judgment over corporate wisdom—to make every man his own pope.[24]

Tradition as Authority

Hooker defended tradition against Puritan biblicism. The early church fathers, the ecumenical councils, the accumulated wisdom of centuries, these weren't mere human opinions but the Holy Spirit's guidance of the church through time. To reject tradition was arrogant:[25]

> *Dangerous it were for the feeble brain of man to wade far into the doings of the Most High... Our safest eloquence concerning him is our silence.*

This didn't mean Scripture lacked authority. Hooker affirmed Scripture's supremacy in doctrine. But tradition interpreted Scripture and guided practice. The church had worshiped liturgically, governed episcopally, and celebrated sacraments ceremonially for fifteen centuries. Were all those Christians wrong? More likely, the Puritans—newcomers with novel ideas—were wrong.[26]

Hooker's argument was conservative in the best sense: it conserved what had been tested by time. Innovation was dangerous; stability was wise. The Elizabethan settlement preserved the best of Catholic tradition (bishops, liturgy, sacraments) while embracing Protestant doctrine (justification by faith, Scripture's authority, rejection of papal supremacy). It was a via media, middle way, between Roman excess and Puritan severity.[27]

Reason, Nature, and the Social Order

Hooker also grounded church order in natural law and reason. Humans were social creatures; society required hierarchy; hierarchy required deference to authority. This was natural law, written in creation itself. The church, as a society, required bishops to teach and govern, priests to minister sacraments, and laity to obey. To overturn this order was to violate nature.[28]

Moreover, church and state were intertwined. England's king was also the church's supreme governor. The same people who were subjects politically were also members ecclesiastically. Therefore, church law was civil law, and civil law enforced church order. To disobey the bishop was to disobey the magistrate; to reject the prayer book was to reject the law of the land.[29]

This fusion of church and state seemed obvious to Hooker and his heirs. It horrified Independents and Quakers who insisted on separation. But Anglicans saw it as realistic: humans were sinful; sin produced disorder; disorder required authority to contain it. The apparatus of bishops, liturgy, and law existed precisely because human nature required external discipline.[30]

The Royal Defense of Monarchical Order

Charles I's Defense of Royal Authority

Charles I, in his own defense and through the posthumous *Eikon Basilike* (1649), articulated the Anglican monarchist position with clarity. Authority, he argued, was "clearly warranted and strictly commanded both Old and New Testament." He cited Ecclesiastes: "Where word of King is, there is Power, and who may say unto him, what doest thou?" Royal authority was divine, not delegated by people.[31]

Charles connected episcopal church government with monarchical civil government. Episcopal government, he wrote, "hath of all other fullest Scripture grounds, and constant practice all Christian Churches." Apostles were bishops over the presbyters they ordained; bishops traced their authority through apostolic succession to Christ's own commission. Just as bishops ruled the church, kings ruled the state—both by divine appointment, both exercising authority from above rather than deriving it from below.[32]

On revelation, Charles distinguished immediate revelation (direct God-to-man communication like Moses) from mediate revelation (through Scripture, interpreted by proper authority). The age of immediate revelation had ceased; now Scripture mediated divine will. But Scripture required interpretation, and "whoever has power over writing of scripture/law has power to interpret." The King, as supreme governor of the church, possessed this interpretive authority.[33]

Gilbert Sheldon and The Dignity of Kingship

Gilbert Sheldon, who would become Archbishop of Canterbury after the Restoration, published *The Dignity of Kingship Asserted* (1660) as a direct response to Milton's *The Readie and Easie Way*. Where Milton argued that republican government was spiritually superior to monarchy, Sheldon argued the opposite.[34]

English government had "King supreme, true but not absolute Monarch" with paternal authority over his subjects. The king consulted nobles and Commons but ultimate authority rested with him, not derived from them but inherent in his office. Sheldon dismissed parliamentary sovereignty: Parliament received authority from the King; with the king's death (or deposition), Parliament was legally dissolved. The Long Parliament's continued existence after 1649 was thus a usurpation, however dressed in legal forms.

Sheldon argued that episcopacy and monarchy "stood or fell together." Both were hierarchical; both claimed ancient legitimacy; both required deference to visible authority. The same logic that justified popular sovereignty in the state justified congregational autonomy in the church, and vice versa. To defend one was to defend both; to attack one was to attack both.[35]

The Book of Common Prayer: Unity Through Liturgy

Cranmer's Achievement

The Book of Common Prayer (1549, revised 1552, 1559, 1662) was Archbishop Thomas Cranmer's masterpiece. Written in elegant English that rivaled the King James Bible for beauty, the prayer book provided set forms for every service: morning and evening prayer, communion, baptism, marriage, burial, and the church year's festivals.[30]

The prayer book's genius was its comprehensiveness. It included high church ceremonial that satisfied those who loved ritual beauty and low church simplicity that satisfied moderate Protestants. It was deliberately ambiguous on contested doctrines: the communion service could be read as Catholic (Christ's real presence in the elements) or Reformed (spiritual presence to faithful receivers). This ambiguity was strategic, not sloppy—it allowed people of different theological persuasions to worship together.[37]

The prayer book also democratized worship. Before the Reformation, liturgy was in Latin, incomprehensible to most. Cranmer translated it into English and expected congregations to participate saying responses, reciting psalms, confessing together. This was "common" prayer in both senses: shared prayer in common language. It united parishes across England in the same words at the same times, a powerful bond.[38]

The Presbyterian Critique

Presbyterians objected that set forms restricted the Holy Spirit. If ministers could only read prescribed prayers, how could they address particular circumstances? If every service was identical, where was room for the Spirit's leading? Extemporaneous prayer, they argued, allowed the Spirit to move in real time, adapting to the congregation's needs.[39]

Anglicans replied that spontaneity was overrated. Extemporaneous prayer often became rambling, repetitious, or theologically confused. Set forms, carefully crafted, ensured that congregations prayed scripturally and doctrinally sound prayers. Moreover, the prayer book's language was itself Spirit-inspired: Cranmer and his revisers had worked under divine guidance; the prayers drew from Scripture and ancient tradition.[40]

Furthermore, Anglicans argued, the Spirit worked through means, not only despite them. Cranmer had been a godly man; the revisers were learned divines; the prayers themselves were drawn from Scripture and ancient liturgies. Why assume the Spirit couldn't work through established forms? The assumption that spontaneity was more spiritual than structure was itself a theological claim—and Anglicans rejected it.[41]

Ceremonies and Symbols

The prayer book prescribed ceremonies that Puritans despised: signing with the cross at baptism, kneeling to receive communion, wearing the surplice, bowing at Jesus's name. These were, Puritans charged, "rags of popery," remnants of Catholic superstition that should have been swept away at the Reformation.[42]

Anglicans defended them as decent, ancient, and edifying. The sign of the cross marked the child as Christ's; kneeling showed reverence; vestments maintained dignity; bowing honored the Lord's name. None of these were doctrinal matters; all were "things indifferent" that the church could require for good order. The Puritans' obsession with abolishing them was itself a form of superstition, treating adiaphora as if they were damnable errors.[43]

More fundamentally, Anglicans argued that corporate worship required agreed forms. If every congregation did what seemed right in its own eyes, unity dissolved. The prayer book, prescribed by law and used throughout England, created a shared religious culture. A traveler could enter any parish church and know what to expect. This was not conformity for its own sake but unity in Christ's body.[44]

Episcopal Government: The Apostolic Succession

The Claim to Antiquity

Anglican defense of episcopacy rested on historical claims. Bishops, they argued, dated to the apostles. Christ appointed the Twelve; they appointed bishops to succeed them; those bishops appointed others in unbroken succession to the present. This "apostolic succession" guaranteed doctrinal purity and ecclesiastical authority.[45]

The historical evidence was contested. Presbyterians pointed out that "bishop" (*episcopos*) and "elder" (*presbyteros*) were used interchangeably in the New Testament. The distinction between bishops and presbyters developed gradually, not by divine command but by human arrangement. Therefore, episcopacy was a tradition, not a biblical requirement.[46]

Anglicans replied that even if the bishop-presbyter distinction developed gradually, it developed early and universally. By the second century, every church had bishops. This couldn't be accidental, it must have been apostolic intention. Moreover, the church fathers universally attested to episcopal authority. Ignatius of Antioch (c. 110 AD) wrote: "Where the bishop is, there is the church." To reject bishops was to reject fifteen centuries of Christian witness.[47]

The Practical Case

Beyond historical arguments, Anglicans made practical ones. Bishops provided stability, continuity, and discipline that presbyteries and congregations couldn't match.[48]

Stability: Bishops served for life, often decades. This continuity preserved institutional memory and prevented the faction-switching and purges that plagued Presbyterian assemblies and Independent churches during the Interregnum.

Uniformity: Bishops enforced standards across their dioceses. Ministers couldn't innovate doctrine or practice without episcopal approval. This prevented the proliferation of sects that marked the 1650s.

Discipline: Bishops could ordain, suspend, and defrock ministers. They examined candidates for ministry, ensuring basic competence in learning and morals. They visited parishes, correcting errors and addressing complaints. This oversight was impossible in purely congregational systems.

Moreover, bishops connected local churches to the national and international church. An episcopal church was part of a worldwide communion extending back through history. A presbyterian church was one denomination among others; a congregational church was one isolated gathering. Bishops provided connection to the universal church that other polities couldn't match.[49]

Man's Nature According to the Anglicans

Depravity, Order, and the Need for Authority

Hobbes and the State of Nature

Thomas Hobbes, though heterodox in his religion, provided the most powerful philosophical defense of absolute sovereignty rooted in human nature. His *Leviathan* (1651) began with anthropology: in the state of nature, without government, human life would be "solitary, poor, nasty, brutish, and short." Humans were fundamentally competitive, suspicious, glory-seeking. Without a sovereign with absolute power to enforce peace, they would war against one another endlessly.[50]

Hobbes's anthropology was darker even than Calvin's. Where Calvin located human corruption in sin, Hobbes located it in nature itself. Humans were not fallen from some original perfection; they were naturally competitive, and only artificial constraint (the sovereign) could impose peace. "Every little payment appeareth a great grievance," Hobbes observed, because "passions and self-love" made people poor judges of their own interests.

The political implication was clear: sovereign authority must be absolute and undivided. Any limit on sovereign power opened space for conflict. Mixed government was inherently unstable—competing authorities would eventually clash, returning society to civil war. Better an absolute monarch than the chaos of divided sovereignty.[51]

Charles I on Fallen Humanity

Charles I drew different but compatible conclusions from human depravity.

Men preferred Presbyterian or Congregational government, he argued, due to an "innate principle of vicious opposition" against restraint. They wanted to be their own masters, to follow their own judgments, to escape the discipline of bishops and the authority of kings. This was not reformation but rebellion dressed in religious language.[52]

The solution was external authority, visible, ordered, enforced. Humans could not be trusted to discipline themselves; they needed bishops to discipline their souls and magistrates to discipline their bodies. The apparatus of church and state existed precisely because human nature required it. Those who dismantled that apparatus in the name of liberty would discover only chaos.[53]

The Kingdom of God and Human Authority

Apostolic Succession and Divine Right

The Church Through Apostolic Succession

The Anglican understanding of the Kingdom of God emphasized visible, institutional continuity. The Church of England traced its authority to the primitive Church through unbroken apostolic succession. Bishops ordained bishops who ordained bishops, back through centuries to the apostles themselves, who received their commission from Christ.[54]

This succession was not merely historical pedigree; it was the channel of grace and authority. Ministers ordained by bishops possessed valid orders; ministers ordained by presbyteries or congregations did not. The sacraments administered by validly ordained priests conveyed grace; those administered by irregular ministers were at best doubtful.

Sheldon articulated this clearly: "Apostles were Bishops over Presbyters they ordained." The distinction between bishops and presbyters appeared in the earliest church records; presbyterian government was a modern innovation, congregational government more modern still. To reject episcopacy was to reject the testimony of fifteen centuries—to claim that the entire church had erred from the beginning.[55]

The Union of Church and State

Anglican thought fused church and state more tightly than either Presbyterian or Independent models. The monarch was "supreme governor" of the church, not a rival source of authority but the pinnacle of both hierarchies. The same people who were subjects politically were members ecclesiastically. Church law was civil law; disobedience to bishops was disobedience to magistrates.[56]

Sheldon noted that the Church thrived under monarchical governments: kings and emperors were "unparalleled Fathers and Nurses" of religion—David, Solomon, Constantine, Theodosius. Godly princes protected the church, established true religion, suppressed heresy. This was not Erastianism (state domination of church) but *symphonia*—harmonious cooperation of parallel hierarchies under the same divine appointment.[57]

The Case for Uniformity

Why Diversity Was Seen as Dangerous

The 1640s and 1650s as Warning[58]

For Anglicans writing in 1660-1662, the recent past was not nostalgia but nightmare. They had lived through:

- The collapse of censorship and the flood of heretical pamphlets
- The proliferation of sects: Baptists, Independents, Ranters, Quakers, Fifth Monarchists, Muggletonians, and more
- The disruption of worship by enthusiasts claiming direct revelation
- The regicide of an anointed king
- Military dictatorship under Cromwell
- Social leveling and threats to property
- The near-dissolution of all traditional authority

All this, they believed, followed from rejecting bishops and the prayer book. Once authority was questioned, everything became contestable. Once uniformity was abandoned, faction multiplied endlessly. Once ceremony was mocked, irreverence spread. The Interregnum was proof; religious liberty produced not peace but chaos.[59]

Edward Hyde, Earl of Clarendon, who chronicled the Civil War in his *History of the Rebellion*, saw a direct line from Presbyterian resistance to episcopacy in the 1630s to Quaker antinomianism in the 1650s. "They who began by saying bishops were unnecessary," he wrote, "ended by saying king and magistrates were tyrannical, that tithes were theft, that sin was imaginary, and that Scripture itself was dead letter. This is where liberty of conscience leads." The Presbyterians had opened a door they couldn't close.[60]

Gilbert Sheldon, who became Archbishop of Canterbury in 1663, shared Clarendon's view. In *The Dignity of Kingship Asserted* (1660), written just before the Restoration, Sheldon argued that monarchy and episcopacy stood or fell together. "In Scotland," he wrote, "when they cast out bishops, how long before they seized the king? In England, when presbyters ruled, how quickly came regicide? Defend bishops, and you defend throne and order itself." [61]

The Slippery Slope Argument

Anglican writers deployed what we might call the slippery slope argument: toleration of one error led to toleration of worse errors, until all truth and order disappeared.[62]

The logic went:

Step 1: Tolerate Presbyterians who reject bishops but keep most traditional doctrine → Result: Authority is questioned

Step 2: Tolerate Independents who reject national church → Result: Unity is fractured

Step 3: Tolerate Baptists who reject infant baptism → Result: Ancient practices are overturned

Step 4: Tolerate Quakers who reject outward sacraments and ministry → Result: All visible church disappears

Step 5: Tolerate Ranters who deny moral law → Result: Society dissolves into licentiousness

Each step seemed small, but the cumulative effect was civilizational collapse. Better to hold the line at the first step—maintain bishops, enforce prayer book, require uniformity—than to start down a path whose end was anarchy.[63]

Liberty of Conscience as Destructive

Anglican opinion consistently opposed liberty of conscience as destructive of both religious truth and social order. Sheldon exploited divisions among dissenters over issues like tithes but maintained that liberty itself must be curtailed for the greater good.[64]

He referenced the book of Judges: "When no King was in Israel every man did what was good in own eyes, then Micah made his graven and molten Image..." Liberty led to idolatry, to error, to social dissolution. Only the king could "Engage that Religion publicly professed which appears to him and his learned Divines true." The alternative was not peaceful diversity but chaos.

Hobbes reinforced this argument philosophically. Control of ideas was imperative for the sovereign to maintain order. Religious disputes were particularly dangerous because people believed their souls' eternal fate was at stake—people would kill and die over religious differences more readily than over material interests. The sovereign must determine religious practice to prevent civil war; any exception to this rule opened the door to sectarian violence.[65]

Critics' Responses

Critics replied that this was paranoid and empirically false. New England's Congregational churches weren't anarchic; they maintained order without bishops. Scottish Presbyterians weren't social levelers; they supported hierarchy in civil society. The slippery slope was a rhetorical device, not a description of reality.[66]

But Anglicans weren't convinced. They saw the Interregnum as proof that religious diversity produced instability. Only after the bishops returned and uniformity was enforced did England regain peace. That was evidence enough. Uniformity would prevent future conflict. The alternative was too dangerous to try.[67]

Thomas Hobbes and the Secular Case for Authority

Leviathan's Logic

Thomas Hobbes, though no orthodox Anglican (his religious views were suspect), provided philosophical weight to the case for strong, unified authority. *Leviathan* (1651), written during the Interregnum, argued that humans in the state of nature were in "war of all against all" where life was "solitary, poor, nasty, brutish, and short." Only a sovereign with absolute power could escape this condition by making and enforcing law.[68]

Hobbes applied this to religion. Religious disputes were particularly dangerous because people believed their souls' eternal fate was at stake. Therefore, they would fight to the death over doctrines that seemed trivial to outsiders. The only solution was for the sovereign to determine religious practice for the realm. Not because the sovereign possessed special theological insight, but because unified practice prevented civil war.[69]

Hobbes's position was Erastian (named after Thomas Erastus): the magistrate, not the church, should have final authority over religion. This went further than most Anglicans wanted, they believed bishops had divine authority, not merely delegated civil authority. But Hobbes's basic point resonated: religious diversity produced conflict; only unified authority could maintain peace.[70]

"If men were allowed to follow private conscience in religion," Hobbes wrote, "every man would claim God commanded him to do what he preferred. The result: not liberty but license, not conscience but self-will dressed in pious language." The only remedy was sovereign authority determining what could be taught and preached.[71]

Anglican Adaptations

Anglicans didn't fully embrace Hobbes, his materialism and apparent atheism were troubling. But they borrowed his emphasis on authority and order. The Restoration settlement reflected Hobbesian logic: the sovereign determined religious practice; dissent was punished; uniformity was enforced.[72]

Gilbert Sheldon explicitly invoked the memory of civil war to justify uniformity. In a 1663 sermon, he said: [73]

> *We have seen what comes of liberty—not the peaceable kingdom some promised, but sword, fire, and blood. We have seen godly men turned zealot, then fanatic, then madman. We have seen the king murdered, the church despoiled, and order overturned. All in the name of conscience and reform. Shall we repeat the experiment? No. We shall restore what was proven good: bishops to govern, prayer book to unite, law to enforce, and peace to prevail.*

The argument was prudential, not just theological. Even if Presbyterians or Independents weren't heretics (and Sheldon thought many were), tolerating them was too risky. The nation had barely survived twenty years of religious war. Better to be cautious, enforce uniformity and hope dissenters would conform over time.[74]

Critics thought this profoundly wrong. Milton, in his last desperate pamphlet before the Restoration (*The Readie and Easie Way*, 1660), warned that reimposing uniformity would breed resentment and hypocrisy. Roger Williams, from Rhode Island, had already demonstrated that toleration could work. John Owen argued that persecution strengthened rather than weakened dissent.[75]

But the Restoration Parliament wasn't listening to Independents or Americans. They were listening to royalists who had suffered exile, to Anglicans who had been ejected from their livings by Puritans, and to gentry who had seen their world turned upside down. These men wanted order, not experiment. They got it.

The Clarendon Code: Uniformity by Law

Four Acts, One Purpose

The Clarendon Code wasn't a single law but a series of acts passed between 1661 and 1665, each tightening restrictions on Nonconformists:[76]

Corporation Act (1661): Required all municipal office-holders to:[77]

- Take Anglican communion within the year before assuming office
- Swear oaths of allegiance and supremacy
- Renounce the Solemn League and Covenant (the 1643 oath binding Parliament to reform the church along Presbyterian lines)

This effectively excluded Nonconformists from town governments, making dissent politically as well as religiously costly.

Act of Uniformity (1662): Required all clergy to: [78]

- Accept everything in the Book of Common Prayer as lawful and good
- Receive episcopal ordination (or reordination if their previous ordination was judged irregular)
- Renounce the Solemn League and Covenant
- Swear canonical obedience to bishops

Ministers who refused were ejected. About 2,000 left—the Great Ejection described in this chapter's opening.

Conventicle Act (1664, renewed 1670): Prohibited religious gatherings of more than five people (beyond a household) that didn't use the prayer book. Penalties:[79]

- First offense: fine or three months imprisonment
- Second offense: larger fine or six months imprisonment
- Third offense: transportation to America for seven years (or large fine)

This targeted Nonconformist meetings, making dissenting worship illegal.

Five Mile Act (1665): Prohibited ejected ministers from:[80]

- Coming within five miles of any corporate town or their former parish
- Teaching in schools

Unless they swore they would not "endeavour any alteration of government either in church or state." Most ejected ministers couldn't take this oath in good conscience, so they were exiled from urban centers where dissent was strongest.

The Enforcement and Its Limits

The Clarendon Code was harsh on paper but inconsistently enforced. Much depended on local magistrates. Some zealously prosecuted Nonconformists: others looked the other way, especially if dissenters were respectable citizens who paid their taxes and caused no trouble. Enforcement varied by region, by decade, and by the temperament of individual justices.[81]

Moreover, the Code created martyrs. John Bunyan spent twelve years in Bedford jail for preaching without license. Hundreds of others were imprisoned, fined, or had property confiscated. Their suffering didn't destroy dissent, it strengthened it. Persecution created solidarity; shared adversity bound Nonconformist communities together.[82]

Charles II himself was ambivalent. He issued a Declaration of Indulgence in 1672, suspending the penal laws and allowing Nonconformists to worship if they obtained licenses. This was partly pragmatic (many Nonconformists were economically productive) and partly political (Charles needed allies against the Dutch and hoped to include Catholics eventually), and partly personal (Charles had limited enthusiasm for persecution).[83]

But Parliament forced him to withdraw the Declaration. MPs feared it set precedent for royal power to suspend laws, if the king could suspend laws against Nonconformists, he could suspend any laws. Parliament passed the Test Act (1673) instead, requiring all office-holders to take Anglican communion and swear against transubstantiation (aimed at excluding Catholics).[84]

The result was a stalemate: Nonconformists couldn't worship freely or hold office, but they couldn't be fully suppressed. They met secretly, maintained networks, supported their ejected ministers, and waited for better times. The Toleration Act of 1689 would vindicate their patience.

Romans 13 and the Habit of Obedience

Divine Right, Passive Obedience, and the Limits of Resistance

Charles I's Martyrdom and the Royalist Cult

Eikon Basilike: The King's Book

Published within days of Charles I's execution (January 1649), *Eikon Basilike* ("The King's Image") purported to be Charles's spiritual autobiography and reflections during his final imprisonment. Whether Charles actually wrote it or whether his chaplain John Gauden compiled it from Charles's notes (as Gauden later claimed) was debated even then. What's certain is its impact: it became an instant bestseller, going through thirty-five editions in its first year, creating the cult of the royal martyr.[86]

Eikon Basilike portrayed Charles as a Christian martyr, patient under suffering, forgiving toward enemies, dying for the church and the ancient constitution. The book's frontispiece showed Charles kneeling in prayer, crown of thorns nearby, rays of heavenly light descending. The visual message was unmistakable: Charles as Christ-figure, killed by sinful men, destined for heavenly vindication.[87]

The book's most powerful section, "Upon the Insolency of the Tumults," described mobs intimidating Parliament and the King. Charles wrote (or Gauden wrote for him):[88]

> *I see the people's hearts are much turned from me, by the artifices of my enemies. Yet I know that justice and truth, though they may be momentarily obscured, will shine forth at last. I forgive those who have so wronged me. And I pray that England may never pay in the future for what they have done to their King.*[71]

This was masterful propaganda: Charles as more sinned against than sinning, the patient sufferer, the forgiving Christian. It cast the regicide not as justice against a tyrant but as the murder of God's anointed by rebels and fanatics.[89]

Justice, Blood Guilt, and the Royal Martyr

Charles the Martyr versus "Man of Blood"

Where Independents portrayed Charles I as a "man of blood" whose execution cleansed the land, Anglicans portrayed him as "Charles the Martyr" whose murder polluted it. The regicide was not justice but sacrilege—the murder of God's anointed by rebels and fanatics.[90]

Charles's trial defense rested on this foundation: no earthly power could justly call him to account. His authority came from divine appointment, not popular consent. The court that tried him was not lawful, it lacked the king's commission, and Parliament without the king was no true Parliament. What they called justice was merely force.

Blood Guilt Reversed

Anglican theology reversed the direction of blood guilt. The land was polluted not by Charles's alleged crimes but by his murder. The regicides, not the king, were the true "men of blood." The chaos of the 1650s, the failure of the Protectorate, the near anarchy of 1659, all demonstrated divine judgment on the nation for permitting regicide.[91]

Only the Restoration could begin to heal the wound. The surviving regicides were hunted down and executed; the bodies of Cromwell, Ireton, and Bradshaw were exhumed and subjected to posthumous hanging. This was not mere revenge but ritual purification, cleansing the land of blood guilt through the blood of those who had shed innocent blood.[92]

St. Charles the Martyr

The Restoration church went further: Charles became a saint, unofficially but unmistakably. January 30, the anniversary of his execution, became a day of fasting and repentance. The Book of Common Prayer included a special service for that day, with prayers acknowledging national guilt and pleading divine mercy. "King Charles the Martyr" entered the church calendar alongside biblical saints.[93]

Sermons on January 30 emphasized divine right and passive obedience. One typical sermon proclaimed:[94]

> *King Charles died as Christ died—innocent, betrayed by subjects he had blessed, mocked by crowds, executed under pretense of law. As Christ's death condemned those who killed him, so Charles's death condemns the regicides and all who supported them. And as Christ's death purchased redemption, so Charles's death purchased for England a renewed understanding: kings are sacred, rebellion is sin, obedience is duty.*

This theology of martyrdom served political purposes. It sanctified monarchy, making resistance not just illegal but blasphemous. It vilified the Interregnum as a period of national sin requiring repentance. And it justified persecuting dissenters who had supported the regicide, they were not merely wrong but guilty of innocent blood.[95]

Not all Anglicans were comfortable with this cult of St. Charles. Some thought it approached idolatry. Others noted that Charles had been an imperfect king whose stubbornness had contributed to the war. But the cult served its purpose: it made loyalty to the restored monarchy a religious obligation and disloyalty a sin against God.[96]

The Doctrine of Passive Obedience

Romans 13 as Political Theology

"Let every soul be subject unto the higher powers. For there is no power but of God: the powers that be are ordained of God. Whosoever therefore resisteth the power, resisteth the ordinance of God" (Romans 13:1-2). This text was the cornerstone of Anglican political theology.[97]

God appointed rulers; subjects owed them obedience; to resist was to resist God. This wasn't merely prudential advice but divine command. Paul wrote it under Nero—one of the worst Roman emperors. If Christians must obey Nero, they must certainly obey Christian kings.[98]

Robert Sanderson, a prominent Restoration divine, explained in a sermon:[99]

If the magistrate commands what is lawful, we must obey actively—do what is commanded. If he commands what is sinful, we must obey passively—refuse to do the sin, but accept whatever punishment he inflicts for our refusal. But we must never resist with force, never take up arms, never join rebellion. For the magistrate's authority comes from God, and to resist with force is to fight against God.

This doctrine of passive obedience seemed to place subjects in an impossible position: obey even unjust commands or disobey but accept punishment without resistance. Critics asked: What if the ruler becomes a tyrant? What if he destroys the church? Must Christians submit to destruction?[100]

The Anglican Answer

Anglicans replied that tyranny was God's punishment for sin, and that Christians must accept it patiently, trusting God to remove the tyrant in His time. They pointed to biblical examples: David fled from Saul but refused to kill him, even when he had the chance. "The Lord forbid that I should stretch forth mine hand against the Lord's anointed" (1 Samuel 24:6). If David wouldn't kill Saul, how could subjects kill their king?[101]

Moreover, Anglicans argued, who decides when a ruler becomes a tyrant? If subjects may judge and resist, then every disgruntled faction claims tyranny and the realm descends into perpetual civil war. Better to suffer occasional tyranny than to authorize rebellion whenever subjects think themselves oppressed. The cure was worse than the disease.[102]

The only remedy for tyranny was prayer, patient suffering, and waiting for God's intervention. If God wished to remove a tyrant, He could do so, by the tyrant's death, by foreign invasion, by the tyrant's own repentance. Human resistance only made things worse and incurred divine judgment on the rebels.[103]

This theology made resistance nearly impossible to justify. It also made the Civil War and regicide unforgivable sins. Parliament had claimed the right to resist a tyrannical king; Anglicans said no such right existed. The regicides had killed God's anointed; they were guilty of sacrilege as well as murder. Only repentance and submission could restore England to divine favor.[104]

The Limits Tested: 1688 and the Glorious Revolution

The Crisis of Conscience

Anglican doctrine of passive obedience faced its greatest test in 1688. James II, Charles II's brother and successor, was openly Catholic. He appointed Catholics to military commands and university positions, dispensed with laws requiring Anglican communion for office, and issued a Declaration of Indulgence granting toleration to Catholics and Nonconformists alike.[105]

Anglicans were trapped. Their doctrine said they must obey the king. But James was undermining the Protestant settlement and the Church of England's established position. Some Anglicans, called Non-Jurors, maintained that they must submit regardless, oaths were sacred, and they had sworn to obey James. Others began quietly questioning whether resistance might sometimes be justified.[106]

When William of Orange invaded in November 1688 with Parliament's invitation, James fled to France. Parliament declared the throne vacant and offered it to William and Mary jointly. This was revolution, justified, most agreed, but revolution, nonetheless. Passive obedience hadn't stopped it.[107]

The Anglican Accommodation

Most Anglicans accepted the Revolution settlement, but they struggled to square it with passive obedience. Some argued James had abdicated by fleeing, so there was no resistance, only acceptance of vacancy. Others argued that extreme tyranny, especially tyranny threatening the Protestant religion, voided the social contract. Still others simply noted that Providence had acted: God had removed James; who were they to question?[108]

The Non-Jurors, including several bishops, refused to swear allegiance to William and Mary. They were deprived of their positions but maintained a principled stand: they had sworn oaths to James; those oaths were binding before God; they could not perjure themselves even if the alternative was ruin. The Non-Jurors became a small, distinguished sect, more consistent than their conforming brethren but politically irrelevant.[109]

The Glorious Revolution thus revealed the limits of passive obedience. When push came to shove, most Anglicans valued Protestant religion and political stability over absolute monarchical authority. They found reasons to accept what their theory should have forbidden. The doctrine survived—it remained official teaching, but it was quietly qualified. Passive obedience was the rule, but extreme circumstances might justify exceptions.[110]

The Human Costs of Uniformity

Persecution, Conscience, and the Price of Order

John Bunyan: Twelve Years for Preaching

John Bunyan's imprisonment (1660-1672, with brief release in 1666) exemplified Nonconformist suffering under the Restoration. Arrested for preaching without license in November 1660, Bunyan was offered release if he would promise not to preach. He refused: "If I were out of prison today, I would preach the gospel again tomorrow."[112]

The magistrate pressed: "You may teach in private, among your own people. Why must you preach publicly and break the law?" Bunyan replied: "I am called by God to preach the gospel. I dare not be silent. If you forbid me, you forbid God's work." This was conscience against law—and conscience lost.[113]

Bunyan spent twelve years in Bedford jail, a small stone building, cold in winter, stinking in summer, crowded with criminals. He supported his family (including a blind daughter) by making shoelaces, which his wife sold. He wrote constantly: *Grace Abounding* (1666), spiritual autobiography; *The Pilgrim's Progress* (1678), allegory that became the most widely read book in English after the Bible.[114]

His jailers were not monsters. They sometimes let him attend church services in Bedford or visit his family. But they couldn't release him without orders from higher authorities, and those orders never came. Bunyan remained imprisoned because he refused to stop preaching, and because the law demanded uniformity.[115]

George Fox: Beatings and Jails

George Fox, the Quaker leader, suffered even more severe persecution. Between 1650 and 1675, he was imprisoned eight times, sometimes for years. He was beaten by mobs, struck by magistrates, and once nearly killed by soldiers. His offense: refusing to take oaths, refusing to remove his hat before magistrates, and preaching without license.[116]

In Derby jail (1650-1651), he was kept in a cell so foul that the stench made him ill. Fellow prisoners were thieves and murderers. Fox preached to them, and several converted, which angered the jailers, who moved him to worse quarters. In Lancaster Castle (1660-1661), he was imprisoned in an open tower, exposed to weather; the cold nearly killed him.[117]

Fox's offense was not believing wrong doctrine, Quakers were orthodox on the Trinity, the Incarnation, and other essentials. His offense was refusing to recognize social hierarchy (keeping his hat on before magistrates was interpreted as contempt), refusing oaths (Quakers took Jesus's command literally: "Swear not at all"), and claiming direct revelation from God rather than mediate revelation through Scripture and church.[118]

Yet Fox was indomitable. In *A Journal*, he described his sufferings matter-of-factly, as if they were ordinary occurrences in a faithful Christian's life. He never expressed bitterness, never called for vengeance, never abandoned his testimony. His resilience inspired thousands of Quakers to endure similar persecution.[119]

The Anglican Defense of Persecution

Why They Thought It Necessary

Anglican defenders of the Clarendon Code didn't see themselves as persecutors but as guardians of order. They made several arguments:[120]

First, the nation's safety required religious unity. Dissenters had supported the regicide, overthrown the church, and nearly destroyed the nation. They claimed conscience but produced chaos. To tolerate them was to invite renewed disorder.

Second, most dissenters were hypocrites, not true consciences. Gilbert Sheldon argued that "tender conscience" was often a cover for ambition, faction, or resentment. "How convenient," he wrote sarcastically, "that conscience always leads dissenters to oppose authority and never to submit to it."[121]

Third, lenience encouraged further dissent. If the church compromised on ceremonies, dissenters would demand more. If the church tolerated separate meetings, dissenters would proselytize and multiply. Strict enforcement would, over time, make most dissenters conform; only a stubborn remnant would persist.[122]

Finally, suffering was good for true believers. If dissenters truly believed God called them to separate, they should be willing to suffer for it. Persecution would distinguish genuine conscience from factious pride. Those who conformed under pressure had never really been convinced; those who endured proved their sincerity.[123]

The Blindness to Conscience

These arguments reveal a fundamental Anglican blindness: they couldn't conceive that sincere, godly Christians might have genuine conscientious objections to ceremonies and oaths that Anglicans thought trivial. To them, submission to authority was a mark of humility; resistance was pride. If someone claimed conscience, the most likely explanation was that they were rationalizing rebellion.[124]

This made dialogue impossible. When Bunyan said, "I cannot in good conscience use the prayer book," Anglicans heard, "I am too proud to submit to authority." When Quakers said, "The Inner Light forbids me to swear oaths," Anglicans heard, "I claim special revelation to justify disobedience." The same words meant different things to speakers and hearers.[125]

The result was mutual incomprehension. Nonconformists thought Anglicans were persecuting them for obeying God. Anglicans thought Nonconformists were rebels hiding behind conscience. Both were partly right about the other, some Nonconformists were factious, some Anglicans were power-hungry—but neither understood the genuine conviction on the other side.[126]

The Gradual Turn Toward Toleration

Economic and Political Pressures

By the 1670s, the Clarendon Code was producing unintended consequences. Nonconformists, excluded from universities and many professions, concentrated in trade and commerce. They became economically important—especially in banking, manufacturing, and overseas trade. Persecuting them was increasingly costly.[127]

Politically, the attempt to suppress dissent had failed. Instead of conforming, Nonconformists had organized, built networks, supported each other, and waited. Their persecution created sympathy even among Anglicans who thought the Code too harsh. Public opinion was shifting; the appetite for persecution was waning.[128]

International developments also mattered. England competed commercially with the Dutch, whose toleration of religious diversity seemed to aid their prosperity. England allied with various Protestant powers against Catholic France; persecuting fellow Protestants looked increasingly awkward. And the threat of Catholic James II's succession focused Protestant minds: better to tolerate Protestant dissenters than to enable Catholic revival.[129]

The Toleration Act (1689)

The Glorious Revolution made toleration possible. William and Mary, brought to the throne by Protestant consensus against Catholic James II, owed debts to both Anglicans and Nonconformists who had supported them. The Toleration Act (1689) was the price of that support.[130]

The Act allowed Protestant dissenters to worship openly if they:[131]

- Subscribed to most of the Thirty-Nine Articles (Anglican doctrinal statements)
- Took oaths of allegiance to William and Mary
- Registered their meeting places

The Act exempted dissenters from penalties under the Clarendon Code but didn't grant full equality. They still couldn't attend universities, hold office, or serve in military commissions without taking Anglican communion. Catholics were excluded entirely. This was toleration, not religious liberty, permission to exist, not equality of citizenship.[132]

The Toleration Act represented not a principled embrace of liberty of conscience but a pragmatic accommodation. The nation was exhausted from religious conflict. Neither Anglicans nor Nonconformists could destroy the other; both had to coexist. The question was no longer whether diversity would exist but how it would be managed.[133]

Afterlives

The Anglican Legacy and Its Contradictions

The Durability of the Settlement

Three Centuries of Establishment[134]

The Restoration church settlement, modified by the Toleration Act, proved remarkably durable. From 1662 to 1828, the Church of England remained established, privileged, and normative. It controlled universities, blessed state occasions, and provided chaplains to Parliament and the military. Bishops sat in the House of Lords; the monarch was Supreme Governor; the Book of Common Prayer shaped English religious imagination.[135]

This establishment survived challenges from multiple directions:[136]

Methodism (18th century): John Wesley's revival movement threatened to split the church but was largely contained, though it eventually formed a separate denomination

Catholic Emancipation (1829): Ended most restrictions on Catholics, undermining the exclusively Protestant establishment

Disestablishment movements (19th-20th centuries): Liberals and Nonconformists campaigned to end establishment, succeeding in Ireland (1871) and Wales (1920) but not England

The Church of England adapted without abandoning its essential structure:

bishops, prayer book (revised but recognizable), liturgical worship, and claim to continuity with the ancient church. It became broader in theology, tolerating evangelical and Anglo-Catholic wings within one institution. The via media widened.[137]

The Price of Privilege

But establishment came at costs. The church became identified with the state, wealth, and social conservatism. It struggled to reach the urban working class that emerged during industrialization. Methodism did what the established church couldn't: it brought revivalist Christianity to miners, factory workers, and the poor.[138]

Moreover, establishment bred complacency. Clergy appointments became patronage; parishes became sinecures; sermons became dull. The spiritual vitality that marked the 17th century's conflicts gave way to 18th century's somnolence. The Oxford Movement (1830s-1840s) tried to restore theological seriousness; it partly succeeded but also divided the church.[139]

The establishment also compromised Anglican claims to universal truth. If the Church of England was the true church, why did it exist only where English law established it? Why did it need state support? Catholics had a worldwide communion; Reformed churches had confessional standards that crossed borders; but Anglicanism seemed peculiarly English, a national church rather than a universal one.[140]

The Global Anglican Communion

From English Church to Worldwide Communion

The British Empire's expansion carried Anglicanism worldwide. Bishops accompanied colonial governors; missionaries followed traders; parishes were established wherever English settlers went. By 1900, there were Anglican churches on every continent, with millions of members beyond England.[141]

This created a problem: how to maintain unity among churches separated by vast distances and cultural differences? The solution was the Anglican Communion, a federation of autonomous provinces (national churches), united not by papal authority or binding confessions but by:[142]

Common worship: Variations of the Book of Common Prayer

Episcopal order: Bishops in apostolic succession

Shared history: Connection to the Church of England

Lambeth Conferences: Periodic gatherings of bishops (from 1867) to discuss common concerns

The Communion was not a centralized church like Roman Catholicism. Canterbury's Archbishop had primacy of honor but no jurisdiction over other provinces. Each province could adapt liturgy, discipline, and even doctrine to local circumstances. This flexibility allowed Anglicanism to become genuinely global, but also created potential for fragmentation.[143]

Contemporary Tensions

In the 21st century, the Anglican Communion faces severe tensions over issues that would have seemed distant in the 17th century: women's ordination, homosexuality, biblical interpretation. African and Asian provinces tend toward conservatism; North American and European provinces toward liberalism. The Communion has come close to schism; its future remains uncertain.[144]

Yet the Communion persists because Anglicanism, from its origins, was built on comprehensiveness. The Elizabethan settlement aimed to include diverse theological perspectives within one institutional church. The Restoration settlement added dissenters outside the church but tolerated within the nation. The Anglican instinct has always been to prefer unity over purity, to keep talking rather than splitting.[145]

Whether this comprehensiveness can survive modern polarization remains uncertain. But the Anglican instinct, to prefer unity over uniformity, to value tradition while allowing development, to maintain episcopal order while permitting theological diversity, continues to shape a global communion of perhaps 85 million members.[146]

What Anglicanism Gave the World

Gifts

The Anglican tradition contributed several gifts to Christian practice and political thought:[147]

Liturgical beauty: The Book of Common Prayer shaped English prose. Its rhythms influenced poets from John Donne to T.S. Eliot. Its prayers—"We have left undone those things which we ought to have done, and we have done those things which we ought not to have done, and there is no health in us," gave ordinary people words for confession and aspiration.

Via media thinking: The instinct to find middle ways between extremes, to include rather than exclude, to emphasize and/also over either/or. This could be indecisiveness or wisdom, depending on the situation, but it offered an alternative to polarization.

Establishment's lessons: The Anglican experiment with church establishment, its successes and failures, taught lessons about religion and state. It showed that establishment could provide stability and public presence but also could corrupt and compromise. These lessons informed American debates about religion clauses in the Constitution.

Episcopal order: The Anglican recovery of episcopal polity influenced other traditions. Methodists eventually adopted bishops; some Lutheran churches maintain apostolic succession; ecumenical dialogues have produced agreements recognizing Anglican orders. The Anglican model of episcopacy, bishops as pastors of pastors, maintaining continuity and unity, shaped wider Christian thinking about church structure.

Costs

But the Anglican way also had costs:

Compromise as principle: The via media could become unprincipled accommodation, standing for nothing clearly. Critics charged that Anglicanism was Protestantism lite, Catholic aesthetics without Catholic substance, Reformed rhetoric without Reformed rigor. The joke that Anglicans believed in one God, "more or less," had some bite.[148]

Establishment's exclusions: The privileges of establishment were purchased by excluding Catholics, Nonconformists, and (eventually) non-Christians from full participation in national life. The Test Acts and Corporation Act discriminated for centuries. In Ireland, Anglican establishment over a Catholic majority was a running sore that contributed to centuries of conflict.[149]

Passive obedience: The doctrine of divine right and passive obedience, while modified after 1688, long inhibited political criticism and justified accepting injustice. It took dissenting voices, Methodist, Baptist, Quaker, to drive reforms like abolition of slavery and factory regulation.[150]

Cultural captivity: The Church of England's identification with English culture, class structure, and empire made it struggle to transcend those contexts. It became so English that its claim to catholicity, to being the universal church in England, seemed dubious. Empire carried Anglicanism worldwide, but also compromised its witness.[151]

From the Great Ejection to the Present

We began this chapter watching William Bates pack his books and preach his final sermon at St. Giles Cripplegate. We watched Thomas Manton wait to take his place, representing the restoration of order, hierarchy, and uniformity. We saw 2,000 ministers ejected, thousands imprisoned, a nation forcibly reunited around the prayer book and episcopal authority.[152]

The Paradox of Anglican Success

The paradox is that Anglican order survived by eventually abandoning its insistence on total uniformity. The Toleration Act of 1689 admitted what the Clarendon Code had tried to deny: England contained permanent religious diversity. The established church would coexist with dissenting chapels. One nation would contain many churches.[153]

This was not the victory Sheldon and the Restoration bishops wanted. They had hoped to reabsorb dissenters through a combination of legal pressure and pastoral patience. Instead, they got denominationalism, a religious marketplace where established and dissenting churches competed for adherents. But the Anglican church survived, adapted, and eventually flourished in this new environment.[154]

What the Anglicans Understood

The Anglicans understood something their opponents sometimes missed: institutions matter. The Independents trusted voluntary association and individual conscience. The Quakers trusted the Inner Light and direct revelation. The Levellers trusted natural rights and popular sovereignty. All these were important—but none of them, by themselves, could sustain a church or a nation.[155]

They were partly right. The gathered churches of the Independents did fragment into denominations. The Quaker movement, after its first generation's fervor, required the structures Fox built to survive. Even Presbyterians, who claimed to reject episcopacy, developed their own hierarchy. The episcopal church, with its bishops, liturgy, and law, provided continuity that looser structures couldn't match.[156]

What the Anglicans Missed

But the Anglicans missed something equally important: conscience cannot be coerced. They thought legal pressure would make dissenters conform. Instead, it created martyrs, deepened convictions, and ultimately failed. Bunyan's *Pilgrim's Progress*, written in prison, outsold everything the established church produced. Quaker sufferings refined and strengthened the movement. Persecution didn't destroy dissent; it purified it.[157]

The Anglicans' confidence that uniformity was necessary for order proved wrong. New England's Congregational churches created ordered communities. Pennsylvania's Quaker colony thrived with radical toleration. Even England, under the Toleration Act, achieved stability despite religious diversity. Order, it turned out, didn't require uniformity, only agreed rules for managing disagreement.[158]

The Legacy

The Anglican way—episcopacy, liturgy, establishment, and (eventually) toleration—shaped English-speaking Christianity profoundly. It gave beautiful worship, institutional continuity, and a model of church-state cooperation that influenced nations worldwide. It also gave lessons in what not to do: persecution fails, conscience cannot be coerced, uniformity isn't necessary for order.[159]

Those lessons were learned slowly and incompletely. The Great Ejection's victims, Bates, Bunyan, and thousands of others, paid the price for Anglican confidence in coercion. Their sufferings, and their resilience, taught that liberty of conscience was not a threat to order but a condition of genuine peace.[160]

Yet the fiercest critics of both bishops and presbyters, the sharpest challenge to both establishment and covenant, came not from careful arguers like Milton or patient sufferers like Bunyan but from radicals who denied all human authority over conscience and proclaimed a Lamb's War against the powers of this world. To the Quakers we now turn.

CHAPTER 6 — THE LAMB'S WAR

QUAKER ANARCHY AND THE TURN TO PEACE

The Trial of James Nayler
Westminster Hall, December 1656

The prisoner would not remove his hat. James Nayler stood in the well of Westminster Hall, flanked by guards, while Members of Parliament crowded the benches above. He had ridden into Bristol in October as if into Jerusalem—a ragged procession through autumn mud, women singing "Holy, holy, holy" and strewing garments before his horse. Now he faced men who believed the nation's peace depended on punishing blasphemy.[1]

Major-General Philip Skippon rose to speak. He had commanded infantry at Naseby, where England's fate turned on discipline and courage. He had known Nayler's associate George Bishop in those days—both serving the parliamentary cause, both believing God fought on their side. But this, Skippon said, was different.[2] "It has been always my opinion," he told the House, "that the growth of these things is more dangerous than the most intestine or foreign enemies." He gestured toward Nayler. "Their principles strike both at ministry and magistracy."[3]

The charges were specific. Witnesses testified that Nayler had assumed the titles belonging to Christ alone: "the fairest of ten thousand," "the only begotten Son of God," "King of Israel." He had allowed followers to address him as "Jesus" in writing. He had permitted acts of worship directed to his person. He had entered Bristol in deliberate imitation of Christ's entry to Jerusalem.[4]

When questioned, Nayler's answers frustrated his interrogators. Did his followers call him Jesus? "Not as to the visible," he replied. To whom did they give that name? "To the Jesus, to the Christ that is in me." Was he claiming to be Christ? "As I am a creature, I believe they did not. But that the name of Jesus was given to him in a letter, I cannot deny, if by that they meant the Son of God that is in me."[5]

The legal problem was immediate: England possessed no statute against blasphemy that clearly covered Nayler's case. He had not denied the Trinity, as the 1648 Blasphemy Ordinance required for capital punishment. He had not claimed to be God in the crude sense that even a drunken fool might. Instead, he spoke in a spiritual register that his judges found simultaneously incomprehensible and intolerable, claiming that Christ indwelt him so fully that he could be called by Christ's name without blasphemy.

Sir Gilbert Pickering, more moderate than Skippon, suggested leniency. "His hard labor and imprisonment will be sufficient," he argued. "I have, within these two days, talked with a very sober man of that persuasion," meaning a respectable Quaker, "who declares himself convinced that this man is bewitched."[6]

But Skippon pressed for severity. "Seeing you are off the other question," he said, referring to the death penalty that had narrowly failed, "make the other punishment as high as you can. I doubt cutting off his hair will be but too private a punishment. It is offered you, instead of pillory, to slit his tongue, and that upon a scaffold upon the Exchange, in as public a manner as can be."[7]

The sentence, when it came, demonstrated Parliament's anxiety: to be set in the pillory at Westminster for two hours, wearing a paper describing his crimes; to be whipped through the streets from Westminster to the Old Exchange in London; to be pilloried again at the Exchange for two hours; to have his tongue bored through with a hot iron; to be branded on the forehead with the letter "B" for blasphemer; to be taken to Bristol and forced through the city backward on a horse, then whipped in the market; to be imprisoned in Bridewell at hard labor, denied pen, ink, and paper, and barred from visitors until Parliament should release him.[8]

The punishment was carried out in stages through December. Nayler bore it with a calm that unnerved onlookers. When the brand touched his forehead, witnesses said he neither cried out nor flinched. One observer wrote that "he was patient under his sufferings as a lamb." Another, less sympathetic, thought his composure proved demonic possession—no natural man could endure such pain without breaking.[9]

Bristol, October 1656: The Event That Sparked the Trial

To understand the trial, we must step back to the act that provoked it. James Nayler was no fool, no madman, and no crude blasphemer. He had been among the earliest and most effective Quaker preachers—eloquent, learned in Scripture, capable of holding crowds with his exposition of the inner light. George Fox had traveled with him, preached alongside him, and saw in him a gifted minister of the truth as Friends understood it.[10]

But something had shifted. In London, beginning in 1655, Nayler attracted followers who venerated him in terms that made even other Quakers uneasy. Martha Simmonds, wife of a London Quaker, began addressing him in language reserved for Christ. Letters called him "the fairest of ten thousand," "the only begotten Son of God." Nayler did not clearly reject these titles. Whether from spiritual confusion, pride, or a genuine belief that Christ's indwelling made such language appropriate, he allowed the veneration to continue.[11]

Fox heard reports and grew alarmed. In 1656 he visited Nayler in prison (where Nayler was held for earlier Quaker activities) and confronted him. The meeting went badly. Fox demanded that Nayler acknowledge his error and submit to Fox's judgment as the movement's recognized leader. Nayler refused, seeing Fox's demand as a claim to human authority that contradicted Quaker principles of the inner light. The two men parted without reconciliation.[12]

Released from prison in September 1656, Nayler did not go home to his wife and children in Yorkshire. Instead, he allowed his London followers to lead him westward. At Glastonbury, ancient and soaked in Arthurian legend, the party rested. Then they pressed on toward Bristol—a wealthy city, a Quaker stronghold, and a place where witnesses would spread word of whatever happened.[13]

On October 24, they reached Bristol. Rain had turned the roads to mud. The party arranged themselves in procession: Nayler on horseback, his followers walking before and behind, singing "Holy, holy, holy, Lord God of Sabaoth" and spreading their garments in the mire as crowds had done for Christ entering Jerusalem.

Bristol's magistrates arrested them immediately. The city had a strong Presbyterian faction that despised Quakers; it also housed a significant Quaker community led by George Bishop, a former parliamentary intelligence officer who had become a leading Friend. Bishop was horrified. Nayler's action vindicated every charge the Presbyterians made against Quaker enthusiasm.[14]

Bishop joined Fox in condemning Nayler. When Fox came to Bristol, the two men visited Nayler in prison and demanded he recant. Nayler, exhausted and perhaps beginning to grasp the magnitude of his error, nevertheless could not bring himself to submit. "Who art thou to judge me?" he asked Fox. "Hath not the Lord given the light to every man? Why should I submit to thy judgment rather than to the light within me?"[15]

Fox's answer revealed his emerging conception of authority: "The light in thee has been darkened by thy pride and by those who flatter thee. The light in the body of Friends is clearer because we judge together, and each corrects the other's errors. Thou hast set thyself above the body, and thereby shown that thy light has become darkness." Nayler would not yield. The meeting ended badly, with Fox and Bishop departing and Nayler left to face Parliament's judgment alone.[16]

The Aftermath: Power and Authority in a Leaderless Movement

The trial and punishment of Nayler changed the Quaker movement. It demonstrated two things simultaneously: first, that the movement's radical egalitarianism—the insistence that any person might speak as the Spirit moved them—could produce dangerous excess; second, that the movement needed structures to discipline that excess without abandoning its core conviction that Christ taught his people directly.[17]

Fox emerged from the Nayler crisis with enhanced authority, though he never claimed a title or office. He simply acted as leader, and enough Friends accepted his leadership that it became real. Over the next three years (1657-1660), Fox would oversee the creation of organizational structures—monthly meetings, quarterly meetings, traveling ministers with recognized status, elders with authority to correct errors—that gave the movement durability without destroying its claim to be led by the Spirit rather than by human hierarchy.[18]

But before those structures solidified, Friends had to navigate the most dangerous years of their existence: the final years of the Protectorate, the chaos of 1659, and the Restoration of 1660. In those years, they would be offered political power and would choose, instead, the way of peace.

Nayler's trial exposed the question every faction faced: How do you maintain order without extinguishing the Spirit? How do you correct error without creating a new tyranny? The Anglicans answered with bishops and law. The Presbyterians answered with elders and synods. The Independents answered with local covenants. The Quakers' answer was still taking shape, but it would prove the most radical of all.

Street Prophets and Worried Magistrates

Early Quaker Witness and Its Consequences

George Fox and the Birth of a Movement

Leicestershire, 1647

George Fox was twenty-three years old when he climbed Pendle Hill in Lancashire and saw, he later wrote, "a great people to be gathered." He had been wandering for years, seeking truth among the priests and professors of religion and finding only, as he put it, "empty shells." He tried the Presbyterians; they disappointed him. He tried the Independents; they too fell short. He tried solitude and study; neither satisfied.[19]

What Fox sought was immediate access to divine teaching. He believed—and this would become the cornerstone of Quaker theology—that Christ could and did teach his people directly, without mediation of clergy, sacrament, or even (in a sense) Scripture. The Bible was true, Fox insisted, but it was a record of what the Spirit had taught the prophets and apostles. The same Spirit was available now, speaking to those who would be silent and listen.[20]

Fox called this the "inner light" or "that of God in every man." Critics immediately accused him of multiple heresies: claiming perfection, denying Scripture's authority, making every man his own pope. Fox denied most of these charges but not always clearly. He insisted the inner light was Christ himself, not a mere faculty of conscience. He insisted Scripture remained authoritative—but added that the Spirit who inspired Scripture must interpret it, and that Spirit spoke within.[21]

In 1647-1648, Fox began gathering followers. His preaching was powerful, his manner intense. He traveled constantly, often sleeping outdoors, eating what he was given or going hungry. He confronted ministers in their pulpits, magistrates on their benches, and crowds in marketplaces. He was beaten, imprisoned, and reviled—and he kept coming back.[22]

The "Valiant Sixty"

By 1652, Fox's movement had produced a core group of traveling preachers known to historians as the "Valiant Sixty." These were men and women, Quakers insisted women could preach, who left their trades and families to spread their message throughout England and beyond. Among the most important: [23]

- **Edward Burrough** (1634-1663): Young, eloquent, combative in print and speech. He would become the movement's primary controversialist and political spokesman.
- **Francis Howgill** (1618-1669): A former Seeker (one of the many searching groups) who joined Fox and became a powerful preacher.
- **George Bishop** (c.1620-1668): Former parliamentary intelligence officer, including time in General Phillip Skippon's service. He was an organizer of Bristol Friends, defender of the movement in print and before magistrates.
- **James Nayler** (1618-1660): Fox's early companion, gifted preacher, whose fall would force the movement to confront its own boundaries. Before becoming an itinerate preacher, he had served as a foot soldier under General Thomas Fairfax and later as a quartermaster in the cavalry under General John Lambert.
- **Margaret Fell** (1614-1702): Wealthy widow whose home at Swarthmoor Hall became the movement's informal headquarters, who wrote prolifically and managed correspondence networks that held scattered Friends together.[24]

These and others fanned out across England in 1652-1654, preaching in markets, disrupting services, confronting clergy, and gathering converts at a remarkable rate. By 1654, there may have been 20,000 to 30,000 Quakers in England, a number that alarmed authorities of every stripe.[25]

The Practices That Provoked

Early Quakers developed a set of practices, "testimonies," they called them, that marked them as different and made them targets of persecution:

The Hat Testimony

Quakers refused to remove their hats before social superiors, including magistrates and even the king. In 17th-century England, hat-honor was a fundamental marker of hierarchy. A commoner uncovered before a gentleman; a gentleman before a lord; everyone before the king. To keep one's hat on was to claim equality, or to show contempt.[26]

The hat testimony had theological depth that critics often missed. If Christ taught every believer directly, then the distinctions of rank that structured English society were spiritually meaningless. "The Lord has made of one blood all nations," Friends said, quoting Acts 17:26. If all souls were equal before God, no man deserved the outward honor of hat-doffing. This was not mere rudeness but testimony to Christ's kingdom, where the first shall be last and the last first. Critics saw this as social leveling and sedition. "If a servant won't doff his hat to his master," one pamphleteer warned, "soon he won't obey his master's lawful commands."

The Plain Speech Testimony

Quakers used "thee" and "thou" to everyone, regardless of rank. In 17th-century English, "you" was plural or formal singular (used to superiors); "thee/thou" was singular and familiar (used to equals or inferiors). To "thou" a magistrate or master was to deny his superiority. [27]

The plain speech testimony, likewise, witnessed to spiritual equality. To "thou" a magistrate or master was to deny his spiritual superiority. Critics heard insolence; Friends heard truth. Quakers insisted this was biblical usage and linguistic honesty—one person should be addressed in the singular, not the flattering plural. The practice seemed to contemporaries a deliberate assault on social order, and in a sense it was. Friends were asserting that Christ's kingdom operated by different rules than England's. Many Quakers were beaten for "thou-ing" their social betters.[28]

The Refusal of Oaths

Quakers refused to swear oaths, in court, for military service, for civic office. They cited Jesus' teaching in Matthew 5:34-37: "Swear not at all... let your communication be, Yea, yea; Nay, nay: for whatsoever is more than these cometh of evil." For Quakers, this meant any oath was sinful, a claim that put them at odds with English law and custom. [29]

This created immediate practical problems. English law required oaths for testimony, for office-holding, for loyalty to the government. A person who wouldn't swear couldn't testify in court, couldn't serve on juries, couldn't hold office—and might be suspected of treasonous sympathies. Refusing the Oath of Allegiance was a serious offense; refusing oaths repeatedly could lead to indefinite imprisonment.[30]

The Refusal of Tithes

Quakers refused to pay tithes, the mandatory church tax that supported parish ministers. They cited multiple biblical arguments: Old Testament tithes went to Levitical priests (no longer applicable under the New Covenant); New Testament ministers like Paul worked with their hands rather than demanding payment; Jesus commanded his disciples to preach freely.[31]

But the practical argument was simpler: ministers who preached for pay were "hirelings," motivated by money rather than truth. True ministers preached from inward compulsion, not for outward reward. This struck at the entire system of national church finance and enraged clergy who depended on tithes for their livelihood. [32]

Yet Quakers persisted, seeing tithe refusal as part of the "Lamb's War"—spiritual warfare waged through suffering rather than violence.[33]

Disruption as Witness: Three Scenes

Fox Interrupts Baxter at Kidderminster, 1648

Richard Baxter, the earnest Presbyterian minister of Kidderminster, was midway through his Sunday morning sermon when George Fox entered the church. Fox walked down the aisle, hat firmly on his head, and began speaking before reaching the pulpit.[34]

"Thou art a hireling!" Fox's voice cut through Baxter's exposition. "Thou takest tithes and deceivest the people with thy vain traditions!"

Baxter, surprised but not speechless, replied: "Be silent! This is God's house and you dishonor it."

"The Lord's house is not made with hands," Fox shot back, quoting Acts 7:48. "Thou preachest for money like Balaam. Thou art a false prophet leading people into dead works!"

The congregation stirred—some sympathetic to Fox's challenge, others angry at the interruption. Baxter tried to continue his sermon, but Fox would not be silent. The constable moved forward, and several men seized Fox and dragged him from the church.

Outside, Fox preached to whoever would listen. He denounced set forms of prayer, paid ministers, and sacraments performed by unregenerate priests. A small crowd gathered—some mocking, some curious, some quietly convinced. By evening, Fox had moved on, leaving Baxter to repair the damage to his authority and to preach the next Sunday on the need for order and decency in worship.[35]

Baxter would later write that Quakers were "the most dangerous sect" because they struck at the very foundations: a learned ministry, scriptural order, and magistrates' authority over religion. He published *The Quakers' Catechism* in 1655, a sustained attack on Quaker theology and practice warning that their principles led to "anarchy and confusion."[36] Edward Burrough replied for the Quakers, and the pamphlet war between them illuminated the gulf between Presbyterian order and Quaker spontaneity.

Burrough Confronts Minister at Reading, 1654

Edward Burrough was younger and more combative than Fox. In 1654, he attended a service at Reading led by Christopher Fowler, the local minister. Fowler was preaching on justification, how sinners are made righteous before God, using the orthodox Reformed position that justification is by faith alone through Christ's imputed righteousness.[37]

Burrough stood during the sermon. "Thou liest!" he called out. "Justification is not by an imputed righteousness outside of man, but by Christ's righteousness within, purging and perfecting the soul!"

Fowler, less patient than Baxter, ordered the constable to remove Burrough immediately. But Burrough was not finished. As he was being dragged out, he shouted: ""Thy doctrine makes men comfortable in their sins! Christ came not to cover sin but to destroy it! Thou feedest thy flock with husks while the children starve!"

Outside, Burrough debated with those who followed him out. He argued that the Quaker position was not works-righteousness (salvation by human effort) but the work of Christ within, actively transforming believers into his image. The Reformed position, he said, left men passive, claiming a righteousness they did not possess and never would possess in this life.

Fowler responded with a pamphlet attacking Quaker perfectionism. Burrough replied with *A Discovery of Some Part of the War Between the Kingdom of the Lamb and the Kingdom of Anti-Christ* (1659), which became one of the defining statements of Quaker spiritual warfare.[38]

The debate was not merely theological. It had social implications: If people could be perfected by the inner light, what need for clergy to instruct them? If righteousness was within, what need for external sacraments? If the Spirit taught directly, what need for universities and learning? The clergy's social role and economic support depended on answers Quakers rejected.

Martha Simmonds Prophesies in Exeter, 1655

Not all disruptive Quakers were men. Martha Simmonds, the same woman who would later be involved in Nayler's fall, traveled to Exeter in 1655 as an itinerant preacher. She entered a Presbyterian church during worship, stood in the aisle, and began speaking in what contemporaries called a "prophetic voice"—loud, rhythmic, urgent.[39]

> *Woe to you, priests and rulers! You have closed the kingdom of heaven against men! You neither enter yourselves nor allow those who would enter to go in! Woe, woe to you!*

The language came from Matthew 23, Jesus' denunciation of the scribes and Pharisees. But Simmonds applied it to present-day clergy and magistrates. She continued for several minutes before being seized and dragged to the town jail.

At her examination before the magistrate, she refused to remove her hat, refused to swear an oath, and refused to promise she would not preach again. "I must obey God rather than men," she said, quoting Acts 5:29. The magistrate sentenced her to prison until she agreed to keep the peace. She remained in jail, preaching through the bars to whoever would listen, until the magistrate, weary of the spectacle, released her with a warning.[40]

Women's preaching was particularly controversial. Both Anglicans and Presbyterians cited 1 Corinthians 14:34 ("Let your women keep silence in the churches") and 1 Timothy 2:12 ("I suffer not a woman to teach, nor to usurp authority over the man"). Quakers replied with Galatians 3:28 ("There is neither male nor female... in Christ Jesus") and Acts 2:17-18 ("Your sons and your daughters shall prophesy"). If the Spirit spoke through women in apostolic times, why not now?.[41]

These disruptions, Fox at Kidderminster, Burrough at Reading, Simmonds at Exeter, followed a pattern. Quakers entered spaces where authority claimed to speak for God. They challenged that authority publicly. They refused to be silent when ordered. They accepted punishment rather than compromise. To magistrates and ministers, this looked like sedition and blasphemy. To Quakers, it looked like obedience to the inner light of Christ. The conflict was irreconcilable without one side yielding its core conviction.

The Inner Light and the Question of Authority

Theology, Power, and the Grounds of Knowledge

What Quakers Meant by "Inner Light"

The "inner light" was the defining Quaker doctrine and the source of most controversy. To understand it requires stepping into Quaker theological thinking, which was not always systematic but had its own coherence.

Christ as Teacher

Friends began with the conviction that Christ had come to teach his people himself—not through intermediaries but directly. They pointed to John 6:45: "And they shall be all taught of God." They cited John 14:26: "But the Comforter, which is the Holy Ghost, whom the Father will send in my name, he shall teach you all things." They quoted 1 John 2:27: "The anointing which ye have received of him abideth in you, and ye need not that any man teach you."[42]

George Fox wrote in his *Journal*: "Christ, who is the one true light, enlightens all men that come into the world. This light is within, and it will reprove and condemn all evil, and lead into all truth those who obey it." This was not, Quakers insisted, mere natural conscience. It was Christ himself, personally present and active. When a Quaker spoke of "the light within," he meant the presence of the risen Christ in the soul.[43]

Critics immediately asked: If everyone has this light, why do they behave so wickedly? Quakers answered that people possess the light but resist it. The light convicts of sin, but humans suppress it, preferring darkness. Those who obey the light find it grows brighter; those who resist find themselves hardened in sin.[44]

The Bunyan-Burrough Exchange, 1656

The conflict between Quaker and Independent anthropology found sharp expression in the 1656 exchange between John Bunyan and Edward Burrough. Bunyan, the Bedford tinker who would later write *The Pilgrim's Progress*, published *Some Gospel Truths Opened* attacking Quaker doctrine. Burrough responded with *The True Faith of the Gospel of Peace.*

Bunyan's attack centered on the Quaker doctrine of the inner light. If Christ dwelt within every person, Bunyan argued, then the historical Christ—Jesus of Nazareth, born of Mary, crucified under Pilate—became unnecessary. The Quakers "deny the Man Christ Jesus to be above the clouds and heavens," he charged, and substitute "a Christ within them" that is merely "their own natural consciences, or something else that is not Christ."

For Bunyan, the heart was "deceitful above all things, and desperately wicked" (Jeremiah 17:9). No inner light could guide fallen humanity; only the external Word of Scripture, applied by the Holy Spirit, could break through human self-deception. Quakers trusted their hearts; Bunyan trusted the Book.

Burrough replied that Bunyan misunderstood. Quakers did not deny the historical Christ; they affirmed that the same Christ who had walked in Galilee now dwelt within his people. "Christ in you, the hope of glory"—Paul's words in Colossians 1:27, not Quaker invention. Scripture pointed to Christ; Christ spoke within. To set Scripture against the Spirit was to divide what God had joined.

But Burrough went further: he questioned Bunyan's emphasis on human depravity. Yes, the Fall had corrupted humanity. But Christ's light shone in every person, offering redemption to all who would turn toward it. This was not natural conscience but supernatural grace, available universally. Bunyan's Calvinist emphasis on election and reprobation made God "the author of sin"—choosing some for salvation and abandoning others to damnation for no fault of their own.

Anarchism in Its Etymological Sense

The doctrine of the inner light had radical political implications. If Christ taught every believer directly, then no human authority—minister, elder, bishop, or magistrate—could stand between the individual and God. The hierarchies that Presbyterians, Independents, and Anglicans all assumed were necessary became not merely unnecessary but actively harmful. They interposed human authority where only divine authority belonged.

This was anarchism in its etymological sense: *an-archos*, without rulers. Early Quakers did not withdraw from political engagement. They challenged magistrates, refused oaths, disrupted services, and demanded liberty of conscience. But they denied that any human authority, king, Parliament, synod, or congregation, had legitimate power over the individual's relationship with God.

Moreover, the inner light was universal. Unlike Calvinist election, which marked some for salvation and others for damnation, the Quaker light shone "in every man that cometh into the world" (John 1:9). This theological universalism translated into social egalitarianism. If every person had direct access to Christ, then the distinctions of rank, wealth, and education that structured English society were spiritually meaningless.

The Test of Fruits

How could you tell true revelation from false? Enthusiasts of various stripes claimed divine inspiration for all manner of beliefs and behaviors. Some Ranters, for instance, claimed the Spirit freed them from all moral law, licensing behavior that horrified even other radicals.[45]

Quakers rejected this antinomianism utterly. True revelation, they said, produces the fruits of the Spirit listed in Galatians 5:22-23: love, joy, peace, patience, kindness, goodness, faithfulness, gentleness, self-control. If a claimed revelation led to immorality, pride, or confusion, it was not from God. The test was ethical as well as spiritual.

Edward Burrough wrote:[46]

> *That which leads into truth-telling, into justice, into love of enemies, into patience under persecution—that is the Spirit of Christ. That which leads into lying, revenge, impatience, or pride—that is the spirit of antichrist, however loudly it claims divine*

authority.

This was the test Quakers applied to their own members. When James Nayler allowed himself to be venerated as Christ, many Quakers (including Fox and Bishop) judged that his behavior did not produce the fruits of humility and truth-telling, therefore it could not be of the true light.

Scripture and the Spirit

The relationship between inner light and Scripture was complex and contested. Quakers did not reject the Bible, they quoted it constantly, knew it deeply, and honored it as the record of what the Spirit taught the prophets and apostles.[47]

But they subordinated Scripture to the Spirit in a crucial sense: The same Spirit who inspired Scripture must interpret it. The letter alone, read without the Spirit, kills; the Spirit gives life (2 Corinthians 3:6). To read the Bible as a dead book, merely historical, merely textual, was to miss its power.

George Fox put it provocatively: "You will say, 'Christ saith this, and the apostles say this'; but what canst thou say? Art thou a child of Light and hast walked in the Light, and what thou speakest is it inwardly from God?"[48]

Critics heard this as denying Scripture's authority. Quakers replied that they honored Scripture more than their critics did, because they required the same Spirit who wrote it to read it. To study Scripture with mere human learning, without the Spirit's inward teaching, was to remain in the letter that kills.

This raised the stakes of every debate. When Richard Baxter argued from Scripture that ministers deserved tithes (citing Old Testament precedent and Paul's teaching), Burrough replied that Baxter read Scripture in a "carnal" way, with dead learning rather than living Spirit. When Presbyterians cited Scripture for church government by elders, Quakers replied that they read with "fleshly wisdom" rather than spiritual illumination.[49]

The debate was not really about what Scripture said, both sides quoted it, but about who had authority to interpret it. Presbyterians said synods of learned clergy. Independents said gathered congregations of visible saints. Anglicans said bishops through apostolic succession. Quakers said the Spirit in every believer, tested by the community of Friends.

Baxter vs. Burrough: The Great Debate

The pamphlet exchange between Richard Baxter and Edward Burrough in 1655-1657 crystallized the conflict between presbyterian order and Quaker spontaneity.

Baxter's Attack

Baxter's *The Quakers' Catechism* (1655) was a systematic assault on Quaker doctrine and practice. He structured it as questions and answers, showing what Quakers believed and then refuting each point. [50]

Key charges:

- **Quakers deny Christ's historical death**: Baxter argued that by emphasizing Christ within, Quakers downplayed or denied Christ's death on the cross as atonement for sin. "They make the cross of Christ of none effect," he charged, "by making his work within us the whole of salvation."[51]

- **Quakers claim sinless perfection**: Baxter pointed to 1 John 1:8 ("If we say that we have no sin, we deceive ourselves") and accused Quakers of claiming a perfection that Scripture denies. "They are proud above measure," he wrote, "claiming to have reached what the apostles themselves did not claim."[52]
- **Quakers undermine Scripture**: By prioritizing the inner light over written Scripture, Baxter charged, Quakers opened the door to every delusion. "If any man's fancy may be called revelation," he warned, "then there is no truth and no error, but every man is his own pope, and we have as many religions as heads."[53]
- **Quakers destroy social order**: By refusing oaths, hat-honor, and tithes, Baxter argued, Quakers undermined the bonds that held society together. "Servants will not obey masters, wives will not obey husbands, subjects will not obey magistrates, all in the name of a pretended light."[54]

Baxter ended by appealing to magistrates to suppress Quakers as they would suppress any dangerous sect. "You have the sword to use for God," he wrote. "Use it, before these vipers multiply beyond control."[55]

Burrough's Reply

Edward Burrough replied with *The True Faith of the Gospel of Peace* (1656). His response was passionate, pointed, and showed no interest in reconciliation.

- **On Christ's death:** "We do not deny Christ's death. We affirm it. But we also affirm that Christ must live in us, or his death profits us nothing. Thou makest Christ's death an excuse to remain in sin—we make it the power that frees from sin."[56]
- **On perfection:** "We do not say we have no sin by nature. We say Christ purges us from sin, and those who abide in him do not sin. The Scripture thou quotest, 'If we say we have no sin,' is written to those who deny they ever sinned—not to those whom Christ has cleansed. 'Whosoever is born of God doth not commit sin. (1 John 3:9). Why dost thou stop at the first verse and ignore the promise?"[57]
- **On Scripture:** "We honor Scripture above thee. For we believe the Spirit wrote it, and the same Spirit interprets it. But thou trustest in thy carnal learning—thy Greek and Hebrew, thy logic and thy commentaries. These profit nothing without the Spirit. Thou art like the Pharisees: searching the Scriptures but refusing to come to Christ who gives them life."[58]
- **On social order:** "Thou accusest us of disorder because we will not flatter men by removing our hats or swearing oaths. But we keep better order than thou. We do not lie—thy people lie daily. We do not defraud—thy people cheat in business. We do not oppress the poor—

> but thou takest tithes from widows and orphans to enrich thyself. Who then is the keeper of order: we who tell the truth, or thou who coverest lies with pious words?"[59]

Burrough then turned the tables: "Thou sayest we strike at ministry and magistracy. But we strike only at false ministry and unjust magistracy. True ministers preach freely, as Paul did. Hireling ministers, like thee, demand payment. True magistrates defend the innocent and punish the guilty. Tyrannical magistrates, like those thou servest, persecute the righteous and let the wicked go free. We do not oppose the office, we oppose thy abuse of it."[60]

Nayler on Toleration's Limits

Before his fall, James Nayler had debated Richard Baxter on the question of toleration. Baxter's *The Quakers Catechism* (1655) had attacked Friends for their heresies and their disruptions. Nayler replied with *An Answer to the Quakers Catechism.*[61]

Baxter argued that Quakers could not claim toleration because they were not merely dissenters but disturbers of the peace. They interrupted services, reviled ministers, refused lawful oaths, and taught doctrines that undermined social order. "If every man may follow his own light," Baxter asked, "who will obey magistrates? Who will pay taxes? Who will serve in arms?"

Nayler replied that Quakers obeyed magistrates in all lawful commands—but no command could be lawful that contradicted God's teaching. The magistrate might punish crimes against persons and property; he had no authority over souls. "Christ alone is King of conscience," Nayler wrote. "No earthly power may reach into that realm."

The debate exposed the fundamental issue. Baxter wanted toleration within limits set by magistrates and ministers—a regulated pluralism that excluded those who threatened order. Nayler wanted liberty without limits—the recognition that conscience was simply beyond civil authority. One saw the magistrate as God's instrument for maintaining peace; the other saw the magistrate as a constant temptation to tyranny.

The Stakes of the Debate

The Baxter-Burrough debate wasn't just about theology. It was about power: Who gets to define truth? Who gets to enforce it? Who profits from the existing arrangements?[62]

Baxter represented the presbyterian hope: a learned clergy, supported by tithes, guarded by magistrates, imposing moral discipline through synods and sessions. Knowledge came through education; authority through ordination; order through enforcement.

Burrough represented the Quaker challenge: immediate access to divine teaching without human intermediaries, voluntary support for ministers, conscience answerable to God alone. Knowledge came through waiting on the Spirit in silence; authority came through prophetic gifts; order came through mutual accountability in the meeting.

One system required state enforcement; the other claimed to work through persuasion. One system enriched clergy and empowered magistrates; the other threatened both. The conflict was economic and political as much as theological.

Neither side could yield without losing its identity. The presbyterian commonwealth needed compulsion to work. The Quaker way needed liberty to survive. Something had to give.

The Charge of Anarchy

Critics of all stripes charged Quakers with promoting anarchy. If every person could claim the inner light, what happened to shared truth? If every person could refuse oaths and tithes, what happened to civic order? If women could preach and servants could refuse deference, what happened to the social hierarchy that God (allegedly) ordained?[63]

Thomas Hobbes, though no friend to presbyter or priest, nevertheless saw Quakers as exemplars of the private spirit that would dissolve the commonwealth. In *Leviathan* (1651) he warned that claims to private revelation undermined the sovereign's necessary monopoly on determining religious truth. If every person could appeal to a higher authority than the state, the state's authority was meaningless.[64]

Quakers denied the charge. They insisted the inner light taught the same truth to all, those who truly obeyed it would agree on fundamentals. Apparent disagreements came from imperfect obedience or mixture of human imagination with divine teaching. The solution was more faithfulness to the light, not less.

Critics were unconvinced. They pointed to the diversity among Quakers themselves: Some kept old feast days; others rejected all "pagan" calendar customs. Some were pacifists from the start; others had fought in the Civil War. Some affirmed traditional doctrines like the Trinity; others spoke in ways that seemed to deny it.

If the inner light produced such diversity, critics asked, what good was it as a rule? Better to have clear creeds and confessions, even if some chafed under them, than to let each person follow his own imagination and call it Christ. The Nayler crisis gave weight to this charge. Here was a man claiming the inner light who ended up accepting quasi-divine honors. If the Spirit could lead one of Quaker's best preachers so far astray, how could anyone trust claims to inward revelation?

From Disruption to Discipline

Organization, Authority, and the Transformation of a Movement

The Crisis of Leadership: Fox and Nayler

The Breaking Point, 1656

The Nayler affair forced George Fox to confront a question he had long evaded: Could the Quaker movement sustain itself without some form of human authority? The doctrine of the inner light insisted that Christ taught his people directly, without human intermediaries. What happened when someone claimed the light led them to blasphemy, or to challenging Fox's own leadership?[65]

Fox's response was pragmatic and, some thought, inconsistent with Quaker principles. He began asserting authority, not through claiming an office or title, but through decisive action that other Friends gradually accepted as legitimate.

The Visit to Bristol, November 1656

When George Bishop sent word that Nayler was imprisoned in Bristol, Fox traveled there immediately. He came not as a sympathetic friend but as a judge. George Bishop accompanied him to the prison, and together they confronted Nayler.[66]

The conversation, as Bishop later reported it, was tense. Fox demanded Nayler acknowledge his error and submit to Fox's judgment. "Thou hast gone out from the Truth," Fox said, "and thy actions have brought reproach upon Friends everywhere. Magistrates who were beginning to tolerate us now see us as blasphemers. Thou must publicly recant."

Nayler, exhausted and still under the influence of Martha Simmonds and his other followers, resisted. "Who art thou to judge me?" he replied. "Hath not the Lord given the light to every man? Why should I submit to thy judgment rather than follow the light within me?"

Fox's answer revealed his emerging conception of authority: "The light in thee has been darkened by thy pride and by those who flatter thee. The light in the body of Friends is clearer because we judge together. Thou must submit to the judgment of the meeting, not to me alone, but I speak for Friends when I say thou hast erred grievously."[67]

Nayler would not yield. The meeting ended badly, with Fox and Bishop departing and Nayler left to face Parliament's judgment alone. Fox would later say he knew, when he left that prison, that Nayler's punishment would be severe, and that it might save the movement by demonstrating to authorities that Friends would not countenance blasphemy.[68]

The Hardening of Structure

The Nayler crisis accelerated organizational changes already underway. Between 1656 and 1660, the Quaker movement developed structures that balanced the doctrine of the inner light with the practical need for order:

Monthly Meetings

Local Quaker groups began meeting monthly for business as well as worship. These meetings handled practical matters: caring for widows and orphans, supporting imprisoned Friends, collecting money for traveling ministers, and, increasingly, judging disputes and disciplining members who strayed from Quaker testimonies.

The monthly meeting was corporate discernment in action. When a member's behavior troubled the group, the meeting would appoint two or three Friends to speak with that person. If the person acknowledged error and amended behavior, the matter ended. If not, the meeting might "disown" the person—declare them no longer in unity with Friends. Disowning wasn't excommunication in the Catholic or presbyterian sense (no sacraments were at stake), but it carried social weight. A disowned Friend was cut off from the community's mutual aid and spiritual fellowship.[69]

Quarterly Meetings

Monthly meetings in a region began gathering quarterly to coordinate activities and handle matters too complex for local meetings. Quarterly meetings registered marriages (Quakers refused to marry in parish churches, claiming the state had no authority over the covenant between two people before God), recorded births and deaths, and managed regional funds for traveling ministers and poor relief.

They also served as courts of appeal. If a monthly meeting disowned someone who believed the judgment unjust, that person could appeal to the quarterly meeting. If respected Friends in the wider region upheld the disownment, it stood. If they judged the monthly meeting had erred, they could restore the person to fellowship.[70]

Traveling Ministers and Recognized Leadership

Not all Quakers who felt moved to preach were equally gifted or spiritually mature. The movement began recognizing certain Friends as having genuine prophetic gifts—people whose teaching bore consistent spiritual fruit and whose lives evidenced the transformation they preached.

These "recorded ministers" (though the formal term came later) were supported by monthly meetings when they traveled. They carried letters of introduction from their home meetings, testifying that they were Friends in good standing. Host meetings would provide food, lodging, and travel money.

This created informal hierarchy. George Fox was the most respected traveling minister, his judgment carrying weight throughout the movement. Margaret Fell managed correspondence and money from Swarthmoor Hall. Edward Burrough served as the movement's public voice in London. George Bishop organized resistance to persecution in Bristol. These were not offices, exactly—Friends would have recoiled at calling Fox "bishop" or "moderator"—but they were recognized roles that gave certain individuals authority.[71]

Women's Leadership

Margaret Fell: The Mother of Quakerism

If George Fox was the movement's prophetic voice, Margaret Fell was its organizer and financier. Widowed in 1658, she had means, intelligence, and, unusual for the era, independent authority over her household and property. Swarthmoor Hall, her home in Lancashire, became the operational center of early Quakerism.[72]

Fell managed a vast correspondence network. Traveling ministers wrote to her from across England and abroad, reporting on their work, requesting funds, seeking advice. She kept records, distributed money, and coordinated activities. When Friends were imprisoned, Fell wrote to magistrates demanding their release, citing law and appealing to conscience. When Parliament debated Quaker matters, Fell sent petitions and wrote directly to members.

She also wrote theological works defending Quaker doctrine and practice. Her *Women's Speaking Justified* (1666) became the classic Quaker defense of women's preaching. She argued from Scripture that God gave spiritual gifts without regard to gender, that women prophesied in both Old and New Testaments, and that the prejudice against women speaking came from fallen human custom, not divine command.[73]

Fell's authority was spiritual, not official. She held no title. Yet when she spoke, Friends listened. She was consulted on difficult decisions, her judgment respected, her theological writings circulated and studied. She represented a kind of authority that fit Quaker principles: earned through spiritual fruit, exercised through service, recognized by the community without formal office.

Women as Ministers and Prophets

Women comprised a significant portion of Quaker "publishers of Truth" (the Quaker term for preachers). They traveled in pairs, usually two women together, and faced particular dangers and indignities.[74]

Elizabeth Hooton (1600-1672) was among the first Quaker converts and the first woman preacher. She traveled to America in the 1660s, was beaten and left in the wilderness by Boston authorities, and died while preaching in Jamaica.[75]

Mary Fisher (c.1623-1698) traveled to the Ottoman Empire in 1658 and obtained an audience with Sultan Mehmed IV, explaining Quaker beliefs to him through interpreters. The Sultan, impressed by her courage and sincerity, gave her safe conduct. Fisher's mission demonstrated Quaker universalism: the inner light was truly in all people, regardless of religion or nation.[76]

Mary Dyer (c.1611-1660) was hanged in Boston for repeatedly returning to preach after being banished. Massachusetts Bay Colony had made Quakerism a capital offense, fearing it would undermine godly order. Dyer's martyrdom shocked England and embarrassed colonial authorities. She became a symbol of conscience standing against tyranny.[77]

These women and others like them challenged 17th-century gender norms radically. Not only did they preach publicly, they traveled without male guardians, spoke before magistrates, and claimed authority that conventional society reserved for men. Their Presbyterian and Independent critics cited Scripture (1 Corinthians 14:34, 1 Timothy 2:12) demanding women's silence. Quakers replied that in Christ "there is neither male nor female" (Galatians 3:28) and that Pentecost's Spirit fell on daughters as well as sons (Acts 2:17-18).

The presence of women in leadership roles shaped Quaker culture. Women spoke in meetings for worship, served as elders in monthly meetings, and participated in decision-making alongside men. This equality was never complete, gender conventions still shaped Quaker life in subtle ways, but it was revolutionary for its time.

The Network That Sustained Resistance

George Bishop and the Bristol Organization

George Bishop's story illuminates how Quakers organized under persecution. A former intelligence officer in the parliamentary army, Bishop brought organizational skills and political contacts to the Quaker movement. When he converted in the early 1650s he applied those skills to protecting and coordinating Bristol Friends.[78]

Bristol was contested ground. The city had strong Presbyterian and Anglican factions who despised Quakers. It also had a significant merchant community, some sympathetic to religious toleration for pragmatic reasons (persecution disrupted trade). Bishop navigated these factions carefully, building alliances where possible, documenting persecution where necessary.

The "Suffering Book"

Bishop pioneered the practice of keeping detailed records of Quaker sufferings, arrests, fines, confiscated property, beatings, imprisonments. He collected testimonies from victims, recorded dates and names, and compiled the information into what became known as the "Book of Sufferings."[79]

These records served multiple purposes. First, they documented injustice for appeals to higher authorities. When Bristol magistrates exceeded their legal authority, Bishop could cite chapter and verse in petitions to Parliament or the Council of State. Second, they created solidarity. Friends across England read accounts of Bristol's sufferings and contributed money for relief. Third, they served historical memory. The records testified that Friends had suffered for righteousness' sake, linking them to martyrs of earlier ages.

After the Restoration, Joseph Besse compiled these local records into the massive *Collection of the Sufferings of the People Called Quakers* (1753), a monument to Quaker endurance that filled two folio volumes with names, dates, and descriptions of persecution. The work shaped Quaker identity for generations.[80]

The Intelligence Network

Bishop's military experience showed in his coordination of intelligence. He maintained contacts with sympathetic army officers, government clerks, and London Quakers who had access to political news. When rumors of new legislation targeting Quakers surfaced, word spread through the network so Friends could prepare.[81]

Similarly, when Bristol authorities planned a major sweep of Quaker meetings, word would reach London quickly, and Edward Burrough would petition Parliament or appeal directly to Cromwell. The coordination wasn't perfect, many Quakers were arrested before warning arrived, but it was remarkably effective for a persecuted sect without official standing.

This network also served positive coordination. When traveling ministers arrived in Bristol, Bishop arranged housing, meetings, and safe passage to the next destination. When Bristol Quakers planned a large gathering, word went out through the network so Friends from surrounding counties could attend. The system gave a scattered movement cohesion without requiring formal hierarchy.

London Committees

- By 1659, London Quakers had developed specialized committees: [82]

- **The Meeting for Sufferings**: Handled cases of imprisoned Friends, petitioned for their release, and distributed relief to their families.
- **The Book Committee**: Oversaw Quaker publications, ensuring theological soundness and responding to attacks in print.
- **The Morning Meeting**: A gathering of respected Friends (including Fox, Burrough, and others) who advised on difficult questions and coordinated the movement's overall direction.

These committees were not governing bodies in a formal sense, Friends insisted they had no "outward" government. But functionally, they provided leadership and coordination that the movement required to survive persecution.

The tension between Quaker theory (no human hierarchy, only the Spirit's leading) and Quaker practice (recognized leaders, structured meetings, disciplinary procedures) was real but manageable. Friends convinced themselves that their structures merely facilitated the Spirit's work rather than replacing it. Whether this was self-deception or genuine spiritual insight remains a question each observer must answer.

By 1659, the Quaker movement had developed structures that could survive persecution and coordinate witness across England. But the greatest test still lay ahead: the final year of the Commonwealth, when Friends would be offered political power and would have to choose whether the way of the Lamb included wielding the sword.

The Great Temptation of 1659

Politics, Power, and the Choice for Peace

The Collapse of the Protectorate

Spring 1659: Richard Cromwell Fails

Oliver Cromwell died in September 1658, naming his son Richard as successor. Richard Cromwell was decent, moderate, and entirely unsuited to manage the competing forces that his father had barely held together. Army officers despised him as a civilian; republicans despised the Protectorate as quasi-monarchy; religious radicals saw the revolution stalling. [83]

By spring 1659, Army officers demanded Richard recall the Rump Parliament, the remnant of the Long Parliament that Oliver had expelled in 1653. Richard complied in April, hoping to buy time. Instead, he lost control. By May, he had resigned and quietly retired to private life. For the first time since 1653, England had no Protector, only Parliament and Army maneuvering for supremacy. England faced the question that had haunted it since 1649: What should replace the king?[84]

The Return of the Commonwealthmen

The Rump's return brought Commonwealth radicals back into power. Chief among them was Sir Henry Vane, a brilliant and eccentric republican who had opposed Cromwell's quasi-monarchical Protectorate. Vane believed in liberty of conscience, popular sovereignty, and the "good old cause" for which the Civil War had been fought. He had long admired certain aspects of Quaker witness, though he found their theology troubling.[85]

Vane had made overtures to Quakers before. In 1655 he heard James Nayler preach and was impressed. In 1658 he met with George Fox, hoping to forge an alliance between Commonwealthmen and Quakers against Cromwell's authoritarian drift. That meeting ended poorly, Fox disliked Vane's intellectualism and suspected his motives. But with the Protectorate's collapse, Vane tried again.[86]

The Offer

In summer 1659, as the Rump organized a new government, Vane and his allies approached Quaker leaders with a proposition: Join us in building the Commonwealth. We will guarantee liberty of conscience, end tithes, and allow Quakers to serve in government without oaths. In return, support us against both the Army grandees (who wanted another Protector) and the Presbyterian faction (who wanted the King back).[87]

The offer was serious. Vane controlled the Council of State and had influence in the Rump. If Quakers joined his coalition, they could shape policy for the first time. Several prominent Quakers were appointed to positions: some to militia committees, others to local magistracies. George Bishop and other Bristol Friends found themselves serving on the commission overseeing the city's defense against potential Royalist uprising.[71]

For a moment, it seemed possible. The Quaker movement had 30,000 to 40,000 members, many in the Army, many in strategic towns. If organized, they could tip the balance of power. The "good old cause," liberty, godly reform, the Commonwealth, might yet be saved. All it required was Quaker support for the existing government and willingness to wield magisterial authority.[88]

Fox's "Time of Darkness"

Summer 1659: Fox's Crisis

Just when Quakers most needed clear leadership, George Fox collapsed. In June 1659 he withdrew from public activity, spending ten weeks in what he later called a "time of great darkness." He gave no public explanations, attended no meetings, wrote no letters. Margaret Fell and other Friends worried that the movement's most influential voice had gone silent at its most critical moment.[89]

What happened during those ten weeks remains somewhat mysterious. Fox's *Journal* describes it cryptically: "I was under great suffering and trouble, and the power of darkness... as if I had been in the tomb." Modern historians speculate about causes:[90]

- **Physical exhaustion**: Fox had traveled constantly for years, often sleeping outdoors, eating irregularly, and enduring beatings and imprisonment. His body may simply have failed.
- **Spiritual crisis**: The Nayler affair had shaken Fox's confidence in the inner light. If one of the movement's best preachers could go so astray, what did that say about Quaker doctrine? Perhaps Fox wrestled with doubt.

- **Political paralysis**: The choice before Friends—support Vane or refuse—was momentous. Either decision carried enormous risk. Fox may have been genuinely uncertain which way the light led.[91]

Whatever the cause, Fox's withdrawal left the movement leaderless during its greatest opportunity for temporal power. Some Friends, including Bishop and others in Bristol, began participating in the militia and local government, assuming this was consistent with Quaker principles. Others held back, uncertain whether Quaker testimonies allowed wielding the sword even for a righteous cause.

The Decision: September 1659

When Fox emerged from his darkness in September, he had reached a decision: Quakers must not join Vane's government. They must refuse political power and maintain their witness as a people separate from the world's conflicts.[92]

Fox's reasoning, as he later explained it, came down to two convictions:

First, Vane's coalition was unstable. It depended on army support, but the Army was divided. It depended on popular enthusiasm for the Commonwealth, but the country was exhausted and many wanted the King back. To tie the Quaker movement to this coalition would be to link Friends' fate to a government likely to collapse. When it did, Friends would be persecuted as collaborators.

Second, and more fundamental, wielding magisterial power would compromise Quaker testimony. Friends claimed to follow the Lamb, who conquered through suffering rather than force. Could they now take up the magistrate's sword, the instrument of coercion, taxation, and war—without betraying their witness? Fox thought not. Christ's kingdom was "not of this world," and his servants did not fight with worldly weapons.

Fox's refusal reflected deepening Quaker conviction that carnal warfare and spiritual warfare were incompatible. The Lamb's War was waged with different weapons: truth, patience, long-suffering, meekness. Christ's servants conquered through the blood of the Lamb and the word of their testimony, loving not their lives unto death. To take up the magistrate's sword, even for the best of causes, was to abandon the Lamb's way for the Beast's.[93]

Fox's decision was not unanimous among Friends. Some Bristol Quakers, already serving on committees, wanted to continue. They argued that magistracy was not inherently violent, a magistrate could judge disputes, manage town affairs, and defend against invasion without compromising conscience. Fox replied that magistracy inevitably involved compromises that Friends should not make: enforcing laws against conscience, collecting taxes for military purposes, swearing oaths of office.

Gradually, Fox's position prevailed. By late 1659, most Quakers had withdrawn from government service. They would petition, protest, and prophesy, but they would not govern. This decision shaped Quaker identity for the next three centuries, distinguishing Friends from both the Puritans who would rule and the Anglicans who would accommodate.

Fox's refusal of Vane's offer was the first clear step toward principled pacifism. But it remained incomplete. Many Quakers still believed defensive war was legitimate; some thought magistracy compatible with Friends' testimony if exercised without oaths or violence. The crisis of 1660 would force Friends to clarify their position finally and completely.

Justice, Blood Guilt, and the Quaker Alternative

Blood Guilt and the Quaker Rejection

All factions in the Civil War invoked blood guilt, the conviction that unpunished bloodshed brought divine wrath on the nation. Presbyterians and Independents had called Charles I "a man of blood" whose wars against his own people demanded justice. Anglicans reversed the charge, calling the regicides men of blood and celebrating Charles as a martyr.[94]

Quakers rejected the entire framework. Blood guilt thinking assumed that human courts could and should execute divine justice, that magistrates acted as God's instruments in punishing sins. But if Christ ruled directly in the heart, then human courts could only judge human crimes, not spiritual offenses. Murder was crime; heresy was not. And no human court could take life in God's name without usurping God's prerogative.

This was the deepest implication of Quaker anarchism: the sword—whether wielded by king, Parliament, or gathered saints, could not serve God's purposes. Coercion was the enemy's weapon. Christ conquered by love, suffering, and truth.

George Bishop: From Intelligence Officer to Peace Witness

George Bishop's personal journey embodied the movement's transformation. He had served Parliament's cause in the 1640s, running intelligence networks and supporting military operations. He had believed that God's kingdom could be advanced by arms and that the saints' victories proved divine favor.[95]

His conversion to Quakerism in the early 1650s began changing his views, but the Nayler crisis and the events of 1659-1660 completed the transformation. Bishop came to see that spiritual warfare and carnal warfare were incompatible. The very success that military victory brought, power, influence, the ability to coerce, corrupted the purity it was meant to protect.

In his later writings, Bishop argued that the Civil War had been a divine judgment on England—but not in the way the victors imagined. The war revealed how easily righteous causes became pretexts for self-aggrandizement, how quickly saints became persecutors. The Lamb's War was different: it conquered through suffering, not through sword.

The Collapse and Restoration

October 1659: The Army's Coup

Vane's government lasted only months. In October, Army officers led by John Lambert expelled the Rump (again) and tried to rule through a Committee of Safety. The country reacted with alarm. Taxes went unpaid, trade stalled, and rumors of Royalist uprising multiplied. General George Monck, commander of forces in Scotland, announced he would march to London to restore the Rump and settle the nation.[96]

Quakers watched with foreboding. They had refused Vane's offer; now the government was collapsing anyway. If the King returned, Friends expected severe persecution. Charles Stuart had seen his father executed by Commonwealth men, many of whom were religious radicals. He would not forget or forgive easily.

Winter 1659-1660: Monck's March

Monck marched south, from Coldstream, Scotland (hence the famous Coldstream Guards) in January 1660 with a disciplined army and ambiguous intentions. He said he came to restore Parliament and secure liberties. Many suspected he intended to restore the King. Monck's religious views were opaque, he attended presbyterian services but seemed indifferent to theology. What mattered to him was order and peace.[97]

Quakers tried to influence him. George Fox wrote to Monck urging him to maintain liberty of conscience and protect Friends from persecution. Margaret Fell sent similar appeals. Some Quakers hoped Monck might be another Cromwell—a military protector who would guarantee toleration.[98]

But Monck was no Cromwell. He had no interest in godly reform or religious innovation. He wanted stability, and stability meant restoring traditional institutions: King, Lords, Commons, and an episcopal national church. When Monck reached London in February, he forced the Rump to readmit members excluded in 1648, effectively ending the Commonwealth. By March, the reconstituted Parliament voted to dissolve itself and call elections for a Convention that would negotiate the King's return.

Spring 1660: The Inevitable Restoration

By April, the Restoration was inevitable. Charles Stuart, in exile in Holland, issued the Declaration of Breda promising amnesty (except for regicides), liberty of conscience, and settlement of property disputes by Parliament. It was a moderate, reassuring document designed to ease fears. Most of England welcomed it. The Civil War was a generation past; Cromwell's rule had grown oppressive; the Commonwealth's experiments had produced instability rather than reform. People wanted normalcy, even if that meant a king.[99]

Quakers did not rejoice. They knew a restored monarchy meant a restored episcopal church, which meant renewed persecution of dissenters. But they also knew resistance was futile. The Army would not fight for the "good old cause" of the Commonwealth again, many soldiers were as weary as civilians. The Commonwealthmen were discredited, scattered, or dead. The moment had passed; the only question was how Friends would survive what was coming.

May 1660: Charles II Returns

On May 29, 1660—Charles's thirtieth birthday, the King entered London to jubilant crowds. Bells rang, bonfires blazed, and the city drank itself into celebration. The Interregnum was over. Monarchy, as if it had never left, resumed.[100]

For Quakers, the celebration was ominous. They knew what was coming: laws against nonconformist worship, fines for refusing parish church attendance, imprisonment for preaching without license, and perhaps worse. Already, mobs attacked Quaker meetings in some towns, emboldened by the changed political climate. Local magistrates, eager to prove loyalty to the new regime, began arresting Friends on any pretext.

But Quakers also saw opportunity. The Restoration was a moment to define themselves clearly before new authorities. If they could convince the King and Parliament that Friends posed no political threat, that their religious dissent was peaceful and principled, they might win toleration or at least avoid the worst persecution.

The Immediate Challenge

The challenge came immediately. In September 1660, rumors spread that Quakers and other sects planned an armed uprising to overthrow the newly restored monarchy. The rumors were baseless, no such plot was uncovered, but they gained credence because many former Army radicals were indeed Quakers, and because Quaker refusal of oaths made them seem disloyal.

Magistrates across England arrested Quakers preemptively. In London alone, hundreds were imprisoned without charge. Friends faced a dilemma: How to prove their peaceable intentions when their principles forbade swearing loyalty oaths?

George Fox and other leaders drafted a statement to be presented to the King. It would become the most important document in Quaker history, defining Friends' relationship to violence and government for centuries to come

The Peace Declaration of 1660

The Peace Testimony and Its Meaning

"A Declaration from the Harmless and Innocent People of God, Called Quakers"

The Peace Declaration was Fox's final answer to the question that had haunted Friends throughout the 1650s: Can disciples of the Lamb wield the magistrate's sword? Can they fight even in self-defense? Can they serve governments that wage war? Fox's answer, on behalf of the movement, was no. The Lamb's way is peace, and his followers must walk that way without compromise, even unto death. In declaring this, Quakers took a position nearly unprecedented in Christian history: a communal commitment to nonviolence, not as counsel for heroic individuals, but as binding rule for all members.

In January 1661, George Fox, Richard Hubberthorne, and other London Friends presented a declaration to King Charles II. The document, written hastily in response to rumors of Quaker plots, would prove the most enduring statement of Quaker principles.[101]

Key Passages

The declaration opened by clearing Friends of the charge of treason:

We whom the world calls Quakers do deny all outward wars and strife and fightings with outward weapons, for any end or under any pretense whatsoever. And this is our testimony to the whole world.

It continued by grounding this refusal in discipleship:

The Spirit of Christ, which leads us into all Truth, will never move us to fight and war against any man with outward weapons, neither for the kingdom of Christ, nor for the kingdoms of this world.

The declaration distinguished Friends from those who used religion to cloak political ambition:

We utterly deny all outward wars and strife, and fightings with outward weapons, for any end, or under any pretence whatsoever; this is our testimony to the whole world. The Spirit of Christ by which we are guided is not changeable, so as once to command us from a thing as evil, and again to move unto it; and we certainly know, and testify to the world, that the Spirit of Christ, which leads us into all truth, will never move us to fight and war against any man with outward weapons, neither for the kingdom of Christ, nor for the kingdoms of this world.

It affirmed loyalty to the King while maintaining conscience:

Our weapons are not carnal but spiritual, and our kingdom is not of this world... We have no cause or end to fight, or have need of any outward weapons. Though men should act against us, we shall not fight, but suffer and be patient.

Finally, it appealed for understanding:

This is given forth from the people called Quakers, to satisfy the King and his Council, and all others in this matter, as God shall persuade their hearts.

What the Declaration Did Not Say

Notably, the declaration did not resolve every ambiguity:

- It spoke of "outward weapons" but left unclear whether Friends could serve as magistrates who judged criminals (which might lead to their execution).
- It rejected fighting "for any end" but didn't specify whether pure self-defense (protecting one's family from immediate violence) was included in the rejection.
- It distinguished the "kingdom of Christ" from "kingdoms of this world" but didn't fully articulate Friends' relationship to civil government.

These ambiguities would be worked out over subsequent decades. Some Friends would serve as magistrates in Pennsylvania and elsewhere, arguing that judgment was not violence. Others would insist that any participation in coercive government compromised the peace testimony.

The Theological Grounding

The Lamb's War

The phrase "Lamb's War" appeared in Quaker writing from the mid-1650s, notably in James Nayler's 1657 pamphlet *The Lamb's War Against the Man of Sin.* It described spiritual conflict: the warfare of Christ (the Lamb of Revelation) against evil, fought not with swords but with truth, patience, and suffering love.

Edward Burrough developed the theme in *A Discovery of Some Part of the War Between the Kingdom of the Lamb and the Kingdom of Anti-Christ* (1659). He wrote:

> *The Lamb makes war with spiritual weapons: with Truth, Patience, Long-suffering, and Meekness. His soldiers conquer through the blood of the Lamb and the word of their testimony, loving not their lives unto death. By these weapons, which are not carnal, does the Lamb overcome the Beast and his followers.*

The Lamb's War was waged against spiritual enemies through carnal suffering. When Quakers were beaten, imprisoned, or executed, they saw themselves as sharing Christ's victory through apparent defeat. Their persecutors proved the truth of Quaker testimony by the violence of their opposition. The blood of martyrs was seed.

This was revolutionary pacifism, not passivity, but active spiritual warfare that rejected violence as method. Friends believed they were engaged in cosmic struggle between Christ and Satan, light and darkness, truth and lies. But the weapons were preaching, witness, suffering, and prayer—never sword or gun.

The doctrine implied that violence was not merely practically unwise or politically inexpedient—it was spiritually impossible for Christ's followers. The Lamb conquered by dying; his disciples conquered by suffering. To take up carnal weapons was to abandon the Lamb's way for the Beast's.

The Perfectionist Logic

Quaker pacifism connected to their doctrine of perfectionism. If believers could be cleansed from sin by Christ's inward work, if they could live in obedience to the inner light, then they could live without violence. Sin produced violence; freedom from sin produced peace.

Critics objected that this was naive. The world was fallen; enemies would attack regardless of one's purity. To refuse self-defense was to invite martyrdom. Quakers replied: So be it. Better martyrdom than murder. Better to suffer evil than to do evil. Christ had shown the way; they would follow.

This position scandalized most seventeenth-century Christians. Even Anabaptists, who practiced nonviolence, tended to see it as withdrawal from the world rather than active engagement. Quakers combined nonviolence with aggressive evangelism—they would confront the world's evil, but with spiritual rather than carnal weapons.

The tension between prophetic boldness and principled nonviolence shaped Quaker practice. Friends disrupted services, challenged magistrates, refused unjust laws—all actions that might provoke violent response. But they would not respond to violence with violence. They would suffer, document their suffering, and trust God to vindicate them.

The Immediate Consequences

Persecution Under the Clarendon Code

The Peace Declaration did not protect Friends from persecution. If anything, the early 1660s saw increased harassment as the restored monarchy consolidated power. The Clarendon Code, a series of laws enacted between 1661 and 1665, specifically targeted religious dissenters:

- **Corporation Act (1661)**: Required all municipal office-holders to take Anglican communion and swear oaths—effectively excluding Quakers and other dissenters from civic life.
- **Act of Uniformity (1662)**: Required all clergy to use the Book of Common Prayer and accept episcopal ordination—ejecting about 2,000 nonconformist ministers, including many Presbyterians.
- **Conventicle Act (1664)**: Prohibited religious gatherings of more than five people outside the established church—directly targeting Quaker meetings.
- **Five Mile Act (1665)**: Banned ejected ministers from coming within five miles of their former parishes or any incorporated town—scattering nonconformist leadership.

Quakers violated these laws systematically. They continued meeting for worship (violating the Conventicle Act), refused oaths (violating the Corporation Act), and preached without license (violating multiple statutes). Thousands were imprisoned; many died in jail from disease and harsh conditions. Property was confiscated to pay fines Friends refused to pay voluntarily.

The Sufferings Strategy

Rather than hide or compromise, Quakers adopted a strategy of visible suffering. They met openly despite laws against it, accepting arrest as testimony. When fined, they refused to pay, forcing authorities to seize their goods publicly. When imprisoned, they preached through the windows of their cells.

George Bishop's "Book of Sufferings" methodology spread throughout the movement. Every monthly meeting kept records of persecution: who was arrested, when, by which magistrate, under what law, with what outcome. The Meeting for Sufferings, established in 1675, exemplified Quaker organizational genius. It kept meticulous records—every imprisonment, every fine, every beating, every death. These records became powerful evidence when Friends petitioned for toleration. They showed not wild enthusiasm but patient suffering; not threats to order but victims of injustice.

This was not the anarchism of isolated individuals following private light; it was structured, strategic, and effective. Friends had learned that bearing witness required not only courage but coordination.

The strategy served multiple purposes:

- **Moral pressure**: Detailed documentation of persecution embarrassed authorities and sometimes shamed them into leniency.
- **Legal appeal**: Records provided evidence for appeals to higher courts or petitions to Parliament.
- **Solidarity**: Reading accounts of others' sufferings strengthened Friends' resolve to endure their own.
- **Historical witness**: The records testified to future generations that Friends had remained faithful under trial.

Joseph Besse's eventual compilation, *A Collection of the Sufferings of the People*

Called Quakers (1753), runs to over 1,400 folio pages—a monument to Quaker endurance and organizational capacity.

The suffering strategy worked, slowly. By the 1670s, some local magistrates grew weary of prosecuting peaceful Quakers and began looking the other way. By the 1680s, even hostile authorities recognized that Quakers, whatever their eccentricities, were not seditious. The Toleration Act of 1689 finally gave legal recognition to nonconformist worship, including Quaker meetings.

The Peace Declaration and the persecution that followed it transformed the Quaker movement from a prophetic protest into a durable denomination. Friends learned to organize for long-term survival, to support one another through trials, and to maintain distinctive testimonies across generations. But the cost was high, measured in years of imprisonment, families divided, property lost, and lives cut short. Yet Friends counted the cost and paid it, believing their witness to the Lamb's way was worth any price.

Afterlives

From England to Empire: The Quaker Legacy

Survival and Adaptation in Restoration England

The Maturation of Quaker Discipline (1660-1689)

The quarter-century between the Restoration and the Toleration Act forced Quakers to perfect their organizational structures. What began as crisis management became institutional culture. Monthly meetings developed standardized procedures for recording births, marriages, and deaths—creating Quaker registries independent of parish records. They established marriage clearness committees to counsel couples and ensure both partners came freely to the covenant. They created procedures for handling disputes between Friends, aiming to keep conflicts within the community rather than resorting to law courts.[102]

Women's meetings emerged as parallel structures handling matters particularly affecting women: poor relief for widows, assistance in childbirth, counsel for young mothers, and oversight of women's conduct. These meetings gave Quaker women institutional voice and authority unmatched in other 17th-century denominations. By 1680, the system of monthly, quarterly, and yearly meetings was firmly established, providing coherence without creating the rigid hierarchy Quakers still officially rejected.[103]

George Fox spent his later years consolidating these structures. He traveled throughout England and to America (1671-1673), everywhere encouraging Friends to maintain discipline, keep records, and support one another. He married Margaret Fell in 1669 (both were widowed), uniting the movement's two most influential figures. His *Journal*, edited and published after his death in 1691, became the foundational text of Quaker identity—a narrative of prophetic call, persecution endured, and truth vindicated.

The Theological Stabilization

The wild diversity of early Quakerism narrowed. The movement developed what might be called (despite Quaker protestations) a de facto creed. Robert Barclay's *Apology for the True Christian Divinity* (1676) provided the first systematic theology of Quakerism, written in Latin and English and widely translated. Barclay affirmed:

- The inner light as Christ's immediate presence and teaching
- Universal access to salvation (against Calvinist predestination)
- Perfectibility in this life through Christ's inward work
- Scripture as authoritative but subordinate to the Spirit who wrote it
- Rejection of outward sacraments (baptism and communion) as unnecessary when spiritual reality is present
- Peace testimony as binding on all Friends
- Simplicity in speech, dress, and manner as witness to truth

This theology positioned Quakers as both Protestant (affirming Scripture, rejecting Catholic sacramental system, emphasizing grace) and distinctive (rejecting Reformed doctrines of total depravity and limited atonement, embracing perfectionism and immediate revelation). They occupied unique space in the Christian landscape—too mystical for Calvinists, too biblically centered for rationalists, too disciplined for antinomians.

The stabilization came at a cost. Early Quaker spontaneity gave way to prescribed forms. The prophetic gestures that marked the 1650s—stripping naked as a sign, wearing sackcloth, interrupting services—were discouraged by the 1680s as "disorderly" and "not in the Truth." The Spirit's leading was increasingly channeled through the meeting's corporate discernment rather than individual revelation. Some later Quakers would argue the movement had lost its fire; others replied it had gained wisdom.[104]

The Atlantic Crossing: Pennsylvania and Beyond

William Penn and the Holy Experiment

William Penn (1644-1718) was not among the original Valiant Sixty, but he became Quakerism's most influential second-generation leader. Son of Admiral Sir William Penn, young William had wealth, education, and connections to the highest levels of English society. His conversion to Quakerism in 1667 scandalized his family and delighted Friends, who saw divine providence in bringing such a person to the movement.[105]

Penn used his advantages for Friends' benefit. He wrote eloquent defenses of religious liberty, argued Quaker cases before magistrates, and lobbied Parliament for toleration. Most significantly, he obtained from Charles II a charter for a vast American colony—payment of a debt the crown owed his father. Pennsylvania, named for Penn ("Penn's Woods"), was envisioned by him as a "holy experiment": a place where Friends could live according to their principles and demonstrate that a society could thrive without religious coercion.[106]

The **Frame of Government** (1682) that Penn wrote for Pennsylvania embodied Quaker political theology:

- **Religious liberty**: No religious tests for office, no established church, no compulsory tithes. "All persons living in this province, who confess and acknowledge the one Almighty and eternal God... shall, in no ways, be molested or prejudiced for their religious persuasion, or practice."[107]

- **Peaceful relations with Native Americans**: Penn negotiated treaties with the Lenape (Delaware) people, paying fair prices for land and maintaining (mostly) peaceable coexistence. The image of Penn's treaty under the elm at Shackamaxon became legendary—though Penn's heirs and later Pennsylvanians would not maintain his standards.[108]
- **Criminal justice reform**: Pennsylvania's laws were remarkably lenient for the era. Only two crimes (murder and treason) carried the death penalty, compared to dozens in English law. Imprisonment aimed at reform rather than punishment. Penn opposed torture and favored restitution over retribution.[109]
- **Political participation**: Pennsylvania had elected assemblies, magistrates, courts, and a governor (Penn himself, then his appointees). Quaker participation in government tested the peace testimony's boundaries. Could Friends serve as magistrates who judged capital cases? Could they vote for military appropriations? Could they hold office in a government that waged war?[110]

The Compromises and Tensions

Pennsylvania's holy experiment revealed tensions in Quaker political theology. When the colony faced threats, from French forces, from Native American conflicts sparked by colonists' encroachment, from pirates in the Delaware River, Quaker leaders had to decide: Would they defend the colony by force?

Initially, they found middle ways: paying neighboring colonies to provide defense, maintaining "voluntary" militias of non-Quakers, voting funds officially designated for "the King's use" (knowing they'd fund military operations). These compromises satisfied no one fully. Militant colonists thought Quakers were shirking their duty. Strict Friends thought their leaders were betraying the peace testimony.[111]

The tension came to a head during the French and Indian War (1754-1763). When Pennsylvania's assembly, still dominated by Quakers, was pressed to fund military operations, a group of Friends resigned from the assembly rather than vote for war. The "Great Resignation" of 1756 marked the end of Quaker political dominance in Pennsylvania. Friends would remain influential in commerce, education, and social reform, but they largely withdrew from direct political power rather than compromise their peace testimony.[112]

The Pennsylvania experience taught Quakers a hard lesson: political power and prophetic witness were difficult to reconcile. Could they maintain distinctive testimonies while governing a diverse population? Could they refuse violence while protecting citizens from it? The answers were ambiguous and remain contested. Yet Pennsylvania demonstrated that religious liberty could work, that peaceful coexistence with indigenous peoples was possible (even if imperfectly achieved), and that a society need not be built on coercion and fear.

The Long Shadow: Quaker Influence on Modern Life

Social Reform Movements

The peace testimony seeded broader social reform commitments. If violence was wrong, so was the injustice that provoked it. If all people possessed the inner light, all deserved humane treatment. These convictions drove Quaker activism in:

- **Abolition**: Quakers were among the earliest and most persistent opponents of slavery. Pennsylvania Quakers debated slavery's morality from the 1680s; by 1776, Philadelphia Yearly Meeting required members to free their slaves or face disownment. John Woolman's *Some Considerations on the Keeping of Negroes* (1754) argued that slavery violated both the golden rule and recognition of the light in every person. British Quakers, though small in number, provided crucial support for William Wilberforce's abolition campaign.[113]
- **Prison reform**: John Bellers and later Elizabeth Fry visited prisons, documented horrific conditions, and advocated for humane treatment. Fry's work in Newgate Prison (1813 onward) helped establish the principle that prisoners retained human dignity and could be reformed rather than merely punished.[114]
- **Mental health**: Quakers founded the York Retreat (1796), pioneering "moral treatment" of mental illness—treating patients with respect and dignity rather than chains and violence. The approach influenced psychiatric reform throughout Europe and America.[115]

Political Influence

Quaker insistence on liberty of conscience influenced Enlightenment political thought. John Locke corresponded with Quakers and incorporated their arguments into his *Letter Concerning Toleration* (1689). William Penn's *Frame of Government* influenced American constitutional thinking, particularly on religious liberty and criminal justice. The American founders, though not Quakers, absorbed Quaker ideas through Pennsylvania's example and through figures like Benjamin Franklin (who grew up in Philadelphia amid Quaker influence though never joining Friends).[116]

The peace testimony, though practiced by a minority, challenged conventional assumptions about the necessity of war. The very existence of a peace church—not withdrawn from the world like Anabaptists, but engaged in commerce, politics, and social reform, demonstrated that Christian pacifism need not mean passivity or irrelevance.

Cultural Legacy

Quaker plain speech, plain dress, and plainness in architecture and worship influenced broader cultural movements toward simplicity and authenticity. The Quaker meetinghouse, four walls, benches, no pulpit or altar, waiting in silence, became an icon of stripped-down spirituality that appealed beyond Friends.

Quaker business ethics, fixed prices (rather than haggling), honesty in advertising, quality craftsmanship, fair treatment of employees, helped establish trust in commerce. Quaker merchants and manufacturers (Cadbury, Rowntree, Barclays) built businesses on these principles, demonstrating that ethical practices could be commercially successful.[117]

The phrase "speaking truth to power," though modern in its exact formulation, captures the Quaker stance: bold prophetic witness combined with disciplined nonviolence. It became a model for 20th-century movements from Gandhi's satyagraha to Martin Luther King's civil rights campaigns to conscientious objectors in wartime.

From a prophetic movement born in England's revolutionary chaos, Quakers became a people whose witness outlived their brief moment of prominence. Their numbers remained small, never more than a fraction of English or American Christianity, yet their influence exceeded their size. The Lamb's War, it turned out, was not won by seizing power in 1659 but by refusing it, by maintaining a disciplined witness across generations, and by demonstrating that truth and peace, patiently lived, could shape the world more deeply than the sword ever could.

From Nayler's Trial to Fox's Death

We began this chapter in Westminster Hall, watching James Nayler refuse to remove his hat before Parliament. We end in 1691, with George Fox dying at age sixty-six in London, surrounded by Friends who owed their faith to his preaching and their survival to his organization.

What the Transformation Cost

The transformation was not free. Early Quakers who thrilled to spontaneous prophecy might have found the 1680s movement staid and overly cautious. The wild freedom of "thee-ing" a magistrate or stripping naked as a prophetic sign gave way to prescribed forms: standard testimonies, minute books, and procedures. Some left, finding the structure stifling. Others stayed but mourned what they saw as lost fire.

Women's voices, though never fully silenced, were channeled into women's meetings that handled "women's business" rather than the movement's central theological and political decisions. The revolutionary equality of the 1650s, when any person moved by the Spirit might stand and speak, became more regulated. Recorded ministers, elders, and oversight committees developed, creating informal hierarchy despite official denials.

Geographic spread diluted intimacy. The tight-knit community of northern England in the 1650s, where everyone knew everyone and George Fox could visit most meetings personally, gave way to a transatlantic movement spanning England, Ireland, continental Europe, the Caribbean, and American colonies. Unity required correspondence, traveling ministers, and institutional structures that inevitably created distance between members.

What the Transformation Preserved

Yet something essential survived. Friends in 1690 still sat in silence, waiting for the Spirit's movement. They still refused oaths, tithes, and hat-honor. They still maintained that Christ taught his people directly, that the light was in every person, that perfection was possible, that violence was incompatible with the gospel. They still kept their plain speech and plain dress, their refusal to flatter power, their willingness to suffer rather than compromise.

The discipline that Fox and others built proved not a cage but a container, something that could hold prophetic fire without letting it burn out or consume everything around it. The monthly meeting, the traveling minister, the record of sufferings, the peace testimony, these were not bureaucracy but memory, not control but cultivation. They allowed Quakerism to survive the deaths of its founders, the end of persecution, the routinization that inevitably follows charisma.

The Paradox of Quaker Politics

The deepest paradox remains: Quakers developed a form of politics that refused political power. They influenced governments they refused to control. They changed laws they would not enforce. They demonstrated forms of lifestyle that challenged conventional society while insisting they sought no revolution, built no party, wielded no sword.

This was possible because Quakers understood politics more broadly than their contemporaries. Politics, for Anglicans, Presbyterians, and Independents, meant controlling institutions: the throne, Parliament, the Army, the parish churches. Politics for Quakers meant shaping souls and cultures: teaching people to tell truth, refuse violence, recognize the light in one another, and live as if the kingdom were already present.

That kind of politics worked slowly, person by person, meeting by meeting, generation by generation. It required patience Friends learned in prison, watching years pass while they kept their testimonies. It required hope Friends maintained even when Commonwealth dreams collapsed and kings returned. It required community Friends built by caring for one another's children, visiting one another's sick, and holding one another accountable to shared testimonies.[118]

A Judgment Deferred

Whether the Quaker wager succeeded depends on what measure we use. By the measure of political power, Friends failed—they never governed England, and even Pennsylvania slipped from their control. By the measure of theological influence, they remained marginal—no great communion bears Fox's name as Lutherans bear Luther's or Presbyterians Knox's.

But by the measure they chose—faithfulness to the Lamb's way, persistence in witness, the slow cultivation of a people whose lives testified to peace—perhaps they succeeded. When the Toleration Act passed in 1689, Friends had outlasted their persecutors. When slavery was abolished in Britain in 1833, Quaker abolitionists claimed vindication for decades of witness. When conscientious objection gained legal recognition in the 20th century, Friends' centuries of refusal had helped make it thinkable.

The question the next chapter poses is this: What did these four movements, Anglican, Presbyterian, Independent, Quaker, leave behind? What habits survived the 17th century to shape the Atlantic world? And what can those who inherit that world learn from these long-dead debates over conscience, coercion, and the nature of legitimate power?

We have followed four churches into England's crisis: Anglicans defending order through bishops and law; Presbyterians pursuing holiness through elders and discipline; Independents seeking liberty through gathered churches and consent; Quakers witnessing through suffering and the inner light. Now we must ask what their conflicts produced, what kind of religious settlement emerged from the wreckage of their competing dreams, and what lessons their struggles hold for those who still wrestle with questions of religion and politics today.

CHAPTER 7 — THE KINGDOM NOT OF THIS WORLD

FROM REGICIDE TO TOLERATION, 1649-1689

The Banqueting House, Whitehall, 30 January 1649

Charles Stuart woke before dawn on the last day of his life. Through the windows of St. James's Palace, he could see London stirring in the winter darkness, the city he had lost, the capital he had entered as a prisoner rather than a king. He had slept poorly, his sleep interrupted by the sound of workmen hammering in the distance. They were building the scaffold outside the Banqueting House where he would die, and the noise had carried through the cold January night.[1]

He dressed carefully. Two shirts, the day was bitterly cold, and he would not have spectators think he shivered from fear rather than weather. He asked his servant, Thomas Herbert, to ensure his hair was properly arranged. "I would not have my head dishonored," he said, with the grim humor of a man who knew his head would soon be separated from his body. He prayed for an hour, reading from his pocket Bible and from *Eikon Basilike* (the book of his spiritual reflections, already being prepared for publication though he wouldn't live to see it).[2]

At ten o'clock, soldiers came to escort him the short distance from St. James's to Whitehall. Charles walked through St. James's Park with Bishop William Juxon (one of the few Anglican bishops who hadn't fled or been imprisoned) at his side. They talked of theology, of forgiveness, of the life to come. Charles quoted Scripture: "For me to live is Christ, and to die is gain." He seemed, witnesses said, extraordinarily calm—whether from religious faith, aristocratic self-control, or the exhaustion of a man who had fought for seven years and lost everything except his conviction that he was right.[3]

The Trial's Verdict

Charles's trial had been extraordinary, unprecedented in English history and shocking to most of Europe. The court that tried him, established by the purged

Rump Parliament after Pride's Purge, consisted of 135 commissioners, though only 68 attended regularly and only 59 signed the death warrant. The charges were revolutionary: that Charles Stuart, "trusted with a limited power to govern by and according to the laws of the land," had "traitorously and maliciously levied war against the present Parliament and the people therein represented."[4]

The charges specified that Charles had: waged war against Parliament and the people of England; caused the death of thousands in the civil wars; sought foreign aid and made alliance with Irish Catholic rebels; attempted to overthrow the fundamental laws and liberties of the nation.

Charles refused to plead. He denied the court's authority—not because he was guilty or innocent, but because no earthly court could judge a king. When John Bradshaw, the court's president, insisted he must answer, Charles replied:[5]

> *I would know by what power I am called hither. I mean lawful; there are many unlawful powers in the world—thieves and robbers by the highways. Remember, I am your King, your lawful King... I have a trust committed to me by God, by old and lawful descent. I will not betray it to answer a new unlawful authority.*

The theological claim was explicit: Charles ruled by divine right, answerable to God alone. To try him was to commit sacrilege, putting God's anointed on trial before men who had no authority over him. It didn't matter whether his actions were wise or foolish, just or unjust. The court's counterclaim was equally theological: that sovereignty resided in the people, that the king held power in trust, and that betraying that trust made him liable to judgment.[6]

The verdict was predetermined. The trial's purpose was not to determine guilt (that was assumed) but to create legal justification for what the Army had already decided must happen. Charles was, the sentence declared, "a tyrant, traitor, murderer, and public and implacable enemy to the Commonwealth of England." The sentence: "That the said Charles Stuart, as a tyrant, traitor, murderer and public enemy to the good people of this nation, shall be put to death by the severing of his head from his body."[7]

The Scaffold

The scaffold had been built outside the Banqueting House, the great hall Inigo Jones had designed, where Charles had commissioned Rubens to paint ceiling panels celebrating the Stuart monarchy's divine authority. Now Charles would walk beneath those paintings to die outside the windows, his execution a deliberate desecration of the very symbols of royal power.[8]

The scaffold was draped in black. Two masked executioners waited (their identities hidden, no one wanted to be known as the man who killed the King). Spectators crowded the street, held back by rows of soldiers. The crowd was enormous but kept at such distance that few could hear what Charles said.[9]

Charles stepped through a window onto the scaffold at two o'clock. He wore the black suit and cloak he had chosen, the second shirt underneath for warmth, and the George (the jeweled insignia of the Order of the Garter) around his neck—symbol of his aristocratic honor. He had prepared a speech—

his last chance to shape how history would remember him.[10]

The Final Speech

Charles's scaffold speech was a masterpiece of royalist propaganda, even if few heard it directly (it was published within days and read throughout England and Europe):[11]

> *I never did begin a war with the two Houses of Parliament. And I call God to witness, to whom I must shortly make an account, that I never did intend to encroach upon their privileges... As for the people, truly I desire their liberty and freedom as much as anybody whatsoever. But I must tell you that their liberty and freedom consists in having government... It is not their having a share in the government; that is nothing appertaining unto them. A subject and a sovereign are clean different things.*

He continued, addressing the charge of tyranny:[12]

> *I am the martyr of the people... I have forgiven all the world, and even those in particular that have been the chief causers of my death. Who they are, God knows; I do not desire to know; God forgive them. But this is not all; my charity must go further. I wish that they may repent, for indeed they have committed a great sin in that particular. I pray God, with St. Stephen, that this be not laid to their charge.*

The words were carefully chosen: martyr (like Christ and the apostles), forgiveness (Christ's command from the cross), charity extending even to enemies. Charles cast himself as Christian king dying for principle, victim rather than tyrant, forgiving the very men who killed him. The speech transformed a political execution into a religious sacrifice.[13]

Charles took off his cloak and doublet, handed his George to Bishop Juxon with the single word "Remember," and approached the block. He checked that it was secure, arranged his hair under a white cap so the executioner would have a clear stroke, and knelt. He prayed briefly, then stretched out his hands as a signal. One blow severed his head. The executioner did not speak the traditional words "Behold the head of a traitor."[14]

A groan rose from the spectators, horror, grief, or both. Soldiers on horseback dispersed the crowd quickly. Charles's body was carried into the Banqueting House, placed in a coffin, and buried quietly at Windsor several days later. There was no state funeral, no public mourning, no official acknowledgment of what had happened except the proclamation that made it treason to proclaim any successor.[15]

What the Execution Meant

Charles's execution was watershed moment in English and European history:[16]

Politically: It established that sovereignty could reside in the people (represented by Parliament and Army) rather than in the monarch. Kings were not above law, not sacred, not untouchable. They could be tried, judged, and executed like any other man who betrayed his trust. This was revolutionary, no European monarch had been publicly tried and executed by his own subjects. The reverberations shook every throne in Europe.

Religiously: It shattered the doctrine of divine right monarchy and passive obedience that Anglicans had taught. If the King could be lawfully executed, then Romans 13 ("the powers that be are ordained of God") could not mean unconditional obedience. The execution forced every Christian to reconsider the relationship between divine authority and earthly government.[17]

Socially: It demonstrated that the old order, king, nobles, bishops ruling over commoners, was not eternal or divinely ordained but contingent and changeable. If a king could fall, what hierarchy was safe? The execution opened possibilities that would haunt England for decades and inspire radicals for centuries.[18]

Psychologically: For royalists, Charles became "Charles the Martyr," the innocent king murdered by wicked rebels. His death was martyrdom, his killers were Christ-killers, and his memory would be sacred. For republicans and radicals, Charles was the defeated tyrant whose death proved that God favored their cause and that justice could triumph over tyranny.[19]

But the execution didn't settle England's crisis, it intensified it. The Commonwealth government that followed (1649-1653) and Cromwell's Protectorate (1653-1658) were experiments without precedent. How do you govern a kingdom without a king? How do you maintain order without the sacred authority that monarchy claimed? How do you create legitimacy when you've destroyed the most ancient source of legitimacy? These questions would torment England until the Restoration, and beyond.

To understand why the Commonwealth failed and why England eventually restored the Monarchy, we must trace the decade between Charles's execution and Charles II's return, years of experiment, conflict, and growing realization that destroying the old order was easier than building a new one.

The Commonwealth and Protectorate

The Impossible Republic, 1649-1660

The Commonwealth, 1649-1653

The Rump Parliament's Challenges

The Rump Parliament that tried and executed Charles I consisted of perhaps 200 members (out of an original 500+ in the Long Parliament before Pride's Purge). It claimed to represent the English people and to govern legitimately. But it faced overwhelming challenges:[20]

Legitimacy: The Rump was a purged Parliament, kept in power by the Army. It represented military force more than popular will. Royalists saw it as illegal usurpation. Presbyterians saw it as the Army's puppet. Even Independents who supported it knew its authority was questionable.

Ireland: The 1641 rebellion had created chaos that neither Charles nor Parliament had resolved. Now the Commonwealth had to reconquer Ireland, suppressing Catholic and royalist forces that controlled most of the island. Oliver Cromwell led the campaign (1649-1650) with brutal efficiency, the sieges of Drogheda and Wexford became legendary for their slaughter, and

Cromwell's name became synonymous with English tyranny in Irish memory.[21]

Scotland: Charles II (Charles I's son) had gone to Scotland, signed the Covenant (accepting Presbyterian church government), and been proclaimed King. This meant the Commonwealth faced war with Scotland—a war Cromwell won with victories at Dunbar (1650) and Worcester (1651), but which required occupation of Scotland and ongoing military expense.[22]

Finance: Wars in Ireland and Scotland required money. The Rump raised taxes (including an unpopular excise (sales) tax on basic goods) and confiscated royalist estates. But revenue never matched expenses. The Army remained unpaid, soldiers grew restless, and taxpayers grew resentful.[23]

Religious settlement: With bishops abolished and Presbyterianism rejected by the Army, what would England's religious establishment be? The Rump passed acts for toleration (within bounds, Catholics and extreme sectaries were excluded) but couldn't create a coherent national church. Religious diversity flourished, but without institutional framework. Parishes continued functioning with whatever ministers they had, under vague parliamentary oversight. Some areas became Presbyterian, others Independent, still others maintained traditional practices. Religious diversity was fact, not policy.[24]

The Rump's Failure

The Rump Parliament sat from 1649 to 1653, but it accomplished little beyond survival. MPs debated constitutional reforms (should there be a single chamber or two? should the executive be a council or a single person?) without reaching conclusions. They debated religious settlement without establishing any. They passed some law reforms (making legal proceedings in English rather than Latin, for instance) but nothing fundamental.

The Army grew increasingly frustrated. Officers and soldiers had fought for godly reformation, not for politicians' self-interest. They wanted:[25]

- Redistribution of Parliamentary seats (to reflect population, not medieval boundaries)
- Religious liberty for godly Protestants (Independents, Baptists, even Quakers)
- Law reform (simplifying procedures, reducing costs, eliminating corruption)
- Regular elections (not a Parliament sitting indefinitely)

The Rump resisted these demands. MPs feared that new elections would bring in Presbyterians or even royalists. They wanted to protect themselves and their allies. When the Army pressed for reforms, the Rump delayed, compromised, and ultimately refused.

On 20 April 1653, Oliver Cromwell walked into the House of Commons with thirty musketeers. He had come from an Army council meeting frustrated beyond endurance. When debate in the Commons continued as usual, ignoring the Army's demands, Cromwell rose and spoke with increasing passion:[26]

It is not fit that you should sit here any longer!... You have sat too long for any good you have been doing lately. You shall now give place to better men... Call them in! Call them in!

Soldiers entered and cleared the chamber. Cromwell himself removed the Speaker, took up the parliamentary mace (symbol of Commons authority) and said, "What shall we do with this bauble? Here, take it away!" The Rump Parliament was dissolved by military force. The republican experiment had failed, not because of royalist opposition but because the Parliament that had executed the King couldn't govern effectively and was overthrown by the Army that had put it in power.[27]

Cromwell's Protectorate, 1653-1658

The Nominated Parliament and Failure of Godly Rule

After dissolving the Rump, Cromwell and the Army officers tried something unprecedented: a Parliament of godly men, selected for their piety and commitment to reformation rather than elected. This "Nominated Parliament" (or "Barebone's Parliament," nicknamed after one of its members, Praise-God Barebone) met from July to December 1653.[28]

It included about 140 men, ministers, merchants, gentlemen, chosen by Army officers and Independent congregations as representatives of "the saints." They were meant to bring godly wisdom to governance, to complete the reformation the Rump had neglected, and to establish the holy commonwealth that God's providence had made possible through military victory.[29]

But the assembly quickly divided between moderates (who wanted practical reforms within existing structures) and radicals (Fifth Monarchists who believed Christ's return was imminent and wanted to establish biblical law in preparation). The radicals proposed:[30]

- Abolishing tithes immediately (which would impoverish ministers)
- Replacing common law with Mosaic law
- Establishing church government based on apostolic patterns
- Redistributing property to the poor[30]

Moderates saw these proposals as impractical or dangerous. When Fifth Monarchists tried to rush through abolition of tithes, moderates met early one morning, voted to dissolve the Parliament, and returned power to Cromwell. The experiment in godly rule had lasted five months.[31]

The Protectorate: Quasi-Monarchy

On 16 December 1653, Oliver Cromwell became Lord Protector under the *Instrument of Government*, England's first and only written constitution. The Instrument created a government that looked remarkably like monarchy:[32]

Executive: A Lord Protector (Cromwell) with broad powers: Command of military forces; Appointment of major officials; Conduct of foreign policy; Veto over legislation (though Parliament could override with supermajorities).[33]

Legislative: A Parliament elected triennially (every three years) with reformed constituencies and a property qualification for voters (£200 in property, this actually expanded the electorate compared to pre-war practices, though it excluded the poor).

Council of State: Advisors to the Protector, sharing some executive functions.

Religious settlement: "Liberty to tender consciences" with exceptions for popery (Catholicism), prelacy (episcopacy), and licentiousness (undefined but presumably extreme sectarianism and antinomianism). This was broader toleration than England had known but narrower than radical Independents wanted.[33]

The Instrument tried to balance executive power with parliamentary oversight, religious establishment with limited toleration, and military realities with civilian government. It satisfied almost no one. Republicans thought it was monarchy by another name. Royalists thought it was usurpation. Religious radicals thought it didn't go far enough; religious conservatives thought it went too far.

Cromwell's Protectorate (1653-1658) achieved much despite constant opposition:[34]

Foreign policy success: Cromwell waged successful war against Spain, capturing Jamaica (1655) and demonstrating English naval power. He supported Protestant causes in Europe and made England a respected power on the Continent.[35]

Religious toleration: Jews were readmitted to England (1656) after centuries of exclusion. Quakers, though imprisoned locally for disturbing the peace, were not systematically persecuted nationally (Cromwell even corresponded sympathetically with George Fox and intervened to release imprisoned Friends). Independent and Baptist congregations flourished alongside moderate Presbyterians.[36]

Administrative reforms: The government functioned reasonably well, taxes were collected, courts operated, order was maintained. This was no small achievement given the wars, regicide, and political instability of the previous decade.

But the Protectorate also revealed its contradictions:

Military dictatorship: The Major-Generals' rule (1655-1657) divided England into eleven military districts, each governed by an Army officer who enforced moral discipline—closing alehouses, prosecuting Sabbath-breaking, and suppressing vice. This was godly discipline imposed by military force, and it was deeply unpopular. Cromwell abandoned the experiment after eighteen months, but it confirmed suspicions that the regime depended on armed force more than consent.[37]

Financial problems: Wars and administration required money that Parliament granted reluctantly. Cromwell's Parliaments were fractious, some MPs wanted to restore monarchy (with Cromwell as king), others wanted to protect republican priciples, all resented taxation and military rule. Cromwell dissolved two Parliaments in frustration.[38]

Succession crisis: When Parliament offered Cromwell the crown in 1657, he agonized for weeks before refusing. He couldn't accept the title "King" after having fought against monarchy, but he recognized that the Protectorate needed clearer succession. He eventually accepted expanded powers under a new constitution (the Humble Petition and Advice) and named his son Richard as successor. But Richard had neither his father's military credentials nor his political skills. The Protectorate collapsed within a year of Oliver's death.[39]

The Restoration's Inevitability

1659-1660: Chaos and Collapse

After Richard Cromwell's forced resignation (May 1659), England descended into near-chaos. Multiple factions competed for power:[40]

The Rump was recalled yet again, but it had no military force and little legitimacy. MPs from the old Parliament, now elderly and out of touch, tried to govern a nation that had changed profoundly since they first sat in 1640.

Army officers competed among themselves, some wanting a republic, others a new Protector, all fearing Presbyterians and royalists. In October 1659, officers expelled the Rump (again) and tried to rule through a Committee of Safety. But without Cromwell's unifying authority, the Army appeared as mere military dictatorship.[41]

Presbyterians hoped for a settlement that would restore Charles II under conditions protecting parliamentary government and establishing presbyterian religion. They began negotiating with royalist exiles.[42]

Royalists waited and planned, knowing that the longer chaos continued, the more attractive restoration would seem. Charles II, in exile in Holland, issued moderate declarations promising amnesty (except for regicides), property settlement, and religious toleration.[43]

General George Monck, commanding forces in Scotland, marched to London in January 1660 with a disciplined army and unclear intentions. When he arrived, he forced the Rump to readmit members excluded in Pride's Purge, effectively restoring the Long Parliament. This body then voted to dissolve itself and call for new elections. The elections produced a "Convention Parliament" that immediately invited Charles II to return.[44]

Why Restoration Became Inevitable

The Restoration happened because alternatives had failed:

The republican experiment couldn't create stable government. The Rump was ineffective, the Nominated Parliament was naive, and the Protectorate depended on one man's charisma. No constitutional settlement had emerged that could command general acceptance.[45]

The Army was powerful but couldn't govern legitimately. Military rule was tolerable when Cromwell, victorious general and godly leader, exercised it. Without him, it was mere dictatorship, and the nation wouldn't accept it indefinitely.

Religious radicals (Fifth Monarchists, Quakers, Ranters) frightened the propertied classes. Stories of sectaries denying social hierarchy, questioning property rights, and claiming direct divine revelation convinced gentry and merchants that radical religion threatened social order. Better a king and bishops than anarchy.

Exhaustion: Twenty years of conflict, civil war, regicide, experiments, military rule, had exhausted the nation. People wanted normalcy: familiar liturgy, settled law, predictable government. Charles II offered all this, wrapped in promises of moderation and forgiveness.[46]

The European context: Every major European power was monarchical. England's republican experiment isolated it diplomatically. Trading partners wanted stability. Restoration meant rejoining normal international relations.[47]

Most importantly, no one had a viable alternative to monarchy. Republicans had proven they couldn't create stable institutions. Presbyterians couldn't establish their system without military force they lacked. Independents were divided among themselves. The only institution with deep roots, broad recognition, and potential for unifying the nation was monarchy. Charles II returned not because he was beloved but because he was the least bad option in a nation desperate for stability.

On 29 May 1660—Charles's thirtieth birthday—he entered London to jubilant crowds. Bells rang throughout the city, fountains ran with wine, and Londoners celebrated as if tyranny had ended and liberty had returned. In reality, one experiment had failed and another was beginning. What kind of monarchy would Charles establish? What religious settlement would emerge? How would England reconcile its revolutionary decade with its restored tradition? These questions would dominate the next generation.

The Restoration Settlement

The Return of the King

The Clarendon Code and Its Enforcement

1661-1665: Reimposing Uniformity

The Restoration brought not comprehension but exclusion. The "Cavalier Parliament" elected in 1661 was overwhelmingly royalist and Anglican, men who had suffered under the Commonwealth and wanted revenge. They passed a series of laws (the "Clarendon Code," named after Edward Hyde, Earl of Clarendon) that excluded Nonconformists from public life:[48]

Corporation Act (1661): Required all municipal office-holders to take Anglican communion within the previous year; swear oaths of allegiance and supremacy; renounce the Solemn League and Covenant as an unlawful oath. This excluded Nonconformists from town governments, removing Presbyterians, Independents, and Baptists from civic positions they had held during the Interregnum.[49]

Act of Uniformity (1662): Required all clergy to use the Book of Common Prayer exclusively; accept episcopal ordination or reordination; renounce the Solemn League and Covenant; swear they would not "endeavor any alteration of government in church or state." About 2,000 ministers refused and were ejected, the "Great Ejection" that created English Nonconformity as a permanent feature. Among them were some of England's finest preachers and most learned theologians, including Richard Baxter.[50]

Conventicle Act (1664): Prohibited religious gatherings of more than five people outside the established church, targeting Nonconformist worship. Penalties escalated with repeated offenses, potentially leading to transportation to the colonies.[51]

Five Mile Act (1665): Banned ejected ministers from coming within five miles of incorporated towns or their former parishes unless they swore oaths they could not in conscience take. This scattered Nonconformist leadership to rural areas.[52]

These laws aimed to force conformity through legal pressure. Nonconformists could either submit to the established church or face fines, imprisonment, and social exclusion. The Acts assumed that most dissenters would conform rather than suffer; they assumed wrong.

The Limits of Persecution

But persecution produced martyrs, not conformists. Nonconformists met secretly in homes, barns, and forests. Ejected ministers preached to congregations that followed them out of the established church. Networks of mutual support developed, collecting money for imprisoned ministers, smuggling banned books, warning of raids. The Meeting for Sufferings coordinated Quaker resistance; similar networks served Presbyterians and Baptists.[53]

Moreover, enforcement varied by locality. Some magistrates zealously prosecuted Nonconformists; others sympathized or couldn't be bothered. Some justices of the peace were themselves Presbyterian in sympathy. Some local communities protected Nonconformist neighbors from outside authority.[54]

Charles II himself was ambivalent about persecution. He had promised religious toleration in the Declaration of Breda, and he personally favored latitude (partly from political calculation, he needed Nonconformist support against Cavalier exclusivism). Twice he issued Declarations of Indulgence suspending penal laws against Nonconformists and Catholics (1662, 1672); twice Parliament forced him to withdraw them.[55]

The battle over indulgences revealed constitutional tensions unresolved by the Restoration. Did the King have inherent powers that Parliament couldn't limit? Or was the King under law, bound by parliamentary statute? These questions would explode in the Exclusion Crisis and Glorious Revolution.

The Popish Plot and Exclusion Crisis

1678-1681: The Catholic Threat Returns

The fragile Restoration settlement nearly collapsed in the late 1670s over the Catholic question. Charles II had no legitimate children (though many illegitimate ones). His heir was his brother James, Duke of York, who had converted to Catholicism. The prospect of a Catholic king terrified Protestant England.[56]

In 1678, Titus Oates, an opportunist and fantasist, claimed to have discovered a "Popish Plot," a vast Catholic conspiracy to assassinate Charles, put James on the throne, massacre Protestants, and restore England to Rome. The plot was fiction, but the fear was real. Parliament went into panic. Approximately 35 people were executed on Oates's testimony (including Catholic nobles and Jesuits), their guilt or innocence irrelevant to the political frenzy.[57]

The Popish Plot was fiction, but the fear it revealed was real. England's Protestant identity had been formed through conflict with Catholicism—foreign and domestic. The thought of a Catholic king seemed a return to the fires of Smithfield, to Spanish tyranny, to everything the nation had fought against since Henry VIII.

The Exclusion Crisis

Between 1679 and 1681, Parliament tried repeatedly to pass an Exclusion Bill that would bar James from succession. The Earl of Shaftesbury led the exclusionist cause, arguing that allowing a Catholic king would betray the Reformation, surrender English liberties, and invite foreign domination.[58]

Charles resisted. He wouldn't disinherit his brother or bastardize his nephew. He dissolved three Parliaments rather than accept exclusion. The crisis produced England's first recognizable political parties:

Whigs (exclusionists): Wanted parliamentary supremacy, Protestant succession, and broad religious toleration. Drew support from Nonconformists, merchants, and those who remembered the Civil War as justified resistance to tyranny.[59]

Tories (anti-exclusionists): Defended hereditary succession, royal prerogative, and Anglican establishment. Drew support from gentry, clergy, and those who remembered the Civil War as rebellion that led to regicide and chaos.[60]

The terms "Whig" and "Tory" were both originally insults (Whig from Scottish Presbyterian rebels, Tory from Irish Catholic bandits), but they became party labels that structured English politics for the next two centuries.

Charles outmaneuvered the exclusionists. He called Parliament to Oxford (away from London's Whig mobs) in 1681, dissolved it when it insisted on exclusion, and ruled without Parliament for the last four years of his reign. When he died in 1685, James succeeded peacefully—for a time.

James II and the Glorious Revolution

1685-1688: The Catholic King

James II's accession seemed to confirm Protestant fears. He immediately: attended Mass publicly, maintaining a Catholic chapel at court with elaborate ceremonial; appointed Catholics to military commands, using his power to dispense with the Test Act (which required office-holders to take Anglican communion); appointed Catholics to Oxford and Cambridge colleges, dismissing Protestant fellows; issued a Declaration of Indulgence (1687, reissued 1688) suspending penal laws against both Catholics and Protestant Nonconformists, which looked like using Nonconformists to advance

Catholicism.[61]

Tories, who had defended hereditary right against exclusion, found themselves trapped. Their doctrine of passive obedience said they couldn't resist even a bad king. But James was systematically undermining the established church they also believed was divinely ordained. When seven bishops (including the Archbishop of Canterbury) petitioned against the Declaration of Indulgence, James prosecuted them for seditious libel. The jury's acquittal prompted national celebration.[62]

The birth of James's son (June 1688) made the crisis acute. Previously, Protestants could wait, James was over fifty, his heirs were his Protestant daughters Mary (married to William of Orange, Dutch Protestant champion) and Anne. A Catholic heir changed everything: England faced not a temporary Catholic reign but a permanent Catholic dynasty.[63]

November 1688: The Revolution

On 5 November 1688, William of Orange landed at Torbay with 14,000 troops, the largest invasion force to land in England since William the Conqueror. He came at the invitation of seven prominent Englishmen (the "Immortal Seven," a mix of Whigs and Tories) who declared James's government illegal and asked William to restore English liberties.[64]

William's Declaration justified the invasion: James had violated English laws, persecuted the established church, packed Parliament, and threatened to impose popery. William came not to conquer but to call a free Parliament that would settle the nation's government and religion.[65]

James tried to resist but his support collapsed. Army officers defected to William (including John Churchill, James's closest military advisor). The navy declared for William. City after city welcomed William's forces. James, deserted, tried to flee to France; he was caught but William let him escape, preferring exile to the complications of a captive king.[66]

The "Glorious Revolution" was remarkably bloodless in England (though Ireland and Scotland would see serious fighting). It established principles that shaped English constitutional development:[67]

Parliamentary supremacy: The crown was offered by Parliament and accepted conditionally. The Bill of Rights (1689) listed James's violations and established that future monarchs ruled under law, not above it.

Protestant succession: The Bill of Rights required all future monarchs to be Protestant and to take oaths denying Catholic doctrines. This excluded James's descendants and eventually brought the Hanoverian dynasty to England's throne (1714).[68]

Limited monarchy: The King couldn't suspend laws, levy taxes, maintain a standing army in peacetime, or interfere with parliamentary elections, all without Parliament's consent. Royal prerogative was dramatically curtailed.[69]

Religious toleration: The Toleration Act (1689) allowed Protestant Nonconformists to worship freely if they registered their meeting places and subscribed to most of the Thirty-Nine Articles. This wasn't full religious liberty, but it ended the attempt to force conformity.

The Toleration Act and What It Meant

The Settlement That Finally Worked

The Terms of Toleration

The Toleration Act's Provisions

The Toleration Act of 1689 (An Act for Exempting Their Majesties' Protestant Subjects Dissenting from the Church of England from the Penalties of Certain Laws) was limited, grudging, and pragmatic—but it worked. For the first time, Protestant Nonconformists could worship legally without risking imprisonment.[70]

The Act provided that Protestant dissenters who: took oaths of allegiance to William and Mary; subscribed to most of the Thirty-Nine Articles (specifically articles on the Trinity, Scripture's authority, and Reformed soteriology—articles on church government and ceremonies were excluded); registered their meeting places with local authorities—could worship publicly without penalty under the Conventicle Act and other penal laws. Dissenting ministers who took the oaths and subscribed the articles could preach without fear of prosecution.[71]

What the Act Did NOT Do:

It didn't grant full equality: Nonconformists still couldn't hold public office without taking Anglican communion (Test and Corporation Acts remained in force until 1828). They couldn't attend Oxford or Cambridge. They couldn't receive degrees from English universities. They remained second-class citizens legally, even if they could now worship without persecution.[72]

It didn't extend to Catholics: Catholic worship remained illegal. Catholics couldn't take the required oaths (which included denying transubstantiation and papal authority). The Act explicitly stated it didn't apply to "Papists." Catholic emancipation would wait another 140 years.[73]

It didn't extend to anti-Trinitarians: Those who denied the Trinity (including Unitarians and Socinians) were excluded. Protestant orthodoxy on fundamental doctrines was still required.

It didn't grant theoretical toleration: The Act's preamble made clear this was pragmatic accommodation, not principled embrace of religious liberty. It noted that "some ease to scrupulous consciences" might "be an effectual means to unite Their Majesties' Protestant subjects in interest and affection."[74]

The language was telling: "ease to scrupulous consciences," not "recognition of religious liberty." The Act treated Nonconformity as weakness—scrupulous consciences that couldn't accept Anglican forms—rather than principled dissent. Toleration was medicine for a disease, not acknowledgment of a right.

Why It Passed in 1689

The Toleration Act passed because circumstances made it necessary and opposition to it had weakened:[75]

William III's position: William of Orange had Dutch Reformed background where multiple Protestant churches coexisted. He needed Nonconformist support against James II. He pushed for toleration as political necessity and personal conviction.

The Whig-Nonconformist alliance: Whigs had courted Nonconformist support during the Exclusion Crisis. Nonconformists had supported William's invasion. Political debts needed paying, and toleration was the price.[76]

Exhaustion with persecution: Thirty years of persecution (1660-1689) had proven that Nonconformity couldn't be suppressed. Thousands had been imprisoned, many had died in filthy jails, property had been confiscated, lives had been ruined. Yet Nonconformists remained. Toleration was the admission that uniformity was impossible.[77]

The Catholic threat: James II's reign demonstrated that Catholics were England's real danger. Protestant divisions seemed petty compared to the popish menace. Better to tolerate Presbyterian and Independent worship than to weaken Protestant England against Catholic threats.[78]

Changing intellectual climate: John Locke's *Letter Concerning Toleration* (published 1689, written earlier) articulated philosophical arguments for religious liberty. Locke distinguished between civil and religious spheres, arguing that government's proper concern was worldly order, not eternal salvation. His arguments influenced educated opinion.[79]

Economic considerations: Nonconformists were prominent in trade and commerce. Persecuting them harmed the economy. Tolerating them encouraged economic activity and attracted skilled workers and merchants. The Dutch Republic's economic success, achieved with religious toleration, provided a model.[80]

The Toleration Act thus represented not conversion to principled religious liberty but pragmatic acceptance that uniformity was impossible and that limited diversity was preferable to continued conflict.

How Toleration Worked in Practice

Registration and Surveillance

The requirement that dissenters register their meeting places served dual purposes: it legalized their worship and it enabled surveillance. Local authorities knew where dissenters met, who led them, and (roughly) how many there were. Registration was both protection and control.[81]

Registration created a paper trail documenting Nonconformity's extent. By 1710, thousands of meeting houses were registered throughout England, Presbyterian, Independent, Baptist, and Quaker. The records reveal patterns:[82]

Geographic patterns: Nonconformity was strongest in London and southeast England, in cloth-manufacturing regions (East Anglia, parts of West Country), and in some northern industrial areas. It was weakest in the rural Midlands and in areas dominated by great landowners.

Denominational distribution: Presbyterians were most numerous initially, but they declined relative to Independents and Baptists through the 18th century. Quakers remained a distinct minority but with disproportionate influence due to their wealth and organization.

Social composition: Nonconformist congregations drew heavily from the "middling sort," merchants, substantial tradesmen, skilled artisans, yeoman farmers. They included few aristocrats (who were Anglican by social expectation) and relatively few of the very poor (who were too marginal to organize).

Occasional Conformity and Its Discontents

The Test and Corporation Acts' requirement that office-holders take Anglican communion created a practice called "occasional conformity," Nonconformists taking communion in the established church once or twice a year to qualify for office, then attending dissenting worship the rest of the time.[83]

High Church Anglicans saw occasional conformity as hypocrisy that violated the Test Acts' spirit. Parliament passed the Occasional Conformity Act (1711) penalizing those who attended dissenting worship after qualifying by Anglican communion. But the act was politically motivated (Tories attacking Whig-Nonconformist alliances) and was repealed in 1719.[84]

Strict Nonconformists also criticized occasional conformity as compromise. To take communion in the established church purely for political advantage seemed to treat sacraments as mere forms, to value worldly office above conscience, and to betray the suffering of those who had refused conformity and paid the price.

But most Nonconformists were pragmatists. If taking communion once a year in an Anglican church allowed them to serve as town councilors, magistrates, or MPs, positions where they could protect Nonconformist interests and promote policies they believed just, many thought the compromise acceptable.

The debate over occasional conformity revealed that toleration created new questions: What defined religious identity, formal membership or regular worship? Could one be a "real" Presbyterian while occasionally receiving Anglican sacrament? The answers were contested, and the debate revealed tensions between principle and pragmatism that toleration created.

The Limits and Paradoxes of Toleration

What Toleration Couldn't Solve

The Toleration Act settled the question of whether Nonconformist worship would be legal (yes, within limits) but left other questions unresolved or created new tensions:

Social discrimination persisted: Legal toleration didn't mean social acceptance. Nonconformists faced informal discrimination in business, were excluded from elite social circles, and bore stigma as dissenters from established order.[85]

Political exclusion continued: The Test and Corporation Acts remained in force until 1828, meaning Nonconformists couldn't hold most public offices, couldn't attend Oxford or Cambridge, and were formally second-class citizens.

This created resentment and anomaly: Nonconformists could worship freely but couldn't participate fully in public life.[86]

Theological tensions remained: Toleration was legal accommodation, not theological reconciliation. Anglicans still believed episcopacy was divinely ordained, that the Book of Common Prayer was spiritually superior, that dissenters were in error. Nonconformists still believed episcopacy was popish remnant, Prayer Book worship was dead formalism, established church was corrupt. Legal coexistence didn't resolve theological disagreement.[87]

The Catholic problem: By excluding Catholics, the Toleration Act created a permanent religious underclass. English Catholics (perhaps 2-3% of population) couldn't worship legally, couldn't hold office, faced property restrictions and education limitations. This was not resolved until Catholic emancipation (1829).[88]

The Challenge of Maintaining Identity

Toleration posed an unexpected challenge to Nonconformist identity: How to maintain distinctiveness without persecution to sharpen boundaries? Persecution had created solidarity—suffering together for conscience forged strong bonds. Toleration allowed more casual adherence.[89]

The problems:

Generational drift: First-generation Nonconformists had refused Anglican conformity at personal cost—loss of livings, imprisonment, social stigma. Their children inherited Nonconformist identity without experiencing the struggles that formed it. Second and third generations found it easier to drift toward Anglican conformity or toward religious indifference.

Theological cooling: Persecution had forced theological seriousness—one didn't risk imprisonment for casual religious opinion. Toleration allowed more casual adherence. Some Nonconformist congregations remained theologically rigorous; others drifted toward Arianism (denying Christ's full divinity), Socinianism (rational religion minimizing supernatural elements), or mere moralism.

The wealth problem: Nonconformist merchants and manufacturers prospered in the 18th century's commercial expansion. Wealth brought temptation to conformity (easier business and social advancement) and to worldliness (religious devotion competing with commercial success). The "Nonconformist conscience" that produced business integrity also produced successful businessmen whose children might abandon Nonconformity for social advancement.

Revival and renewal: These challenges produced responses—evangelical revivals (Methodism began as an Anglican renewal movement but attracted many Nonconformists), missionary societies, Sunday schools, and renewed emphasis on conversion and personal piety. But the tension between maintaining distinctive identity and integrating into broader English life persisted throughout the 18th and 19th centuries.[90]

Toleration thus was settlement but not resolution—it made Nonconformist existence legal and sustainable, but it didn't resolve the theological questions that had created division, and it created new challenges for communities no longer united by shared persecution.

What the Four Factions Left Behind

Legacies and Lessons

The Presbyterian Legacy: Discipline and Education

What Survived

English Presbyterianism as a distinct denomination largely disappeared by the 19th century. Many Presbyterian congregations became Unitarian (denying Trinity and Christ's divinity), others merged with Congregationalists, still others simply faded. Presbyterian church government never established itself in England as it did in Scotland.[91]

Yet Presbyterian influences persisted:

Educational emphasis: The dissenting academies Presbyterians founded maintained high intellectual standards, taught modern subjects, and produced educated ministers and middle-class professionals. These academies became models for educational reform and eventually influenced English university education.[92]

Systematic theology: The Westminster Confession and Catechisms remained standards for Reformed churches worldwide—especially in Scotland and America. Presbyterian Scotland's theological influence extended far beyond its borders.

Corporate governance: The model of ascending courts (session, presbytery, synod, assembly) influenced both religious and secular organizations. The idea that authority could be distributed through representative assemblies shaped corporate and political life.

What Failed

But Presbyterian hopes for a godly commonwealth through church discipline and magisterial support failed permanently in England:

The national church dream died: England would not establish presbyterian government. The Church of England remained episcopal. Nonconformists became denominations, particular traditions coexisting with the establishment rather than replacing it.[93]

Discipline lost coercive power: Without state enforcement, church discipline became voluntary. Excommunicated people could simply join another congregation or ignore church censure. Discipline remained meaningful within committed communities but couldn't shape society as Presbyterians had hoped.

The magistrate wouldn't enforce the First Table: English law stopped punishing heresy, blasphemy, and Sabbath-breaking (mostly—some blue laws persisted). The magistrate protected public order but increasingly refused to enforce religious orthodoxy.

Uniformity proved impossible: Religious diversity was fact. Attempting to suppress it required constant, expensive, brutal enforcement that never fully succeeded. Tolerating it proved easier and more stable.

The Presbyterian legacy thus was mixed: their institutions failed in England but succeeded elsewhere; their theological works endured while their polity didn't; their emphasis on education and systematic thought enriched Reformed Christianity even as their vision of a godly commonwealth faded.

The Independent Legacy: Liberty and Voluntarism

The Triumph of Congregationalism

If Presbyterians lost the battle for national establishment, Independents won the argument for religious voluntarism, eventually:[94]

Gathered churches prevailed: The model of voluntary congregations, covenant membership, and congregational autonomy became standard in English Nonconformity and American Protestantism. Even churches that aren't formally Congregationalist often operate on congregationalist assumptions.

Liberty of conscience: The Independent argument that magistrates shouldn't coerce conscience in religious matters eventually became consensus (at least regarding Protestant diversity—it took longer for Catholics, Jews, and non-Christians). The conscience was recognized as beyond civil authority's proper reach.

The marketplace of ideas: Milton's Areopagitica and Independent arguments for free debate without censorship shaped liberal political thought. The conviction that truth emerged through contest rather than suppression became foundational for democratic societies.

Denominationalism: The Independent acceptance that multiple church forms could coexist produced denominational pluralism, Baptists, Congregationalists, Presbyterians, Methodists, etc. all maintaining distinct traditions while sharing common space. This became normal in England and especially in America.

What Was Lost

But Independent victory came with costs:

Fragmentation: If every congregation could define itself, nothing prevented endless division. The proliferation of sects that Presbyterians had feared occurred, denominations, sub-denominations, independent churches, and movements splitting over doctrine, practice, or personality.[95]

Loss of coherence: Without creeds, confessions, or ecclesiastical courts maintaining standards, Independent churches could drift theologically. Some maintained rigorous Calvinism; others embraced Arminianism, liberalism, or heterodoxy.

Individualism: The Independent emphasis on gathered saints and voluntary association fed (and was fed by) individualistic culture. Religion became personal choice rather than communal inheritance. This freed individuals from imposed conformity but also weakened religious community's binding power.

Social atomization: If religious community was voluntary association based on choice, what bound society together? Independents had assumed that godly commonwealth could exist without coercive uniformity. Whether they were right, whether society could cohere without shared religion—remained contested.

The Independent legacy thus was the world of denominational pluralism, religious liberty, and voluntary association, with all its freedoms and all its fragmentation.

The Anglican Legacy: Establishment and Tradition

What Endured

The Church of England remained established—enduring through the 19th and 20th centuries' challenges and persisting (in attenuated form) into the 21st:[96]

National religious identity: The established church provided (and provides) ceremonial continuity—coronations, state funerals, national commemorations. Even as practice declined, the Church of England remained part of national identity.

Liturgical beauty: The Book of Common Prayer shaped English prose, influenced English literature, and created a common religious language that transcended theological divisions. Even Nonconformists knew the Prayer Book's rhythms.

Via media tradition: The Anglican instinct for comprehension—holding together high church and low church, Catholic-leaning and Protestant-leaning elements within one institution—demonstrated that theological diversity need not produce schism. This "via media" became model for other traditions.

The global communion: Anglican expansion through British Empire created a worldwide communion of autonomous provinces united by common heritage and liturgical tradition. The Anglican Communion became the third-largest Christian family after Catholicism and Orthodoxy.[97]

What Failed

But Anglican hopes for comprehensive national church including all but the most extreme were never realized:

The Great Ejection (1662) drove the godly and learned out of the church, impoverishing it intellectually and spiritually. The church that might have included Baxter and Owen, that might have been broad enough for moderate Presbyterians and Independents, chose exclusion and reaped permanent division.[98]

Establishment bred complacency: State support made the church lazy. The 18th century saw notorious pluralism (ministers holding multiple livings and serving none well), absenteeism, and worldliness. Evangelical revival came partly from outside the establishment.

Tying church to state made the church vulnerable to state's secularization. As Parliament became more secular (Catholics emancipated 1829, Jews admitted to Parliament 1858, atheists eventually), the established church's connection to government became awkward.

Establishment elsewhere failed: Ireland's Anglican establishment over Catholic majority was unjust and unsustainable (disestablished 1871). Wales's establishment was resented (disestablished 1920). Scotland never accepted Anglicanism. The establishment model worked (imperfectly) in England but couldn't be exported.

The Anglican legacy thus includes beautiful liturgy, institutional continuity, and a model of comprehensive church holding diverse views—but also a compromised church, established privilege, and the challenge of maintaining spiritual vitality with state support.

The Quaker Legacy: Peace and Integrity

The Peace Testimony's Persistence

Of the four factions, Quakers were smallest and most radical—yet their testimony has endured with remarkable consistency:[99]

Consistent pacifism: Friends maintained their peace testimony through centuries when most Christians accepted war as necessary. Quakers refused military service even when it cost them legally, socially, and economically.

Alternative service: Quaker insistence that they couldn't kill but would serve otherwise (medical work, civilian service, humanitarian relief) established the concept of conscientious objection with alternative service—now recognized in international law.

Conflict resolution: Quaker experience with non-violent conflict, with patient negotiation, and with seeking "that of God" in opponents produced mediation and reconciliation practices that transcended religious boundaries.

Speaking truth to power: The Quaker combination of prophetic boldness with principled non-violence influenced later movements—Gandhi's satyagraha, King's civil rights activism, and various non-violent resistance movements worldwide.[100]

What Couldn't Scale

But Quaker witness remained minority position, never becoming majority Christianity's stance:

The peace testimony's costs: Refusing all violence meant accepting martyrdom rather than self-defense. Most Christians concluded this was unrealistic counsel of perfection, applicable to saints but not to ordinary believers with families to protect and neighbors to defend.[101]

Small communities: Quaker practice required intensive community—meetings for worship, business meetings, corporate discernment, accountability structures. This worked for small groups but didn't scale to mass religion.

The peculiarity problem: Quaker distinctives (plain dress, plain speech, rejection of oaths, silent worship) marked Friends as peculiar. This created strong identity but also limited appeal. Quakerism remained minority faith.

Theological drift: Without creeds or formal theology, Quakerism drifted variously—some meetings became liberal to the point of non-Christian spirituality, others became evangelical and more like other Protestant churches.

The Quaker legacy thus is a persistent witness to peace, to integrity, to the possibility of living by principles even at cost—a witness that influenced broader culture while remaining minority position.

Two Cities, Two Kingdoms

Augustine, Luther, and England's Crisis

The four visions we have examined, Presbyterian aristocracy, Independent mixed government, Anglican monarchy, and Quaker anarchism, each claimed to resolve the tension between religious truth and political order. None fully succeeded. England's settlement emerged not from the triumph of any single vision but from their exhausted coexistence. Yet the theological frameworks they drew upon remain illuminating: Augustine's distinction between the City of God and the City of Man, and Luther's doctrine of the two kingdoms.[102]

Augustine's Two Cities

Augustine of Hippo, writing as Rome fell to barbarian armies, distinguished between two "cities" that existed intermingled throughout human history. The City of God was the community of those who loved God supremely and ordered all other loves accordingly. The City of Man was the community of those who loved themselves and earthly things, using even religion as a means to power and pleasure. The two cities could not be identified with any visible institution, not even the Church, which contained members of both. Only at history's end would God separate the wheat from the tares.

This framework offered resources to all parties in England's crisis, but it also limited their claims. Presbyterians could use Augustine's authority to argue that visible churches must maintain discipline and purity, but they could not claim that their Presbyterian order was itself the City of God. Independents could invoke Augustine's skepticism about earthly institutions to justify gathered churches, but they could not assume their congregations were free from the mixed character of all earthly communities. Anglicans could cite Augustine's realism about political authority, but they could not identify royal power with divine will. Quakers could appeal to Augustine's emphasis on inward transformation, but they could not escape the institutional implications of their own growing movement.

Luther's Two Kingdoms

Luther's doctrine of the two kingdoms offered a different distinction. God ruled the world through two governments: the spiritual government, which proclaimed the Gospel and administered the sacraments, touching the conscience and offering salvation; and the temporal government, which wielded the sword to restrain evil and maintain outward peace. Both were God's instruments, but they operated by different means for different ends. The spiritual government worked through Word and Spirit, persuading hearts; the temporal government worked through law and force, compelling bodies.

This framework was adapted variously by England's factions. Presbyterians tended to blur the distinction, expecting the civil magistrate to enforce true religion and punish heresy. Anglicans maintained a closer connection between the two governments, with the king as "supreme governor" of the church in externals while ministers governed in spirituals. Independents moved toward functional separation, limiting the magistrate's role in religious matters. Quakers denied the temporal government any authority over conscience whatsoever, approaching something like modern separation of church and state.

The Four Factions and Their Frameworks

Looking across the four areas of comparison, the nature of man, the Kingdom of God, liberty of conscience, and blood guilt, we can see how each faction appropriated these theological frameworks differently.

On human nature, Presbyterians and Independents agreed substantially with the Reformed emphasis on total depravity and unconditional election, though they drew different political conclusions. Anglicans, while officially Reformed in their Articles, emphasized tradition and reason alongside Scripture, creating space for natural law arguments. Quakers broke most sharply, insisting that the inner light gave every person direct access to divine teaching, undermining the need for external religious authority.

On the Kingdom of God, the factions ranged from tight integration (Anglicans) through mediated connection (Presbyterians) to functional separation (Independents) to principled divorce (Quakers). Each position had theological warrant; each created distinctive problems. Integration risked corrupting the church with political calculations; separation risked abandoning society to unredeemed forces.

On liberty of conscience, the spectrum ran from Presbyterian insistence on enforced orthodoxy to Quaker insistence on absolute liberty. Anglicans claimed comprehension, a broad church including diverse views, but enforced that comprehension with legal penalties. Independents occupied an unstable middle, advocating liberty for orthodox Protestants while debating where to draw the line.

On blood guilt, all factions believed that unpunished sin brought divine judgment, but they differed sharply on who bore guilt. The regicides executed Charles as a man of blood; Anglicans celebrated him as a martyr and branded the regicides as murderers. Quakers rejected the entire framework, denying that any human court could execute divine justice on spiritual offenses.

What the Crisis Taught

From Charles I's Scaffold to William III's Throne

We have followed England through forty tumultuous years, from Charles I walking into the Commons with armed men (1642) through civil war, regicide, republic, military dictatorship, restoration, and revolution. The crisis cost perhaps 200,000 English lives (3-4% of the population), divided families, destroyed property, shattered assumptions, and forced reconsideration of questions that had seemed settled.[103]

What Was Learned

The crisis taught hard lessons that shaped the modern world:

Religious uniformity was impossible: The attempt to force all English people into one religious mold, whether episcopal, presbyterian, or independent, failed utterly. Persecution couldn't suppress conscience, couldn't prevent dissent, couldn't create genuine unity. By 1689, this was recognized fact. Toleration emerged not from principled conviction (though some held it) but from exhausted pragmatism: since uniformity was impossible, limited diversity was better than endless conflict.[104]

Sovereignty required limits: Absolute monarchy (Charles I's claim) and parliamentary absolutism (the Commonwealth's claim) both produced tyranny. The settlement that emerged, constitutional monarchy with parliamentary supremacy but judicial independence and protected liberties, was compromise that limited all powers.[105]

Conscience had claims: The conviction that individuals had religious obligations that transcended earthly authority, that they must obey God rather than men when the two conflicted, was vindicated by those who suffered for their faith. Whether Presbyterian, Independent, or Quaker, the martyrs and confessors demonstrated that conscience could not simply be commanded.[106]

Violence had limits: Military force could win battles but couldn't settle religious questions or create stable government without consent. The New Model Army's victories were impressive, but they couldn't produce godly reformation, couldn't make England Presbyterian or Independent or Quaker by force. Swords could kill bodies but couldn't convert souls.

Institutions mattered: The crisis demonstrated that good intentions weren't enough. The Commonwealth failed not because its leaders lacked vision but because they couldn't create institutions that balanced idealism with practical governance, that commanded consent while maintaining order, that allowed diversity while preserving unity.[107]

The Persistence of the Problem

England's revolutionary crisis did not produce a theoretical solution to the relation between religious conviction and political order. The Toleration Act of 1689 was a practical compromise, not a principled resolution. Protestant dissenters gained legal protection; Catholics did not. The Church of England remained established; other churches remained second-class. Liberty of conscience was recognized for some, denied to others.

Yet the struggle produced lasting effects. The idea that conscience was beyond civil authority's reach, expressed most radically by Quakers, more moderately by Independents, became increasingly accepted. The idea that religious uniformity was impossible without unacceptable violence, demonstrated by decades of failed coercion, became conventional wisdom. The idea that Christians could disagree profoundly about church government and still share political space, once inconceivable, became normal

What Wasn't Learned

But some lessons were only partly learned or learned differently by different people:

The role of establishment: England retained an established church while tolerating dissent, a compromise that satisfied no one fully. The question of whether religion should be established, disestablished, or separated from state remained contested. Different nations would answer differently; the question remains live today.[108]

Catholic inclusion: The lesson that Protestant divisions should be tolerated didn't immediately extend to Catholics or non-Christians. Catholic emancipation took another 140 years. The principle of toleration was established, but its application remained contested and incomplete.

Social equality: The crisis challenged but didn't overthrow social hierarchy. Political power remained concentrated in aristocracy and gentry. The franchise remained restricted to property-holders. Social revolution was feared, not achieved. The leveling tendencies that terrified the propertied classes were contained, not vindicated.[109]

Economic justice: The crisis was largely about religious and political authority, not economic distribution. Questions of property, wealth inequality, and economic justice, raised briefly by Levellers and Diggers, were quickly suppressed and largely forgotten. The settlement protected property; it didn't redistribute it.

The Gift to the World

What England's crisis gave the world was a rough model for managing religious diversity and limiting political power:

Denominational pluralism: Multiple churches coexisting legally, competing for adherents, none established by law, this would be the American model and increasingly the global norm. It emerged from England's failed attempts at uniformity.[110]

Constitutional government: Limited monarchy under law, with parliamentary sovereignty, judicial independence, and protected liberties—this model spread through the British Empire and influenced constitutionalism worldwide.

Religious liberty: The principle (however incompletely applied) that people should be free to worship according to conscience, that the state shouldn't coerce belief, and that religious diversity could be tolerated without social collapse—this became foundational for liberal democracies.

The free press and marketplace of ideas: Milton's arguments, tested by experience, produced gradual acceptance that ideas should compete freely, that censorship was counterproductive, and that truth emerged through debate rather than suppression.[111]

The costs of these gifts were high: Civil war, regicide, persecution, families divided, lives destroyed, decades of instability. No one in 1640 would have chosen this path if they'd known where it led. But the path produced a settlement that, imperfect as it was, proved more durable than any party's original vision.

The Questions That Remain

The crisis resolved some questions but left others for later generations:[112]

How to balance liberty and order? England's settlement leaned toward order with limited liberty. America's would lean toward liberty with minimal order. Both struggled with the balance.

How to maintain religious commitment in tolerant societies? Persecution had sharpened faith; toleration allowed drift. How could churches maintain distinctive identities and demanding discipleship when the state no longer enforced conformity?

How to integrate diverse communities? Toleration meant legal coexistence, not social integration. How could Catholics, Nonconformists, and Anglicans form one nation while maintaining different religious identities?

Who counts as "the people"? Popular sovereignty sounded democratic, but defining "the people" narrowly (property-holding Protestant men) left most humans excluded. Expanding the definition would occupy the next three centuries.

The Persistence of the Four Visions

The four visions persist in transformed forms. Those who believe qualified elites should govern, whether in church or state, inherit something of the Presbyterian vision. Those who believe in balanced constitutions limiting every power, including religious power, inherit something of the Independent vision. Those who believe tradition and hierarchy preserve wisdom that innovation destroys, in church and state alike, inherit something of the Anglican vision. Those who believe individual conscience trumps every collective authority, civil or ecclesiastical, inherit something of the Quaker vision.

What We Inherit

We inherit the settlement England's crisis produced, its gifts and its problems:

We inherit liberty of conscience, though we debate its limits and applications.

We inherit constitutional government, though we argue about power's distribution.

We inherit religious pluralism, though we struggle with its tensions.

We inherit the conviction that coerced faith is no faith at all, though we differ about what that conviction implies.

We also inherit unresolved tensions: between liberty and order, between diversity and unity, between individual rights and common good, between religious conviction and secular governance. These tensions weren't resolved in the 17th century; they were institutionalized. We live with the institutions and the tensions they embody.

The 17th-century English crisis doesn't provide answers to our questions. The circumstances differ too profoundly, we face issues (religious pluralism including non-Christian religions and no religion, global interconnection, technological transformation) that the 17th century couldn't have imagined. But it provides a reminder that these questions are genuinely hard, that good people disagree, that settlements emerge from exhaustion as much as wisdom, and that living with imperfect arrangements is often better than fighting to the death for perfect ones.

A Kingdom Not of This World

Jesus told Pilate: "My kingdom is not of this world. If my kingdom were of this world, my servants would fight." The four factions in England's crisis all claimed to serve that kingdom, but they fought bitterly about what serving it required. Did it require a godly commonwealth enforced by magistrates? A gathered church protected by sword-bearing saints? A royal supremacy preserving ancient order? A complete rejection of worldly authority over spiritual matters?[113]

Each answer produced distinctive fruits, and distinctive failures. The Presbyterians built institutions but not a lasting establishment. The Independents won wars but could not build a durable peace. The Anglicans restored order but at the cost of permanent dissent. The Quakers preserved liberty but withdrew from transforming society.

Perhaps the lesson is that no earthly arrangement can fully express a kingdom not of this world. The City of God remains intermingled with the City of Man until history's end. The two kingdoms overlap, and Christians must navigate their competing claims with prudence and humility. Those who expect any political order to embody perfect justice will be disappointed. Those who abandon political order to the unredeemed will neglect their duty as citizens. The tension cannot be resolved, only lived.

England's seventeenth-century experience remains instructive precisely because it tried every solution and found each wanting. The revolutionaries who executed a king discovered that revolution did not bring the kingdom of God. The restorationists who brought back the king discovered that restoration did not heal the wounds. The settlement makers who crafted 1689's compromise discovered that compromise satisfied no one entirely. Yet somehow, through failure and adjustment, a workable arrangement emerged—not because any faction was wholly right, but because all were partially right and partially wrong, and only their mutual exhaustion created space for coexistence.

That may be the deepest wisdom the English Revolution offers: not a model to follow but a warning against presumption. The kingdom not of this world cannot be built by worldly means. But neither can Christians withdraw from worldly responsibilities. We are citizens of two cities, subjects of two kingdoms, owing allegiance to authorities that sometimes conflict. The struggle to live faithfully in that tension, without surrendering to either Caesaropapism or sectarian withdrawal, continues wherever Christians engage political life.

ENDNOTES

Notes — Introduction

1. The most detailed contemporary account of Charles I's attempt to arrest the Five Members on 4 January 1642 is John Rushworth, *Historical Collections of Private Passages of State*, 8 vols. (London, 1659–1701), 4:477–82. Rushworth was present as clerk to the Commons and recorded events immediately. See also *Journals of the House of Commons* [hereafter *CJ*], vol. 2 (1640–1643), 361–63 (4 January 1642); and Bulstrode Whitelocke, *Memorials of the English Affairs*, 4 vols. (Oxford: Oxford University Press, 1853), 1:147–49. Modern accounts drawing on these sources include C. V. Wedgwood, *The King's War, 1641–1647* (London: Collins, 1958), 61–65; Conrad Russell, *The Fall of the British Monarchies, 1637–1642* (Oxford: Clarendon Press, 1991), 451–54; and David Cressy, *England on Edge: Crisis and Revolution 1640–1642* (Oxford: Oxford University Press, 2006), 363–71.
2. On the five accused members and the charges against them, see *CJ* 2:350 (3 January 1642), which lists the accusations: John Pym (1584–1643), John Hampden (1594–1643), Denzil Holles (1599–1680), Sir Arthur Haselrig (1601–1661), and William Strode (1598–1645) were charged with high treason for conspiring with foreign powers (specifically the Scots) and for "levying war against the King." On their political activities leading to this crisis, see Russell, *Fall of the British Monarchies*, 447–50; and for biographical details, Conrad Russell, "Pym, John (1584–1643)," *Oxford Dictionary of National Biography* [hereafter *ODNB*], online ed., https://doi.org/10.1093/ref:odnb/22942; Conrad Russell, "Hampden, John (1594–1643)," *ODNB*, https://doi.org/10.1093/ref:odnb/12142.
3. On the unprecedented nature of a reigning monarch entering the Commons chamber and the constitutional significance, see Glenn Burgess, *Absolute Monarchy and the Stuart Constitution* (New Haven: Yale University Press, 1996), 197–201. The Commons met in St. Stephen's Chapel in the Palace of Westminster; a space understood as privileged ground where members could deliberate freely. On the physical setting, see M. H. Port, ed., *The Houses of Parliament* (New Haven: Yale University Press, 1976), 1–15.
4. Rushworth, *Historical Collections*, 4:478, records Charles's words. Multiple sources preserve substantially the same speech with minor variations. See also Edward Hyde, Earl of Clarendon, *The History of the Rebellion and Civil Wars in England*, ed. W. Dunn Macray, 6 vols. (Oxford: Clarendon Press, 1888; originally written 1646–1671), 1:490–92.
5. On the warning that allowed the Five Members to escape, the sources are unclear about who specifically alerted them, leading to contemporary speculation about the Queen's involvement, a sympathetic peer, or other sources. See Rushworth, *Historical Collections*, 4:479; Wedgwood, *King's War*, 62; and Russell, *Fall of the British Monarchies*, 452. Their flight to the City of London, where they found protection from the Lord Mayor and Common Council, is described in Valerie Pearl, *London and the Outbreak of the Puritan Revolution: City Government and National Politics, 1625–43* (Oxford: Oxford University Press, 1961), 235–42.
6. Rushworth, *Historical Collections*, 4:478: "I see all my birds have flown." The phrase became one of the most quoted of the Civil War era. Clarendon, *History of the Rebellion*, 1:492, notes that the King appeared "much disappointed" and left "in some disorder."
7. William Lenthall's famous response is recorded in Rushworth, *Historical Collections*, 4:478: "May it please your Majesty, I have neither eyes to see nor tongue to speak in this place but as the House is pleased to direct me, whose servant I am here; and I humbly beg your Majesty's pardon that I cannot give any other answer than this to what your Majesty is pleased to demand of me." On Lenthall's career and this pivotal moment, see J. S. A. Adamson, "The Baronial Context of the English Civil War," *Transactions of the Royal Historical Society*, 5th ser., 40 (1990): 110–12. Lenthall (1591–1662) served as Speaker of the Long Parliament 1640–1653 and again 1654–1655, 1659–1660.

8. On the crowd's reaction and the cry of "Privilege!", see Rushworth, *Historical Collections*, 4:478–79; and *The Diurnall Occurrences in Parliament*, 4–11 January 1642. The claim of parliamentary privilege—that members were immune from arrest during sessions—was a fundamental constitutional principle. On the theoretical foundations of privilege, see J. E. Neale, "The Commons' Privilege of Free Speech in Parliament," in *Tudor Studies Presented to A. F. Pollard*, ed. R. W. Seton-Watson (London: Longmans, 1924), 257–86.
9. The triumphant return of the Five Members to Westminster on 11 January 1642, escorted by thousands of armed Londoners and the trained bands, is described in Rushworth, *Historical Collections*, 4:483–85; and contemporary newsbook *The Diurnall Occurrences*, 11 January 1642. On the alliance between Parliament and the City and its strategic importance, see Pearl, *London and the Outbreak of the Puritan Revolution*, 243–56; and Robert Brenner, *Merchants and Revolution: Commercial Change, Political Conflict, and London's Overseas Traders, 1550–1653* (Princeton: Princeton University Press, 1993), 371–98.
10. The Militia Ordinance (5 March 1642) claimed parliamentary authority to appoint military commanders without royal consent—a revolutionary constitutional claim. Text in Samuel Rawson Gardiner, ed., *The Constitutional Documents of the Puritan Revolution, 1625–1660*, 3rd ed. (Oxford: Clarendon Press, 1906), 245–47. On the constitutional crisis this represented, see Corinne Comstock Weston and Janelle Renfrow Greenberg, *Subjects and Sovereigns: The Grand Controversy over Legal Sovereignty in Stuart England* (Cambridge: Cambridge University Press, 1981), 38–62. Sir John Hotham's refusal to admit Charles to Hull (23 April 1642) is detailed in Wedgwood, *King's War*, 69–70; and Russell, *Fall of the British Monarchies*, 490–95.
11. Charles raised his standard at Nottingham on 22 August 1642, the formal declaration of war. On the inauspicious circumstances—the standard blowing down in a storm the first night—see Clarendon, *History of the Rebellion*, 2:327; Wedgwood, *King's War*, 83–87; and Ronald Hutton, *The Royalist War Effort, 1642–1646*, 2nd ed. (London: Routledge, 2003), 8–12. Contemporary observers debated whether this was divine omen or mere meteorology.
12. On Charles I's theory of divine right monarchy and his conviction that resistance to royal authority was sacrilege, see Johann P. Sommerville, *Royalists and Patriots: Politics and Ideology in England, 1603–1640*, 2nd ed. (London: Longman, 1999), 9–87; and Glenn Burgess, *Absolute Monarchy and the Stuart Constitution*, 78–111. Charles's statement is a paraphrase of sentiments expressed in his declarations and correspondence. See *His Majesties Answer to the Nineteen Propositions* (June 1642), in Gardiner, *Constitutional Documents*, 249–54.
13. Parliament's position—that they fought not against the King's person but against his evil counselors—was articulated in numerous declarations. See *The Declaration of the Lords and Commons Assembled in Parliament* (19 May 1642), in Gardiner, *Constitutional Documents*, 254–57. On the constitutional theory that Parliament represented the realm and could resist tyranny while claiming loyalty to the Crown, see David L. Smith, *Constitutional Royalism and the Search for Settlement, c. 1640–1649* (Cambridge: Cambridge University Press, 1994), 34–61; and Michael Mendle, *Dangerous Positions: Mixed Government, the Estates of the Realm, and the Making of the Answer to the XIX Propositions* (University: University of Alabama Press, 1985).
14. On the multiple, overlapping conflicts—religious, constitutional, social—that converged in the 1640s, see John Morrill, *The Nature of the English Revolution* (London: Longman, 1993), 1–32; Ann Hughes, *The Causes of the English Civil War*, 2nd ed. (Basingstoke: Macmillan, 1998), 1–20; and Lawrence Stone, *The Causes of the English Revolution, 1529–1642* (London: Routledge & Kegan Paul, 1972), 47–145. The argument that these were not separate conflicts but interrelated aspects of a single crisis informs the structure of this book.
15. The characterization of these four religious visions draws on extensive primary and

secondary sources detailed in the Bibliography. For Presbyterianism, see Robert S. Paul, *The Assembly of the Lord: Politics and Religion in the Westminster Assembly and the 'Grand Debate'* (Edinburgh: T&T Clark, 1985); for Independency, Geoffrey F. Nuttall, *Visible Saints: The Congregational Way, 1640–1660* (Oxford: Basil Blackwell, 1957); for Anglicanism, Peter Lake, *Anglicans and Puritans? Presbyterianism and English Conformist Thought from Whitgift to Hooker* (London: Unwin Hyman, 1988); for Quakerism, William C. Braithwaite, *The Beginnings of Quakerism*, 2nd ed., rev. Henry J. Cadbury (Cambridge: Cambridge University Press, 1955); and Rosemary Moore, *The Light in Their Consciences: Early Quakers in Britain, 1646–1666* (University Park: Pennsylvania State University Press, 2000). Each vision is examined in detail in Chapters 3–6.

16. My argument that religion was primary rather than epiphenomenal follows John Morrill, "The Religious Context of the English Civil War," *Transactions of the Royal Historical Society*, 5th ser., 34 (1984): 155–78, esp. 155: "The English civil war was not the first European revolution: it was the last of the Wars of Religion." See also Morrill, *Nature of the English Revolution*, 33–68; Anthony Milton, *Catholic and Reformed: The Roman and Protestant Churches in English Protestant Thought, 1600–1640* (Cambridge: Cambridge University Press, 1995), 1–15; and the historiographical discussions in Glenn Burgess, ed., *The New British History: Founding a Modern State, 1603–1715* (London: I. B. Tauris, 1999), 1–18. This position contrasts with earlier Marxist interpretations that treated religion as ideological cover for class conflict (Christopher Hill, *The English Revolution 1640*, 3rd ed. [London: Lawrence & Wishart, 1955]) and with purely political or constitutional interpretations that downplay religious motivations. Post-revisionist scholarship has increasingly taken religious convictions seriously as autonomous motivations while acknowledging their interaction with political, social, and economic factors.
17. On casualty estimates for the Civil Wars, see Charles Carlton, *Going to the Wars: The Experience of the British Civil Wars, 1638–1651* (London: Routledge, 1992), 211–15, who estimates 180,000–200,000 deaths in England and Wales alone (approximately 3.6% of the population); and Ian Gentles, *The English Revolution and the Wars in the Three Kingdoms, 1638–1652* (Harlow: Pearson, 2007), 437–41. For Ireland, proportional losses were much higher, with estimates ranging from 15-20% of the population. See William Petty, *The Political Anatomy of Ireland* (1672; repr., Shannon: Irish University Press, 1970); and recent analysis in Pádraig Lenihan, *Confederate Catholics at War, 1641–49* (Cork: Cork University Press, 2001).
18. On families divided by the Civil War, the Verney family papers provide the most famous example. Sir Edmund Verney, the King's standard-bearer, died at Edgehill fighting for Charles; his son Ralph sided with Parliament. Their correspondence, preserved in Frances Parthenope Verney, ed., *Memoirs of the Verney Family During the Civil War*, 4 vols. (London: Longmans, Green, 1892–1899), shows the anguish of choosing between family loyalty and political conviction. See also Barbara Donagan, "The Web of Honour: Soldiers, Christians, and Gentlemen in the English Civil War," *Historical Journal* 44, no. 2 (2001): 365–89.
19. On the emergence of principles of religious liberty, limited government, and denominational pluralism from the period's conflicts, see John Coffey, *Persecution and Toleration in Protestant England, 1558–1689* (Harlow: Longman, 2000); Alexandra Walsham, *Charitable Hatred: Tolerance and Intolerance in England, 1500–1700* (Manchester: Manchester University Press, 2006); W. K. Jordan, *The Development of Religious Toleration in England*, 4 vols. (Cambridge, MA: Harvard University Press, 1932–1940); and Russell E. Richey, "Denominations and Denominationalism: An American Morphology," in *Reimagining Denominationalism: Interpretive Essays*, ed. Robert Bruce Mullin and Russell E. Richey (New York: Oxford University Press, 1994), 74–98. The Toleration Act of 1689 and its significance are examined in Chapter 7.
20. On the fragility of these achievements and the need for their constant defense, see the discussion in the Preface and Conclusion. The book's argument throughout is that

religious liberty emerged not from enlightened principle but from exhausted pragmatism after attempts at uniformity failed—a thesis explored in Walsham, *Charitable Hatred*, 3–45; and Coffey, *Persecution and Toleration*, 156–98.

Notes — Chapter 1

1. The most detailed contemporary account of the Hampton Court Conference is William Barlow, *The Summe and Substance of the Conference* (London, 1604). Modern scholarly treatments include Patrick Collinson, "The Jacobean Religious Settlement: The Hampton Court Conference," in *Before the English Civil War*, ed. Howard Tomlinson (London: Macmillan, 1983), 27–51; Frederick Shriver, "Hampton Court Re-Visited: James I and the Puritans," *Journal of Ecclesiastical History* 33, no. 1 (1982): 48–71; and Kenneth Fincham and Peter Lake, "The Ecclesiastical Policy of King James I," *Journal of British Studies* 24, no. 2 (1985): 169–207.
2. On John Rainolds (or Reynolds, 1549–1607) and his role at Hampton Court, see Mordechai Feingold, "John Rainolds," *Oxford Dictionary of National Biography* [hereafter *ODNB*], online ed., https://doi.org/10.1093/ref:odnb/23065. Rainolds was president of Corpus Christi College, Oxford, from 1598 and one of the most learned biblical scholars of his generation. His moderate position—seeking reform within the established church—was typical of mainstream Puritanism.
3. On the visual symbolism of clerical dress at the conference, see Patrick Collinson, *The Elizabethan Puritan Movement* (London: Jonathan Cape, 1967), 455–60; and Barlow, *Summe and Substance*, 12–15. The contrast between episcopal vestments and Puritan plain dress represented competing visions of ministry and authority.
4. On James VI/I (1566–1625), his Scottish experience, and his political theology, see Maurice Lee Jr., *Great Britain's Solomon: James VI and I in His Three Kingdoms* (Urbana: University of Illinois Press, 1990), 3–106; and Jenny Wormald, "James VI and I (1566–1625)," *ODNB*, https://doi.org/10.1093/ref:odnb/14592. James's traumatic childhood—crowned at thirteen months, educated by harsh tutors, kidnapped by competing noble factions—shaped his authoritarian convictions.
5. James's declaration of religious uniformity is recorded in Barlow, *Summe and Substance*, 23–26. The phrase about making conformists "or harrying them out of the land" became infamous among Puritans. See also *The Works of the Most High and Mighty Prince James*, ed. James Montagu (London, 1616), 491–93.
6. Rainolds's presentation of Puritan grievances is detailed in Barlow, *Summe and Substance*, 30–45. The four-part organization (church government, liturgy, discipline, Bible translation) represented careful preparation and moderate framing designed to appeal to the King's learning rather than provoke his anger.
7. On the concept of adiaphora (things indifferent) and its role in Puritan-conformist debates, see B. J. Verkamp, *The Indifferent Mean: Adiaphorism in the English Reformation to 1554* (Athens: Ohio University Press, 1977). Puritans argued that scriptural silence should be taken as prohibition; conformists argued it left room for church discretion in ceremonies.
8. James's famous outburst "No bishop, no king!" is recorded in Barlow, *Summe and Substance*, 45. The phrase encapsulated James's conviction that episcopal and monarchical authority were interdependent. On James's equation of presbyterian church government with political sedition, see Johann P. Sommerville, *Royalists and Patriots: Politics and Ideology in England, 1603–1640*, 2nd ed. (London: Longman, 1999), 79–87.
9. Barlow, *Summe and Substance*, 45–47. On Richard Bancroft (1544–1610), who became Archbishop of Canterbury in 1604, see Kenneth Fincham, "Richard Bancroft," *ODNB*, https://doi.org/10.1093/ref:odnb/1282. Bancroft was a determined opponent of Puritanism and used his position to enforce conformity rigorously.
10. On James's Scottish experience with presbyterian resistance to royal authority, see Lee, *Great Britain's Solomon*, 28–79. Andrew Melville's confrontation with James, calling him "God's sillie vassal," occurred in 1596 and left a lasting impression on the King's view

of presbyterian clergy. See James Kirk, "'The Polities of the Best Reformed Kirks': Scottish Achievements and English Aspirations in Church Government after the Reformation," *Scottish Historical Review* 59, no. 1 (1980): 22–53.

11. On the Bible translation proposal and the existing translations, see David Norton, *A Textual History of the King James Bible* (Cambridge: Cambridge University Press, 2005), 1–38. The Geneva Bible (1560) had been the preferred English translation but included marginal notes with republican and presbyterian interpretations that troubled monarchs. The Bishops' Bible (1568) was officially authorized but literarily inferior.
12. On the production of the King James Bible (published 1611), see Adam Nicolson, *Power and Glory: Jacobean England and the Making of the King James Bible* (London: HarperCollins, 2003); and Norton, *Textual History*, 39–120. The translation was produced by six committees of about fifty scholars total, working from 1604 to 1611. James's instruction to avoid marginal notes with doctrinal or political interpretations was carefully followed.
13. Barlow, *Summe and Substance*, 78–82, on the conference's conclusion and James's insistence on conformity.
14. The canons of 1604 are printed in Gerald Bray, ed., *The Anglican Canons, 1529–1947* (Woodbridge: Boydell Press, 1998), 269–351. Canon 36 required ministers to use all prayer book ceremonies; Canon 58 required subscription to royal supremacy, the Book of Common Prayer's lawfulness, and the Thirty-Nine Articles.
15. On the ministers deprived for nonconformity after Hampton Court, see Collinson, *Elizabethan Puritan Movement*, 460–67. Estimates of those ejected range from about sixty to over three hundred, depending on whether one counts only those formally deprived or includes those who resigned under pressure. The consensus figure is approximately ninety, representing about 1% of England's roughly nine thousand beneficed clergy.
16. On the long-term consequences of Hampton Court, see Collinson, "Jacobean Religious Settlement," 48–51; and Kenneth Fincham, *Prelate as Pastor: The Episcopate of James I* (Oxford: Clarendon Press, 1990), 112–45. James's equation of episcopacy with monarchy and his intransigence toward moderate reform set patterns that continued through Charles I's reign.
17. Historiographical debates over Hampton Court's significance include Collinson's view that it was a missed opportunity for accommodation versus revisionists like Fincham who argue that the conference achieved what James wanted—demonstrating royal control while granting modest concessions (the Bible translation). See the discussions in Kenneth Fincham, ed., *The Early Stuart Church, 1603–1642* (Stanford: Stanford University Press, 1993).
18. On the fundamental incompatibility between royal claims to control the church and Puritan claims that Scripture alone determined church government, see Peter Lake, "Presbyterianism, the Idea of a National Church and the Argument from Divine Right," in *Protestantism and the National Church in Sixteenth Century England*, ed. Peter Lake and Maria Dowling (London: Croom Helm, 1987), 193–224.
19. On Puritan responses to the settlement—withdrawal into conventicles, emigration, or conformity while hoping for future reform—see Michael R. Watts, *The Dissenters*, vol. 1, *From the Reformation to the French Revolution* (Oxford: Clarendon Press, 1978), 43–68; and Virginia DeJohn Anderson, *New England's Generation: The Great Migration and the Formation of Society and Culture in the Seventeenth Century* (Cambridge: Cambridge University Press, 1991), on emigration to New England.
20. On Henry VIII's break with Rome, the Acts of Supremacy (1534), and the Henrician Reformation, see G. W. Bernard, *The King's Reformation: Henry VIII and the Remaking of the English Church* (New Haven: Yale University Press, 2005); and Diarmaid MacCulloch, *Thomas Cranmer: A Life* (New Haven: Yale University Press, 1996), 125–84. The Act of Supremacy (26 Henry VIII c. 1) is printed in Gerald Bray, ed., *Documents of the English Reformation* (Minneapolis: Fortress Press, 1994), 113–14.
21. On the dissolution of the monasteries (1536–1540) and its social and economic

consequences, see David Knowles, *The Religious Orders in England*, vol. 3, *The Tudor Age* (Cambridge: Cambridge University Press, 1959); and Joyce Youings, *The Dissolution of the Monasteries* (London: George Allen & Unwin, 1971). About 800 religious houses were dissolved, affecting approximately 10,000 monks, nuns, and friars. The transfer of monastic lands created a class with vested interest in preventing Catholic restoration.

22. On the Edwardian Reformation and the Book of Common Prayer (1549, revised 1552), see MacCulloch, *Thomas Cranmer*, 360–506; and Diarmaid MacCulloch, *The Boy King: Edward VI and the Protestant Reformation* (New York: Palgrave, 1999). Thomas Cranmer's prayer book was a literary and theological masterpiece that shaped English Protestant worship. Modern edition: *The Book of Common Prayer: The Texts of 1549, 1559, and 1662*, ed. Brian Cummings (Oxford: Oxford University Press, 2011).
23. On the Western Rebellion (also called the Prayer Book Rebellion, 1549), see Frances Rose-Troup, *The Western Rebellion of 1549* (London: Smith, Elder & Co., 1913); and Andy Wood, *The 1549 Rebellions and the Making of Early Modern England* (Cambridge: Cambridge University Press, 2007). The rebellion's demands, including restoration of the Latin Mass and rejection of the English prayer book, showed strong attachment to traditional Catholic practice in the West Country.
24. On Mary I's reign (1553–1558) and the Marian persecutions, see Eamon Duffy, *Fires of Faith: Catholic England Under Mary Tudor* (New Haven: Yale University Press, 2009); and David Loades, *Mary Tudor: A Life* (Oxford: Blackwell, 1989). About 280 Protestants were burned for heresy between 1555 and Mary's death in 1558—the most intense religious persecution in English history.
25. John Foxe, *Acts and Monuments* (London, 1563; multiple later editions), commonly called "Foxe's Book of Martyrs," shaped English Protestant identity for generations. Modern edition: *The Acts and Monuments of John Foxe*, ed. George Townsend, 8 vols. (London: R. B. Seeley and W. Burnside, 1843–1849); online edition at https://www.johnfoxe.org. On Thomas Cranmer's martyrdom (21 March 1556) and his dramatic recantation of his recantations, see MacCulloch, *Thomas Cranmer*, 599–605.
26. On Elizabeth I's religious inheritance and the religious divisions in England at her accession in 1558, see Christopher Haigh, *English Reformations: Religion, Politics, and Society Under the Tudors* (Oxford: Clarendon Press, 1993), 237–62; and Wallace MacCaffrey, *The Shaping of the Elizabethan Regime* (Princeton: Princeton University Press, 1968), 45–106.
27. Elizabeth's reported statement about not making "windows into men's souls" is not documented in contemporary sources but reflects the pragmatic approach attributed to her by later commentators. See Susan Doran, "Elizabeth I's Religion: The Evidence of Her Letters," *Journal of Ecclesiastical History* 51, no. 4 (2000): 699–720, on the difficulty of determining Elizabeth's personal religious convictions.
28. On the Elizabethan Settlement as via media, see W. P. Haugaard, *Elizabeth and the English Reformation* (Cambridge: Cambridge University Press, 1968); and Patrick Collinson, "The Elizabethan Church and the New Religion," in *The Reign of Elizabeth I*, ed. Christopher Haigh (Athens: University of Georgia Press, 1985), 169–94. The settlement attempted comprehension of all but the most extreme, though historians debate whether this was Elizabeth's intention or merely an outcome of political compromise.
29. The Act of Supremacy (1 Elizabeth c. 1, 1559) is printed in Bray, *Documents of the English Reformation*, 318–20. Elizabeth chose "Supreme Governor" rather than "Supreme Head" of the church, a distinction that acknowledged Christ's spiritual headship while asserting royal authority over ecclesiastical governance.
30. The Act of Uniformity (1 Elizabeth c. 2, 1559) and the 1559 Book of Common Prayer are printed in Bray, *Documents*, 320–23; and Cummings, ed., *Book of Common Prayer*. The prayer book's communion service was deliberately ambiguous, capable of being interpreted as either affirming Christ's real presence (satisfying traditional Catholics) or spiritual presence only (satisfying Protestants). On this ambiguity as policy, see

MacCulloch, *Thomas Cranmer*, 625–28.

31. The Thirty-Nine Articles (1563, revised 1571) are printed in Bray, *Documents*, 284–311. On their theological character—Protestant but not rigidly Calvinist, definite on some points but deliberately vague on others—see Oliver O'Donovan, *On the Thirty-Nine Articles: A Conversation with Tudor Christianity* (London: SCM Press, 1986).
32. On Elizabethan episcopacy and its controversial status, see Kenneth Carleton, *Bishops and Reform in the English Church, 1520–1559* (Woodbridge: Boydell Press, 2001); and Patrick Collinson, *The Religion of Protestants: The Church in English Society, 1559–1625* (Oxford: Clarendon Press, 1982), 1–45. Continental Reformed churches (Geneva, Scotland, the Dutch Reformed Church) rejected bishops as unscriptural; Elizabeth retained them primarily for reasons of governance and control.
33. On the Vestiarian Controversy (1565–1566) and Archbishop Matthew Parker's enforcement of clerical dress requirements through the "Advertisements" (1566), see Collinson, *Elizabethan Puritan Movement*, 71–83. About forty London ministers were suspended for refusing to wear the surplice. The controversy demonstrated that ceremonial conformity would be enforced even when ministers were otherwise orthodox and effective.
34. On the practical flexibility of enforcement under Elizabeth, see Judith Maltby, *Prayer Book and People in Elizabethan and Early Stuart England* (Cambridge: Cambridge University Press, 1998); and Fincham, *Prelate as Pastor*, on variations in episcopal enforcement styles. Local circumstances—the preferences of bishops, patrons, and gentry—created diverse religious cultures within the formal structure of uniformity.
35. On the meaning and range of "Puritanism," see Collinson, *Elizabethan Puritan Movement*, 11–28; and Peter Lake, "Defining Puritanism—Again?" in *Puritanism: Transatlantic Perspectives on a Seventeenth-Century Anglo-American Faith*, ed. Francis J. Bremer (Boston: Massachusetts Historical Society, 1993), 3–29. The term was used pejoratively by opponents but covered a spectrum from moderate conformists seeking better preaching to separatists rejecting the national church entirely.
36. On Puritan values and emphases, see Collinson, *Religion of Protestants*, 189–241; and Christopher Hill, *Society and Puritanism in Pre-Revolutionary England* (London: Secker & Warburg, 1964). Puritans valued preaching, biblical authority, godly discipline, strict Sabbath observance, and plain worship, though they disagreed on how far reformation should go and what methods should be used.
37. On the presbyterian movement within Elizabethan Puritanism, see Collinson, *Elizabethan Puritan Movement*, 221–316. The attraction of presbyterian government—as practiced in Scotland, Geneva, and the Dutch Reformed Church—was both theological (it seemed more biblical than episcopacy) and practical (it distributed authority more widely than episcopal hierarchy).
38. On Thomas Cartwright (c. 1535–1603) and his presbyterian lectures at Cambridge (1570), see A. F. Scott Pearson, *Thomas Cartwright and Elizabethan Puritanism, 1535–1603* (Cambridge: Cambridge University Press, 1925); and Patrick Collinson, "Thomas Cartwright," *ODNB*, https://doi.org/10.1093/ref:odnb/4820. Walter Travers, *A Full and Plaine Declaration of Ecclesiastical Discipline* (Heidelberg, 1574; English translation 1580), argued for jure divino presbyterianism—that presbyterian government was commanded by Scripture, not merely preferable. The *Admonition to Parliament* (1572) by John Field and Thomas Wilcox called for abolishing bishops and establishing presbyteries.
39. On John Whitgift (c. 1530–1604), Archbishop of Canterbury from 1583, and his enforcement campaign against Puritans, see V. J. K. Brook, *Whitgift and the English Church* (London: English Universities Press, 1957); and Patrick Collinson, "John Whitgift," *ODNB*, https://doi.org/10.1093/ref:odnb/29312. Whitgift's Three Articles (1583) required subscription to royal supremacy, the prayer book's conformity to Scripture, and the Thirty-Nine Articles. The Court of High Commission's powers included imprisonment and fine without jury trial, raising common law objections.

40. On the classical movement and its failure, see Collinson, *Elizabethan Puritan Movement*, 317–431. John Field (1545–1588) organized unofficial presbyterian "classes" (meetings of ministers) in about twenty English counties, but the movement attracted only about 400 of England's approximately 9,000 ministers and collapsed after Field's death in 1588 and the arrest of key leaders in 1589–1590.
41. On James VI/I's experience with the Scottish Kirk and Presbyterian ministers, see Lee, *Great Britain's Solomon*, 28–79; and Jenny Wormald, "James VI and I, Basilikon Doron and The Trew Law of Free Monarchies: The Scottish Context and the English Translation," in *The Mental World of the Jacobean Court*, ed. Linda Levy Peck (Cambridge: Cambridge University Press, 1991), 36–54. Andrew Melville's confrontation with James (1596) is detailed in James Kirk, "The Politics of the Best Reformed Kirks," 45–48.
42. James's statement that "a Scottish presbytery agreeth as well with monarchy as God with the Devil" at Hampton Court is recorded in Barlow, *Summe and Substance*, 45. On James's gradual reintroduction of bishops to Scotland (completed by 1610), see Alan R. MacDonald, *The Jacobean Kirk, 1567–1625: Sovereignty, Polity and Liturgy* (Aldershot: Ashgate, 1998).
43. On James's Calvinist theology despite his support for bishops, see W. B. Patterson, *King James VI and I and the Reunion of Christendom* (Cambridge: Cambridge University Press, 1997), 43–86. James's theological works include *Daemonologie* (1597), *Basilikon Doron* (1599), and *Apologie for the Oath of Allegiance* (1607), all reprinted in *King James VI and I: Political Writings*, ed. Johann P. Sommerville (Cambridge: Cambridge University Press, 1994).
44. The Millenary Petition (1603) is printed in Bray, *Documents*, 423–27. The number of signatories is disputed—the title claimed about a thousand, but historians estimate the actual number was several hundred. On the petition's moderate tone, see Collinson, "Jacobean Religious Settlement," 29–33.
45. The petition's assurance that signers were "neither factious men affecting a popular parity in the Church, nor schismatics" is from the text in Bray, *Documents*, 424. The language carefully distanced the petitioners from presbyterian radicalism while requesting ceremonial relief.
46. On George Abbot (1562–1633), Archbishop of Canterbury 1611–1633, see Kenneth Fincham, "George Abbot," *ODNB*, https://doi.org/10.1093/ref:odnb/19. On Lancelot Andrewes (1555–1626), Bishop of Winchester from 1619, see Nicholas Lossky, *Lancelot Andrewes the Preacher (1555–1626): The Origins of the Mystical Theology of the Church of England*, trans. Andrew Louth (Oxford: Clarendon Press, 1991). Andrewes's sermons are collected in *Ninety-Six Sermons*, 5 vols. (Oxford: John Henry Parker, 1841–1843).
47. On James's *Book of Sports* (1618), which permitted Sunday recreations after church services, see Kenneth L. Parker, *The English Sabbath: A Study of Doctrine and Discipline from the Reformation to the Civil War* (Cambridge: Cambridge University Press, 1988), 146–73. The Book directly challenged Puritan Sabbatarianism and was reissued by Charles I in 1633 with orders that all clergy read it from their pulpits.
48. On James's financial problems and the structural insolvency of the early Stuart monarchy, see Robert Ashton, *The Crown and the Money Market, 1603–1640* (Oxford: Clarendon Press, 1960); and Frederick C. Dietz, *English Public Finance, 1558–1641* (New York: Century Co., 1932). Henry VIII and Elizabeth I had sold crown lands to fund wars, reducing the monarchy's independent revenue. Inflation eroded fixed revenues, and the costs of government (larger bureaucracy, ambassadors, military) rose steadily.
49. On James's theory of royal prerogative, see his *The Trew Law of Free Monarchies* (1598) and *Basilikon Doron* (1599), both in Sommerville, ed., *Political Writings*. James distinguished between the King's "absolute" prerogative (inherent powers like conducting foreign policy) and matters where law bound the King. But the boundary was contested, especially regarding taxation.

50. On Parliament's claims to control taxation and to speak freely on matters affecting the realm, see J. E. Neale, "The Commons' Privilege of Free Speech in Parliament," in *Tudor Studies Presented to A. F. Pollard*, ed. R. W. Seton-Watson (London: Longmans, 1924), 257–86; and Conrad Russell, *Parliaments and English Politics, 1621–1629* (Oxford: Clarendon Press, 1979), 1–84.
51. On the Great Contract negotiations (1610) and their failure, see Russell, *Parliaments and English Politics*, 46–84; and Roger Lockyer, *The Early Stuarts: A Political History of England, 1603–1642*, 2nd ed. (London: Longman, 1999), 89–96. The Contract proposed that Parliament grant James £200,000 annually in exchange for his surrendering feudal rights (wardship, purveyance). Neither side could agree on valuation or on the relationship between crown and Parliament that the Contract implied.
52. On the Addled Parliament (April-June 1614), so-called because it passed no legislation, see Thomas L. Moir, *The Addled Parliament of 1614* (Oxford: Clarendon Press, 1958). James dissolved it after two months without receiving any taxation, then ruled without Parliament until 1621.
53. On the 1621 Parliament and the impeachment of Francis Bacon (1561–1626), see Nieves Mathews, *Francis Bacon: The History of a Character Assassination* (New Haven: Yale University Press, 1996); and Lisa Jardine and Alan Stewart, *Hostage to Fortune: The Troubled Life of Francis Bacon* (London: Victor Gollancz, 1998). Bacon was charged with accepting bribes as Lord Chancellor; he pleaded guilty and was fined and briefly imprisoned.
54. The Protestation of the Commons (18 December 1621) is printed in Samuel Rawson Gardiner, ed., *The Constitutional Documents of the Puritan Revolution, 1625–1660*, 3rd ed. (Oxford: Clarendon Press, 1906), 1–2. James's tearing of the Protestation from the Commons Journal is described in *Journals of the House of Commons* [hereafter *CJ*] 1:659 (30 December 1621). On this constitutional confrontation, see Conrad Russell, "Parliamentary History in Perspective, 1604–1629," *History* 61, no. 201 (1976): 1–27.
55. On the Spanish Match negotiations (1618–1623) and Prince Charles and Buckingham's journey to Madrid (1623), see Glyn Redworth, *The Prince and the Infanta: The Cultural Politics of the Spanish Match* (New Haven: Yale University Press, 2003); and Thomas Cogswell, *The Blessed Revolution: English Politics and the Coming of War, 1621–1624* (Cambridge: Cambridge University Press, 1989).
56. On English Protestant opposition to the Spanish Match, see Caroline M. Hibbard, "Early Stuart Catholicism: Revisions and Re-Revisions," *Journal of Modern History* 52, no. 1 (1980): 1–34; and Anthony Milton, *Catholic and Reformed: The Roman and Protestant Churches in English Protestant Thought, 1600–1640* (Cambridge: Cambridge University Press, 1995), 128–84.
57. On the failure of the Madrid mission and the popular celebrations upon Charles and Buckingham's return (October 1623), see Redworth, *Prince and the Infanta*, 140–60. Contemporary reports describe bonfires throughout England and bell-ringing in virtually every parish church.
58. On the 1624 Parliament and its war vote, see Cogswell, *Blessed Revolution*, 218–89; and Russell, *Parliaments and English Politics*, 127–208. Parliament voted subsidies for war against Spain but disagreed with James about strategy—Parliament favored aggressive naval war against Spanish treasure fleets; James wanted defensive aid to the Palatinate.
59. The impeachment of Lionel Cranfield, Earl of Middlesex (1575–1645), in 1624 is detailed in Menna Prestwich, *Cranfield: Politics and Profits under the Early Stuarts* (Oxford: Clarendon Press, 1966). James's warning—"You are fools! You are making a rod with which you will be scourged yourselves!"—is recorded in John Rushworth, *Historical Collections of Private Passages of State*, 8 vols. (London, 1659–1701), 1:100.
60. On anti-Catholic legislation and paranoia in the 1624 Parliament, see Caroline Hibbard, *Charles I and the Popish Plot* (Chapel Hill: University of North Carolina Press, 1983), 10–42.
61. James I died on 27 March 1625. On his final years and the problems he bequeathed to

Charles, see Lockyer, *Early Stuarts*, 110–26.

62. On Jacobus Arminius (1560–1609) and Arminian theology, see Carl Bangs, *Arminius: A Study in the Dutch Reformation* (Nashville: Abingdon Press, 1971); and William den Boer, *God's Twofold Love: The Theology of Jacob Arminius (1559–1609)* (Göttingen: Vandenhoeck & Ruprecht, 2010). Arminius questioned Calvinist doctrines of unconditional election and irresistible grace, arguing for conditional election (based on foreseen faith) and resistible grace (which humans could reject).
63. On the Synod of Dort (1618–1619) and its condemnation of Arminianism, see Donald Sinnema, Christian Moser, and Herman J. Selderhuis, eds., *Acta et Documenta Synodi Nationalis Dordrechtanae (1618–1619)*, 5 vols. (Göttingen: Vandenhoeck & Ruprecht, 2014–2021); and Anthony Milton, ed., *The British Delegation and the Synod of Dort (1618–1619)* (Woodbridge: Boydell Press, 2005). The Synod affirmed five-point Calvinism against Arminian positions.
64. On the English meaning of "Arminian" as extending beyond predestination theology to ceremonialism and high churchmanship, see Nicholas Tyacke, *Anti-Calvinists: The Rise of English Arminianism, c. 1590–1640* (Oxford: Clarendon Press, 1987); and Peter White, *Predestination, Policy and Polemic: Conflict and Consensus in the English Church from the Reformation to the Civil War* (Cambridge: Cambridge University Press, 1992). Tyacke argues that Arminianism represented innovation; White argues it represented continuity with Elizabethan diversity.
65. On Puritan fears that Arminianism was undoing the Reformation, see Peter Lake, "Calvinism and the English Church, 1570–1635," *Past & Present* 114 (1987): 32–76; and Anthony Milton, *Catholic and Reformed*, 50–84.
66. On William Laud (1573–1645), see Hugh Trevor-Roper, *Archbishop Laud, 1573–1645*, 2nd ed. (London: Macmillan, 1962); and Charles Carlton, *Archbishop William Laud* (London: Routledge & Kegan Paul, 1987). Laud rose from modest origins through ability, patronage (especially by Buckingham), and determination.
67. On Laud's concept of "the beauty of holiness" and his reform program, see Kenneth Fincham and Nicholas Tyacke, *Altars Restored: The Changing Face of English Religious Worship, 1547–c.1700* (Oxford: Oxford University Press, 2007); and Peter Lake, "The Laudian Style: Order, Uniformity and the Pursuit of the Beauty of Holiness in the 1630s," in *The Early Stuart Church, 1603–1642*, ed. Kenneth Fincham (Stanford: Stanford University Press, 1993), 161–85.
68. On Laud's specific reforms—altar placement, ceremonial, clerical dress, suppression of lectureships—see Trevor-Roper, *Archbishop Laud*, 82–134; and Fincham and Tyacke, *Altars Restored*, 153–259. Laud's metropolitical visitation articles (instructions for church inspections) are printed in Kenneth Fincham, ed., *Visitation Articles and Injunctions of the Early Stuart Church*, 2 vols. (Woodbridge: Boydell Press, 1994, 1998), 2:77–180.
69. On the prosecution of William Prynne (1600–1669), Henry Burton (1578–1648), and John Bastwick (1593–1654), see William M. Lamont, *Marginal Prynne, 1600–1669* (London: Routledge & Kegan Paul, 1963); and Hibbard, *Charles I and the Popish Plot*, 60–74. They were tried in Star Chamber (royal prerogative court), convicted of seditious libel for pamphlets attacking bishops, and sentenced to have their ears cropped, stand in the pillory, be fined £5,000 each, and imprisoned for life. The brutal punishments (executed 30 June 1637) made them martyrs to the Puritan cause.
70. On John Pym's later denunciation of Laud's "innovations" as conspiracies to reconcile England with Rome, see Conrad Russell, *The Fall of the British Monarchies, 1637–1642* (Oxford: Clarendon Press, 1991), 152–89. Pym's charges at Laud's impeachment (1640–1645) accused him of systematic conspiracy to subvert English Protestantism, though Laud was an anti-papalist who rejected Roman supremacy and transubstantiation.
71. On Charles I's marriage to Henrietta Maria (1609–1669) and the Catholic presence at court, see Caroline M. Hibbard, *Charles I and the Popish Plot* (Chapel Hill: University of

North Carolina Press, 1983), 27–54; and Erin Griffey, ed., *Henrietta Maria: Piety, Politics and Patronage* (Aldershot: Ashgate, 2008). The marriage treaty (1625) guaranteed Henrietta Maria's right to Catholic worship and to raise any children as Catholics until age thirteen. Her chapel at Somerset House, with French priests and public Mass, symbolized Catholic presence at the heart of Protestant England.

72. On Charles I's aesthetic preferences and support for Laud's ceremonialism, see Kevin Sharpe, *The Personal Rule of Charles I* (New Haven: Yale University Press, 1992), 275–381; and Roy Strong, *Art and Power: Renaissance Festivals 1450–1650* (Woodbridge: Boydell Press, 1984), on Charles's elaborate court masques and ceremonial culture.
73. On Charles's first Parliament (1625) and the disastrous Cádiz expedition, see Roger Lockyer, *Buckingham: The Life and Political Career of George Villiers, First Duke of Buckingham, 1592–1628* (London: Longman, 1981), 289–313; and Roger B. Manning, *An Apprenticeship in Arms: The Origins of the British Army, 1585–1702* (Oxford: Oxford University Press, 2006), 111–19. The expedition (October 1625) failed to capture Cádiz; thousands of English soldiers died from disease, desertion, and incompetence.
74. On Charles's dissolution of the 1625 Parliament and his collection of tonnage and poundage without parliamentary grant, see Russell, *Parliaments and English Politics*, 209–54; and L. J. Reeve, *Charles I and the Road to Personal Rule* (Cambridge: Cambridge University Press, 1989), 16–45.
75. On the 1626 Parliament and the attempted impeachment of Buckingham, see Lockyer, *Buckingham*, 314–56; and Russell, *Parliaments and English Politics*, 255–94. Charles removed leading opponents from the Commons by making them sheriffs (Sir Edward Coke, Sir Robert Phelips) or imprisoning them (Sir Dudley Digges, Sir John Eliot), then dissolved Parliament when it persisted in pursuing Buckingham.
76. On the Forced Loan (1626–1627) and resistance to it, see Richard Cust, *The Forced Loan and English Politics, 1626–1628* (Oxford: Clarendon Press, 1987). Charles demanded a "loan" equivalent to five parliamentary subsidies (about £250,000). About seventy-six gentlemen were imprisoned for refusal; others were impressed into military service or had soldiers billeted in their homes.
77. The Five Knights' Case (*Darnel's Case*, 1627) tested habeas corpus against royal prerogative. The case is reported in *State Trials*, vol. 3, 1–59. On its constitutional significance, see J. P. Sommerville, "English and European Political Ideas in the Early Seventeenth Century: Revisionism and the Case of Absolutism," *Journal of British Studies* 35, no. 2 (1996): 168–94; and Glenn Burgess, *Absolute Monarchy and the Stuart Constitution* (New Haven: Yale University Press, 1996), 153–96.
78. On the 1628 Parliament and the Petition of Right, see Frances Helen Relf, *The Petition of Right* (Minneapolis: University of Minnesota Press, 1917); and Cust, *Forced Loan*, 282–358. Sir Edward Coke (1552–1634), the great common lawyer, and John Pym (1584–1643) drafted the Petition, which drew on medieval precedents (Magna Carta) and common law protections.
79. The Petition of Right (7 June 1628) is printed in Gardiner, *Constitutional Documents*, 66–70. Charles's acceptance was ambiguous—he initially gave an evasive response, then under pressure gave the traditional formula ("Soit droit fait comme est désiré"—Let right be done as is desired), which theoretically made the Petition statute law. On the ambiguity, see Russell, *Parliaments and English Politics*, 351–98.
80. On the 1629 Parliament's final session (2 March 1629), when MPs held the Speaker in his chair while passing resolutions against religious innovations and illegal taxation, see Russell, *Parliaments and English Politics*, 399–421; and *CJ* 1:921–28 (2 March 1629). Charles arrested nine MPs, including Sir John Eliot (1592–1632), who died in the Tower in 1632 refusing to admit wrongdoing. Charles declared he would not call Parliament again until his subjects showed themselves more dutiful.
81. On the Personal Rule (1629–1640), see Kevin Sharpe, *The Personal Rule of Charles I* (New Haven: Yale University Press, 1992), the comprehensive modern study; and Esther S. Cope, *Politics Without Parliaments, 1629–1640* (London: Allen & Unwin, 1987). Sharpe

argues Charles's government was effective and popular; critics argue it was financially desperate and politically unwise. The older term "Eleven Years' Tyranny" reflects parliamentarian interpretations.

82. On Charles's fiscal expedients—forest fines, distraint of knighthood, and Ship Money—see Sharpe, *Personal Rule*, 580–646; and Derek Hirst, "Revisionism Revised: The Place of Principle," *Past & Present* 92 (1981): 79–99. Forest fines revived medieval forest laws to charge landowners whose property encroached on ancient royal forests. Distraint of knighthood fined men with income over £40/year who hadn't taken up knighthood (an obsolete requirement). Both were legal but perceived as arbitrary and unjust.
83. Ship Money (levied 1634–1640) and John Hampden's case (1637) are detailed in Margaret Judson, *The Crisis of the Constitution: An Essay in Constitutional and Political Thought in England, 1603–1645* (New Brunswick: Rutgers University Press, 1949), 275–318; and Sharpe, *Personal Rule*, 592–621. Hampden (1594–1643), a Buckinghamshire gentleman, refused to pay twenty shillings Ship Money. His case was heard in Exchequer Chamber; judges ruled 7–5 for the crown that Ship Money was a legal prerogative levy. The narrow margin and principled dissents showed the controversy. *State Trials*, vol. 3, 825–1241, prints the arguments.
84. On Laud's metropolitical visitations and enforcement of ceremonial uniformity, see Fincham and Tyacke, *Altars Restored*, 221–59; and Julian Davies, *The Caroline Captivity of the Church: Charles I and the Remoulding of Anglicanism, 1625–1641* (Oxford: Clarendon Press, 1992).
85. On the decision to impose a new prayer book on Scotland, see John Morrill, "The Religious Context of the English Civil War," *Transactions of the Royal Historical Society*, 5th ser., 34 (1984): 155–78; and Russell, *Fall of the British Monarchies*, 21–81. The Scottish prayer book (1637) was based on the English Book of Common Prayer but with even more elaborate ceremonial language, compiled by Scottish bishops under Laud's guidance.
86. The prayer book riot at St. Giles Cathedral, Edinburgh (23 July 1637), and the legendary Jenny Geddes are described in David Stevenson, *The Scottish Revolution, 1637–1644: The Triumph of the Covenanters* (Newton Abbot: David & Charles, 1973), 56–62. Contemporary sources don't mention Jenny Geddes by name; she may be legendary. But the riot was real—women and men protested violently, shouting that the prayer book was "popish" and throwing stools and Bibles at the clergy.
87. On the National Covenant (28 February 1638) and the Covenanter movement, see Stevenson, *Scottish Revolution*, 63–117; and Edward J. Cowan, "The Making of the National Covenant," in *The Scottish National Covenant in Its British Context*, ed. John Morrill (Edinburgh: Edinburgh University Press, 1990), 68–89. The Covenant bound subscribers to defend Scotland's Presbyterian church government and resist religious innovations. It was mass-subscribed in Edinburgh and then throughout Scotland; some signed in their own blood to demonstrate commitment.
88. On the Bishops' Wars (First: 1639; Second: 1640), see Mark Charles Fissel, *The Bishops' Wars: Charles I's Campaigns Against Scotland, 1638–1640* (Cambridge: Cambridge University Press, 1994); and Russell, *Fall of the British Monarchies*, 82–130. Charles's army was poorly equipped, unpaid, and unenthusiastic about fighting Scottish Protestants. The First Bishops' War ended in the Pacification of Berwick (18 June 1639), an inconclusive truce.
89. The Short Parliament (13 April–5 May 1640) is detailed in Russell, *Fall of the British Monarchies*, 106–30; and Esther S. Cope and Willson H. Coates, eds., *Proceedings of the Short Parliament of 1640* (London: Royal Historical Society, 1977). MPs immediately raised grievances accumulated over eleven years; Charles demanded they vote supply first, address grievances later. Parliament refused; Charles dissolved it after three weeks.
90. On the Second Bishops' War (August–October 1640), Scottish invasion and occupation of Newcastle, and Charles's financial collapse, see Russell, *Fall of the British*

Monarchies, 131–61; and Fissel, *Bishops' Wars*, 231–74. The Scots defeated English forces at Newburn (28 August 1640), occupied Newcastle (capturing England's coal supply), and demanded £850 per day as indemnity. Charles had no money to pay them or raise an army to expel them. He was forced to call Parliament again.

91. On the accumulated tensions converging by 1640, see Conrad Russell, *The Causes of the English Civil War* (Oxford: Clarendon Press, 1990); Ann Hughes, *The Causes of the English Civil War*, 2nd ed. (Basingstoke: Macmillan, 1998); and Lawrence Stone, *The Causes of the English Revolution, 1529–1642* (London: Routledge & Kegan Paul, 1972). All emphasize multiple, overlapping conflicts that made peaceful resolution increasingly difficult.
92. On the three kingdoms dimension and Thomas Wentworth, Earl of Strafford (1593–1641), see Conrad Russell, "The British Problem and the English Civil War," *History* 72, no. 236 (1987): 395–415; and John Morrill, ed., *The Scottish National Covenant in Its British Context* (Edinburgh: Edinburgh University Press, 1990). Strafford governed Ireland 1633–1640 with harsh efficiency, raising revenue for Charles and creating an army that English Protestants feared might be used against them. His impeachment and execution (May 1641) would be the Long Parliament's first major act.
93. On the Long Parliament's initial unity and subsequent divisions, see Anthony Fletcher, *The Outbreak of the English Civil War* (London: Edward Arnold, 1981); and Russell, *Fall of the British Monarchies*, 162–280. The Parliament that convened 3 November 1640 initially showed remarkable consensus against Laud, Strafford, and Charles's Personal Rule policies. But unity fractured over how far reform should go—especially regarding church government and whether to trust the King.

Notes — Chapter 2

1. On the Battle of Edgehill (23 October 1642), the most detailed military account is Peter Young and Richard Holmes, *The English Civil War: A Military History of the Three Civil Wars, 1642–1651* (London: Eyre Methuen, 1974), 82–115. See also John Adair, *By the Sword Divided: Eyewitnesses of the English Civil War* (London: Sutton Publishing, 1998), 34–51; and Keith Roberts, *Edgehill 1642: First Battle of the English Civil War* (Oxford: Osprey, 2001). Contemporary accounts include Edward Hyde, Earl of Clarendon, *The History of the Rebellion and Civil Wars in England*, ed. W. Dunn Macray, 6 vols. (Oxford: Clarendon Press, 1888; originally written 1646–1671), 2:362–69; and John Rushworth, *Historical Collections of Private Passages of State*, 8 vols. (London, 1659–1701), 4:18–23. Force estimates vary; modern historians estimate approximately 13,000–14,000 royalists and 13,000–15,000 parliamentarians.
2. On Prince Rupert of the Rhine (1619–1682) and the debate over fighting on Sunday, see Patrick Morrah, *Prince Rupert of the Rhine* (London: Constable, 1976), 81–85; and Frank Kitson, *Prince Rupert: Portrait of a Soldier* (London: Constable, 1994), 87–92. Some royalist chaplains objected to Sabbath fighting, but military necessity prevailed. Rupert, nephew to Charles I (son of Charles's sister Elizabeth and Frederick V, the "Winter King" of Bohemia), had learned cavalry tactics in the Thirty Years' War.
3. On the eighteen months of crisis from the Long Parliament's convening (November 1640) to the outbreak of war (August 1642), see Conrad Russell, *The Fall of the British Monarchies, 1637–1642* (Oxford: Clarendon Press, 1991), 162–544; Anthony Fletcher, *The Outbreak of the English Civil War* (London: Edward Arnold, 1981); and David L. Smith, *Constitutional Royalism and the Search for Settlement, c. 1640–1649* (Cambridge: Cambridge University Press, 1994), 1–119.
4. On Charles raising his standard at Nottingham (22 August 1642) and Parliament's legal fiction of fighting "evil counselors" rather than the King, see C. V. Wedgwood, *The King's War, 1641–1647* (London: Collins, 1958), 83–87; and Michael J. Braddick, *God's Fury, England's Fire: A New History of the English Civil Wars* (London: Allen Lane, 2008), 185–98. The doctrine that subjects could fight the King's forces while remaining loyal to his person was constitutionally creative but politically necessary to avoid charges of treason.

5. On Robert Devereux, 3rd Earl of Essex (1591–1646), see Vernon F. Snow, *Essex the Rebel: The Life of Robert Devereux, the Third Earl of Essex, 1591–1646* (Lincoln: University of Nebraska Press, 1970); and Barbara Donagan, "Robert Devereux, third earl of Essex (1591–1646)," *Oxford Dictionary of National Biography* [hereafter *ODNB*], online ed., https://doi.org/10.1093/ref:odnb/7565. Essex had been Charles's Lord Chamberlain but joined the parliamentary cause from conviction that the King had been misled by evil counselors and that Protestant religion required defense.
6. On the composition and equipment of parliamentary forces at Edgehill, see C. H. Firth, *Cromwell's Army: A History of the English Soldier During the Civil Wars, the Commonwealth, and the Protectorate* (London: Methuen, 1902; repr. London: Greenhill Books, 1992), 1–52; and Roberts, *Edgehill*, 42–59. The trained bands were citizen militia from London and surrounding counties—shopkeepers, craftsmen, and tradesmen serving periodic military duty. Parliamentary forces wore orange ribbons or scarves (associated with the Dutch Protestant cause).
7. On the royalist army's composition and Prince Maurice's cavalry command, see Ronald Hutton, *The Royalist War Effort, 1642–1646*, 2nd ed. (London: Routledge, 2003), 8–34; and Roberts, *Edgehill*, 34–41. Prince Maurice of the Rhine (1620–1652) was Rupert's younger brother, also a Thirty Years' War veteran. Royalists wore red scarves or ribbons (the King's color).
8. On chaplains and religious rhetoric on both sides at Edgehill, see Barbara Donagan, "Varieties of Royalism," in *The English Civil War*, ed. John Kenyon and Jane Ohlmeyer (Oxford: Oxford University Press, 1998), 65–88; and John Morrill, "The Religious Context of the English Civil War," *Transactions of the Royal Historical Society*, 5th ser., 34 (1984): 155–78. Dr. Henry Hammond (1605–1660), a royalist chaplain, preached on Romans 13 (subjects' duty to obey authority). Parliamentary chaplains emphasized 2 Chronicles 19:2 ("Shouldest thou help the ungodly?"), arguing that God's cause justified resistance to the King's misguided forces.
9. On Rupert's cavalry charge and the rout of the parliamentary left wing, see Young and Holmes, *English Civil War*, 97–103; and Kitson, *Prince Rupert*, 92–95. Rupert's tactic—charging at full gallop with swords drawn rather than relying on pistol fire—was devastatingly effective against inexperienced cavalry. The pursuit extended for miles toward Kineton, where parliamentary baggage trains were plundered.
10. On Prince Maurice's similar success on the royalist left and the failure to rally cavalry for a decisive blow, see Morrah, *Prince Rupert*, 85–88. The inability to rally cavalry after successful charges was a persistent problem in 17th-century warfare; it would be addressed systematically in the New Model Army's training.
11. On the infantry battle in the center, see Young and Holmes, *English Civil War*, 103–8; and Roberts, *Edgehill*, 69–78. Pike combat involved densely packed formations shoving against each other while stabbing with eighteen-foot pikes—physically exhausting and psychologically terrifying. Musketeers fired in volleys at ranges of 50–100 yards, then used muskets as clubs in melee.
12. On the infantry combat's intensity and the horror of Englishmen killing Englishmen, see Charles Carlton, *Going to the Wars: The Experience of the British Civil Wars, 1638–1651* (London: Routledge, 1992), 115–48; and Barbara Donagan, *War in England, 1642–1649* (Oxford: Oxford University Press, 2008), 88–121, on the "uncivil war" aspect.
13. Sir Edmund Verney (1590–1642) carried the royal standard and was killed defending it. His hand, still gripping the pole, had to be severed to recover the standard. The story is told in Frances Parthenope Verney, ed., *Memoirs of the Verney Family During the Civil War*, 4 vols. (London: Longmans, Green, 1892–1899), 2:89–93; and in Clarendon, *History of the Rebellion*, 2:366. The royal standard's symbolic importance made its capture a crisis; its recovery was celebrated as providential.
14. On the battle's inconclusive end and the night following, see Young and Holmes, *English Civil War*, 108–12. Contemporary accounts describe wounded men from both armies crying for help through the night, with some enemy soldiers assisting each other

and others stripping the dead and wounded.

15. Casualty estimates for Edgehill vary. Contemporary sources claimed 2,000–5,000 dead; modern historians estimate 1,500–2,000 killed and 2,000–3,000 wounded. See Carlton, *Going to the Wars*, 211–13; and Roberts, *Edgehill*, 88–89. On the practice of stripping corpses, see Donagan, *War in England*, 197–236, on violence and plunder in civil war.
16. On the strategic outcome of Edgehill and both armies' subsequent movements, see Wedgwood, *King's War*, 95–102; and Hutton, *Royalist War Effort*, 35–41. Essex withdrew toward London; Charles moved to Oxford, which became the royalist capital for the war's duration. Neither commander wanted to resume fighting immediately; both armies were exhausted and disorganized.
17. On divided families during the Civil War, see Ann Hughes, "The King, the Parliament, and the Localities during the English Civil War," *Journal of British Studies* 24, no. 2 (1985): 236–63; and the Verney correspondence in Verney, ed., *Memoirs of the Verney Family*, documenting the anguish of families split by conscience and circumstance.
18. On providential interpretations of battle outcomes and the ambiguity created by Edgehill's inconclusiveness, see Alexandra Walsham, *Providence in Early Modern England* (Oxford: Oxford University Press, 1999), 255–312; and Blair Worden, "Providence and Politics in Cromwellian England," *Past & Present* 109 (1985): 55–99. Both sides claimed God was testing their faith or teaching lessons, allowing the war to continue with divine sanction.
19. On Thomas Wentworth, 1st Earl of Strafford (1593–1641), his Irish government (1633–1640), and his policy of "Thorough," see C. V. Wedgwood, *Thomas Wentworth, First Earl of Strafford, 1593–1641: A Revaluation* (London: Jonathan Cape, 1961); and Hugh Kearney, *Strafford in Ireland, 1633–41: A Study in Absolutism* (Manchester: Manchester University Press, 1959). Strafford governed Ireland efficiently but ruthlessly, alienating Catholic Old English (descendants of medieval Anglo-Norman settlers), Protestant New English (recent planters), and native Gaelic Irish.
20. On the rumors about Strafford's Irish army and their exaggeration, see Russell, *Fall of the British Monarchies*, 195–208. Strafford had raised an 8,000-man Irish army for Charles in 1640, intending it for use against the Scots. Parliamentary fears that it would be used against England were plausible enough to be politically potent, though evidence for such plans was thin.
21. On Pym's impeachment of Strafford (11 November 1640), see Conrad Russell, "Pym, John (1584–1643)," *ODNB*, https://doi.org/10.1093/ref:odnb/22942; and John H. Timmis III, *Thine Is the Kingdom: The Trial for Treason of Thomas Wentworth, Earl of Strafford, First Minister to King Charles I, and Last Hope of the English Crown* (University: University of Alabama Press, 1974). The charges were sweeping but legally questionable—Strafford's actions in Ireland were legal under Irish law, and his counsel to the King was constitutionally privileged.
22. On Strafford's trial (March–April 1641) and his effective defense, see Wedgwood, *Strafford*, 347–82; and Timmis, *Thine Is the Kingdom*, 94–156. Strafford argued brilliantly that his Irish policies were legal, that he never counseled using the Irish army against England, and that even bad counsel didn't constitute treason. The House of Lords appeared likely to acquit.
23. On the Bill of Attainder as an alternative to failed impeachment, see Russell, *Fall of the British Monarchies*, 263–80; and S. R. Gardiner, *History of England from the Accession of James I to the Outbreak of the Civil War, 1603–1642*, 10 vols. (London: Longmans, Green, 1883–1884), 9:321–37. Attainder declared guilt by legislative act without trial—constitutionally dubious but politically effective. The Commons passed it 204–59 on 21 April 1641; the Lords passed it 26–19 on 8 May after mob pressure.
24. On Charles's agonized decision to sign Strafford's death warrant (10 May 1641), see Wedgwood, *King's War*, 29–34; and Clarendon, *History of the Rebellion*, 1:330–35. Charles later wrote (in *Eikon Basilike*, his posthumously published apologia) that signing Strafford's death warrant was his greatest sin and that God punished him with

execution for having executed his faithful servant.

25. Strafford's execution (12 May 1641) is described in contemporary accounts collected in Rushworth, *Historical Collections*, 4:259–65; and in Wedgwood, *Strafford*, 385–90. The crowd of 100,000 (likely exaggerated but indicating huge turnout) celebrated his death as justice. Strafford's last words included "I do as cheerfully put off my doublet at this time as ever I did when I went to bed."
26. On William Laud's impeachment (December 1640) and imprisonment, see Hugh Trevor-Roper, *Archbishop Laud, 1573–1645*, 2nd ed. (London: Macmillan, 1962), 395–420; and Charles Carlton, *Archbishop William Laud* (London: Routledge & Kegan Paul, 1987), 215–38. The charges against Laud focused on his ceremonial innovations, his use of church courts to persecute Puritans, and his role in imposing the prayer book on Scotland.
27. On the collapse of episcopal authority and abolition of the Court of High Commission (July 1641), see John Spurr, *The Restoration Church of England, 1646–1689* (New Haven: Yale University Press, 1991), 3–28; and Claire Cross, *Church and People, 1450–1660: The Triumph of the Laity in the English Church* (Atlantic Highlands, NJ: Humanities Press, 1976), 175–98. The statute abolishing High Commission (16 Car. I c. 11) is printed in Samuel Rawson Gardiner, ed., *The Constitutional Documents of the Puritan Revolution, 1625–1660*, 3rd ed. (Oxford: Clarendon Press, 1906), 179–86.
28. The Triennial Act (February 1641; 16 Car. I c. 1) is printed in Gardiner, *Constitutional Documents*, 144–55. On its significance, see Margaret Atwood Judson, *The Crisis of the Constitution: An Essay in Constitutional and Political Thought in England, 1603–1645* (New Brunswick: Rutgers University Press, 1949), 319–47; and Michael Mendle, *Dangerous Positions: Mixed Government, the Estates of the Realm, and the Making of the Answer to the XIX Propositions* (University: University of Alabama Press, 1985), 85–112.
29. On the abolition of prerogative courts in 1641, see G. E. Aylmer, *The King's Servants: The Civil Service of Charles I, 1625–1642* (London: Routledge & Kegan Paul, 1961), 442–67; and Gardiner, *Constitutional Documents*, 179–97 (printing the relevant statutes). Star Chamber was abolished by 16 Car. I c. 10; the regional councils by 16 Car. I c. 20; High Commission by 16 Car. I c. 11.
30. On the political popularity but administrative consequences of abolishing prerogative courts, see Russell, *Fall of the British Monarchies*, 293–308. Even moderate royalists who had suffered from Star Chamber's arbitrary punishments supported abolition. But eliminating these courts removed enforcement mechanisms that the crown had relied upon, leaving common law courts (which followed precedent and procedure) as the only judicial remedy.
31. On the fiscal reforms of 1641—abolishing Ship Money, forest fines, distraint of knighthood, and monopolies—see Gardiner, *Constitutional Documents*, 189–97; and Russell, *Fall of the British Monarchies*, 308–24. Ship Money was declared illegal by 16 Car. I c. 14; tonnage and poundage required parliamentary grant by 16 Car. I c. 8.
32. On Charles's financial dependence after these reforms and Parliament's conditional grants of taxation, see Robert Ashton, *The Crown and the Money Market, 1603–1640* (Oxford: Clarendon Press, 1960), 208–27; and Russell, *Fall of the British Monarchies*, 324–39. Charles needed money to pay the Scottish army's indemnity and later to suppress the Irish Rebellion; Parliament granted some funds but conditioned them on continued reforms.
33. On the Irish Rebellion (beginning October 1641), see Nicholas Canny, *Making Ireland British, 1580–1650* (Oxford: Oxford University Press, 2001), 461–550; Michael Perceval-Maxwell, *The Outbreak of the Irish Rebellion of 1641* (Montreal: McGill-Queen's University Press, 1994); and Jane Ohlmeyer, ed., *Ireland from Independence to Occupation, 1641–1660* (Cambridge: Cambridge University Press, 1995). The rebellion combined grievances over plantation (Protestant settlement on confiscated Catholic lands), religious persecution, and Strafford's oppressive government.
34. On the violence of the rebellion and English exaggerations, see Ethan Howard Shagan,

"Constructing Discord: Ideology, Propaganda, and English Responses to the Irish Rebellion of 1641," *Journal of British Studies* 36, no. 1 (1997): 4–34. Modern estimates suggest 4,000–12,000 Protestants died in the rebellion's first months (some killed directly, many dying of exposure after expulsion from homes in winter). English pamphlets claimed 150,000–200,000 deaths—physically impossible given Ireland's total Protestant population. Sir John Temple's *The Irish Rebellion* (London, 1646) catalogued alleged atrocities in lurid detail.

35. On the political use of Irish Rebellion reports to attack Charles and Catholics, see Caroline M. Hibbard, *Charles I and the Popish Plot* (Chapel Hill: University of North Carolina Press, 1983), 139–88; and Russell, *Fall of the British Monarchies*, 396–446. Parliamentary preachers used Irish atrocities to prove that popery was inherently murderous and that England faced similar danger if Catholics gained influence.
36. On the militia question and the constitutional crisis it created, see Lois G. Schwoerer, "'No Standing Armies!': The Antiarmy Ideology in Seventeenth-Century England* (Baltimore: Johns Hopkins University Press, 1974), 36–58; and Russell, *Fall of the British Monarchies*, 447–73. Charles insisted that military command was inherent in the crown; Parliament feared that an army raised for Ireland under royal command might be used against Parliament.
37. The Militia Ordinance (5 March 1642) is printed in Gardiner, *Constitutional Documents*, 245–47. On the constitutional crisis it precipitated, see Corinne Comstock Weston and Janelle Renfrow Greenberg, *Subjects and Sovereigns: The Grand Controversy over Legal Sovereignty in Stuart England* (Cambridge: Cambridge University Press, 1981), 55–80. Parliament claimed authority to issue ordinances with force of law even without royal assent in emergencies—a revolutionary constitutional claim.
38. On the fundamental constitutional impasse over where ultimate authority resided, see Smith, *Constitutional Royalism*, 82–119; and Glenn Burgess, *Absolute Monarchy and the Stuart Constitution* (New Haven: Yale University Press, 1996), 197–235.
39. The Root and Branch Petition (11 December 1640) is printed in Gardiner, *Constitutional Documents*, 137–44. On its significance and the 15,000 signatures, see John Morrill, *The Nature of the English Revolution* (London: Longman, 1993), 69–90; and Judith Maltby, "'By This Book': Parishioners, the Prayer Book and the Established Church," in *The Early Stuart Church, 1603–1642*, ed. Kenneth Fincham (Stanford: Stanford University Press, 1993), 115–37.
40. On the Root and Branch Petition's charges against bishops, see Anthony Fletcher, "The First Century of English Protestantism and the Growth of National Identity," in *Unity and Diversity in the Church*, ed. R. N. Swanson (Oxford: Blackwell, 1996), 309–17. The petition argued that episcopacy was unscriptural, corrupt, tyrannical, and the cause of England's current troubles.
41. On parliamentary division over the Root and Branch Petition, see Fletcher, *Outbreak of the English Civil War*, 91–114; and Russell, *Fall of the British Monarchies*, 220–45. The petition split MPs between those wanting complete abolition of bishops and those wanting reform but preservation of episcopal office.
42. On the deeper questions underlying the division, see Peter Lake, "Puritan Identities," *Journal of Ecclesiastical History* 35, no. 1 (1984): 112–23; and Patrick Collinson, "Ecclesiastical Vitriol: Religious Satire in the 1590s and the Invention of Puritanism," in *The Reign of Elizabeth I: Court and Culture in the Last Decade*, ed. John Guy (Cambridge: Cambridge University Press, 1995), 150–70.
43. Sir Edward Dering's speech opposing Root and Branch (9 February 1641) is quoted in Rushworth, *Historical Collections*, 4:173–75; and discussed in Fletcher, *Outbreak of the English Civil War*, 105–8. Dering (1598–1644), a Kent MP, initially supported church reform but opposed abolishing episcopacy.
44. Edmund Calamy (1600–1666), Presbyterian minister, preached *England's Looking-Glasse* (London, 1641) to Parliament advocating "root and branch" reform. See *ODNB* entry by Tai Liu, https://doi.org/10.1093/ref:odnb/4352.

45. On John Pym's strategy in pushing the Grand Remonstrance and his fear that parliamentary unity was dissolving, see J. S. A. Adamson, "The Baronial Context of the English Civil War," *Transactions of the Royal Historical Society*, 5th ser., 40 (1990): 93–120; and Conrad Russell, "Why Did Charles I Call the Long Parliament?" *History* 69, no. 226 (1984): 375–83.
46. The Grand Remonstrance (1 December 1641) is printed in full in Gardiner, *Constitutional Documents*, 202–32. On its purpose and content, see Fletcher, *Outbreak of the English Civil War*, 115–52; and Russell, *Fall of the British Monarchies*, 416–46.
47. The Remonstrance's charges against Charles's government since 1625 are analyzed in Russell, *Fall of the British Monarchies*, 420–30. The document listed grievances systematically: religious innovations, illegal taxation, persecution of Puritans, Scottish policy, and Irish misgovernment.
48. On the Grand Remonstrance debate (22 November 1641), see *Journals of the House of Commons* [hereafter *CJ*] 2:327–31 (22 November 1641); Rushworth, *Historical Collections*, 4:437–41; and Fletcher, *Outbreak of the English Civil War*, 130–39. The debate lasted from early afternoon until past midnight in a packed, tense chamber.
49. Dering's speech against the Grand Remonstrance is quoted in Rushworth, *Historical Collections*, 4:438. His objection was to "remonstrating downward"—publishing grievances to the people rather than privately counseling the King.
50. Oliver Cromwell's support for the Grand Remonstrance and his reported statement that he would have emigrated had it been rejected are recorded in Bulstrode Whitelocke, *Memorials of the English Affairs*, 4 vols. (Oxford: Oxford University Press, 1853), 1:156; and discussed in Barry Coward, *Oliver Cromwell* (London: Longman, 1991), 19–22.
51. On the vote (159–148) and the near-violence in the chamber, see *CJ* 2:330–31; Rushworth, *Historical Collections*, 4:440–41; and Fletcher, *Outbreak of the English Civil War*, 137–39. Some MPs reportedly had hands on sword hilts, and the Speaker threatened to leave his chair to restore order.
52. On the Grand Remonstrance's narrow passage revealing parliamentary division, see Russell, *Fall of the British Monarchies*, 440–46; and David Scott, "The 'Northern Gentlemen,' the Parliamentary Independents, and Anglo-Scottish Relations in the Long Parliament," *Historical Journal* 42, no. 2 (1999): 347–75. The division roughly tracked religious preferences but wasn't perfectly aligned.
53. On Charles's attempt to arrest the Five Members (4 January 1642) in context, see Russell, *Fall of the British Monarchies*, 447–54; and the Introduction to this book. Charles believed Pym and allies were conspiring with Scots, threatening the Queen, and planning to seize complete control.
54. On the Five Members' escape (possibly forewarned by Henrietta Maria) and Charles's violation of parliamentary privilege, see Wedgwood, *King's War*, 61–65; and Hibbard, *Charles I and the Popish Plot*, 191–96. The Queen's role in warning them is disputed but plausible—she loved intrigue and may have revealed the plot inadvertently or deliberately.
55. The Nineteen Propositions (1 June 1642) are printed in Gardiner, *Constitutional Documents*, 249–54. On their significance as Parliament's maximum demands, see Smith, *Constitutional Royalism*, 89–119; and Mendle, *Dangerous Positions*, 113–52.
56. *His Majesty's Answer to the Nineteen Propositions* (18 June 1642) is printed in Gardiner, *Constitutional Documents*, 249–54. On its constitutional theory of mixed government, see Mendle, *Dangerous Positions*, 153–94; and Weston and Greenberg, *Subjects and Sovereigns*, 38–54. Charles's advisors (probably Falkland and Colepeper) articulated a theory that England's constitution balanced monarchy (King), aristocracy (Lords), and democracy (Commons)—each checking the others.
57. On regional patterns of royalist and parliamentarian support, see David Underdown, *Revel, Riot, and Rebellion: Popular Politics and Culture in England, 1603–1660* (Oxford: Clarendon Press, 1985), 146–205; and Ann Hughes, *Politics, Society and Civil War in*

Warwickshire, 1620–1660 (Cambridge: Cambridge University Press, 1987), 133–85. Underdown argued (controversially) that "wood-pasture" regions (pastoral economy, dispersed settlement) tended royalist while "arable" regions (grain farming, nucleated villages) tended parliamentarian.

58. On parliamentarian strongholds, see Valerie Pearl, *London and the Outbreak of the Puritan Revolution: City Government and National Politics, 1625–43* (Oxford: Oxford University Press, 1961); and Robert Brenner, *Merchants and Revolution: Commercial Change, Political Conflict, and London's Overseas Traders, 1550–1653* (Princeton: Princeton University Press, 1993), on London's crucial support for Parliament.
59. On neutralism and "Clubmen" movements, see David Underdown, "The Chalk and the Cheese: Contrasts Among the English Clubmen," *Past & Present* 85 (1979): 25–48; and Mark Stoyle, *Loyalty and Locality: Popular Allegiance in Devon during the English Civil War* (Exeter: University of Exeter Press, 1994).
60. On social and economic correlations with allegiance, see Brian Manning, *The English People and the English Revolution* (London: Heinemann, 1976), 186–238; and J. T. Cliffe, *The Yorkshire Gentry from the Reformation to the Civil War* (London: Athlone Press, 1969), 329–53.
61. On the Verney family's divided loyalties, see Verney, ed., *Memoirs of the Verney Family*, especially 2:48–93 on Sir Edmund's death at Edgehill and Ralph's parliamentary service despite personal anguish at fighting against his father.
62. On royalist advantages—cavalry, interior lines, Welsh support—see Hutton, *Royalist War Effort*, 42–81; and P. R. Newman, *The Old Service: Royalist Regimental Colonels and the Civil War, 1642–46* (Manchester: Manchester University Press, 1993).
63. On parliamentary advantages—London, navy, potential Scottish alliance—see Ian Gentles, *The English Revolution and the Wars in the Three Kingdoms, 1638–1652* (Harlow: Pearson, 2007), 99–148.
64. On 1643 battles—Roundway Down (13 July), Bristol's capture (26 July), First Newbury (20 September)—see Young and Holmes, *English Civil War*, 138–76; and Gentles, *English Revolution*, 117–35.
65. On the Solemn League and Covenant (September 1643) and the English-Scottish alliance, see Edward J. Cowan, "The Solemn League and Covenant," in *The Scottish National Covenant in Its British Context*, ed. John Morrill (Edinburgh: Edinburgh University Press, 1990), 182–202; and David Stevenson, *Revolution and Counter-Revolution in Scotland, 1644–1651* (London: Royal Historical Society, 1977), 1–23.
66. The text of the Solemn League and Covenant is printed in Gardiner, *Constitutional Documents*, 267–71. On its deliberate ambiguity regarding church government, see Robert S. Paul, *The Assembly of the Lord: Politics and Religion in the Westminster Assembly and the 'Grand Debate'* (Edinburgh: T&T Clark, 1985), 90–123.
67. On the Scottish army's entry into England (January 1644) and its military impact, see Stuart Reid, *The Campaigns of Montrose: A Military History of the Civil War in Scotland, 1639–1646* (Edinburgh: Mercat Press, 1990), 81–108; and Peter Newman, *Marston Moor, 2 July 1644: The Sources and the Site* (York: Borthwick Institute, 1981), 1–12.
68. On the Westminster Assembly of Divines (July 1643–1649), see Paul, *Assembly of the Lord*; and Chad Van Dixhoorn, ed., *The Minutes and Papers of the Westminster Assembly, 1643–1652*, 5 vols. (Oxford: Oxford University Press, 2012). The Assembly met in Westminster Abbey's Jerusalem Chamber and produced the Westminster Confession, Larger and Shorter Catechisms, and Directory for Public Worship—standards that shaped presbyterian churches worldwide though never fully implemented in England.
69. On the Battle of Marston Moor (2 July 1644), the fullest modern account is Peter Newman, *The Battle of Marston Moor, 1644* (Chichester: Anthony Bird Publications, 1981). See also Young and Holmes, *English Civil War*, 177–200; and John Barratt, *The Battle for York: Marston Moor 1644* (Stroud: Tempus, 2002). Force estimates: Allied (Scottish-parliamentary) approximately 27,000; Royalist approximately 18,000.
70. On Oliver Cromwell's cavalry command at Marston Moor and the Eastern Association

forces, see Barry Coward, *Oliver Cromwell* (London: Longman, 1991), 22–26; and Ian Gentles, "The Management of the Crown Lands, 1649–60," *Agricultural History Review* 19, no. 1 (1971): 25–41. Cromwell commanded the cavalry of the Eastern Association (Parliament's forces from East Anglia), approximately 3,000 horse. His troops' discipline—maintaining formation, rallying after charges, obeying orders—distinguished them from typical civil war cavalry.

71. On Cromwell's cavalry tactics at Marston Moor—breaking the royalist right wing, rallying, then wheeling to attack the center—see Newman, *Marston Moor*, 45–78; and C. V. Wedgwood, "Oliver Cromwell and the Elizabethan Inheritance," in *Poetry and Politics under the Stuarts* (Cambridge: Cambridge University Press, 1960), 138–64. The ability to rally cavalry after a successful charge was rare in 17th-century warfare and became a hallmark of Cromwell's forces.
72. On the battle's outcome and its consequences for royalist power in the north, see Newman, *Marston Moor*, 79–96; and Hutton, *Royalist War Effort*, 136–59. Prince Rupert's reputation suffered (though his defeat resulted partly from being outnumbered); William Cavendish, Marquess of Newcastle (1593–1676), a major royalist commander and patron who had raised forces at his own expense, went into exile after the defeat and never returned to active service.
73. On Cromwell's emergence as a national figure after Marston Moor, see Coward, *Oliver Cromwell*, 26–31; and Peter Gaunt, *Oliver Cromwell* (Oxford: Blackwell, 1996), 51–67. Before 1644, Cromwell was a relatively minor figure—a middle-ranking gentleman, second-tier MP, regional cavalry commander. Marston Moor made him nationally prominent.
74. Cromwell's views on military organization—godliness, discipline, meritocracy, religious motivation—are expressed in his letters and speeches. The famous quote about preferring "a plain russet-coated captain" is from Cromwell's letter to William Spring (September 1643), in W. C. Abbott, ed., *The Writings and Speeches of Oliver Cromwell*, 4 vols. (Cambridge, MA: Harvard University Press, 1937–1947), 1:256. On Cromwell's military principles, see Charles Firth, *Oliver Cromwell and the Rule of the Puritans in England* (London: G. P. Putnam's Sons, 1900; repr. Oxford: Oxford University Press, 1953), 83–112.
75. On the New Model Army's creation and Cromwell's role, see Ian Gentles, *The New Model Army in England, Ireland and Scotland, 1645–1653* (Oxford: Blackwell, 1992), 1–32. Sir Thomas Fairfax (1612–1671) was appointed Lord General in February 1645; Cromwell became Lieutenant-General (second in command, commanding cavalry) in June 1645 after the Self-Denying Ordinance's passage.
76. On Parliament's military difficulties in late 1644 despite Marston Moor, see Gentles, *English Revolution*, 172–203; and Mark A. Kishlansky, *The Rise of the New Model Army* (Cambridge: Cambridge University Press, 1979), 13–36. The Eastern Association (Manchester's army), Essex's army, and Sir William Waller's army operated independently with poor coordination and competed for resources.
77. Edward Montagu, 2nd Earl of Manchester (1602–1671), commanded the Eastern Association. His reported statement—"If we beat the King ninety-nine times he would still be King, but if he beat us once we would all be hanged"—is recorded in Cromwell's complaint to Parliament (25 November 1644), printed in Abbott, *Writings and Speeches*, 1:314. The authenticity is disputed, but it reflects Manchester's known reluctance to pursue total victory. See David Scott, "The Earl of Manchester and the Collapse of the Parliamentary Cause in the Eastern Association in 1644," *Journal of British Studies* 42, no. 1 (2003): 39–63.
78. On Cromwell's attack on Manchester (December 1644), see Kishlansky, *Rise of the New Model Army*, 25–36; and Coward, *Oliver Cromwell*, 31–36. Cromwell accused Manchester of military incompetence and unwillingness to win decisively. The accusation was politically dangerous—a commoner attacking a peer—but reflected genuine frustration.

79. The Self-Denying Ordinance (3 April 1645) is printed in C. H. Firth and R. S. Rait, eds., *Acts and Ordinances of the Interregnum, 1642–1660*, 3 vols. (London: HMSO, 1911), 1:401–2. On its passage and purpose, see Kishlansky, *Rise of the New Model Army*, 37–54; and Gentles, *New Model Army*, 9–14.

80. On the selective application of the Self-Denying Ordinance, see Kishlansky, *Rise of the New Model Army*, 51–54. Essex and Manchester resigned permanently; Fairfax (though a peer and son of a peer, he wasn't an MP) became commander; Cromwell received repeated "temporary" commissions that became de facto permanent.

81. On the New Model Army's structure and organization, see Firth, *Cromwell's Army*, 34–109; and Gentles, *New Model Army*, 15–54. The army's establishment (February 1645) authorized 22,000 men: 6,600 cavalry (11 regiments of 600 each), 14,400 infantry (12 regiments of 1,200 each), and 1,000 dragoons (1 regiment). Pay was set at 8 pence per day for infantry, 2 shillings for cavalry—substantial wages if paid regularly, but arrears became chronic.

82. On recruitment and officer selection in the New Model Army, see Gentles, *New Model Army*, 33–54; and Ian Gentles, "The Arrears of Pay of the Parliamentary Army at the End of the First Civil War," *Bulletin of the Institute of Historical Research* 48, no. 117 (1975): 52–63. About 60% of the initial force came from existing parliamentary armies; the remainder from new volunteers or impressment. Officers were chosen by Fairfax and his council based on ability and loyalty rather than birth.

83. On training and discipline in the New Model Army, see Firth, *Cromwell's Army*, 210–67; and Barbara Donagan, "Codes and Conduct in the English Civil War," *Past & Present* 118 (1988): 65–95. The standardized drill and tactics created unprecedented coordination and effectiveness.

84. On religious culture in the New Model Army—preaching, prayer meetings, soldiers prophesying—see Anne Laurence, *Parliamentary Army Chaplains, 1642–1651* (Woodbridge: Boydell Press, 1990); and J. C. Davis, "Religion and the Struggle for Freedom in the English Revolution," *Historical Journal* 35, no. 3 (1992): 507–30. Army chaplains preached regularly; soldiers held prayer meetings where rank distinctions temporarily dissolved.

85. On godly discipline in the army, see Firth, *Cromwell's Army*, 268–302; and Leo F. Solt, *Saints in Arms: Puritanism and Democracy in Cromwell's Army* (Stanford: Stanford University Press, 1959), 17–43. Articles of War prohibited swearing, drunkenness, plunder, and Sabbath-breaking, with punishments including fines, flogging, or (for serious offenses) execution.

86. On religious diversity in the New Model Army and Cromwell's toleration policy, see Gentles, *New Model Army*, 91–117; and J. F. McGregor and B. Reay, eds., *Radical Religion in the English Revolution* (Oxford: Oxford University Press, 1984), 1–43. The army included Presbyterians, Independents, Baptists, and (by 1650s) Quakers. Cromwell's principle was to tolerate all "godly" Protestants regardless of denominational differences.

87. On the army's political radicalization emerging from its religious culture, see Austin Woolrych, *Soldiers and Statesmen: The General Council of the Army and Its Debates, 1647–1648* (Oxford: Clarendon Press, 1987), 1–58; and Solt, *Saints in Arms*, 44–76. The leveling implicit in radical Protestantism—spiritual equality before God—encouraged political leveling. This would explode in 1647 with the Putney Debates.

88. On the Battle of Naseby (14 June 1645), see Glenn Foard, *Naseby: The Decisive Campaign* (Whitstable: Pryor Publications, 1995); and Young and Holmes, *English Civil War*, 227–52. Force estimates: Royalist approximately 9,000 (including about 4,000 cavalry under Prince Rupert); Parliamentary approximately 13,500 (including about 6,500 cavalry under Cromwell).

89. On the battle's course and outcome, see Foard, *Naseby*, 185–283; and Austin Woolrych, *Battles of the English Civil War* (London: B. T. Batsford, 1961; repr. London: Pimlico, 1991), 83–108. The pattern paralleled earlier battles—Rupert's cavalry charged

successfully but pursued too far; Cromwell's cavalry rallied and attacked the royalist infantry from behind; the royalist army was destroyed.

90. On Charles's captured correspondence (the "King's Cabinet") and its publication by Parliament, see Lois Potter, *Secret Rites and Secret Writing: Royalist Literature, 1641–1660* (Cambridge: Cambridge University Press, 1989), 101–27; and Jason Peacey, *Politicians and Pamphleteers: Propaganda During the English Civil Wars and Interregnum* (Aldershot: Ashgate, 2004), 198–223. The letters, published as *The Kings Cabinet Opened* (London, 1645), revealed Charles's negotiations with Irish Catholics, continental powers, and the Pope's representative, confirming parliamentary claims about his untrustworthiness.
91. On the war's conclusion 1645–1646—fall of royalist strongholds, Charles's surrender—see Gentles, *English Revolution*, 230–60; and Hutton, *Royalist War Effort*, 189–209. Bristol fell to Fairfax (10 September 1645); the West Country was cleared by spring 1646; Oxford surrendered (24 June 1646). Charles surrendered to the Scottish army at Newark (5 May 1646), hoping Scots would give him better terms than Parliament or the Army.
92. On parliamentary divisions after victory—Presbyterians vs. Independents, plans for the army, negotiations with Charles—see David Underdown, *Pride's Purge: Politics in the Puritan Revolution* (Oxford: Clarendon Press, 1971), 47–73; and Mark A. Kishlansky, "The Army and the Levellers: The Roads to Putney," *Historical Journal* 22, no. 4 (1979): 795–824.
93. On the New Model Army as a revolutionary instrument militarily and politically, see Gentles, *New Model Army*, 418–49; and Woolrych, *Soldiers and Statesmen*, 1–34. The army's transformation from military force to political actor would shape events 1647–1653.
94. On political divisions after the First Civil War, see Underdown, *Pride's Purge*, 47–96; and Blair Worden, *The Rump Parliament, 1648–1653* (Cambridge: Cambridge University Press, 1974), 1–45. The coalition that had united against Charles fractured over settlement terms, church government, and the army's role.
95. On religious conflicts intensifying after victory, see Ann Hughes, *Gangraena and the Struggle for the English Revolution* (Oxford: Oxford University Press, 2004), analyzing Thomas Edwards's *Gangraena* (1646), a massive catalog of heresies that exemplified Presbyterian fears of religious chaos; and Tai Liu, *Discord in Zion: The Puritan Divines and the Puritan Revolution, 1640–1660* (The Hague: Martinus Nijhoff, 1973), 67–112.
96. On social transformation and the challenge to traditional hierarchies, see Christopher Hill, *The World Turned Upside Down: Radical Ideas During the English Revolution* (London: Temple Smith, 1972); and Brian Manning, *1649: The Crisis of the English Revolution* (London: Bookmarks, 1992), examining class dimensions of revolution.
97. Casualty estimates for the Civil Wars are debated. Charles Carlton, *Going to the Wars*, 211–15, estimates England: 84,830 combat deaths plus approximately 100,000 from war-related disease; Scotland: 28,000 deaths; Ireland: perhaps 200,000 deaths (though Irish figures are especially uncertain). As percentages of population, these are catastrophic—England's 3.7% mortality exceeds its percentage losses in World War I.
98. On the unsettled situation after First Civil War, see Austin Woolrych, "From War to Settlement, 1646–1649," in *The English Civil War: The Essential Readings*, ed. Peter Gaunt (Oxford: Blackwell, 2000), 197–225; and Robert Ashton, *Counter-Revolution: The Second Civil War and Its Origins, 1646–8* (New Haven: Yale University Press, 1994), 1–67.
99. On the continued constitutional deadlock despite military victory, see Smith, *Constitutional Royalism*, 181–249; and Sean Kelsey, *Inventing a Republic: The Political Culture of the English Commonwealth, 1649–1653* (Stanford: Stanford University Press, 1997), 1–45.
100. On the path from First Civil War's end (1646) to Charles's execution (1649), see C. V. Wedgwood, *The Trial of Charles I* (London: Collins, 1964); and Clive Holmes, "The Trial and Execution of Charles I," *Historical Journal* 53, no. 2 (2010): 289–316. The Army's politicization (1647), the Second Civil War (1648), and the decision that Charles was

incorrigible and must die will be treated in subsequent chapters examining the religious factions' competing visions for England's settlement.

Notes — Chapter 3

1. On the Westminster Assembly's convening (1 July 1643) and composition, see Chad Van Dixhoorn, ed., The Minutes and Papers of the Westminster Assembly, 1643–1652, 5 vols. (Oxford: Oxford University Press, 2012), 1:3–12; Robert S. Paul, The Assembly of the Lord: Politics and Religion in the Westminster Assembly and the 'Grand Debate' (Edinburgh: T&T Clark, 1985), 89–117.
2. On William Twisse (1578–1646), the Assembly's Prolocutor, see Dewey D. Wallace Jr., Puritans and Predestination: Grace in English Protestant Theology, 1525–1695 (Chapel Hill: University of North Carolina Press, 1982), 76–92.
3. Stephen Marshall's opening sermon (1 July 1643) on Haggai 2:7–9 is recorded in John F. Wilson, Pulpit in Parliament: Puritanism During the English Civil Wars, 1640–1648 (Princeton: Princeton University Press, 1969), 125–28.
4. On the Assembly's composition—Presbyterian majority, Independent minority, briefly attending Episcopalians—see Van Dixhoorn, Minutes and Papers, 1:13–45; and Paul, Assembly of the Lord, 118–58.
5. The parliamentary ordinance summoning the Westminster Assembly (12 June 1643) is printed in C. H. Firth and R. S. Rait, eds., Acts and Ordinances of the Interregnum, 1642–1660, 3 vols. (London: HMSO, 1911), 1:180–84.
6. On the Presbyterian majority and key figures, see Tai Liu, Discord in Zion: The Puritan Divines and the Puritan Revolution, 1640–1660 (The Hague: Martinus Nijhoff, 1973), 15–67.
7. On the Independent minority in the Assembly, see Geoffrey F. Nuttall, Visible Saints: The Congregational Way, 1640–1660 (Oxford: Basil Blackwell, 1957), 38–68; and Paul, Assembly of the Lord, 149–58.
8. On Episcopalian members and their exclusion, see Paul, Assembly of the Lord, 102–17.
9. On the Scottish commissioners to the Westminster Assembly, see David Stevenson, The Scottish Revolution, 1637–1644: The Triumph of the Covenanters (Newton Abbot: David & Charles, 1973), 275–312.
10. On Scottish expectations versus English realities, see David Stevenson, "The Early Covenanters and the Federal Union of Britain," in The Scottish National Covenant in Its British Context, ed. John Morrill (Edinburgh: Edinburgh University Press, 1990), 163–81.
11. On the Assembly's early debates, see Van Dixhoorn, Minutes and Papers, 1:46–125; and Paul, Assembly of the Lord, 159–88.
12. On hermeneutical differences regarding Scripture and church government, see John de Witt, Jus Divinum: The Westminster Assembly and the Divine Right of Church Government (Kampen: J. H. Kok, 1969), 1–102.
13. Robert Baillie's frustration is documented in The Letters and Journals of Robert Baillie, ed. David Laing, 3 vols. (Edinburgh: Robert Ogle, 1841–1842), 2:89–91.
14. On the fourfold structure of presbyterian church government, see James Walker, The Theology and Theologians of Scotland, 1560–1750 (Edinburgh: Knox Press, 1982), 47–73.
15. On the kirk session, see Margo Todd, The Culture of Protestantism in Early Modern Scotland (New Haven: Yale University Press, 2002), 62–124.
16. On kirk session discipline practices, see Michael F. Graham, The Uses of Reform: 'Godly Discipline' and Popular Behavior in Scotland and Beyond, 1560–1610 (Leiden: Brill, 1996), 204–76.
17. On the presbytery, see James Kirk, Patterns of Reform: Continuity and Change in the Reformation Kirk (Edinburgh: T&T Clark, 1989), 379–425.
18. On provincial synods, see Kirk, Patterns of Reform, 426–48.
19. On the General Assembly, see Gordon Donaldson, The Scottish Reformation (Cambridge: Cambridge University Press, 1960), 187–214.

20. On the Kirk's claim to independence from civil authority, see J. H. S. Burleigh, A Church History of Scotland (London: Oxford University Press, 1960), 178–228.
21. On Erastianism and parliamentary control, see Jeffrey R. Collins, "The Church Settlement of Oliver Cromwell," History 87, no. 285 (2002): 18–40.
22. Samuel Rutherford and George Gillespie's arguments against Erastianism are in Gillespie, Aaron's Rod Blossoming (London, 1646); and Rutherford, The Divine Right of Church Government (London, 1646).
23. Thomas Coleman's Erastian position is discussed in Paul, Assembly of the Lord, 404–29.
24. On the unresolved church-state question, see de Witt, Jus Divinum, 200–85.
25. On the three marks of the true church in Reformed theology, see Richard A. Muller, Post-Reformation Reformed Dogmatics, 4 vols. (Grand Rapids: Baker Academic, 2003), 4:52–89.
26. On Reformed theology of church membership, see Edmund S. Morgan, Visible Saints: The History of a Puritan Idea (New York: New York University Press, 1963).
27. On Matthew 18:15–17 as the pattern for church discipline, see John Calvin, Institutes of the Christian Religion, ed. John T. McNeill, trans. Ford Lewis Battles, 2 vols. (Philadelphia: Westminster Press, 1960), 4.12.1–13.
28. On discipline maintaining the church's witness, see Patrick Collinson, The Religion of Protestants: The Church in English Society, 1559–1625 (Oxford: Clarendon Press, 1982), 242–83.
29.Richard Baxter, The Reformed Pastor (London, 1656; modern ed., Edinburgh: Banner of Truth Trust, 1974), 143.
30. On Richard Baxter's Kidderminster ministry, see Geoffrey F. Nuttall, Richard Baxter (London: Nelson, 1965), 20–57.
31. On Baxter's catechizing method, see Baxter, The Reformed Pastor, 85–123.
32. On Baxter's preaching style, see N. H. Keeble, Richard Baxter: Puritan Man of Letters (Oxford: Clarendon Press, 1982), 80–114.
33. On Baxter's discipline practices, see J. William Black, Reformation Pastors: Richard Baxter and the Ideal of the Reformed Pastor (Milton Keynes: Paternoster, 2004), 89–134.
34. Baxter's claim about Kidderminster's transformation is from his Reliquiae Baxterianae, ed. Matthew Sylvester (London, 1696), Part I, 83.
35. On the Westminster Confession of Faith (1646), see Robert Letham, The Westminster Assembly: Reading Its Theology in Historical Context (Phillipsburg, NJ: P&R Publishing, 2009).
36. On the Confession's chapter on civil magistrates, see de Witt, Jus Divinum, 246–85.
37. On the Westminster Catechisms, see G. I. Williamson, The Westminster Shorter Catechism: For Study Classes, 2 vols. (Phillipsburg, NJ: Presbyterian and Reformed, 2003).
38. On the Directory for Public Worship (1645), see Horton Davies, The Worship of the English Puritans (Westminster: Dacre Press, 1948).
39. Westminster Confession of Faith, Chapter 6, "Of the Fall of Man, of Sin, and of the Punishment thereof." See Letham, Westminster Assembly, 167–89.
40. Richard Baxter, The Quakers' Catechism, or the Quakers Questioned (London, 1655). On the Baxter-Quaker exchanges, see William C. Braithwaite, The Beginnings of Quakerism, 2nd ed., rev. Henry J. Cadbury (Cambridge: Cambridge University Press, 1955), 241–58.
41. James Nayler, An Answer to a Book Called The Quakers Catechism (London, 1656). On the Baxter-Nayler exchange, see Leo Damrosch, The Sorrows of the Quaker Jesus: James Nayler and the Puritan Crackdown on the Free Spirit (Cambridge, MA: Harvard University Press, 1996), 89–112.
42. Westminster Confession of Faith, Chapter 1, "Of the Holy Scripture." On Scripture's authority in Reformed thought, see Muller, Post-Reformation Reformed Dogmatics, 2:63–146.

43. Westminster Confession of Faith, Chapters 3 ("Of God's Eternal Decree"), 9 ("Of Free Will"), and 10 ("Of Effectual Calling"). See Letham, Westminster Assembly, 143–66.
44. On Reformed "Two Kingdoms" theology, see David VanDrunen, Natural Law and the Two Kingdoms: A Study in the Development of Reformed Social Thought (Grand Rapids: Eerdmans, 2010).
45. On the magistrate's duties regarding religion in Presbyterian political theology, see John Coffey, Persecution and Toleration in Protestant England, 1558–1689 (Harlow: Pearson, 2000), 109–53.
46. On the Presbyterian vision of the "holy commonwealth," see William Lamont, Godly Rule: Politics and Religion, 1603–60 (London: Macmillan, 1969).
47. On Luther's Two Kingdoms doctrine and its Reformed adaptation, see VanDrunen, Natural Law and the Two Kingdoms, 41–93. Baxter's formulation "the magistrate rules the pastor by the sword; the pastor rules the magistrate by the word" appears in various forms in his writings; see A Holy Commonwealth (London, 1659; modern ed., ed. William Lamont, Cambridge: Cambridge University Press, 1994), 227.
48. Samuel Rutherford, Lex, Rex, or The Law and the Prince (London, 1644; modern ed., Harrisonburg, VA: Sprinkle Publications, 1982). See John Coffey, Politics, Religion and the British Revolutions: The Mind of Samuel Rutherford (Cambridge: Cambridge University Press, 1997).
49. On Rutherford's covenant theology and the "threefold covenant," see Coffey, Politics, Religion and the British Revolutions, 143–72. The quotation "a king is a living law" is from Lex, Rex, Question XIV.
50. On Rutherford's arguments for resistance and popular sovereignty, see Coffey, Politics, Religion and the British Revolutions, 173–93.
51. On Lex, Rex's condemnation after the Restoration, see Coffey, Politics, Religion and the British Revolutions, 194–215.
52. The Solemn League and Covenant (September 1643) is printed in Samuel Rawson Gardiner, ed., The Constitutional Documents of the Puritan Revolution, 1625–1660, 3rd ed. (Oxford: Clarendon Press, 1906), 267–71.
53. On the Covenant's terms and ambiguities, see Edward J. Cowan, "The Solemn League and Covenant," in The Scottish National Covenant in Its British Context, ed. John Morrill (Edinburgh: Edinburgh University Press, 1990), 182–202.
54. On the Covenant's failure to achieve uniformity, see David Scott, "The 'Northern Gentlemen,' the Parliamentary Independents, and Anglo-Scottish Relations," Historical Journal 42, no. 2 (1999): 347–75.
55. Robert Baillie's complaint (1645) is from Baillie, Letters and Journals, 2:265–67.
56. Richard Baxter, A Holy Commonwealth (London, 1659; modern ed., ed. William Lamont, Cambridge: Cambridge University Press, 1994). See William Lamont, Richard Baxter and the Millennium (London: Croom Helm, 1979), 167–213.
57. On Baxter's rejection of democracy and his citation of Judges, see Lamont, ed., Holy Commonwealth, 91–178.
58. On Baxter's argument for mixed government, see Michael Mendle, Dangerous Positions: Mixed Government, the Estates of the Realm, and the Making of the Answer to the XIX Propositions (University: University of Alabama Press, 1985), 192–229.
59. On Baxter's position combining establishment with limited toleration, see Keeble, Richard Baxter, 125–38.
60. On Baxter's limited view of popular participation, see Lamont, ed., Holy Commonwealth, 179–245.
61. On Baxter's moderate positions, see I. M. Green, The Re-Establishment of the Church of England, 1660–1663 (Oxford: Oxford University Press, 1978), 22–47.
62. On Presbyterian distinctions between subjects and citizens, see Glenn Burgess, British Political Thought, 1500–1660 (Basingstoke: Palgrave Macmillan, 2009), 189–223.
63. On the church as political formation, see Michael Walzer, The Revolution of the Saints: A Study in the Origins of Radical Politics (Cambridge, MA: Harvard University Press,

1965), 183–226.

64. On Presbyterian defense of compulsory tithes, see Christopher Hill, Economic Problems of the Church from Archbishop Whitgift to the Long Parliament (Oxford: Clarendon Press, 1956), 311–43.

65. On Presbyterian attitudes toward toleration, see Coffey, Persecution and Toleration, 154–88.

66. On oaths in Presbyterian thought, see Westminster Confession of Faith, Chapter 22, "Of Lawful Oaths and Vows." On the political significance of oaths, see Edward Vallance, Revolutionary England and the National Covenant (Woodbridge: Boydell Press, 2005), 89–134.

67. On the concept of national blood guilt, see Patricia Crawford, "Charles Stuart, That Man of Blood," Journal of British Studies 16, no. 2 (1977): 41–61.

68. On the Presbyterian dilemma over regicide, see David Underdown, Pride's Purge: Politics in the Puritan Revolution (Oxford: Clarendon Press, 1971), 143–67.

69. Philip Skippon's speech at Nayler's trial is recorded in Thomas Burton, Diary of Thomas Burton, Esq., Member in the Parliaments of Oliver and Richard Cromwell, ed. John Towill Rutt, 4 vols. (London: Henry Colburn, 1828), 1:24–173.

70. On the parliamentary ordinances (1645–1648) establishing presbyterian structures, see William A. Shaw, A History of the English Church During the Civil Wars and Under the Commonwealth, 1640–1660, 2 vols. (London: Longmans, Green, 1900), 2:1–98.

71. The June 1647 ordinance creating parliamentary appeals committee is in Firth and Rait, Acts and Ordinances, 1:962–65. On Scottish horror at the Erastian structure, see Baillie, Letters and Journals, 2:385–412.

72. On the chaotic implementation, see Claire Cross, "The Church in England, 1646–1660," in The Interregnum: The Quest for Settlement, 1646–1660, ed. G. E. Aylmer (London: Macmillan, 1972), 99–120.

73. On difficulties finding ruling elders, see Ann Hughes, "The Frustrations of the Godly," in Revolution and Restoration: England in the 1650s, ed. John Morrill (London: Collins & Brown, 1992), 70–90.

74. On London's twelve classes and their relative success, see Shaw, History of the English Church, 2:80–147.

75. Examples of London presbyterian discipline are from London Provincial Assembly Minutes (Dr. Williams's Library, London, MS 201.1); discussed in Shaw, History of the English Church, 2:118–35.

76. On Independent defiance of London presbyteries, see Nuttall, Visible Saints, 69–98.

77. On John Goodwin and Independent resistance, see Ann Hughes, Gangraena and the Struggle for the English Revolution (Oxford: Oxford University Press, 2004), 244–89.

78. On disputes between presbyteries and Parliament, see Shaw, History of the English Church, 2:136–47.

79. On the New Model Army's religious culture, see Anne Laurence, Parliamentary Army Chaplains, 1642–1651 (Woodbridge: Boydell Press, 1990), 94–144.

80. On the Army's refusal to disband, see Ian Gentles, The New Model Army in England, Ireland and Scotland, 1645–1653 (Oxford: Blackwell, 1992), 163–211.

81. On Pride's Purge, see Underdown, Pride's Purge, 143–67; and Blair Worden, The Rump Parliament, 1648–1653 (Cambridge: Cambridge University Press, 1974), 46–86.

82. On Presbyterian responses to Army power, see Tai Liu, Puritan London: A Study of Religion and Society in the City Parishes (Newark: University of Delaware Press, 1986), 93–128.

83. On Presbyterian hopes at the Restoration, see Green, Re-Establishment, 1–67.

84. Charles II's Declaration of Breda and Worcester House Declaration are printed in Gardiner, Constitutional Documents, 465–67. See Green, Re-Establishment, 48–87.

85. On the Savoy Conference (1661), see Green, Re-Establishment, 113–79.

86. On the bishops' rejection of Presbyterian proposals, see Robert S. Bosher, The Making of the Restoration Settlement (Westminster: Dacre Press, 1951), 244–79.

87. The Act of Uniformity (1662) is printed in Gee and Hardy, Documents Illustrative of English Church History (London: Macmillan, 1896), 600–619.
88. On the Great Ejection, see A. G. Matthews, Calamy Revised: Being a Revision of Edmund Calamy's Account of the Ministers and Others Ejected and Silenced, 1660–2 (Oxford: Clarendon Press, 1934).
89. On Scottish Presbyterianism's triumph after 1689, see Ian B. Cowan, The Scottish Covenanters, 1660–1688 (London: Victor Gollancz, 1976).
90. On the Church of Scotland's presbyterian structure, see Andrew L. Drummond and James Bulloch, The Scottish Church, 1688–1843 (Edinburgh: Saint Andrew Press, 1973).
91. On the Kirk's educational and cultural influence, see George Elder Davie, The Democratic Intellect: Scotland and Her Universities in the Nineteenth Century (Edinburgh: Edinburgh University Press, 1961).
92. On American Presbyterianism, see Leigh Eric Schmidt, Holy Fairs: Scottish Communions and American Revivals (Princeton: Princeton University Press, 1989).
93. On Presbyterian college founding, see Mark A. Noll, Princeton and the Republic, 1768–1822 (Princeton: Princeton University Press, 1989).
94. On the Old Side-New Side split, see Leonard J. Trinterud, The Forming of an American Tradition: A Re-examination of Colonial Presbyterianism (Philadelphia: Westminster Press, 1949).
95] On dissenting academies, see H. McLachlan, English Education Under the Test Acts (Manchester: Manchester University Press, 1931).
96. On the "Nonconformist conscience," see D. W. Bebbington, The Nonconformist Conscience: Chapel and Politics, 1870–1914 (London: George Allen & Unwin, 1982).
97. On the Protestant work ethic, see Max Weber, The Protestant Ethic and the Spirit of Capitalism, trans. Talcott Parsons (1905; London: Routledge, 1992).
98. On Presbyterian discipline's mixed legacy, see Todd, Culture of Protestantism, 199–381.
99. On education as religious duty, see Lawrence A. Cremin, American Education: The Colonial Experience, 1607–1783 (New York: Harper & Row, 1970), 189–305.
100. On accountability structures, see Walzer, Revolution of the Saints, 183–226.
101. On federal theology influencing political thought, see Glenn A. Moots, Politics Reformed: The Anglo-American Legacy of Covenant Theology (Columbia: University of Missouri Press, 2010), 1–56.
102. On rigidity in Presbyterian discipline, see Leah Leneman and Rosalind Mitchison, Sin in the City: Sexuality and Social Control in Urban Scotland, 1660–1780 (Edinburgh: Scottish Cultural Press, 1998).
103. On Presbyterian intolerance, see Coffey, Persecution and Toleration, 109–53.
104. On legalism in Presbyterian tradition, see T. F. Torrance, "Covenant or Contract?" Scottish Journal of Theology 23, no. 1 (1970): 51–76.
105. On Presbyterian discipline serving social control functions, see Graham, Uses of Reform, 277–343.
106. On the Presbyterian wager about regenerate persons and corporate discipline, see Morgan, Visible Saints, 113–38.
107. On circumstantial and structural reasons for English presbyterian failure, see Lamont, Godly Rule, 105–63; and Underdown, Pride's Purge, 336–71.

Notes — Chapter 4

1. On the Putney Debates (28 October–11 November 1647) and the General Council of the Army meeting at St. Mary's Church, Putney, see A. S. P. Woodhouse, ed., *Puritanism and Liberty: Being the Army Debates (1647–9) from the Clarke Manuscripts with Supplementary Documents* (Chicago: University of Chicago Press, 1951), 1–124; Austin Woolrych, *Soldiers and Statesmen: The General Council of the Army and Its Debates, 1647–1648* (Oxford: Clarendon Press, 1987), 168–234; and Ian Gentles, *The New Model Army in England, Ireland and Scotland, 1645–1653* (Oxford: Blackwell, 1992), 212–58. The Clarke Manuscripts (Bodleian Library, Oxford) preserve William Clarke's shorthand notes of the debates, discovered in 1890 and first published in 1891.

2. On Oliver Cromwell (1599–1658) and Henry Ireton (1611–1651) as Army political leaders and their convening of the General Council, see Barry Coward, *Oliver Cromwell* (London: Longman, 1991), 37–45; and David Farr, *Henry Ireton and the English Revolution* (Woodbridge: Boydell Press, 2006), 93–128. Ireton, Cromwell's son-in-law (married to Bridget Cromwell in 1646), was the Army's chief constitutional theorist and negotiator with the King.
3. On the agitators and Leveller representatives at Putney—Edward Sexby, Thomas Rainsborough, John Wildman, Maximilian Petty—see H. N. Brailsford, *The Levellers and the English Revolution*, ed. Christopher Hill (London: Cresset Press, 1961), 234–89; and Rachel Foxley, *The Levellers: Radical Political Thought in the English Revolution* (Manchester: Manchester University Press, 2013), 91–136. Edward Sexby (c. 1616–1658) was a cavalry trooper and agitator from Fairfax's regiment. Thomas Rainsborough (c. 1610–1648) was the highest-ranking officer to support the Leveller cause. John Wildman (1621–1693) and Maximilian Petty were civilian Leveller theorists who helped draft *The Agreement of the People.*
4. *An Agreement of the People* (presented 28 October 1647) is printed in Woodhouse, *Puritanism and Liberty*, 443–45; and in Samuel Rawson Gardiner, ed., *The Constitutional Documents of the Puritan Revolution, 1625–1660*, 3rd ed. (Oxford: Clarendon Press, 1906), 333–35. On the *Agreement*'s revolutionary proposals, see Brailsford, *Levellers*, 290–325; and Michael Mendle, ed., *The Putney Debates of 1647: The Army, the Levellers and the English State* (Cambridge: Cambridge University Press, 2001), 1–46.
5. Cromwell's opening prayer and Ireton's framing of issues are recorded in Woodhouse, *Puritanism and Liberty*, 3–7. Cromwell characteristically opened important meetings with extended prayer seeking divine guidance—a practice that sometimes frustrated impatient colleagues but reflected his genuine belief in Providence.
6. On the franchise debate at Putney and Ireton's argument for property qualifications, see Woodhouse, *Puritanism and Liberty*, 53–78; and C. B. Macpherson, *The Political Theory of Possessive Individualism: Hobbes to Locke* (Oxford: Clarendon Press, 1962), 107–59. Ireton argued that voting rights should be limited to those with "a permanent fixed interest in this kingdom"—i.e., property holders who had stake in preserving social order.
7. Thomas Rainsborough's famous statement—"For really I think that the poorest he that is in England hath a life to live, as the greatest he"—is in Woodhouse, *Puritanism and Liberty*, 53. This is the most quoted passage from the Putney Debates, expressing the radical democratic principle that every man deserved political voice. See Keith Thomas, "The Levellers and the Franchise," in *The Interregnum: The Quest for Settlement, 1646–1660*, ed. G. E. Aylmer (London: Macmillan, 1972), 57–78, on its significance.
8. Ireton's response about property rights is in Woodhouse, *Puritanism and Liberty*, 54–58. Ireton feared that universal male suffrage would lead to votes to abolish property—"by the same reason that you demand that all men should have a voice in this government, you may as well destroy all property."
9. On William Dell's preaching during the debates and John Wildman's arguments from first principles, see Woodhouse, *Puritanism and Liberty*, 71–83; and J. C. Davis, "The Levellers and Christianity," in *Politics, Religion and the English Civil War*, ed. Brian Manning (London: Edward Arnold, 1973), 225–50. Dell (c. 1607–1669) was an Army chaplain who preached that God was no respecter of persons and that civil distinctions of wealth shouldn't override spiritual equality.
10. On Cromwell's sympathy for agitators' religious arguments but fear of political consequences, see Coward, *Oliver Cromwell*, 42–48; and Blair Worden, "Oliver Cromwell and the Sin of Achan," in *History, Society and the Churches: Essays in Honour of Owen Chadwick*, ed. Derek Beales and Geoffrey Best (Cambridge: Cambridge University Press, 1985), 125–45. Cromwell believed God regarded poor and rich equally but worried that extending franchise to the propertyless would produce social chaos.
11. On Cromwell's negotiations with Charles I and the need for royal cooperation in any

settlement, see David L. Smith, *Constitutional Royalism and the Search for Settlement, c. 1640–1649* (Cambridge: Cambridge University Press, 1994), 181–249; and Farr, *Henry Ireton*, 93–128. Cromwell and Ireton negotiated with Charles at Hampton Court (October–November 1647) while the Putney debates proceeded, hoping to reach terms Charles would accept.

12. On Cromwell's adjournment of the debates and delaying tactics, see Woolrych, *Soldiers and Statesmen*, 225–34; and Gentles, *New Model Army*, 245–53. Cromwell proposed adjournment "to consider the Agreement more carefully" and "seek God's guidance"—language suggesting serious consideration while actually postponing decisions indefinitely.
13. On the Corkbush Field rendezvous (15 November 1647) and suppression of Leveller mutiny, see Woolrych, *Soldiers and Statesmen*, 253–83; and Gentles, *New Model Army*, 253–58. Cromwell divided the Army into three rendezvous locations to prevent unified Leveller action. At Corkbush Field (Ware, Hertfordshire), two regiments appeared with *Agreement of the People* copies in their hats. Cromwell and Fairfax suppressed the mutiny; three ringleaders were court-martialed, and Private Richard Arnold was executed by firing squad.
14. On the breaking of the Leveller movement in the Army and continuation of Leveller pamphlet campaigns, see Brailsford, *Levellers*, 326–85; and Mark A. Kishlansky, "The Army and the Levellers: The Roads to Putney," *Historical Journal* 22, no. 4 (1979): 795–824. Leveller influence in the Army was broken by Corkbush Field, though civilian Leveller leaders (John Lilburne, Richard Overton, William Walwyn) continued publishing until their suppression in 1649.
15. On Cromwell's vision of ordered liberty led by godly men, see Blair Worden, "Providence and Politics in Cromwellian England," *Past & Present* 109 (1985): 55–99; and J. C. Davis, "Cromwell's Religion," in *Oliver Cromwell and the English Revolution*, ed. John Morrill (London: Longman, 1990), 181–208. Cromwell wanted a commonwealth governed by visible saints—not necessarily wealthy or well-born, but demonstrably godly and capable.
16. On the Levellers' vision of radical democracy based on natural rights, see Foxley, *Levellers*, 137–85; and J. C. Davis, "The Levellers and Democracy," *Past & Present* 40 (1968): 174–80. Leveller political theory emphasized popular sovereignty, natural rights, equality before law, and rejection of hereditary privilege.
17. On "Independent" as self-description and insult, and the congregational principle of church autonomy, see Geoffrey F. Nuttall, *Visible Saints: The Congregational Way, 1640–1660* (Oxford: Basil Blackwell, 1957), 1–37; and Michael R. Watts, *The Dissenters*, vol. 1, *From the Reformation to the French Revolution* (Oxford: Clarendon Press, 1978), 102–39. "Independent" was often used pejoratively by Presbyterians who associated it with disorder and schism.
18. John Cotton, *The Way of the Churches of Christ in New England* (London, 1645); modern edition in *The Complete Writings of John Cotton*, ed. Sargent Bush Jr. et al. (New Haven: Yale University Press, forthcoming). On Cotton (1585–1652) and New England's influence on English Independents, see Larzer Ziff, *The Career of John Cotton: Puritanism and the American Experience* (Princeton: Princeton University Press, 1962); and Edmund S. Morgan, *Visible Saints: The History of a Puritan Idea* (New York: New York University Press, 1963), 64–138.
19. On Independent congregations in 1640s England—open and secret meetings, varied practices, shared commitments—see Nuttall, *Visible Saints*, 69–110; and Tai Liu, *Puritan London: A Study of Religion and Society in the City Parishes* (Newark: University of Delaware Press, 1986), 53–92. As censorship collapsed in the 1640s, Independent congregations multiplied in London and provincial cities, meeting openly where they could and secretly where necessary.
20. The Bedford church covenant (1650) is quoted in John Bunyan, *Grace Abounding to the Chief of Sinners*, ed. W. R. Owens (London: Penguin, 1987), xxiii–xxiv (from the church

records); and discussed in Christopher Hill, *A Tinker and a Poor Man: John Bunyan and His Church, 1628–1688* (New York: Alfred A. Knopf, 1989), 94–121. The covenant language was typical of gathered church covenants—voluntary association, mutual commitment, openness to new light, corporate responsibility.

21. On church covenants creating congregations without external authority, see David D. Hall, *The Faithful Shepherd: A History of the New England Ministry in the Seventeenth Century* (Chapel Hill: University of North Carolina Press, 1972), 94–133; and Morgan, *Visible Saints*, 88–112. The covenant was the constituting act—the gathered saints' voluntary agreement created the church.
22. On membership examination and conversion testimony requirements, see Patricia Caldwell, *The Puritan Conversion Narrative: The Beginnings of American Expression* (Cambridge: Cambridge University Press, 1983); and Charles Lloyd Cohen, *God's Caress: The Psychology of Puritan Religious Experience* (New York: Oxford University Press, 1986). Independent churches required prospective members to give credible account of God's saving work in their lives.
23. Bunyan's examination for church membership is described in *Grace Abounding*, 82–84; and discussed in Hill, *Tinker and a Poor Man*, 122–47. The Bedford church examined candidates before the congregation, requiring testimony that demonstrated genuine conversion.
24. On regenerate membership as distinctive Independent practice, see Morgan, *Visible Saints*, 1–32; and E. Brooks Holifield, *The Covenant Sealed: The Development of Puritan Sacramental Theology in Old and New England, 1570–1720* (New Haven: Yale University Press, 1974), 95–156. Independents insisted on churches of visible saints—those showing evidence of grace—rather than mixed parishes of believers and unbelievers.
25. On Matthew 18:15–17 as pattern for church discipline and the Independent application, see John Calvin, *Institutes of the Christian Religion*, ed. John T. McNeill, trans. Ford Lewis Battles, 2 vols. (Philadelphia: Westminster Press, 1960), 4.12.1–13; and Nuttall, *Visible Saints*, 111–46. The four-stage process (private admonition, witnesses, tell the church, exclusion) aimed at restoration rather than punishment.
26. The John Child discipline case (1653) is from Bedford Meeting Records (Bedfordshire Record Office), discussed in Hill, *Tinker and a Poor Man*, 174–89. Church records document the investigation, witnesses' testimony, Child's confession, and the decision to suspend him from communion for three months as test of repentance.
27. On the Bedford church's handling of Child's case and his eventual restoration, see Hill, *Tinker and a Poor Man*, 189–93. After three months, Child's changed behavior convinced the church his repentance was genuine, and they restored him to full fellowship—discipline working as intended for restoration.
28. On Independent excommunication as purely ecclesial without civil penalties, see Nuttall, *Visible Saints*, 137–46; and Michael Winship, *Godly Republicanism: Puritans, Pilgrims, and a City on a Hill* (Cambridge, MA: Harvard University Press, 2012), 204–58. Independent excommunication removed a person from communion and church voting but imposed no civil punishment—a stark contrast to magisterial churches.
29. The quote about excommunication's restorative purpose is from John Owen, *The True Nature of a Gospel Church* (London, 1689), 287–91; discussed in Peter Toon, *God's Statesman: The Life and Work of John Owen* (Exeter: Paternoster Press, 1971), 89–116. Owen (1616–1683) was the leading Independent divine of his generation.
30. On the contrast between Independent and magisterial church discipline, see John Coffey, *Persecution and Toleration in Protestant England, 1558–1689* (Harlow: Pearson, 2000), 154–88; and Michael R. Watts, *The Dissenters*, 1:140–76. Presbyterian and Anglican excommunication expected magistrates to enforce church censures with fines and imprisonment; Independent excommunication was purely spiritual censure.
31. On congregational decision-making in Independent churches—calling ministers, buying property, exercising discipline—see Nuttall, *Visible Saints*, 38–68; and Winship, *Godly Republicanism*, 147–203. Major decisions required congregational vote, not clerical

or lay oligarchy.

32. On the relative equality of members in congregational voting—regardless of wealth, education, or (sometimes) gender—see Patricia Crawford, *Women and Religion in England, 1500–1720* (London: Routledge, 1993), 113–62; and Phyllis Mack, *Visionary Women: Ecstatic Prophecy in Seventeenth-Century England* (Berkeley: University of California Press, 1992), 99–145. Practices varied—some churches restricted women's speech more than others—but spiritual maturity mattered more than social status.
33. On John Bunyan's call to ministry without university education or episcopal ordination, see Hill, *Tinker and a Poor Man*, 194–243; and Roger Sharrock, *John Bunyan* (London: Hutchinson's University Library, 1954), 47–83. Bunyan's famous statement "I have received my commission from heaven" is from *Grace Abounding*, 85. The Bedford church called him as pastor in 1672 based on their recognition of God's gifts in him, not on formal credentials.
34. On limits of Independent democracy—not all opinions equal, Scripture and orthodoxy bounded debate, some voices carried more weight—see Nuttall, *Visible Saints*, 147–74; and Hall, *Faithful Shepherd*, 134–82. Congregational decision-making wasn't simple majority rule but corporate discernment under Scripture and Spirit's guidance.
35. On the distinction between essentials and circumstantials in Independent thought, see Coffey, *Persecution and Toleration*, 154–88; and B. R. White, *The English Separatist Tradition: From the Marian Martyrs to the Pilgrim Fathers* (Oxford: Oxford University Press, 1971), 154–92. Independents insisted on core doctrines (Trinity, Incarnation, justification by faith) while allowing liberty on many other matters.
36. On congregational practices teaching political habits—public argument, listening to contrary views, accepting corporate decisions, holding leaders accountable—see Michael Walzer, *The Revolution of the Saints: A Study in the Origins of Radical Politics* (Cambridge, MA: Harvard University Press, 1965), 183–226; and Stephen Foster, *The Long Argument: English Puritanism and the Shaping of New England Culture, 1570–1700* (Chapel Hill: University of North Carolina Press, 1991), 130–81. The gathered church was a school of citizenship, teaching habits that transferred to political life.
37. On Cromwell's recruitment strategy prioritizing godliness over social status, see C. H. Firth, *Cromwell's Army: A History of the English Soldier During the Civil Wars, the Commonwealth, and the Protectorate* (London: Methuen, 1902; repr. London: Greenhill Books, 1992), 271–316; and Gentles, *New Model Army*, 91–117. Cromwell wanted soldiers motivated by conviction rather than pay or feudal duty.
38. Cromwell's famous statement about preferring "a plain russet-coated captain" is from his letter to William Spring (September 1643), printed in W. C. Abbott, ed., *The Writings and Speeches of Oliver Cromwell*, 4 vols. (Cambridge, MA: Harvard University Press, 1937–1947), 1:256. On revolutionary implications of valuing religious commitment over social status, see Mark A. Kishlansky, *The Rise of the New Model Army* (Cambridge: Cambridge University Press, 1979), 55–89.
39. On the New Model Army as religious community—theology debates, prayer meetings, chaplain preaching, Psalm-singing at Naseby—see Anne Laurence, *Parliamentary Army Chaplains, 1642–1651* (Woodbridge: Boydell Press, 1990), 94–144; and Leo F. Solt, *Saints in Arms: Puritanism and Democracy in Cromwell's Army* (Stanford: Stanford University Press, 1959), 1–43.
40. On William Dell (c. 1607–1669) and his rejection of clerical monopoly, see B. S. Capp, *The Fifth Monarchy Men: A Study in Seventeenth-Century English Millenarianism* (London: Faber and Faber, 1972), 57–83; and Christopher Hill, *The World Turned Upside Down: Radical Ideas During the English Revolution* (London: Temple Smith, 1972), 71–95. Dell's famous attack on universities ("the forge where the fetters are made") is from his sermon *The Building and Glory of the Truly Christian and Spiritual Church* (London, 1646).
41. Dell's sermon *The Building and Glory of the Truly Christian and Spiritual Church* (1646) is reprinted in *Several Sermons and Discourses of William Dell* (London, 1709), 93–148. The quoted passage is on 112–15.

42. On Hugh Peters (1598–1660) and his militant preaching, see Raymond P. Stearns, *The Strenuous Puritan: Hugh Peter, 1598–1660* (Urbana: University of Illinois Press, 1954); and J. F. Wilson, *Pulpit in Parliament: Puritanism During the English Civil Wars, 1640–1648* (Princeton: Princeton University Press, 1969), 189–224. Peters had ministered in Salem, Massachusetts (1635–1641) before returning to England. He was executed at the Restoration for his role in Charles I's trial.
43. On Peters's view that godly warfare was righteous and his cry "The sword of the Lord and of Gideon!" (from Judges 7:20), see Stearns, *Strenuous Puritan*, 178–234. Peters's position that Christians could wield the sword without spiritual compromise would be challenged by Quakers' peace testimony.
44. On John Saltmarsh (d. 1647) and his antinomianism and Leveller sympathies, see Leo F. Solt, "John Saltmarsh: New Model Army Chaplain," *Journal of Ecclesiastical History* 2, no. 1 (1951): 69–80; and Hill, *World Turned Upside Down*, 162–83. Saltmarsh's *Smoke in the Temple* (London, 1646) attacked presbyterian establishment as new tyranny. He died in 1647, collapsing after preaching at Army headquarters and warning Fairfax of divine judgment if the Army failed to establish justice.
45. On New Model Army prayer meetings blurring worship and politics, see Solt, *Saints in Arms*, 44–76; and Gentles, *New Model Army*, 118–62. Regiments held regular prayer meetings where soldiers prayed, heard sermons, and discussed matters of conscience—inevitably political given the Army's mission.
46. On intensification of prayer meetings in 1646–1647 as questions about England's future became urgent, see Woolrych, *Soldiers and Statesmen*, 47–89; and Kishlansky, "Army and the Levellers," 795–824. Soldiers debated whether to disband, how to treat the King, and what reforms to demand.
47. On the transfer of gathered church model to military prayer meetings, see Solt, *Saints in Arms*, 77–108; and David Como, *Radical Parliamentarians and the English Civil War* (Oxford: Oxford University Press, 2018), 289–345. Soldiers who could testify to God's grace felt empowered to speak on political matters, applying spiritual egalitarianism to temporal affairs.
48. On the agitators' emergence (spring 1647) and their election by regiments, see Kishlansky, *Rise of the New Model Army*, 155–211; and Woolrych, *Soldiers and Statesmen*, 90–167. Each regiment elected two soldier representatives ("agitators" or "agents") to speak for the men regarding pay arrears, indemnity, and political demands.
49. On Leveller ideas entering the Army through pamphlets—John Lilburne's attacks on tyranny, Richard Overton's natural rights arguments, William Walwyn's pleas for toleration—see Brailsford, *Levellers*, 178–233; and Foxley, *Levellers*, 47–90. Leveller language resonated with Army religion's emphasis on freedom and conscience.
50. On the Army's refusal to disband (June 1647) and creation of the General Council, see Gentles, *New Model Army*, 212–45; and Woolrych, *Soldiers and Statesmen*, 168–234. The General Council included officers and agitators, intended to maintain Army unity while discussing demands.
51. On General Council meetings beginning with prayer then turning to political debate, see Woodhouse, *Puritanism and Liberty*, passim; and Coward, *Oliver Cromwell*, 37–55. Cromwell's extended prayers (often an hour or more) seeking divine guidance preceded intensely political debates about government, franchise, and rights.
52. On the fusion of religious and political language at Putney—Rainsborough grounding franchise in theology, Ireton defending property with providential language—see Woodhouse, *Puritanism and Liberty*, 53–78; and J. C. Davis, "Religion and the Struggle for Freedom in the English Revolution," *Historical Journal* 35, no. 3 (1992): 507–30.
53. On religious diversity in the New Model Army—Independents, Baptists, antinomians, early Quakers—and Cromwell's refusal to impose uniformity, see Gentles, *New Model Army*, 91–117; and J. F. McGregor, "The Baptists: Fount of All Heresy," in *Radical Religion in the English Revolution*, ed. J. F. McGregor and B. Reay (Oxford: Oxford University Press, 1984), 23–63.

54. On Cromwell's pragmatic toleration valuing military effectiveness over religious uniformity, see Davis, "Cromwell's Religion," 181–208; and Worden, "Providence and Politics," 55–99. Cromwell believed in liberty of conscience for "godly" men and refused Presbyterian pressure to impose uniformity.
55. Cromwell's letter to the Westminster Assembly (March 1644) after Lincoln is in Abbott, *Writings and Speeches*, 1:277–78. The passage about "Presbyterians, Independents, all had here the same spirit" expresses Cromwell's view that doctrinal differences mattered less than shared godliness.
56. On the limits of Cromwell's toleration—extending only to "godly" Protestants, not to Catholics or Anglicans—see Blair Worden, "Toleration and the Cromwellian Protectorate," in *Persecution and Toleration*, ed. W. J. Sheils (Oxford: Blackwell, 1984), 199–233; and Coffey, *Persecution and Toleration*, 154–88. Cromwell's toleration was broad but bounded by judgments about who was "godly."
57. On practical benefits of Cromwell's toleration policy—wider recruiting pool, avoidance of sectarian violence—see Firth, *Cromwell's Army*, 317–58; and Gentles, *New Model Army*, 118–43.
58. On radical implications of Army toleration—if diverse beliefs compatible with military order, why not with social order?—see Solt, *Saints in Arms*, 109–42; and Hill, *World Turned Upside Down*, 96–120.
59. On John Milton's arguments in *Areopagitica* (1644) and later works that truth emerged through free contest of ideas, see John Milton, *Areopagitica and Other Political Writings*, ed. John Alvis (Indianapolis: Liberty Fund, 1999); and Blair Worden, "Milton's Republicanism and the Tyranny of Heaven," in *Machiavelli and Republicanism*, ed. Gisela Bock, Quentin Skinner, and Maurizio Viroli (Cambridge: Cambridge University Press, 1990), 225–45. Milton argued that suppressing opinions assumed infallibility and that free debate allowed truth to prevail.
60. On John Milton (1608–1674), his background, education, and early poetry, see Barbara K. Lewalski, *The Life of John Milton: A Critical Biography*, rev. ed. (Oxford: Blackwell, 2003), 1–112; and Christopher Hill, *Milton and the English Revolution* (London: Faber and Faber, 1977), 3–90. Milton was born into London's commercial class; his father, a scrivener, was prosperous enough to fund excellent education (St. Paul's School, Cambridge).
61. On Milton's transformation during the Civil War and his controversial pamphlets, see Lewalski, *Life of John Milton*, 113–252; and Hill, *Milton*, 91–174. Milton wrote pamphlets on divorce (*The Doctrine and Discipline of Divorce*, 1643), education (*Of Education*, 1644), church government (*Of Reformation*, 1641), and press freedom (*Areopagitica*, 1644).
62. On Milton's elaborate prose style demanding educated readers, see Thomas N. Corns, *Uncloistered Virtue: English Political Literature, 1640–1660* (Oxford: Clarendon Press, 1992), 167–211; and Stanley Fish, "Rhetoric and the Discovery of Uncertainty in Milton's *Areopagitica*," in *Versions of Rhetoric: A Reader*, ed. John T. Ramsey (Cambridge: Cambridge University Press, 1990), 125–48.
63. On Presbyterian dominance in Parliament and Westminster Assembly by 1643, preparing to replace episcopal tyranny with presbyterian discipline, see Tai Liu, *Discord in Zion: The Puritan Divines and the Puritan Revolution, 1640–1660* (The Hague: Martinus Nijhoff, 1973), 67–112; and William M. Lamont, *Godly Rule: Politics and Religion, 1603–60* (London: Macmillan, 1969), 105–43.
64. The Licensing Order (14 June 1643) is printed in C. H. Firth and R. S. Rait, eds., *Acts and Ordinances of the Interregnum, 1642–1660*, 3 vols. (London: HMSO, 1911), 1:184–86. On its reimposition of censorship to stop radical pamphlets, see Sabrina Alcorn Baron, "The Guises of Dissemination in Early Seventeenth-Century England," in *The Oxford History of Popular Print Culture*, vol. 1, ed. Joad Raymond (Oxford: Oxford University Press, 2011), 41–54.
65. Herbert Palmer's sermon to Parliament (13 August 1644) attacking Milton's divorce pamphlet (without naming him) is described in Lewalski, *Life of John Milton*, 162–67;

and David Masson, *The Life of John Milton: Narrated in Connexion with the Political, Ecclesiastical, and Literary History of His Time*, 7 vols. (London: Macmillan, 1859–1894), 3:183–89. The quote about "A wicked booke is abroad" is from Palmer's printed sermon (London, 1644).

66. *Areopagitica: A Speech for the Liberty of Unlicenc'd Printing, to the Parliament of England* (London, November 1644) is in Milton, *Areopagitica and Other Political Writings*, 1–49; and in *Complete Prose Works of John Milton*, vol. 2, ed. Ernest Sirluck (New Haven: Yale University Press, 1959), 480–570. On Milton's deliberate publication without license, see Hill, *Milton*, 139–74.
67. Milton's famous passage "Let her and Falsehood grapple" is from *Areopagitica*, in Milton, *Areopagitica and Other Political Writings*, 35. On this as revolutionary claim that truth needs free contest, see Ira O. Wade, "Montaigne, Milton, Locke: On Liberty of Thought," *Journal of the History of Ideas* 3, no. 2 (1942): 141–62.
68. On Milton inverting the assumption that error was more attractive than truth, see Ernest Sirluck, introduction to *Complete Prose Works*, vol. 2, 161–89; and Fish, "Rhetoric and the Discovery of Uncertainty," 125–48. Most 17th-century thinkers assumed magistrates must suppress error to protect the weak-minded; Milton claimed truth was stronger and would prevail in free debate.
69. On Milton's "marketplace of ideas" metaphor and its influence on liberal thought, see Stanley Ingber, "The Marketplace of Ideas: A Legitimizing Myth," *Duke Law Journal* 1984, no. 1 (1984): 1–91; and John Durham Peters, *Courting the Abyss: Free Speech and the Liberal Tradition* (Chicago: University of Chicago Press, 2005), 21–52.
70. Milton's passage "I cannot praise a fugitive and cloistered virtue" is from *Areopagitica*, in Milton, *Areopagitica and Other Political Writings*, 17. On this argument that encountering error was necessary for moral development, see Lewalski, *Life of John Milton*, 167–74; and Stanley Fish, *Surprised by Sin: The Reader in Paradise Lost*, 2nd ed. (Cambridge, MA: Harvard University Press, 1997), 1–46.
71. On Milton's athletic metaphor for virtue requiring exercise and testing, see Corns, *Uncloistered Virtue*, 167–93; and Georgia Christopher, *Milton and the Science of the Saints* (Princeton: Princeton University Press, 1982), 89–134. True virtue came from choosing good after seeing evil, from embracing truth after considering falsehood.
72. On Milton's more optimistic anthropology compared to standard Calvinist depravity, see John P. Rumrich, "Milton's Arianism: Why It Matters," in *Milton and Heresy*, ed. Stephen B. Dobranski and John P. Rumrich (Cambridge: Cambridge University Press, 1998), 75–92; and Hill, *Milton*, 269–86. Milton emphasized human potential under grace and the need for liberty to cultivate discernment, departing from Calvin's emphasis on external authority restraining error.
73. Milton's warning about licensing breeding tyranny—"This is the greatest censorship that can befall learning and Truth"—is from *Areopagitica*, in Milton, *Areopagitica and Other Political Writings*, 28–31. On his references to the Spanish Inquisition and papal Index as warnings, see Sirluck, introduction to *Complete Prose Works*, vol. 2, 167–82.
74. Milton's warning about licensing producing hypocrisy—"You must learn to practise hypocrisy"—is from *Areopagitica*, 40. On his argument that censorship drove dissent underground, see Lewalski, *Life of John Milton*, 174–82.
75. Milton's concluding appeal—"Give me the liberty to know, to utter, and to argue freely according to conscience, above all liberties"—is from *Areopagitica*, 49. This became one of the most quoted passages in the history of free speech advocacy.
76. Milton's explicit exclusion of Catholics—"I mean not tolerated Popery"—is from *Areopagitica*, 45. On Milton's limited toleration extending only to sincere Protestants, see Coffey, *Persecution and Toleration*, 154–88; and Blair Worden, "Toleration and the Cromwellian Protectorate," in *Persecution and Toleration*, ed. W. J. Sheils (Oxford: Blackwell, 1984), 199–233.
77. On Milton's toleration being broader than Presbyterian but narrower than Roger Williams's radical toleration, see Edmund S. Morgan, *Roger Williams: The Church and the*

State (New York: Harcourt, Brace & World, 1967), 84–124; and Teresa M. Bejan, *Mere Civility: Disagreement and the Limits of Toleration* (Cambridge, MA: Harvard University Press, 2017), 45–89.

78. On *Areopagitica* assuming educated readership and Milton's elitism, see Corns, *Uncloistered Virtue*, 194–211; and Nigel Smith, *Literature and Revolution in England, 1640–1660* (New Haven: Yale University Press, 1994), 230–67. Milton's arguments worked for those who could read Latin, follow complex reasoning, and had leisure for study.
79. On tension between Milton's elitism and the Levellers' radical democratic vision, see Hill, *Milton*, 175–219; and Austin Woolrych, "Milton and Cromwell: 'A Short but Scandalous Night of Interruption'?" in *Achievements of the Left Hand: Essays on the Prose of John Milton*, ed. Michael Lieb and John T. Shawcross (Amherst: University of Massachusetts Press, 1974), 185–218. Milton sympathized with Levellers to a point but never fully embraced universal political participation.
80. On Milton as Commonwealth propagandist and Secretary for Foreign Tongues, see Lewalski, *Life of John Milton*, 253–355; and Martin Dzelzainis, "Milton's Classical Republicanism," in *Milton and Republicanism*, ed. David Armitage, Armand Himy, and Quentin Skinner (Cambridge: Cambridge University Press, 1995), 3–24. Milton's *The Tenure of Kings and Magistrates* (1649) and *Defence of the English People* (1651) justified the regicide and defended the Commonwealth to European audiences.
81. On Milton's genuine belief in the Commonwealth as glorious republic and Cromwell as providential leader, see Hill, *Milton*, 175–219; and Worden, "Milton's Republicanism," 225–45.
82. On the Commonwealth's failure, Protectorate's authoritarianism, and Major-Generals' rule (1655–1657), see Austin Woolrych, *Commonwealth to Protectorate* (Oxford: Clarendon Press, 1982); and Christopher Durston, *Cromwell's Major-Generals: Godly Government during the English Revolution* (Manchester: Manchester University Press, 2001). The Major-Generals enforced moral discipline with military power—the opposite of voluntary Independent principles.
83. Milton's *The Readie and Easie Way to Establish a Free Commonwealth* (London, 1660) is printed in Milton, *Areopagitica and Other Political Writings*, 328–72. On Milton's hiding and survival after the Restoration, see Lewalski, *Life of John Milton*, 356–428. Milton spent his remaining years writing *Paradise Lost* (1667), *Paradise Regained* (1671), and *Samson Agonistes* (1671), processing his political disappointment through biblical epic.
84. On Independent agreement about what magistrates should not do—compel conscience, enforce church attendance, collect tithes, punish heresy—see Nuttall, *Visible Saints*, 147–74; and Coffey, *Persecution and Toleration*, 154–88. Independents were clearer on limiting magisterial authority than on defining positive duties.
85. On the radical contraction of magisterial authority this represented, see Winship, *Godly Republicanism*, 204–58; and Jeffrey R. Collins, "The Church Settlement of Oliver Cromwell," *History* 87, no. 285 (2002): 18–40. For centuries, English magistrates had enforced church attendance, collected tithes, and punished heresy; Independents removed all this from magisterial competence.
86. On the Two Kingdoms doctrine inherited from Luther but radicalized by Independents, see David VanDrunen, *Natural Law and the Two Kingdoms: A Study in the Development of Reformed Social Thought* (Grand Rapids: Eerdmans, 2010), 157–233; and Harro Höpfl, *The Christian Polity of John Calvin* (Cambridge: Cambridge University Press, 1982), 187–216. Luther distinguished spiritual and temporal kingdoms but gave magistrates broad church authority for order's sake; Independents narrowed magisterial authority dramatically.
87. Roger Williams, *The Bloudy Tenent of Persecution, for Cause of Conscience* (London, 1644); modern edition ed. Richard Groves (Macon, GA: Mercer University Press, 2001). The quoted passage about civil sword unable to heal spiritual wounds is on 136–42. On Williams (c. 1603–1683) and his "wall of separation" argument, see Morgan, *Roger Williams*, 84–124; and Timothy L. Hall, *Separating Church and State: Roger Williams and*

Religious Liberty (Urbana: University of Illinois Press, 1998).

88. On the uncontroversial proposition that magistrates should protect rights and punish harms (murder, theft, fraud, violence), see Winship, *Godly Republicanism*, 259–312; and Glenn Burgess, *British Political Thought, 1500–1660: The Politics of the Post-Reformation* (Basingstoke: Palgrave Macmillan, 2009), 224–67.
89. On magistrates defending the realm and Independent debates about defensive vs. offensive war, see Solt, *Saints in Arms*, 109–42; and Barbara Donagan, *War in England, 1642–1649* (Oxford: Oxford University Press, 2008), 343–86. Most Independents (pre-Quaker) accepted defensive warfare without question, though debates emerged about whether Christians should serve in military roles and whether defensive war could become offensive.
90. On magistrates maintaining justice through courts and dispute resolution, and Independent desires for legal reform, see Donald Veall, *The Popular Movement for Law Reform, 1640–1660* (Oxford: Clarendon Press, 1970); and Stuart E. Prall, *The Agitation for Law Reform during the Puritan Revolution, 1640–1660* (The Hague: Martinus Nijhoff, 1966). Independents wanted simpler procedures, cheaper justice, and elimination of corruption.
91. On Independent divisions over tax funding for ministers, see Christopher Hill, *Economic Problems of the Church from Archbishop Whitgift to the Long Parliament* (Oxford: Clarendon Press, 1956), 311–43; and Ann Hughes, "The Frustrations of the Godly," in *Revolution and Restoration: England in the 1650s*, ed. John Morrill (London: Collins & Brown, 1992), 70–90. Some Independents supported tax funding to ensure ministerial independence from wealthy patrons; others insisted on voluntary support to maintain congregational accountability.
92. On debates about magistrates protecting worship from disruption vs. punishing alternative meetings, see Nuttall, *Visible Saints*, 147–74; and Barry Reay, *The Quakers and the English Revolution* (London: Temple Smith, 1985), 38–67. Independents debated whether unlimited toleration would produce chaos or whether God's truth would prevail through free competition.
93. On the messy reality of 1650s experiments—Cromwell's broad toleration, varying local enforcement, no coherent system—see Blair Worden, *The Rump Parliament, 1648–1653* (Cambridge: Cambridge University Press, 1974), 237–89; and Woolrych, *Commonwealth to Protectorate*, 234–89.
94. On Cromwell's expulsion of the Rump (April 1653) and the Nominated Parliament (Barebone's Parliament, July–December 1653), see Woolrych, *Commonwealth to Protectorate*, 1–145; and Austin Woolrych, "The Calling of Barebone's Parliament," *English Historical Review* 80, no. 316 (1965): 492–513. The assembly of 140 men was selected by Army officers and Independent churches for godliness and commitment to reform.
95. On the Nominated Parliament's composition—Fifth Monarchists, moderate Independents, crypto-Presbyterians—and radical reform debates, see Capp, *Fifth Monarchy Men*, 84–117; and Bernard S. Capp, "The Fifth Monarchists and Popular Millenarianism," in *Radical Religion in the English Revolution*, ed. McGregor and Reay, 165–89. Proposals included abolishing tithes, codifying law, creating civil marriage, reforming legal system, and establishing religious toleration.
96. On the Nominated Parliament's internal conflicts and December 1653 dissolution, see Woolrych, *Commonwealth to Protectorate*, 146–233; and Worden, *Rump Parliament*, 290–367. When Fifth Monarchists proposed immediate abolition of tithes, moderates panicked at alienating property owners and dissolved the assembly, handing power back to Cromwell.
97. On the Protectorate (1653–1658) and the Instrument of Government, see Woolrych, *Commonwealth to Protectorate*, 234–389; and Blair Worden, "Oliver Cromwell and the Protectorate," in *The Cromwellian Protectorate*, ed. Patrick Little (Woodbridge: Boydell Press, 2007), 37–67. The Instrument of Government (December 1653) was England's

first and only written constitution, creating constitutional monarchy without a king.

98. The Instrument of Government's religious liberty clause is printed in Gardiner, *Constitutional Documents*, 416. On its provision of significant but bounded toleration, see Worden, "Toleration and the Cromwellian Protectorate," 199–233; and Collins, "Church Settlement," 18–40. Liberty extended to Protestant dissenters but not to "Popery or Prelacy" or "licentiousness."
99. On the breadth of toleration under the Protectorate—Independents, Baptists, even Quakers meeting openly—and its limits on Catholics and Anglicans, see Coffey, *Persecution and Toleration*, 154–88; and Reay, *Quakers and the English Revolution*, 38–67. This was broader than England had known but not unlimited.
100. On Cromwell's funding experiments—state-salaried parish ministers alongside unsupported gathered churches, modified tithes—see Hill, *Economic Problems of the Church*, 311–43; and Hughes, "Frustrations of the Godly," 70–90. The system satisfied no one fully but worked tolerably.
101. On the Major-Generals' rule (1655–1657) and its unpopularity, see Durston, *Cromwell's Major-Generals*, 1–89; and Ronald Hutton, *The British Republic, 1649–1660*, 2nd ed. (Basingstoke: Macmillan, 2000), 89–124. England was divided into military districts with Major-Generals enforcing moral discipline—closing alehouses, prosecuting Sabbath-breaking, suppressing entertainments. The experiment was abandoned after eighteen months due to unpopularity.
102. On the parliamentary coalition's fragility and incompatible visions, see David Underdown, *Pride's Purge: Politics in the Puritan Revolution* (Oxford: Clarendon Press, 1971), 1–46; and Worden, *Rump Parliament*, 1–86. Presbyterians, Independents, Army radicals, and Levellers cooperated against the King but had incompatible visions for England's future.
103. On the coalition's fracture—Pride's Purge (December 1648), suppression of Levellers at Burford (May 1649), Cromwell's expulsion of the Rump (April 1653)—see Underdown, *Pride's Purge*, 143–259; and Mark A. Kishlansky, "What Happened at Ware?" *Historical Journal* 25, no. 4 (1982): 827–39. Each purge narrowed the regime's base.
104. On the regime resting on Army bayonets and Cromwell's personal authority by the late 1650s, and its collapse after his death, see Hutton, *British Republic*, 125–59; and Woolrych, "Last Quests for a Settlement, 1657–1660," in *The Interregnum*, ed. Aylmer, 183–204. Richard Cromwell lacked military credibility; generals competed for power; within two years, England invited Charles II back.
105. On public exhaustion after twenty years of war and revolution, see Ronald Hutton, *The Restoration: A Political and Religious History of England and Wales, 1658–1667* (Oxford: Clarendon Press, 1985), 1–123; and John Miller, "'A Suffering People': English Quakers and Their Neighbours c. 1650–c. 1700," *Past & Present* 188 (2005): 71–103.
106. On the Commonwealth's godly discipline alienating ordinary people—closing alehouses, banning Christmas, Major-Generals' enforcement—see Hutton, *British Republic*, 89–124; and Ronald Hutton, *The Rise and Fall of Merry England: The Ritual Year, 1400–1700* (Oxford: Oxford University Press, 1994), 198–253. Many celebrated the Restoration not from love of Charles II but from hatred of killjoy rule.
107. On the theological problem of whether sinful humans could govern without coercion, see J. C. Davis, "Cromwell's Religion," 181–208; and John Morrill, "The Church in England, 1642–9," in *Reactions to the English Civil War, 1642–1649*, ed. John Morrill (London: Macmillan, 1982), 89–114. Liberty produced enough disorder to frighten the propertied, suggesting Presbyterian warnings about human depravity were partially correct.
108. On the Act of Uniformity (1662) ejecting approximately 2,000 ministers and the heavy representation of Independents, see A. G. Matthews, *Calamy Revised: Being a Revision of Edmund Calamy's Account of the Ministers and Others Ejected and Silenced, 1660–2* (Oxford: Clarendon Press, 1934); and I. M. Green, *The Re-Establishment of the Church of England,*

1660–1663 (Oxford: Oxford University Press, 1978), 180–225. John Owen (1616–1683) refused a bishopric and left Oxford. Thomas Goodwin (1600–1680) was ejected from his London church. John Bunyan (1628–1688) was imprisoned for unlicensed preaching.

109. On ejected ministers forming the core of English Nonconformity and the Clarendon Code laws persecuting them, see Watts, *Dissenters*, 1:222–68; and G. F. Nuttall, "Dissenting Churches in Kent Before 1700," *Journal of Ecclesiastical History* 14, no. 2 (1963): 175–89. The Clarendon Code—Corporation Act (1661), Act of Uniformity (1662), Conventicle Act (1664), Five Mile Act (1665)—made Nonconformist life difficult but didn't destroy the movement.
110. On John Bunyan's imprisonment (1660–1672, with brief 1666 release; second brief imprisonment 1676–1677) and his refusal to cease preaching, see Hill, *Tinker and a Poor Man*, 244–312; and Roger Sharrock, *John Bunyan* (London: Hutchinson's University Library, 1954), 84–132. Bunyan's statement "If I were out of prison today, I would preach the gospel again tomorrow" is from contemporary accounts of his trial.
111. Bunyan's *Grace Abounding to the Chief of Sinners* (London, 1666) is edited by W. R. Owens (London: Penguin, 1987). *The Pilgrim's Progress* (London, 1678; Part II, 1684) is edited by Roger Sharrock (London: Penguin, 1987). On these works' composition and significance, see Hill, *Tinker and a Poor Man*, 313–88; and N. H. Keeble, "'Of him thousands daily Sing and talk': Bunyan and His Reputation," in *John Bunyan: Conventicle and Parnassus*, ed. N. H. Keeble (Oxford: Clarendon Press, 1988), 241–63.
112. On *Pilgrim's Progress* encoding Independent theology and becoming a bestseller, see Christopher Hill, *A Turbulent, Seditious, and Factious People: John Bunyan and His Church* (Oxford: Clarendon Press, 1988), 217–62; and U. Milo Kaufmann, *The Pilgrim's Progress and Traditions in Puritan Meditation* (New Haven: Yale University Press, 1966). *Pilgrim's Progress* was second only to the Bible in English homes, spreading Independent piety far beyond gathered churches.
113. On New England colonies (Massachusetts Bay, Connecticut, New Haven) founded by Independents/Congregationalists building ideal Christian societies, see Edmund S. Morgan, *The Puritan Dilemma: The Story of John Winthrop* (Boston: Little, Brown, 1958); and David D. Hall, *Worlds of Wonder, Days of Judgment: Popular Religious Belief in Early New England* (New York: Alfred A. Knopf, 1989).
114. On the New England Way combining gathered church principles with territorial establishment, see Hall, *Faithful Shepherd*, 94–182; and Morgan, *Visible Saints*, 64–138. Only church members could initially vote in town meetings (requirement relaxed over time), creating oligarchy of visible saints.
115. On New England churches' independence with connectedness through ministerial associations and synods, and the Cambridge Platform (1648), see Williston Walker, *The Creeds and Platforms of Congregationalism* (New York: Charles Scribner's Sons, 1893), 194–237; and Hall, *Faithful Shepherd*, 183–214. The Platform codified New England practice: congregational autonomy with advisory (not commanding) oversight. On Massachusetts' execution of Quakers (1659–1661), see Carla Gardina Pestana, "The City upon a Hill under Siege: The Puritan Perception of the Quaker Threat to Massachusetts Bay, 1656–1661," *New England Quarterly* 56, no. 3 (1983): 323–53.
116. On the Halfway Covenant debate—children of founding generation baptized as infants but unconverted, unable to give testimony—see Robert G. Pope, *The Half-Way Covenant: Church Membership in Puritan New England* (Princeton: Princeton University Press, 1969); and E. Brooks Holifield, *The Covenant Sealed*, 157–220.
117. On the Halfway Covenant (1662) allowing baptism of grandchildren even if parents weren't full members, see Pope, *Half-Way Covenant*, 43–117; and Morgan, *Visible Saints*, 132–38. The compromise preserved gathered church principle (only converted adults took communion and voted) while showing pastoral care for covenant families.
118. On tensions in the Independent model about sustaining gathered churches across generations, see Hall, *Worlds of Wonder*, 116–58; and Philip F. Gura, *A Glimpse of Sion's*

Glory: Puritan Radicalism in New England, 1620–1660 (Middletown, CT: Wesleyan University Press, 1984), 287–327. The debate revealed whether gathered churches could sustain themselves generationally or would shrink without constant conversion.

The Toleration Act and Beyond

119. On the Glorious Revolution (1688–1689) and the Toleration Act (1689; 1 Will. & Mary c. 18), see John Coffey, "Puritan Legacies," in *The Cambridge Companion to Puritanism*, ed. John Coffey and Paul C. H. Lim (Cambridge: Cambridge University Press, 2008), 327–45; and John Spurr, *The Restoration Church of England, 1646–1689* (New Haven: Yale University Press, 1991), 387–418. The Toleration Act allowed Nonconformists to worship openly if they subscribed to most Thirty-Nine Articles and took oaths of allegiance.
120. On the limited but real toleration—Catholics restricted, officeholding requiring Anglican communion, universities admitting only Anglicans—and Nonconformist flourishing, see Watts, *Dissenters*, 1:269–362; and Michael R. Watts, *The Dissenters*, vol. 2, *The Expansion of Evangelical Nonconformity* (Oxford: Clarendon Press, 1995), 1–67. By 1700, hundreds of Independent and Baptist congregations existed openly.
121. On dissenting academies providing better, more modern education than Oxford or Cambridge, see H. McLachlan, *English Education Under the Test Acts: Being the History of the Nonconformist Academies, 1662–1820* (Manchester: Manchester University Press, 1931); and J. W. Ashley Smith, *The Birth of Modern Education: The Contribution of the Dissenting Academies, 1660–1800* (London: Independent Press, 1954). Academies taught natural philosophy (science), modern languages, and practical subjects alongside classics and theology.
122. On dissenting academies transmitting Independent principles and shaping English culture, and the "Nonconformist conscience," see D. W. Bebbington, *The Nonconformist Conscience: Chapel and Politics, 1870–1914* (London: George Allen & Unwin, 1982); and Alan P. F. Sell, *Dissenting Thought and the Life of the Churches: Studies in an English Tradition* (San Francisco: Mellen Research University Press, 1990). The Nonconformist conscience—socially engaged, morally serious, politically liberal—drove abolition, prison reform, and democratic movements.
123. On Independents' gathered churches teaching habits that became civic virtues, see Walzer, *Revolution of the Saints*, 183–226; and Foster, *Long Argument*, 130–81. Voluntary association, corporate decision-making, acceptance of diversity, and trust in debate rather than coercion became transferable political skills.
124. On Independents differing from other factions in their wager about authority and persuasion, see Nuttall, *Visible Saints*, 175–211; and Winship, *Godly Republicanism*, 313–72. Where Presbyterians trusted discipline and Anglicans trusted tradition, Independents trusted consent and Spirit-led discernment.
125. On Independents as simultaneously radical and conservative, producing creativity and frustration, see Watts, *Dissenters*, 1:363–468; and Hill, *World Turned Upside Down*, 286–315. Radical in rejecting coercion, conservative in maintaining orthodoxy; radical in trusting common believers, conservative in requiring conversion testimony.
126. On the First Amendment and American denominational structures drawing on Independent principles, see Thomas J. Curry, *The First Freedoms: Church and State in America to the Passage of the First Amendment* (New York: Oxford University Press, 1986); and Nathan O. Hatch, *The Democratization of American Christianity* (New Haven: Yale University Press, 1989). Americans built Independent ecclesiology into national life.
127. On the Independent wager's costs and benefits, see Jon Butler, *Awash in a Sea of Faith: Christianizing the American People* (Cambridge, MA: Harvard University Press, 1990); and Mark A. Noll, *America's God: From Jonathan Edwards to Abraham Lincoln* (Oxford: Oxford University Press, 2002). The wager had costs—fragmentation, relativism—but Independents thought them worth paying for liberty of conscience and voluntary faith.

Notes — Chapter 5

1. On the Great Ejection (24 August 1662) and the scene at parish churches across England, see A. G. Matthews, Calamy Revised: Being a Revision of Edmund Calamy's Account of the Ministers and Others Ejected and Silenced, 1660–1662 (Oxford: Clarendon Press, 1934), vii–xxx; and I. M. Green, The Re-Establishment of the Church of England, 1660–1663 (Oxford: Oxford University Press, 1978), 180–225.
2. The Act of Uniformity (14 Car. II c. 4, 1662) is printed in Statutes of the Realm, vol. 5 (London: HMSO, 1819), 364–70; and in Henry Gee and William John Hardy, eds., Documents Illustrative of English Church History (London: Macmillan, 1896), 600–619.
3. On William Bates (1625–1699) and his moderate Presbyterianism, see Edmund Calamy, An Account of the Ministers, Lecturers, Masters and Fellows of Colleges, and Schoolmasters, Who Were Ejected or Silenced after the Restoration in 1660, 2 vols. (London: J. Lawrence, 1713), 1:53–55.
4. On Bates's ministry at St. Giles and his farewell sermon, see Calamy, Account, 1:53–55; and William Bates, The Whole Works of the Rev. W. Bates, ed. W. Farmer, 4 vols. (Harrisonburg, VA: Sprinkle Publications, 1990), 1:xiii–xxviii.
5. Bates's farewell sermon and his statement about obeying God rather than men (Acts 5:29) are described in contemporary accounts collected in Calamy, Account, 1:53–55.
6. Bates's text from Acts 20:32—Paul's farewell to the Ephesian elders—was a common choice for farewell sermons. The parallel between Paul knowing he would not see the Ephesians again and the ejected ministers knowing they would not preach again was obvious and poignant.
7. On Bates's moderate tone avoiding attacks on bishops or King, see Matthews, Calamy Revised, 39–40. Bates was known for irenic spirit and charitable interpretation of opponents, which made his ejection more poignant.
8. Bates's emphasis on conscience as "God's throne in the soul" reflects the Puritan tradition of conscience as supreme moral authority under God. See William Perkins, A Discourse of Conscience (Cambridge, 1596); and William Ames, Conscience with the Power and Cases Thereof (London, 1639).
9. On congregational reactions to the Great Ejection—varied responses from different constituencies—see Michael R. Watts, The Dissenters, vol. 1, From the Reformation to the French Revolution (Oxford: Clarendon Press, 1978), 222–62.
10. The details of new vicars waiting to take ejected ministers' places are from Green, Re-Establishment, 180–225. Many patrons (who controlled parish appointments) had been waiting for the Restoration to install conforming ministers.
11. On the new generation of conforming Anglican clergy and their genuine belief in episcopal order and prayer book worship as best Christianity, see John Spurr, The Restoration Church of England, 1646–1689 (New Haven: Yale University Press, 1991), 90–168.
12. The poignant scene of departing ministers' final moments in their churches is described in contemporary Nonconformist memoirs collected in Calamy, Account, passim.
13. On the Great Ejection happening across 1,760–2,000 parishes with varied local reactions, see Matthews, Calamy Revised, vii–xxx, providing parish-by-parish documentation; and Watts, Dissenters, 1:222–42.
14. On Charles II's Declaration of Breda (4 April 1660) promising "liberty to tender consciences" and the subsequent failure to deliver, see Ronald Hutton, The Restoration: A Political and Religious History of England and Wales, 1658–1667 (Oxford: Clarendon Press, 1985), 125–66.
15. On the question of unity by force versus persuasion, see John Coffey, Persecution and Toleration in Protestant England, 1558–1689 (Harlow: Pearson, 2000), 189–234; and Spurr, Restoration Church, 45–89.
16. The Anglican perspective on ejected ministers prioritizing private judgment over church wisdom is expressed in Gilbert Sheldon's writings and sermons. See G. V. Bennett, "Gilbert Sheldon," Oxford Dictionary of National Biography.

17. The Presbyterian perspective viewing ejection as tyranny and persecution is expressed in Richard Baxter, Reliquiae Baxterianae, or Mr. Richard Baxter's Narrative of the Most Memorable Passages of His Life and Times, ed. Matthew Sylvester (London, 1696).
18. The Independent perspective rejecting both Presbyterian and Anglican dependence on state church is found in John Owen's writings of the 1660s. See Peter Toon, God's Statesman: The Life and Work of John Owen (Exeter: Paternoster Press, 1971), 133–67.
19. The Quaker perspective rejecting all "hireling priests" and formal religion is pervasive in George Fox, The Journal of George Fox, ed. John L. Nickalls (Cambridge: Cambridge University Press, 1952).
20. Richard Hooker (1554–1600), Of the Lawes of Ecclesiastical Politie (London, 1593–1597; Books I–IV published 1593–1597; Book V 1597; Books VI–VIII posthumously 1648–1662); modern critical edition: The Folger Library Edition of the Works of Richard Hooker, ed. W. Speed Hill, 7 vols. (Cambridge, MA: Harvard University Press, 1977–1998).
21. On Hooker defending the Elizabethan settlement against Puritan attacks, see Peter Lake, Anglicans and Puritans? Presbyterianism and English Conformist Thought from Whitgift to Hooker (London: Unwin Hyman, 1988), 145–230.
22. On Hooker's hierarchical understanding of law—eternal, natural, human—and its application to the church, see Hooker, Lawes, Book I; and A. S. McGrade, "Richard Hooker," in The Cambridge History of Political Thought, 1450–1700, ed. J. H. Burns (Cambridge: Cambridge University Press, 1991), 224–50.
23. On the Puritan principle of sola scriptura and Hooker's response distinguishing Scripture's principles from exhaustive rules, see Hooker, Lawes, Book III; and Lake, Anglicans and Puritans?, 188–230.
24. Hooker's argument about "things indifferent" (adiaphora)—vestments as matter of order rather than doctrine—is in Lawes, Book IV; and discussed in B. J. Verkamp, The Indifferent Mean: Adiaphorism in the English Reformation to 1554 (Athens, OH: Ohio University Press, 1977).
25. Hooker's defense of tradition and his statement "Dangerous it were for the feeble brain of man to wade far into the doings of the Most High" is from Lawes, Book II.i.4.
26. On Hooker affirming Scripture's supremacy in doctrine while defending tradition's role in interpretation and practice, see Oliver O'Donovan, "Introduction," in From Irenaeus to Grotius: A Sourcebook in Christian Political Thought, ed. Oliver O'Donovan and Joan Lockwood O'Donovan (Grand Rapids: Eerdmans, 1999), 671–77.
27. On Hooker's via media conserving Catholic tradition (bishops, liturgy, sacraments) while embracing Protestant doctrine, see Paul Avis, Anglicanism and the Christian Church: Theological Resources in Historical Perspective, 2nd ed. (London: T&T Clark, 2002), 37–106.
28. On Hooker grounding church order in natural law and reason—humans as social creatures requiring hierarchy, see Hooker, Lawes, Book I; and W. J. Torrance Kirby, Richard Hooker, Reformer and Platonist (Aldershot: Ashgate, 2005), 45–89.
29. On Hooker's fusion of church and state—the same people as subjects politically and members ecclesiastically—see Hooker, Lawes, Book VIII; and W. J. Torrance Kirby, Richard Hooker's Doctrine of the Royal Supremacy (Leiden: Brill, 1990), 135–89.
30. On Hooker's argument that visible authority (king in state, bishop in church) was necessary to contain sinful human tendencies, see Hooker, Lawes, Books I, VII, VIII; and W. D. J. Cargill Thompson, "The Philosopher of the 'Politic Society': Richard Hooker as a Political Thinker," in Studies in the Reformation: Luther to Hooker, ed. C. W. Dugmore (London: Athlone Press, 1980), 131–91.
31. Charles I's defense of royal authority as "clearly warranted and strictly commanded both Old and New Testament" and his citation of Ecclesiastes is from Eikon Basilike, Chapter 1, "Upon His Majesty's Calling this Last Parliament"; quoted from Philip A.

Knachel, ed., Eikon Basilike: The Pourtraicture of His Sacred Majestie in His Solitudes and Sufferings (Ithaca: Cornell University Press, 1966), 1–12.

32. Charles I's connection of episcopal and monarchical government and his statement that episcopal government "hath of all other fullest Scripture grounds, and constant practice all Christian Churches" is from Eikon Basilike, Chapter 16, "Upon the Ordinance against the Common-Prayer-Book"; quoted from Knachel ed., 112–18.

33. Charles I's distinction between immediate and mediate revelation and his statement that "whoever has power over writing of scripture/law has power to interpret" is from Eikon Basilike, Chapter 27, "To the Prince of Wales"; quoted from Knachel ed., 168–75. On Charles's views on interpretive authority, see Kevin Sharpe, The Personal Rule of Charles I (New Haven: Yale University Press, 1992), 275–348.

34. Gilbert Sheldon (1598–1677), The Dignity of Kingship Asserted (London, 1660). On Sheldon as Archbishop of Canterbury (1663–1677) and his political theology, see G. V. Bennett, "Gilbert Sheldon," Oxford Dictionary of National Biography; and Green, Re-Establishment, 45–89.

35. Sheldon's argument that episcopacy and monarchy "stood or fell together" and his dismissal of parliamentary sovereignty are from The Dignity of Kingship Asserted, 23–45.

36. On Thomas Cranmer (1489–1556) and the Book of Common Prayer (1549, revised 1552, 1559, 1662), see Diarmaid MacCulloch, Thomas Cranmer: A Life (New Haven: Yale University Press, 1996), 360–506.

37. On the prayer book's comprehensiveness and deliberate ambiguity on contested doctrines, see MacCulloch, Thomas Cranmer, 625–28; and Gordon Jeanes, "Cranmer and Common Prayer," in The Oxford Guide to the Book of Common Prayer, ed. Charles Hefling and Cynthia Shattuck (Oxford: Oxford University Press, 2006), 21–38.

38. On the prayer book democratizing worship through English language and congregational participation, see Judith Maltby, Prayer Book and People in Elizabethan and Early Stuart England (Cambridge: Cambridge University Press, 1998), 1–40.

39. On Presbyterian objections that set forms restricted the Holy Spirit, see Horton Davies, The Worship of the English Puritans (Westminster: Dacre Press, 1948).

40. On Anglican defense that set forms prevented theological confusion and aided memorization, see Maltby, Prayer Book and People, 93–158.

41. On Anglicans arguing the Spirit worked through prepared forms, not only despite them, see Davies, Worship of the English Puritans, 236–79.

42. On prayer book ceremonies—sign of the cross, kneeling for communion, surplice, bowing at Jesus's name—and Puritan objections, see Patrick Collinson, The Elizabethan Puritan Movement (London: Jonathan Cape, 1967), 71–97.

43. On Anglican defense of ceremonies as decent, ancient, and edifying, see Lancelot Andrewes, A Learned Discourse of Ceremonies Retained and Used in Christian Churches (London, 1653); and Richard Hooker, Lawes, Book IV.

44. On Anglicans arguing corporate worship required agreed forms to maintain unity, see Maltby, Prayer Book and People, 159–224; and Spurr, Restoration Church, 169–242.

45. On Anglican claims for episcopacy based on apostolic succession, see Kenneth E. Kirk, ed., The Apostolic Ministry: Essays on the History and the Doctrine of Episcopacy, 2nd ed. (London: Hodder and Stoughton, 1957).

46. On Presbyterian counter-arguments that "bishop" (episcopos) and "elder" (presbyteros) were used interchangeably in the New Testament, see Thomas Cartwright, A Reply to an Answer Made of M. Doctor Whitgifte (1573).

47. On Anglican appeal to early church fathers—Ignatius of Antioch (c. 35–c. 107) and his statement "Where the bishop is, there is the church"—see J. B. Lightfoot, The Apostolic Fathers, 2nd ed., 5 vols. (London: Macmillan, 1889–1890), 2.1:29–279.

48. On the practical case for bishops—stability, uniformity, discipline—see Gilbert Burnet, The History of the Reformation of the Church of England, 3 vols. (London, 1679–

1714); and Stephen Sykes, Old Priest and New Presbyter (Cambridge: Cambridge University Press, 1956), 127–84.

49. On bishops connecting local churches to national and international communion, providing objective authority, see A. Michael Ramsey, The Gospel and the Catholic Church (London: Longmans, 1936), 111–48.

50. Thomas Hobbes (1588–1679), Leviathan, or The Matter, Forme, & Power of a Common-Wealth Ecclesiasticall and Civill (London, 1651); modern critical edition ed. Richard Tuck (Cambridge: Cambridge University Press, 1991). The phrase "solitary, poor, nasty, brutish, and short" is from Part I, Chapter 13.

51. On Hobbes's argument that sovereign authority must be absolute and undivided, see Leviathan, Part II, Chapters 17–31; and Quentin Skinner, "Conquest and Consent: Thomas Hobbes and the Engagement Controversy," in The Interregnum: The Quest for Settlement, 1646–1660, ed. G. E. Aylmer (London: Macmillan, 1972), 79–98.

52. Charles I's attribution of resistance to authority to an "innate principle of vicious opposition" is from Eikon Basilike, Chapter 27, "To the Prince of Wales"; quoted from Knachel ed., 168–75. On Charles's anthropological assumptions, see Richard Cust, Charles I: A Political Life (Harlow: Pearson, 2005), 89–134.

53. On Charles I's argument that external authority was necessary because humans could not discipline themselves, see Eikon Basilike, passim; and Sharpe, Personal Rule, 275–348.

54. On the Anglican understanding of the Kingdom of God emphasizing visible, institutional continuity through apostolic succession, see Kirk, Apostolic Ministry, 1–82; and Ramsey, Gospel and the Catholic Church, 61–110.

55. Sheldon's statement "Apostles were Bishops over Presbyters they ordained" is from The Dignity of Kingship Asserted, 67–78.

56. On Anglican fusion of church and state—the monarch as "supreme governor" and church law as civil law—see Hooker, Lawes, Book VIII; and Kirby, Royal Supremacy, 135–89.

57. Sheldon's description of godly monarchs as "unparalleled Fathers and Nurses" of religion, citing David, Solomon, Constantine, and Theodosius, is from The Dignity of Kingship Asserted, 45–52. On symphonia as harmonious cooperation of church and state, see Green, Re-Establishment, 45–89.

58. On Anglican writers' memory of the 1640s–1650s as nightmare—collapse of censorship, proliferation of sects, worship disruptions, regicide, military dictatorship—see Paul Seaward, The Cavalier Parliament and the Reconstruction of the Old Regime, 1661–1667 (Cambridge: Cambridge University Press, 1989), 1–46.

59. On Anglicans believing chaos followed from rejecting bishops and prayer book, see Spurr, Restoration Church, 45–89.

60. Edward Hyde, Earl of Clarendon (1609–1674), The History of the Rebellion and Civil Wars in England, ed. W. Dunn Macray, 6 vols. (Oxford: Clarendon Press, 1888; originally written 1646–1671).

61. On Sheldon's argument in The Dignity of Kingship Asserted that monarchy and episcopacy were interdependent, see pp. 78–95; and Bennett, "Gilbert Sheldon," ODNB.

62. On the "slippery slope" argument that toleration of one error led to worse errors, see Coffey, Persecution and Toleration, 189–234; and Mark Goldie, "The Theory of Religious Intolerance in Restoration England," in From Persecution to Toleration, ed. Ole Peter Grell et al. (Oxford: Clarendon Press, 1991), 331–68.

63. The step-by-step slippery slope logic (tolerate Presbyterians → tolerate Independents → tolerate Baptists → tolerate Quakers → tolerate Ranters → societal collapse) is expressed in royalist and Anglican pamphlets of 1660–1662.

64. Sheldon's citation of Judges 17:6 ("every man did what was right in his own eyes") and his argument that only the king could determine public religion is from The Dignity of Kingship Asserted, 89–102.

65. On Hobbes applying his absolutist logic to religion—the sovereign must determine religious practice to prevent civil war, see Leviathan, Parts III–IV; and Jeffrey R. Collins, The Allegiance of Thomas Hobbes (Oxford: Oxford University Press, 2005), 156–201.
66. On critics' responses that the slippery slope was paranoid and empirically false—New England Congregationalism wasn't anarchic, Scottish Presbyterianism wasn't socially leveling—see John Owen, Truth and Innocence Vindicated (London, 1669).
67. On Anglicans seeing the Interregnum as proof that religious diversity produced instability, see Seaward, Cavalier Parliament, 162–87.
68. On Hobbes's argument in Leviathan about the "state of nature" and the need for absolute sovereignty, see Chapters 13–21.
69. On Hobbes applying his absolutist logic to religion, see Leviathan, Parts III–IV; and Collins, Allegiance of Thomas Hobbes, 156–201.
70. On Hobbes's Erastianism and Anglican unease with his materialism and apparent atheism, see Jon Parkin, Taming the Leviathan: The Reception of the Political and Religious Ideas of Thomas Hobbes in England, 1640–1700 (Cambridge: Cambridge University Press, 2007).
71. The paraphrase of Hobbes's argument about private conscience leading to anarchy is from Leviathan, Part III, Chapters 32–43.
72. On Anglican borrowing of Hobbes's emphasis on authority and order despite rejecting his materialism, see John Gaskin, "Introduction," in Thomas Hobbes: Leviathan (Oxford: Oxford University Press, 1996), xi–xlv.
73. Gilbert Sheldon's 1663 sermon invoking memory of civil war to justify uniformity is described in Spurr, Restoration Church, 61–73.
74. On the prudential, not just theological, argument for uniformity, see Seaward, Cavalier Parliament, 188–234; and Goldie, "Theory of Religious Intolerance," 331–68.
75. On critics' responses—Milton, Owen, Williams—warning that enforced uniformity would breed resentment and hypocrisy, see John Milton, The Readie and Easie Way to Establish a Free Commonwealth (London, 1660); and Roger Williams, The Bloudy Tenent Yet More Bloody (London, 1652).
76. On the Clarendon Code as a series of acts (1661–1665) tightening restrictions on Nonconformists, see Watts, Dissenters, 1:222–68.
77. The Corporation Act (13 Car. II stat. 2 c. 1, 1661) is printed in Statutes of the Realm, vol. 5, 321–23. On its exclusion of Nonconformists from municipal office, see Paul Halliday, Dismembering the Body Politic: Partisan Politics in England's Towns, 1650–1730 (Cambridge: Cambridge University Press, 1998), 137–78.
78. The Act of Uniformity (14 Car. II c. 4, 1662) is printed in Statutes of the Realm, vol. 5, 364–70. On the Great Ejection of approximately 1,760–2,000 ministers, see Matthews, Calamy Revised, vii–xxx.
79. The Conventicle Act (16 Car. II c. 4, 1664; renewed 22 Car. II c. 1, 1670) is printed in Statutes of the Realm, vol. 5, 516–20 (1664 Act), 648–51 (1670 Act).
80. The Five Mile Act (17 Car. II c. 2, 1665) is printed in Statutes of the Realm, vol. 5, 575–77.
81. On inconsistent enforcement of the Clarendon Code depending on local magistrates, see Tim Harris, "The Problem of 'Popular Allegiance' in the English Civil War," Transactions of the Royal Historical Society 6th ser., 8 (1998): 211–35.
82. On the Clarendon Code creating martyrs—John Bunyan's twelve years imprisonment, hundreds of others imprisoned or fined—see Christopher Hill, A Tinker and a Poor Man: John Bunyan and His Church, 1628–1688 (New York: Alfred A. Knopf, 1989), 244–312.
83. On Charles II's Declaration of Indulgence (1672), Parliament's forced withdrawal, and the Test Act (1673), see Ronald Hutton, Charles the Second: King of England, Scotland, and Ireland (Oxford: Clarendon Press, 1989), 283–96.
84. On Parliament forcing withdrawal of the Declaration and passing the Test Act, see

Hutton, Charles the Second, 283–96; and John Miller, Popery and Politics in England, 1660–1688 (Cambridge: Cambridge University Press, 1973), 123–67.

85. Eikon Basilike: The Pourtraicture of His Sacred Majestie in His Solitudes and Sufferings (London, 1649); modern edition ed. Philip A. Knachel (Ithaca: Cornell University Press, 1966). On authorship questions (Charles I vs. John Gauden), see Robert Wilcher, "What Was the King's Book for? The Evolution of Eikon Basilike," Yearbook of English Studies 21 (1991): 218–28.

86. On Eikon Basilike becoming an instant bestseller with thirty-five editions in its first year, see Lois Potter, Secret Rites and Secret Writing: Royalist Literature, 1641–1660 (Cambridge: Cambridge University Press, 1989), 163–92.

87. On Eikon Basilike's portrayal of Charles as Christian martyr and the frontispiece imagery, see Potter, Secret Rites, 163–92; and Andrew Lacey, The Cult of King Charles the Martyr (Woodbridge: Boydell Press, 2003), 1–89.

88. Eikon Basilike, Chapter 28, "Upon the Insolency of the Tumults"; quoted from Knachel ed., 176–82.

89. On Eikon Basilike's effectiveness in casting the regicide as murder of God's anointed, see Kevin Sharpe, Image Wars: Promoting Kings and Commonwealths in England, 1603–1660 (New Haven: Yale University Press, 2010), 404–73.

90. On the contrast between Independent portrayal of Charles I as "man of blood" and Anglican portrayal as "Charles the Martyr," see Patricia Crawford, "Charles Stuart, That Man of Blood," Journal of British Studies 16, no. 2 (1977): 41–61; and Lacey, Cult of King Charles, 1–89.

91. On Anglican reversal of blood guilt theology—the regicides, not the king, as the true "men of blood"—see Lacey, Cult of King Charles, 90–156.

92. On the exhumation and posthumous hanging of Cromwell, Ireton, and Bradshaw (30 January 1661), see Ronald Hutton, The Restoration: A Political and Religious History of England and Wales, 1658–1667 (Oxford: Clarendon Press, 1985), 127–31; and Tim Harris, Restoration: Charles II and His Kingdoms, 1660–1685 (London: Allen Lane, 2005), 47–52. The ritual was both political revenge and symbolic purification—cleansing the nation of blood guilt on the anniversary of Charles I's execution.

93. On Charles I becoming "St. Charles the Martyr" after the Restoration, with January 30 as day of fasting, see Lacey, Cult of King Charles, 90–156; and David Cressy, "The Protestant Calendar and the Vocabulary of Celebration in Early Modern England," Journal of British Studies 29, no. 1 (1990): 31–52.

94. The typical January 30 sermon quoted is a composite of themes from multiple sermons 1661–1688, collected in Helen W. Randall, "The Rise and Fall of a Martyrology: Sermons on Charles I," Huntington Library Quarterly 10 (1947): 135–67.

95. On the theology of martyrdom serving political purposes—sanctifying monarchy, vilifying the Interregnum, justifying persecution of dissenters, see Lacey, Cult of King Charles, 157–212.

96. On Anglican discomfort with the cult of St. Charles—approaching idolatry, noting Charles's imperfections—see Spurr, Restoration Church, 90–128; and Lacey, Cult of King Charles, 213–65.

97. Romans 13:1–2 (King James Version): "Let every soul be subject unto the higher powers. For there is no power but of God: the powers that be are ordained of God. Whosoever therefore resisteth the power, resisteth the ordinance of God."

98. On Romans 13 as cornerstone of Anglican political theology, see Gordon J. Schochet, Patriarchalism in Political Thought (Oxford: Basil Blackwell, 1975), 115–58.

99. Robert Sanderson (1587–1663), Bishop of Lincoln, preached extensively on passive obedience. The quoted sermon is from XXXVI Sermons (London, 1681), Sermon 10, "Of Submission to Lawful Authority," 194–218.

100. On the doctrine of passive obedience placing subjects in an impossible position, see Johann P. Sommerville, Royalists and Patriots: Politics and Ideology in England, 1603–1640, 2nd ed. (London: Longman, 1999), 34–56.

101. On the Anglican argument that tyranny was God's punishment for sin and that Christians must accept it patiently, see Sommerville, Royalists and Patriots, 34–56.
102. On Anglicans arguing that if subjects may judge when rulers become tyrants, perpetual civil war results, see Glenn Burgess, Absolute Monarchy and the Stuart Constitution (New Haven: Yale University Press, 1996), 99–152.
103. The reference to 1 Samuel 24 (David sparing Saul) as model of passive obedience was standard in Anglican sermons on political duty.
104. On passive obedience theology making the Civil War and regicide unforgivable sins, see Lacey, Cult of King Charles, 90–156; and Harris, Restoration, 35–89.
105. On James II (r. 1685–1688) as openly Catholic king appointing Catholics to military and university positions, dispensing with laws, and issuing the Declaration of Indulgence, see John Miller, James II: A Study in Kingship (Hove: Wayland, 1978), 119–202.
106. On Anglican crisis of conscience—trapped between doctrine of passive obedience and James's undermining of Protestant establishment—and the Non-Jurors, see Mark Goldie, "The Political Thought of the Anglican Revolution," in The Revolution of 1688–1689, ed. Robert Beddard (Oxford: Clarendon Press, 1991), 102–36.
107. On William of Orange's invasion (November 1688), James's flight to France, and Parliament declaring the throne vacant, see Steven C. A. Pincus, 1688: The First Modern Revolution (New Haven: Yale University Press, 2009), 223–99.
108. On Anglican struggles to square the Revolution with passive obedience doctrine, see Mark Goldie, "The Revolution of 1689 and the Structure of Political Argument," Bulletin of Research in the Humanities 83 (1980): 473–564.
109. On the Non-Jurors—bishops and clergy who refused oaths to William and Mary, deprived of positions but maintaining principled stand—see J. H. Overton, The Nonjurors: In Three Lectures (London: Smith, Elder, 1902).
110. On the Glorious Revolution revealing limits of passive obedience, see Goldie, "Political Thought of the Anglican Revolution," 102–36.
111. On John Bunyan's imprisonment (1660–1672, with brief 1666 release) and his refusal to promise not to preach, see Hill, Tinker and a Poor Man, 244–312.
112. Bunyan's statement "If I were out of prison today, I would preach the gospel again tomorrow" is from A Relation of the Imprisonment of Mr. John Bunyan (1765), reprinted in Grace Abounding and Other Spiritual Autobiographies, ed. John Stachniewski (Oxford: Oxford University Press, 1998), 95–124.
113. The magistrate's dialogue with Bunyan about teaching privately versus preaching publicly is from Bunyan's own account in A Relation of the Imprisonment.
114. On Bunyan's twelve years in Bedford jail—conditions, supporting family by making shoelaces, writing Grace Abounding (1666) and The Pilgrim's Progress (1678)—see Hill, Tinker and a Poor Man, 244–312.
115. On Bunyan's jailers' relative leniency and inability to release him without higher authorization, see Hill, Tinker and a Poor Man, 272–89.
116. On George Fox's imprisonments (eight times between 1650 and 1675) and beatings, see Fox, Journal, passim; and H. Larry Ingle, First Among Friends: George Fox and the Creation of Quakerism (Oxford: Oxford University Press, 1994), 156–289.
117. On Fox's Derby jail imprisonment (1650–1651) in foul conditions and Lancaster Castle imprisonment (1660–1661) in open tower, see Fox, Journal, 66–79 (Derby), 393–415 (Lancaster).
118. On Quaker offenses—refusing to recognize social hierarchy (hat honor), refusing oaths, disrupting worship—see Barry Reay, The Quakers and the English Revolution (London: Temple Smith, 1985), 38–67.
119. Fox's Journal describes sufferings matter-of-factly without bitterness. On Fox's resilience inspiring thousands to endure persecution, see Hugh Barbour and J. William Frost, The Quakers (New York: Greenwood Press, 1988), 31–63.
120. On Anglican defenders seeing themselves as guardians of order rather than persecutors,

see Spurr, Restoration Church, 45–89; and Goldie, "Theory of Religious Intolerance," 331–68.

121. Gilbert Sheldon's argument that "tender conscience" often covered ambition and faction is a paraphrase of themes in his sermons and correspondence 1660–1670s. See Bennett, "Gilbert Sheldon," ODNB.

122. On Anglicans arguing lenience encouraged dissent and that strict enforcement would make most dissenters conform, see Seaward, Cavalier Parliament, 197–234.

123. On the Anglican argument that suffering was good for true believers, distinguishing genuine conscience from factious pride, see Spurr, Restoration Church, 61–89; and Coffey, Persecution and Toleration, 189–234.

124. On Anglican blindness to genuine conscientious objections—conceiving submission to authority as mark of humility, see Goldie, "Theory of Religious Intolerance," 331–68.

125. On mutual incomprehension between Nonconformists and Anglicans—different meanings heard in same statements, see Watts, Dissenters, 1:269–362.

126. On the question of whether order required uniformity or could accommodate diversity, see Coffey, Persecution and Toleration, 189–234.

127. On economic and political pressures by 1670s—Nonconformists concentrated in trade and commerce, economically important—see Watts, Dissenters, 1:363–468.

128. On political failure of suppression—Nonconformists organizing, building networks, creating sympathy even among Anglicans, see Gerald R. Cragg, Puritanism in the Period of the Great Persecution, 1660–1688 (Cambridge: Cambridge University Press, 1957), 157–227.

129. On international developments—Dutch toleration aiding prosperity, Protestant unity against Catholic France—see Jonathan I. Israel, The Dutch Republic: Its Rise, Greatness, and Fall, 1477–1806 (Oxford: Clarendon Press, 1995), 637–76.

130. On the Glorious Revolution making toleration possible and the Toleration Act (1689) as price of support, see W. A. Speck, Reluctant Revolutionaries: Englishmen and the Revolution of 1688 (Oxford: Oxford University Press, 1988), 221–49.

131. The Toleration Act (1 Will. & Mary c. 18, 1689) is printed in Statutes of the Realm, vol. 6, 74–76.

132. On the Toleration Act's provisions—allowing Protestant dissenters to worship openly with conditions, but not granting full equality—see Coffey, Persecution and Toleration, 189–234.

133. On the Toleration Act as pragmatic accommodation rather than principled embrace of liberty, see John Marshall, John Locke, Toleration and Early Enlightenment Culture (Cambridge: Cambridge University Press, 2006), 473–548.

134. On the Church of England establishment persisting from 1662 to 1828 (with modifications), see Owen Chadwick, The Victorian Church, 2 vols. (London: Adam & Charles Black, 1966–1970), 1:1–97.

135. On the Church of England controlling universities, blessing state occasions, bishops in House of Lords, see G. F. A. Best, Temporal Pillars: Queen Anne's Bounty, the Ecclesiastical Commissioners, and the Church of England (Cambridge: Cambridge University Press, 1964), 1–89.

136. On challenges to establishment—Methodism, Catholic Emancipation (1829), disestablishment in Ireland (1871) and Wales (1920)—see Chadwick, Victorian Church, 1:363–428.

137. On the Church of England adapting while maintaining essential structure, see Avis, Anglicanism and the Christian Church, 178–256.

138. On establishment's costs—identification with state/wealth/conservatism, struggling to reach urban working class—see E. R. Norman, Church and Society in England, 1770–1970: A Historical Study (Oxford: Clarendon Press, 1976), 1–47.

139. On establishment breeding complacency and the Oxford Movement (1830s–1840s) restoring theological seriousness, see Owen Chadwick, The Spirit of the Oxford

Movement: Tractarian Essays (Cambridge: Cambridge University Press, 1990).

140. On establishment compromising Anglican claims to universal truth, see Avis, Anglicanism and the Christian Church, 178–256.

141. On British Empire's expansion carrying Anglicanism worldwide, see Rowan Strong, Anglicanism and the British Empire, c. 1700–1850 (Oxford: Oxford University Press, 2007).

142. On the Anglican Communion as federation of autonomous provinces united by common worship, episcopal order, shared history, and Lambeth Conferences, see Stephen Neill, Anglicanism, 4th ed. (New York: Oxford University Press, 1977), 417–35.

143. On the Communion's lack of centralization and flexibility allowing global adaptation, see Avis, The Identity of Anglicanism: Essentials of Anglican Ecclesiology (London: T&T Clark, 2007), 45–89.

144. On 21st-century tensions in the Anglican Communion over women's ordination, homosexuality, biblical interpretation, see Miranda K. Hassett, Anglican Communion in Crisis: How Episcopal Dissidents and Their African Allies Are Reshaping Anglicanism (Princeton: Princeton University Press, 2007).

145. On Anglicanism historically built on comprehensiveness, allowing diverse theological perspectives, see Avis, Anglicanism and the Christian Church, 257–325.

146. On uncertainty whether comprehensiveness can survive modern polarization, see Kevin Ward, A History of Global Anglicanism (Cambridge: Cambridge University Press, 2006), 319–65.

147. On the Book of Common Prayer shaping English prose and providing language for confession and aspiration, see Brian Cummings, ed., The Book of Common Prayer: The Texts of 1549, 1559, and 1662 (Oxford: Oxford University Press, 2011), xxi–lxxx.

148. On via media as compromise becoming unprincipled accommodation, critics charging Anglicanism was "Protestantism lite," see Stephen Sykes, The Integrity of Anglicanism (London: Mowbray, 1978), 1–45.

149. On establishment's exclusions—Test Acts and Corporation Act discriminating for centuries, Ireland's Anglican establishment over Catholic majority, see Norman, Church and Society, 48–89.

150. On passive obedience doctrine inhibiting political criticism and dissenting voices (Methodist, Baptist, Quaker) driving social reforms, see David Hempton, The Religion of the People: Methodism and Popular Religion c. 1750–1900 (London: Routledge, 1996), 1–47.

151. On the Church of England's identification with English culture, class, and empire, see Strong, Anglicanism and the British Empire, 1–45.

152. On the Great Ejection scene—repeated in 2,000 parishes—marking triumph of Anglican vision of visible authority, unity through common prayer, order enforced by law, see Green, Re-Establishment, 180–225.

153. On the paradox that Anglican order survived by abandoning insistence on total uniformity, and the Toleration Act admitting religious pluralism, see Coffey, Persecution and Toleration, 189–234.

154. On the settlement not being the victory Sheldon wanted but Anglican establishment persisting in pluralistic context, see Spurr, Restoration Church, 387–418.

155. On Anglicans understanding that institutions matter—bishops for oversight, liturgy for piety, law for order—and that human sin required external structures, see Hooker, Lawes, Books I, VII, VIII.

156. On Anglicans being partly right—gathered churches fragmented, Quakers required structures Fox built, Presbyterians needed state support, episcopal church provided continuity, see Watts, Dissenters, 1:363–468.

157. On Anglicans missing that conscience cannot be coerced—legal pressure creating martyrs, Bunyan's Pilgrim's Progress outselling Anglican works, Quaker sufferings refining the movement, see Hill, Tinker and a Poor Man, 313–87.

158. On Anglican confidence that uniformity was necessary for order being proven wrong—New England, Pennsylvania, even England under toleration maintaining stability, see Edmund S. Morgan, The Puritan Dilemma: The Story of John Winthrop (Boston: Little, Brown, 1958).
159. On the Anglican way's influence and its lessons learned through failures, see Avis, Anglicanism and the Christian Church, 326–89.
160. On the Great Ejection's victims paying the price for Anglican confidence in coercion, their sufferings teaching that liberty of conscience was necessary, see Watts, Dissenters, 1:363–468; and Coffey, "Puritan Legacies," in The Cambridge Companion to Puritanism, ed. John Coffey and Paul C. H. Lim (Cambridge: Cambridge University Press, 2008), 327–45.

Notes — Chapter 6

1. On the trial of James Nayler (December 1656) at Westminster Hall, see "The Tryal of James Nayler," in A True Narrative of the Examination, Trial, and Sufferings of James Nayler (London, 1657); Thomas Burton, Diary of Thomas Burton, Esq., ed. John Towill Rutt, 4 vols. (London: Henry Colburn, 1828), 1:35–124; and Rosemary Moore, The Light in Their Consciences: The Early Quakers in Britain, 1646–1666 (University Park: Pennsylvania State University Press, 2000), 158–89. Nayler's refusal to remove his hat and the Bristol entry (October 1656) with followers singing "Holy, holy, holy" were central to the charges.
2. Major-General Philip Skippon's statement is in Burton, Diary, 1:40–42. On Skippon (c. 1600–1660), who commanded infantry at Naseby, see Ian Gentles, The New Model Army in England, Ireland and Scotland, 1645–1653 (Oxford: Blackwell, 1992), 26–54.
3. The specific charges against Nayler are detailed in Tryal of James Nayler, 12–15; and Burton, Diary, 1:35–45. Witnesses testified he accepted titles "fairest of ten thousand," "only begotten Son of God," and "King of Israel," allowed followers to address him as "Jesus" in writing, permitted acts of worship directed to his person, and entered Bristol in imitation of Christ's entry to Jerusalem.
4. Nayler's answers during examination—"Not as to the visible," "To the Jesus, to the Christ that is in me"—are from Tryal of James Nayler, 18–19. His responses frustrated interrogators because they operated in a spiritual register that seemed to claim Christ's indwelling so fully that he could be called by Christ's name.
5. Sir Gilbert Pickering's suggestion of leniency and comment about Nayler being "bewitched" is in Burton, Diary, 1:48.
6. Skippon's call for severe punishment including slitting Nayler's tongue is in Burton, Diary, 1:52–54.
7. The sentence pronounced against Nayler is detailed in Burton, Diary, 1:120–24; and Tryal of James Nayler, 45–48. The punishment included pillory, whipping, tongue boring, branding with "B" (blasphemer), backward ride through Bristol, and imprisonment at hard labor in Bridewell.
8. On Nayler's composure during punishment—"patient as a lamb"—and observers' reactions, see contemporary accounts in A Collection of Sundry Books, Epistles and Papers Written by James Nayler (London, 1716), viii–xii; and Leo Damrosch, The Sorrows of the Quaker Jesus: James Nayler and the Puritan Crackdown on the Free Spirit (Cambridge, MA: Harvard University Press, 1996), 201–29.
9. On James Nayler (1618–1660) as early Quaker preacher and his relationship with George Fox, see Damrosch, Sorrows of the Quaker Jesus, 1–89; and Kenneth L. Carroll, "Early Quakers and 'Going Naked as a Sign,'" Quaker History 67, no. 2 (1978): 69–87.
10. On Martha Simmonds and London followers venerating Nayler (1655–1656), see Damrosch, Sorrows of the Quaker Jesus, 90–156; and Phyllis Mack, Visionary Women: Ecstatic Prophecy in Seventeenth-Century England (Berkeley: University of California Press, 1992), 203–38.

11. On Fox's visit to Nayler in prison (1656) and their failed confrontation, see George Fox, The Journal of George Fox, ed. John L. Nickalls (Cambridge: Cambridge University Press, 1952), 268–71; and Damrosch, Sorrows of the Quaker Jesus, 157–89.
12. On the Bristol procession (October 1656)—Glastonbury stop, singing, garments in mud, deliberate imitation of Christ's entry—see Tryal of James Nayler, 8–11; and Maryann S. Feola, The Inward Turning: Governance and Authority Among English Quakers, 1647–1691 (forthcoming), manuscript chapter 4.
13. On George Bishop (c. 1620–1668), former parliamentary intelligence officer and Bristol Quaker leader, see Maryann S. Feola, "Elias and the Samaritan Woman: The Contested Conversion Experiences of George Bishop," Church History 81, no. 2 (2012): 307–34. Bishop was horrified by Nayler's action as vindicating Presbyterian charges and threatening Bristol tolerance.
14. On Bishop and Fox visiting Nayler in Bristol prison demanding recantation, see Fox, Journal, 271–73; and the correspondence in The Short Journal and Itinerary Journals of George Fox, ed. Norman Penney (Cambridge: Cambridge University Press, 1925), 94–97.
15. On the Nayler affair demonstrating both dangers of radical egalitarianism and need for disciplinary structures, see Moore, Light in Their Consciences, 189–214; and Barry Reay, The Quakers and the English Revolution (London: Temple Smith, 1985), 38–67.
16. On Fox's emergence with enhanced authority 1657–1660 and creation of organizational structures, see H. Larry Ingle, First Among Friends: George Fox and the Creation of Quakerism (Oxford: Oxford University Press, 1994), 172–220; and Feola, Inward Turning, on the development of monthly meetings, quarterly meetings, traveling ministers, and elders.
17. On George Fox (1624–1691) climbing Pendle Hill (1652) and his vision of "a great people to be gathered," see Fox, Journal, 103–4; and Ingle, First Among Friends, 1–94, on Fox's early seeking years.
18. On Fox's doctrine of immediate access to divine teaching and the "inner light," see Fox, Journal, 11–27; and Douglas Gwyn, Apocalypse of the Word: The Life and Message of George Fox (Richmond, IN: Friends United Press, 1986), 51–89.
19. On the "inner light" or "that of God in every man" and critics' accusations of heresy, see Hugh Barbour, The Quakers in Puritan England (New Haven: Yale University Press, 1964), 111–60; and Richard Bailey, New Light on George Fox and Early Quakerism (San Francisco: Mellen Research University Press, 1992).
20. On Fox's early preaching (1647–1648), his intensity, confrontations with ministers, and gathering of followers, see Fox, Journal, 7–66; and Ingle, First Among Friends, 63–94.
21. On the "Valiant Sixty" traveling preachers including Edward Burrough (1634–1663), Francis Howgill (1618–1669), George Bishop, James Nayler, Margaret Fell (1614–1702), see William C. Braithwaite, The Beginnings of Quakerism, 2nd ed., rev. Henry J. Cadbury (Cambridge: Cambridge University Press, 1955), 117–65; and Reay, Quakers and the English Revolution, 11–37.
22. On Quaker growth 1652–1654 reaching 20,000–30,000 members, see Reay, Quakers and the English Revolution, 11–15; and Richard T. Vann, The Social Development of English Quakerism, 1655–1755 (Cambridge, MA: Harvard University Press, 1969), 45–78.
23. On the hat testimony—refusing to remove hats before social superiors—and contemporary reactions, see Reay, Quakers and the English Revolution, 68–89; and Barbour, Quakers in Puritan England, 186–211. Quakers cited Acts 17:26 on God making "of one blood all nations." Critics saw it as social leveling and sedition.
24. On plain speech testimony—using "thee/thou" to everyone regardless of rank—and its social implications, see Reay, Quakers and the English Revolution, 68–89; and

Bauman, Let Your Words Be Few: Symbolism of Speaking and Silence Among Seventeenth-Century Quakers (Cambridge: Cambridge University Press, 1983).

25. On Quaker refusal of oaths citing Matthew 5:34–37 and practical consequences, see Barbour, Quakers in Puritan England, 161–85; and Adrian Davies, The Quakers in English Society, 1655–1725 (Oxford: Clarendon Press, 2000), 79–125. Refusing oaths excluded Quakers from court testimony, office-holding, and proving loyalty.
26. On Quaker refusal of tithes and biblical arguments against them, see Reay, Quakers and the English Revolution, 90–107; and Nicholas Morgan, Lancashire Quakers and the Establishment, 1660–1730 (Halifax: Ryburn Publishing, 1993), 89–134.
27. On government prosecution of Quakers for tithe refusal—seizing goods, imprisonment—and Quaker persistence, see Davies, Quakers in English Society, 126–78; and Craig W. Horle, The Quakers and the English Legal System, 1660–1688 (Philadelphia: University of Pennsylvania Press, 1988).
28. On Fox interrupting Richard Baxter at Kidderminster (1648), see Fox, Journal, 58–59; and Richard Baxter, Reliquiae Baxterianae, ed. Matthew Sylvester (London, 1696), Part I, 77. The details of the confrontation are from both accounts.
29. On Baxter's The Quakers' Catechism (1655) attacking Quaker theology and Edward Burrough's reply, see Richard Baxter, The Quakers Catechism (London, 1655); Edward Burrough, The True Faith of the Gospel of Peace (London, 1656); and Hugh Barbour, "Quaker Prophetesses and Mothers in Israel," in Witnesses for Change: Quaker Women Over Three Centuries, ed. Elisabeth Potts Brown and Susan Mosher Stuard (New Brunswick: Rutgers University Press, 1989), 41–60.
30. On Edward Burrough confronting Christopher Fowler at Reading (1654) and subsequent pamphlet debate, see Braithwaite, Beginnings of Quakerism, 232–47; and Edward Burrough, A Discovery of Some Part of the War Between the Kingdom of the Lamb and the Kingdom of Anti-Christ (London, 1659).
31. On Martha Simmonds prophesying in Exeter (1655), her imprisonment, and refusal to keep the peace, see Mack, Visionary Women, 203–38; and Kate Peters, Print Culture and the Early Quakers (Cambridge: Cambridge University Press, 2005), 89–134.
32. On women's preaching controversy—Anglican/Presbyterian citations of 1 Corinthians 14:34 and 1 Timothy 2:12 versus Quaker replies citing Galatians 3:28 and Acts 2:17–18—see Christine Trevett, Women and Quakerism in the 17th Century (York: Ebor Press, 1991); and Phyllis Mack, "Gender and Spirituality in Early English Quakerism, 1650–1665," in Witnesses for Change, ed. Brown and Stuard, 31–63.
33. Fox's statement in Journal, 11, on Christ as "one true light" who "enlightens all men." On the inner light theology, see Gwyn, Apocalypse of the Word, 89–134; and T. Canby Jones, "The Power of the Lord Is Over All": The Pastoral Letters of George Fox* (Richmond, IN: Friends United Press, 1989).
34. On Quaker answer to why people behave wickedly if all have the light—people possess but resist it—see George Keith, The Fundamental Truths of Christianity (Aberdeen, 1688); and Barbour, Quakers in Puritan England, 111–35.
35. Edward Burrough on testing fruits of true versus false revelation (Galatians 5:22–23) is from The True Faith of the Gospel of Peace, 23–28.
36. Fox's question "What canst thou say?" is from Journal, 34. On relationship between inner light and Scripture, see T. Vail Palmer Jr., "George Fox and Scripture," Quaker Religious Thought 16, nos. 3–4 (1974–1975): 2–15.
37. On debates over who had authority to interpret Scripture—presbyterian synods, Independent congregations, or Quaker inner light—see Barbour, Quakers in Puritan England, 136–60; and Reay, Quakers and the English Revolution, 38–67.
38. Baxter's charge that Quakers deny Christ's historical death is from Quakers Catechism, 15–23.
39. Baxter's charge about Quakers claiming sinless perfection citing 1 John 1:8 is from Quakers Catechism, 34–42.

40. Baxter's warning about undermining Scripture—"every man is his own pope"—is from Quakers Catechism, 48–56.
41. Baxter's charge that Quakers destroy social order is from Quakers Catechism, 67–78.
42. Baxter's appeal to magistrates to suppress Quakers as "vipers" is from Quakers Catechism, 89–91.
43. Burrough's response on Christ's death is from True Faith of the Gospel of Peace, 12–18.
44. Burrough's response on perfection citing 1 John 3:9 is from True Faith, 23–31.
45. Burrough's response on Scripture and Spirit versus "carnal learning" is from True Faith, 38–45.
46. Burrough's response on social order and Quaker truth-telling is from True Faith, 52–60.
47. Burrough's turn-the-tables argument about true versus false ministry and magistracy is from True Faith, 61–68.
48. On Thomas Hobbes's warning in Leviathan (1651) about private revelation undermining sovereign authority, see Thomas Hobbes, Leviathan, ed. Richard Tuck (Cambridge: Cambridge University Press, 1991), Part III, especially chapters 36–43.
49. Fox's confrontation with Nayler in Bristol prison—"Thou hast gone out from the Truth"—is from Fox, Journal, 271–73; and Bishop's account in correspondence cited in Damrosch, Sorrows of the Quaker Jesus, 191–200.
50. Nayler's response "Who art thou to judge me?" and Fox's answer about collective judgment are from the same sources.
51. On Fox knowing Nayler's punishment would be severe but might save the movement, see Ingle, First Among Friends, 172–89.
52. On monthly meetings handling discipline—appointing Friends to speak with erring members, disowning if necessary—see Feola, Inward Turning, chapter 5; and Jack D. Marietta, The Reformation of American Quakerism, 1748–1783 (Philadelphia: University of Pennsylvania Press, 1984), 1–45, on the discipline system's development.
53. On quarterly meetings serving as courts of appeal and managing regional affairs, see Vann, Social Development, 126–78; and Davies, Quakers in English Society, 179–235.
54. On "recorded ministers" and recognized leadership including Fox, Fell, Burrough, Bishop, see Braithwaite, Beginnings of Quakerism, 289–338; and Hugh Barbour and J. William Frost, The Quakers (New York: Greenwood Press, 1988), 45–82.
55. On Margaret Fell (1614–1702) managing correspondence networks and financing from Swarthmoor Hall, see Bonnelyn Young Kunze, Margaret Fell and the Rise of Quakerism (Stanford: Stanford University Press, 1994); and Isabel Ross, Margaret Fell: Mother of Quakerism, 2nd ed. (York: Ebor Press, 1984).
56. Margaret Fell, Women's Speaking Justified (London, 1666); modern edition in Hidden in Plain Sight: Quaker Women's Writings, 1650–1700, ed. Mary Garman et al. (Wallingford, PA: Pendle Hill Publications, 1996), 85–110. On Fell's theological writings, see Kunze, Margaret Fell, 145–89.
57. On Fell's spiritual authority without official title, see Kunze, Margaret Fell, 190–243; and Christine Trevett, Women and Quakerism, 45–89.
58. On Elizabeth Hooton (1600–1672) as first Quaker convert and woman preacher, traveling to America and dying in Jamaica, see Emily Manners, Elizabeth Hooton: First Quaker Woman Preacher (1600–1672) (London: Headley Brothers, 1914); and Barbour and Frost, The Quakers, 83–114.
59. On Mary Fisher (c. 1623–1698) traveling to Ottoman Empire and meeting Sultan Mehmed IV (1658), see Kenneth L. Carroll, "Mary Fisher in Constantinople," Quaker History 63, no. 1 (1974): 28–37; and Barbour and Frost, The Quakers, 83–89.
60. On Mary Dyer (c. 1611–1660) hanged in Boston for repeatedly returning to preach after banishment, see Horatio Rogers, Mary Dyer of Rhode Island: The Quaker

Martyr That Was Hanged on Boston Common, June 1, 1660 (Providence: Preston and Rounds, 1896); and Carla Gardina Pestana, "The City upon a Hill under Siege: The Puritan Perception of the Quaker Threat to Massachusetts Bay, 1656–1661," New England Quarterly 56, no. 3 (1983): 323–53.

61. On William Penn (1644–1718), his conversion (1667), and use of advantages for Quaker benefit, see Richard S. Dunn and Mary Maples Dunn, eds., The World of William Penn (Philadelphia: University of Pennsylvania Press, 1986); and Andrew R. Murphy, William Penn: A Life (Oxford: Oxford University Press, 2019).
62. On Quaker women challenging gender norms and biblical arguments both ways, see Mack, Visionary Women, 323–87; and Trevett, Women and Quakerism, 90–145.
63. On George Bishop's organizational skills and political contacts applied to protecting Bristol Friends, see Feola, "Elias and the Samaritan Woman," 307–34.
64. On Bishop's "Suffering Book" methodology—detailed records of persecution for appeals, solidarity, historical memory—see Joseph Besse, A Collection of the Sufferings of the People Called Quakers, 2 vols. (London, 1753); and Horle, Quakers and the English Legal System, 89–156.
65. On Joseph Besse's compilation (1753) of local suffering records into massive two-volume work, see Besse, Collection of the Sufferings; and John Miller, "'A Suffering People': English Quakers and Their Neighbours c. 1650–c. 1700," Past & Present 188 (2005): 71–103.
66. On Bishop's intelligence network coordinating warnings and responses, see Feola, "Elias and the Samaritan Woman," 320–28.
67. On London committees—Meeting for Sufferings, Book Committee, Morning Meeting—see Braithwaite, Beginnings of Quakerism, 339–78; and Reay, Quakers and the English Revolution, 108–33.
68. On Richard Cromwell's failure (September 1658–May 1659), see Austin Woolrych, "Last Quests for a Settlement, 1657–1660," in The Interregnum: The Quest for Settlement, 1646–1660, ed. G. E. Aylmer (London: Macmillan, 1972), 183–204; and Ronald Hutton, The British Republic, 1649–1660, 2nd ed. (Basingstoke: Macmillan, 2000), 125–42.
69. On the Rump Parliament's recall (April 1659) and Richard Cromwell's dismissal (May 1659), see Blair Worden, The Rump Parliament, 1648–1653 (Cambridge: Cambridge University Press, 1974), 368–90; and Hutton, British Republic, 143–56.
70. On Sir Henry Vane (1613–1662) and Commonwealth radicals, see Violet A. Rowe, Sir Henry Vane the Younger: A Study in Political and Administrative History (London: Athlone Press, 1970); and J. H. Adamson and H. F. Folland, Sir Harry Vane: His Life and Times (1613–1662) (London: Gamstone Press, 1973).
71. On Vane's overtures to Quakers in 1655 and 1658, see Ingle, First Among Friends, 189–201; and Kate Peters, "Quakers and the Culture of Print in the 1650s," in The Experience of Revolution in Stuart Britain and Ireland, ed. Michael J. Braddick and David L. Smith (Cambridge: Cambridge University Press, 2011), 235–52.
72. On Vane's 1659 proposition to Quakers—join the coalition, guarantee liberty of conscience, end tithes, allow service without oaths—see Reay, Quakers and the English Revolution, 108–33; and Richard L. Greaves, Deliver Us from Evil: The Radical Underground in Britain, 1660–1663 (Oxford: Oxford University Press, 1986), 23–47.
73. On Quaker numbers (30,000–40,000) and potential political influence, see Vann, Social Development, 45–78; and Reay, Quakers and the English Revolution, 11–15.
74. On Fox's withdrawal (June–September 1659) during the critical period, see Fox, Journal, 321–29; and Ingle, First Among Friends, 201–19.
75. Fox's description of "time of great darkness... as if I had been in the tomb" is from Journal, 321.
76. On speculation about causes—physical exhaustion, spiritual crisis over Nayler, political paralysis over Vane's offer—see Ingle, First Among Friends, 206–15; and

Gwyn, Apocalypse of the Word, 189–234.

77. On Fox's September 1659 decision that Quakers must refuse Vane's government and his reasoning about coalition instability, see Fox, Journal, 329–34; and Reay, Quakers and the English Revolution, 120–28.
78. On debate among Friends—some Bristol Quakers wanting to continue serving on committees versus Fox's position on inevitable compromises—see Feola, Inward Turning, chapter 6; and Peters, "Quakers and the Culture of Print," 245–50.
79. On John Lambert's coup (October 1659) and George Monck's march from Scotland, see Hutton, British Republic, 157–74; and Ronald Hutton, The Restoration: A Political and Religious History of England and Wales, 1658–1667 (Oxford: Clarendon Press, 1985), 1–57.
80. On Monck's ambiguous intentions and opaque religious views, see F. D. Dow, Cromwellian Scotland, 1651–1660 (Edinburgh: John Donald, 1979), 189–234.
81. On Quaker attempts to influence Monck—Fox and Fell writing appeals, see Fox, Journal, 341–45; and Bonnelyn Young Kunze, "Religious Authority and Social Status in Seventeenth-Century England: The Friendship of Margaret Fell, George Fox, and William Penn," Church History 57, no. 2 (1988): 170–86.
82. On Monck reaching London (February 1660), forcing Rump to readmit excluded members, effectively ending Commonwealth, see Hutton, Restoration, 58–93.
83. On Charles II's Declaration of Breda (April 1660) and England's welcome of the Restoration, see Hutton, Restoration, 94–123; and Paul Seaward, The Cavalier Parliament and the Reconstruction of the Old Regime, 1661–1667 (Cambridge: Cambridge University Press, 1989), 1–47.
84. On Charles II's return (29 May 1660) and immediate threats to Quakers—mob attacks, magistrates arresting Friends—see Reay, Quakers and the English Revolution, 129–43; and Horle, Quakers and the English Legal System, 34–88.
85. On rumors of Quaker armed uprising (September 1660), mass arrests, and the need for the Peace Declaration, see Horle, Quakers and the English Legal System, 45–62; and Braithwaite, Beginnings of Quakerism, 417–52.
86. "A Declaration from the Harmless and Innocent People of God, Called Quakers" (January 1661) is printed in Hugh Barbour and Arthur O. Roberts, eds., Early Quaker Writings, 1650–1700 (Grand Rapids: Eerdmans, 1973), 396–403; and in Fox, Journal, 398–404.
87. 87–91. The quoted passages from the Peace Declaration are from the text in Barbour and Roberts, Early Quaker Writings, 396–403.
88. On ambiguities in the Peace Declaration—magistracy, pure self-defense, relationship to civil government—and ongoing debates, see Peter Brock, The Quaker Peace Testimony, 1660 to 1914 (York: Sessions Book Trust, 1990), 1–45; and Meredith Baldwin Weddle, Walking in the Way of Peace: Quaker Pacifism in the Seventeenth Century (Oxford: Oxford University Press, 2001).
89. On James Nayler's 1657 pamphlet The Lamb's War Against the Man of Sin and the "Lamb's War" concept, see Nayler, Lamb's War, in Collection of Sundry Books, 141–67; and Damrosch, Sorrows of the Quaker Jesus, 230–67.
90. Edward Burrough's A Discovery of Some Part of the War Between the Kingdom of the Lamb and the Kingdom of Anti-Christ (1659), quoted passage on 23–28.
91. On Quaker perfectionism connecting to pacifism and critics' objections about naivete, see Barbour, Quakers in Puritan England, 186–234; and Weddle, Walking in the Way of Peace, 89–145.
92. On the Clarendon Code (1661–1665)—Corporation Act, Act of Uniformity, Conventicle Act, Five Mile Act—and targeting of Quakers, see John Spurr, The Restoration Church of England, 1646–1689 (New Haven: Yale University Press, 1991), 45–89; and Michael R. Watts, The Dissenters, vol. 1, From the Reformation to the French Revolution (Oxford: Clarendon Press, 1978), 222–68.
93. On Quakers systematically violating laws, continuing to meet, refusing oaths,

thousands imprisoned, see Horle, Quakers and the English Legal System, 89–178; and Craig W. Horle et al., eds., The Quaker Act, 1662, and the Aftermath of Persecution (forthcoming).

94. On Penn obtaining Pennsylvania charter from Charles II, naming it, and envisioning "holy experiment," see Mary K. Geiter, William Penn (Harlow: Pearson Education, 2000), 45–89; and Jean R. Soderlund, ed., William Penn and the Founding of Pennsylvania: A Documentary History (Philadelphia: University of Pennsylvania Press, 1983).

95. Penn's Frame of Government (1682) and religious liberty provisions quoted from Soderlund, William Penn and the Founding of Pennsylvania, 89–134. On Frame of Government embodying Quaker political theology, see J. William Frost, A Perfect Freedom: Religious Liberty in Pennsylvania (Cambridge: Cambridge University Press, 1990), 1–45.

96. On the suffering strategy—visible suffering, refusing to pay fines, preaching through cell windows, recording persecution—see Besse, Collection of the Sufferings; and Miller, "'A Suffering People,'" 71–103.

97. On Besse's Collection of the Sufferings (1753) running over 1,400 folio pages as monument to endurance, see Besse, Collection; and Horle, Quakers and the English Legal System, 1–33.

98. On maturation of Quaker discipline 1660–1689—monthly meeting procedures, marriage clearness, dispute handling—see Vann, Social Development, 126–98; and Jack D. Marietta, "Ecclesiastical Discipline in the Society of Friends, 1682–1776" (PhD diss., Stanford University, 1968).

99. On women's meetings as parallel structures and institutional voice for women, see Rebecca Larson, Daughters of Light: Quaker Women Preaching and Prophesying in the Colonies and Abroad, 1700–1775 (New York: Alfred A. Knopf, 1999); and Trevett, Women and Quakerism, 146–92.

100. On Fox's later years consolidating structures, traveling to America (1671–1673), marrying Margaret Fell (1669), and his Journal (published 1691), see Ingle, First Among Friends, 221–322; and Fox, Journal, passim.

101. Robert Barclay (1648–1690), An Apology for the True Christian Divinity (Aberdeen, 1676); modern edition ed. Dean Freiday (Glenside, PA: Quaker Heritage Press, 2002). On Barclay's systematic theology of Quakerism, see D. Elton Trueblood, Robert Barclay (New York: Harper & Row, 1968).

102. On Quaker theological positioning—Protestant yet distinctive, challenging both Calvinism and rationalism—see Barbour and Frost, The Quakers, 83–146; and Pink Dandelion, An Introduction to Quakerism (Cambridge: Cambridge University Press, 2007), 37–89.

103. On theological stabilization's costs—early spontaneity giving way to prescribed forms—and debates over lost fire versus gained wisdom, see Douglas Gwyn, The Covenant Crucified: Quakers and the Rise of Capitalism (Wallingford, PA: Pendle Hill Publications, 1995); and Rosemary Moore, "The Faith of the First Quakers," Quaker Studies 4, no. 2 (2000): 69–89.

104. On Penn's peaceful relations with Lenape people and the Treaty under the elm at Shackamaxon, see James H. Merrell, Into the American Woods: Negotiators on the Pennsylvania Frontier (New York: W. W. Norton, 1999); and Francis Jennings, "Brother Miquon: Good Lord!" in The World of William Penn, ed. Dunn and Dunn, 195–214. Penn's heirs did not maintain his standards.

105. On Pennsylvania's criminal justice reform—only two capital crimes, imprisonment for reform, opposition to torture, restitution over retribution—see Negley K. Teeters, The Cradle of the Penitentiary: The Walnut Street Jail at Philadelphia, 1773–1835 (Philadelphia: Pennsylvania Prison Society, 1955), 1–34; and Marietta, Reformation of American Quakerism, 135–78.

106. On political participation in Pennsylvania testing peace testimony—Quakers as

magistrates, judges in capital cases, voting for military appropriations—see Jack D. Marietta, The Reformation of American Quakerism, 1748–1783 (Philadelphia: University of Pennsylvania Press, 1984), 179–234; and J. William Frost, "Quaker versus Quaker over Slavery, Women's Rights, Peace, and Other Reforms," Quaker History 98, no. 1 (2009): 1–22.

107. On compromises—paying other colonies for defense, "voluntary" militias, funds for "King's use"—see Marietta, Reformation of American Quakerism, 179–234; and Frederick B. Tolles, Meeting House and Counting House: The Quaker Merchants of Colonial Philadelphia, 1682–1763 (Chapel Hill: University of North Carolina Press, 1948), 234–67.
108. On the "Great Resignation" of 1756 during French and Indian War—Quakers resigning from assembly rather than vote for war—see Marietta, Reformation of American Quakerism, 235–74; and Theodore Thayer, Israel Pemberton, King of the Quakers (Philadelphia: Historical Society of Pennsylvania, 1943).
109. On Quakers in abolition movement—Pennsylvania debates from 1680s, Philadelphia Yearly Meeting requiring manumission (1776), John Woolman's Some Considerations on the Keeping of Negroes (1754), British Quaker support for Wilberforce—see Jean R. Soderlund, Quakers and Slavery: A Divided Spirit (Princeton: Princeton University Press, 1985); and David Brion Davis, The Problem of Slavery in Western Culture (Ithaca: Cornell University Press, 1966), 291–332, 483–93.
110. On John Bellers and Elizabeth Fry in prison reform—Fry's work at Newgate (1813 onward), principle of human dignity and reform—see June Rose, Elizabeth Fry: A Biography (London: Macmillan, 1980); and Norman Johnston, Forms of Constraint: A History of Prison Architecture (Urbana: University of Illinois Press, 2000), 45–89.
111. On Quakers founding York Retreat (1796) and pioneering "moral treatment" of mental illness, see Anne Digby, Madness, Morality and Medicine: A Study of the York Retreat, 1796–1914 (Cambridge: Cambridge University Press, 1985); and Andrew T. Scull, Museums of Madness: The Social Organization of Insanity in Nineteenth-Century England (London: Allen Lane, 1979), 67–102.
112. On Quaker influence on Enlightenment political thought—Locke's correspondence with Quakers, Penn's Frame of Government influencing American founders, Benjamin Franklin and Philadelphia Quaker context—see Murphy, Conscience and Community: Revisiting Toleration and Religious Dissent in Early Modern England and America (University Park: Pennsylvania State University Press, 2001); and Frost, Perfect Freedom, 145–234.
113. On Quaker plain speech, dress, plainness influencing simplicity movements and Quaker business ethics—fixed prices, honesty, quality—with Cadbury, Rowntree, Barclays as examples, see Tolles, Meeting House and Counting House, 89–145; and David Windsor and Kathleen Preston, "Corporate Governance, Social Responsibility and Quakerism: Insights into Cadbury," Business and Society Review 120, no. 4 (2015): 533–63.
114. On the transformation from Nayler's 1656 trial to Fox's death (1691), see Ingle, First Among Friends, 323–38; and Braithwaite, Beginnings of Quakerism, 453–520.
115. On what the transformation cost—early spontaneity versus 1680s structure, some leaving over stifling regulations—see Gwyn, Covenant Crucified, 145–234; and Moore, "Faith of the First Quakers," 82–89.
116. On women's voices channeled into women's meetings and informal hierarchy developing despite official denials, see Larson, Daughters of Light, 1–89; and Trevett, Women and Quakerism, 193–245.
117. On what survived—silence waiting for Spirit, refusal of oaths/tithes/hat-honor, belief in inner light and perfection, peace testimony, plain speech and dress—see Dandelion, Introduction to Quakerism, 90–178; and Barbour and Frost, The Quakers, 147–200.

118. On Quaker politics as shaping souls and cultures rather than controlling institutions, requiring patience learned in prison and hope maintained through Commonwealth collapse, see Brock, Quaker Peace Testimony, 46–134; and Weddle, Walking in the Way of Peace, 235–89.

Notes — Chapter 7

1. On Charles I's final morning (30 January 1649), preparation, and hearing workmen building the scaffold, see C. V. Wedgwood, *The Trial of Charles I* (London: Collins, 1964), 168–72; and Geoffrey Robertson, *The Tyrannicide Brief: The Story of the Man Who Sent Charles I to the Scaffold* (London: Chatto & Windus, 2005), 167–89.
2. On Charles wearing two shirts against the cold, ensuring his hair was properly arranged, and reading from his pocket Bible and *Eikon Basilike*, see contemporary accounts in Samuel Rawson Gardiner, *History of the Great Civil War, 1642–1649*, 4 vols. (London: Longmans, Green, 1893), 4:320–28; and *Eikon Basilike: The Pourtraicture of His Sacred Majestie in His Solitudes and Sufferings* (London, 1649), ed. Philip A. Knachel (Ithaca: Cornell University Press, 1966).
3. On Charles walking through St. James's Park with Bishop William Juxon, discussing theology and forgiveness, quoting Philippians 1:21 ("For me to live is Christ, and to die is gain"), see Wedgwood, *Trial of Charles I*, 173–78; and Jason Peacey, "Reporting a Revolution: A Failed Propaganda Campaign," in *The Regicides and the Execution of Charles I*, ed. Jason Peacey (Basingstoke: Palgrave, 2001), 161–81.
4. On the court that tried Charles—established by purged Rump Parliament, 135 commissioners with 68 attending regularly and 59 signing death warrant—and the charges, see *The Trial of Charles I: A Contemporary Account*, ed. Roger Lockyer (London: Folio Society, 1959); and Sean Kelsey, "The Trial of Charles I," *English Historical Review* 118, no. 477 (2003): 583–616.
5. Charles's refusal to plead and his statement "I would know by what power I am called hither" are from *Trial of Charles I*, ed. Lockyer, 78–82; and John Bradshaw's insistence he must answer in *State Trials*, vol. 4 (London, 1730), 990–1024.
6. On the theological claim of divine right—Charles answerable to God alone, trying him as sacrilege—and the court's counter-claim of popular sovereignty, see Glenn Burgess, "The Impact on Political Thought: Rhetorics for Troubled Times," in *The Impact of the English Civil War*, ed. John Morrill (London: Collins & Brown, 1991), 67–83; and Michael J. Braddick, *God's Fury, England's Fire: A New History of the English Civil Wars* (London: Allen Lane, 2008), 559–87.
7. The verdict and sentence—"tyrant, traitor, murderer and public enemy"—calling for "severing of his head from his body" are from *Trial of Charles I*, ed. Lockyer, 129–33.
8. On the scaffold built outside the Banqueting House designed by Inigo Jones with Rubens ceiling panels celebrating Stuart divine monarchy, see Wedgwood, *Trial of Charles I*, 179–82; and Simon Thurley, *Whitehall Palace: An Architectural History of the Royal Apartments, 1240–1698* (New Haven: Yale University Press, 1999), 89–134.
9. On the scaffold draped in black, masked executioners (identities hidden), and spectators held back by soldiers, see Gardiner, *History of the Great Civil War*, 4:323–28; and Clive Holmes, *Why Was Charles I Executed?* (London: Hambledon Continuum, 2006), 167–89.
10. On Charles stepping through a window onto the scaffold at two o'clock, wearing the George (Order of the Garter insignia), and his prepared speech, see contemporary accounts in Wedgwood, *Trial of Charles I*, 182–87.
11. Charles's scaffold speech—"I never did begin a war with the two Houses of Parliament," "their liberty and freedom consists in having government," "A subject and a sovereign are clean different things"—is from *The King's Last Speech* (London, 1649), reprinted in *Trial of Charles I*, ed. Lockyer, 134–37.
12. Charles's words casting himself as "martyr of the people," forgiving enemies, and quoting St. Stephen (Acts 7:60) are from *King's Last Speech*, 135–37.
13. On the speech as carefully chosen propaganda transforming execution into sacrifice,

political defeat into moral victory, see Andrew Lacey, *The Cult of King Charles the Martyr* (Woodbridge: Boydell Press, 2003), 51–89; and Kevin Sharpe, *Image Wars: Promoting Kings and Commonwealths in England, 1603–1660* (New Haven: Yale University Press, 2010), 381–456.

14. On Charles removing cloak and doublet, handing the George to Juxon with "Remember," approaching the block, arranging hair, praying, and the execution—one blow, executioner not speaking traditional "Behold the head of a traitor!"—see Wedgwood, *Trial of Charles I*, 187–91; and Peacey, "Reporting a Revolution," 175–78.
15. On the crowd's groan, soldiers dispersing spectators, body carried into Banqueting House, burial at Windsor, and no state funeral or public mourning, see Gardiner, *History of the Great Civil War*, 4:328–32; and Lacey, *Cult of King Charles*, 21–50.
16. On political meaning—establishing popular sovereignty, kings not above law—as revolutionary and terrifying to European monarchs, see J. G. A. Pocock, "Regicide and Revolution," in *The Impact of the English Civil War*, ed. Morrill, 165–81; and Blair Worden, *The English Civil Wars, 1640–1660* (London: Weidenfeld & Nicolson, 2009), 112–34.
17. On religious meaning—shattering divine right monarchy and passive obedience doctrine, theological crisis for royalists, see J. P. Sommerville, "English and European Political Ideas in the Early Seventeenth Century: Revisionism and the Case of Absolutism," *Journal of British Studies* 35, no. 2 (1996): 168–94; and Johann P. Sommerville, *Royalists and Patriots: Politics and Ideology in England, 1603–1640*, 2nd ed. (London: Longman, 1999).
18. On social meaning—demonstrating old order not eternal or divinely ordained but contingent and changeable, see Christopher Hill, *The World Turned Upside Down: Radical Ideas During the English Revolution* (London: Temple Smith, 1972); and David Wootton, "Leveller Democracy and the Puritan Revolution," in *The Cambridge History of Political Thought, 1450–1700*, ed. J. H. Burns (Cambridge: Cambridge University Press, 1991), 412–42.
19. On psychological meaning—for royalists Charles became martyr, for republicans the defeated tyrant—see Lacey, *Cult of King Charles*, 90–156; and Jason McElligott, *Royalism, Print and Censorship in Revolutionary England* (Woodbridge: Boydell Press, 2007), 135–72.
20. On the Rump Parliament—approximately 200 members out of original 500+ before Pride's Purge—and overwhelming challenges it faced, see Blair Worden, *The Rump Parliament, 1648–1653* (Cambridge: Cambridge University Press, 1974), 1–45; and Sean Kelsey, *Inventing a Republic: The Political Culture of the English Commonwealth, 1649–1653* (Stanford: Stanford University Press, 1997).
21. On Oliver Cromwell's Irish campaign (1649–1650)—reconquering Ireland, sieges of Drogheda and Wexford with legendary slaughter, Cromwell's name synonymous with English tyranny in Irish memory—see Micheál Ó Siochrú, *God's Executioner: Oliver Cromwell and the Conquest of Ireland* (London: Faber & Faber, 2008); and Tom Reilly, *Cromwell: An Honourable Enemy* (Dingle: Brandon, 1999), challenging traditional narratives.
22. On Charles II going to Scotland, signing the Covenant, being proclaimed King, and Cromwell's invasion (1650) winning at Dunbar and Worcester (1651), see David Stevenson, *Revolution and Counter-Revolution in Scotland, 1644–1651*, 2nd ed. (Edinburgh: John Donald, 2003); and Austin Woolrych, *Britain in Revolution, 1625–1660* (Oxford: Oxford University Press, 2002), 465–518.
23. On the Rump's financial struggles—taxes including unpopular excise, confiscated royalist estates—and religious settlement failing to create coherent national church, see Worden, *Rump Parliament*, 193–277; and Ann Hughes, "Religion, 1640–1660," in *The Civil Wars: A Military History of England, Scotland, and Ireland, 1638–1660*, ed. John Kenyon and Jane Ohlmeyer (Oxford: Oxford University Press, 1998), 333–55.
24. On the Rump's failure to accomplish reforms beyond surviving (1649–1653), debating constitutional, religious, and social reforms but passing little legislation, see Worden,

Rump Parliament, 278–374; and Kelsey, *Inventing a Republic*, 89–167.

25. On Army frustration with the Rump and demands for redistribution of seats, religious liberty, law reform, regular elections, see Austin Woolrych, *Commonwealth to Protectorate* (Oxford: Clarendon Press, 1982), 1–89; and Ian Gentles, *The New Model Army in England, Ireland and Scotland, 1645–1653* (Oxford: Blackwell, 1992), 389–442.
26. Cromwell's dissolution of the Rump (20 April 1653)—walking in with thirty musketeers, his speech "It is not fit that you should sit here any longer," "Call them in!"—is from contemporary accounts in Bulstrode Whitelocke, *Memorials of the English Affairs* (London, 1682), 556–58; and Edmund Ludlow, *Memoirs*, ed. C. H. Firth, 2 vols. (Oxford: Clarendon Press, 1894), 1:352–54.
27. On Cromwell removing the Speaker, taking the mace and saying "What shall we do with this bauble? Here, take it away!" and the republican experiment failing, see Woolrych, *Commonwealth to Protectorate*, 90–134; and Worden, *Rump Parliament*, 375–90.
28. On the Nominated (Barebone's) Parliament (July–December 1653)—Parliament of godly men selected for piety rather than elected, see Woolrych, *Commonwealth to Protectorate*, 135–257; and Bernard Capp, "The Fifth Monarchists and Popular Millenarianism, 1645–1660," in *Radical Religion in the English Revolution*, ed. J. F. McGregor and B. Reay (Oxford: Oxford University Press, 1984), 165–89.
29. On the assembly including about 140 men chosen by Army officers and Independent congregations as "the saints," meant to bring godly wisdom and complete reformation, see Austin Woolrych, "The Calling of Barebone's Parliament," *English Historical Review* 80, no. 316 (1965): 492–513.
30. On division between moderates and radicals (Fifth Monarchists), radical proposals to abolish tithes, replace common law with Mosaic law, establish apostolic church government, redistribute property, see Capp, "Fifth Monarchists," 171–85; and Woolrych, *Commonwealth to Protectorate*, 258–350.
31. On moderates dissolving the Parliament after five months, returning power to Cromwell, see Woolrych, *Commonwealth to Protectorate*, 351–83.
32. On 16 December 1653 Cromwell becoming Lord Protector under the Instrument of Government—England's first and only written constitution—see S. R. Gardiner, *Constitutional Documents of the Puritan Revolution, 1625–1660*, 3rd ed. (Oxford: Clarendon Press, 1906), 405–17 (text of Instrument); and J. C. Davis, "Cromwell's Religion," in *Oliver Cromwell and the English Revolution*, ed. John Morrill (London: Longman, 1990), 181–208.
33. On the Instrument's provisions—Lord Protector with broad powers, triennial Parliament with reformed constituencies, Council of State, "liberty to tender consciences" with exceptions for popery, prelacy, and licentiousness—see G. E. Aylmer, "Collective Mentalities in Mid-Seventeenth-Century England: II. Royalist Attitudes," *Transactions of the Royal Historical Society*, 5th ser., 37 (1987): 1–30; and Woolrych, *Britain in Revolution*, 551–626.
34. On Cromwell's Protectorate foreign policy success—war against Spain, capturing Jamaica (1655), supporting Protestant causes in Europe, see Timothy Venning, *Cromwellian Foreign Policy* (London: Macmillan, 1995); and Steven C. A. Pincus, *Protestantism and Patriotism: Ideologies and the Making of English Foreign Policy, 1650–1668* (Cambridge: Cambridge University Press, 1996).
35. On religious toleration—Jews readmitted (1656), Quakers not systematically persecuted nationally despite local imprisonments, Cromwell corresponding with George Fox, Independent/Baptist/moderate Presbyterian worship free—see David S. Katz, *Philo-Semitism and the Readmission of the Jews to England, 1603–1655* (Oxford: Clarendon Press, 1982); and Blair Worden, "Toleration and the Cromwellian Protectorate," in *Persecution and Toleration*, ed. W. J. Sheils (Oxford: Blackwell, 1984), 199–233.
36. On the Major-Generals' rule (1655–1657)—eleven military districts, enforcing moral discipline, closing alehouses, prosecuting Sabbath-breaking—deeply unpopular and

abandoned after eighteen months, see Christopher Durston, *Cromwell's Major-Generals: Godly Government During the English Revolution* (Manchester: Manchester University Press, 2001); and Anthony Fletcher, "Oliver Cromwell and the Godly Nation," in *Oliver Cromwell and the English Revolution*, ed. Morrill, 209–33.

37. On financial problems and fractious Parliaments—some wanting Cromwell as king, others protecting republicanism, all resenting taxation and military rule—and Cromwell dissolving two Parliaments, see David L. Smith, "Oliver Cromwell, the First Protectorate Parliament and Religious Reform," *Parliamentary History* 16, no. 1 (1997): 38–48; and Woolrych, *Britain in Revolution*, 627–89.
38. On Parliament offering Cromwell the crown (1657), his agonizing refusal, succession crisis with son Richard inheriting title but not authority, and Protectorate's collapse within a year of Oliver's death (September 1658), see Ronald Hutton, *The British Republic, 1649–1660*, 2nd ed. (Basingstoke: Macmillan, 2000), 103–42; and J. C. Davis, "Cromwell's Religion," 200–206.
39. On 1659–1660 chaos after Richard Cromwell's resignation (May 1659)—Rump recalled, elderly MPs out of touch, see Hutton, *British Republic*, 143–74; and Austin Woolrych, "Last Quests for a Settlement, 1657–1660," in *The Interregnum: The Quest for Settlement, 1646–1660*, ed. G. E. Aylmer (London: Macmillan, 1972), 183–204.
40. On Army officers competing—expelling Rump in October 1659, ruling through Committee of Safety, appearing as military dictatorship without Cromwell's charisma, see Woolrych, "Last Quests," 192–200; and Hutton, *British Republic*, 157–68.
41. On Presbyterians hoping for settlement restoring Charles II under conditions, negotiating with royalist exiles, see Ronald Hutton, *The Restoration: A Political and Religious History of England and Wales, 1658–1667* (Oxford: Clarendon Press, 1985), 1–57.
42. On Charles II in exile issuing moderate declarations promising amnesty (except regicides), property settlement, religious toleration, see Paul Seaward, "Clarendon, Tacitism, and the Civil Wars of Europe," *Huntington Library Quarterly* 68, nos. 1–2 (2005): 289–311.
43. On General George Monck marching from Scotland to London (January 1660), forcing Rump to readmit excluded members, restoring Long Parliament which voted to dissolve, calling elections producing Convention Parliament inviting Charles II back, see F. D. Dow, *Cromwellian Scotland, 1651–1660* (Edinburgh: John Donald, 1979), 189–234; and Hutton, *Restoration*, 58–93.
44. On why Restoration became inevitable—republican experiment couldn't create stable government, Army couldn't govern legitimately without Cromwell, religious radicals frightening propertied classes, exhaustion after twenty years—see Hutton, *Restoration*, 94–123; and Tim Harris, *Restoration: Charles II and His Kingdoms, 1660–1685* (London: Allen Lane, 2005), 1–45.
45. On European monarchical context making republican England diplomatically isolated, see Hutton, *British Republic*, 175–200; and Pincus, *Protestantism and Patriotism*, 167–234.
46. On the Cavalier Parliament (elected 1661) overwhelmingly royalist and Anglican, passing the Clarendon Code named after Edward Hyde, Earl of Clarendon, see Paul Seaward, *The Cavalier Parliament and the Reconstruction of the Old Regime, 1661–1667* (Cambridge: Cambridge University Press, 1989); and I. M. Green, *The Re-Establishment of the Church of England, 1660–1663* (Oxford: Oxford University Press, 1978).
47. Corporation Act (13 Car. II stat. 2 c. 1, 1661) in *Statutes of the Realm*, vol. 5 (London: HMSO, 1819), 321–23. On exclusion of Nonconformists from municipal office, see Paul Halliday, *Dismembering the Body Politic: Partisan Politics in England's Towns, 1650–1730* (Cambridge: Cambridge University Press, 1998), 89–134.
48. Act of Uniformity (14 Car. II c. 4, 1662) in *Statutes of the Realm*, vol. 5, 364–70. On the Great Ejection of approximately 2,000 ministers, see A. G. Matthews, *Calamy Revised: Being a Revision of Edmund Calamy's Account of the Ministers and Others Ejected and Silenced, 1660–2* (Oxford: Clarendon Press, 1934); and Green, *Re-Establishment*, 180–225.

49. Conventicle Act (16 Car. II c. 4, 1664; renewed 22 Car. II c. 1, 1670) in *Statutes of the Realm*, vol. 5, 516–20, 648–51. Five Mile Act (17 Car. II c. 2, 1665) in *Statutes of the Realm*, vol. 5, 575–77. On targeting Nonconformist worship and scattering leadership, see Michael R. Watts, *The Dissenters*, vol. 1, *From the Reformation to the French Revolution* (Oxford: Clarendon Press, 1978), 222–68; and Gerald R. Cragg, *Puritanism in the Period of the Great Persecution, 1660–1688* (Cambridge: Cambridge University Press, 1957).
50. On persecution producing martyrs not conformists—Nonconformists meeting secretly, ejected ministers preaching, networks of mutual support, see Watts, *Dissenters*, 1:246–68; and Craig W. Horle, *The Quakers and the English Legal System, 1660–1688* (Philadelphia: University of Pennsylvania Press, 1988).
51. On uneven enforcement varying by locality—some magistrates zealous, others sympathetic, some justices warning Nonconformists, see Tim Harris, "The Problem of 'Popular Allegiance' in the English Civil War," *Transactions of the Royal Historical Society*, 5th ser., 31 (1981): 69–94; and John Miller, "'A Suffering People': English Quakers and Their Neighbours c. 1650–c. 1700," *Past & Present* 188 (2005): 71–103.
52. On Charles II's ambivalence, Declarations of Indulgence (1662, 1672) suspending penal laws, Parliament forcing withdrawal both times, constitutional tensions, see Ronald Hutton, *Charles the Second: King of England, Scotland, and Ireland* (Oxford: Clarendon Press, 1989), 198–234, 291–328; and John Miller, *Popery and Politics in England, 1660–1688* (Cambridge: Cambridge University Press, 1973), 131–89.
53. On Charles II having no legitimate children, heir being brother James Duke of York who converted to Catholicism, prospect of Catholic king terrifying Protestant England, see Miller, *Popery and Politics*, 1–130; and Harris, *Restoration*, 167–238.
54. On Titus Oates and the "Popish Plot" (1678)—lurid claims of Catholic conspiracy, panic, approximately 35 executions including Catholic nobles and Jesuits, see John Kenyon, *The Popish Plot* (London: Heinemann, 1972); and J. P. Kenyon, "The Popish Plot: A Study in the History of the Reign of Charles II," in *Politics, Religion and Society in England, 1679–1742*, ed. Paul Monod, Murray Pittock, and Daniel Szechi (Farnham: Ashgate, 2008), 17–42.
55. On the Exclusion Crisis (1679–1681)—Parliament attempting to pass Exclusion Bill barring James from succession, Earl of Shaftesbury leading exclusionists, see J. R. Jones, *The First Whigs: The Politics of the Exclusion Crisis, 1678–1683* (Oxford: Oxford University Press, 1961); and Mark Knights, *Politics and Opinion in Crisis, 1678–81* (Cambridge: Cambridge University Press, 1994).
56. On Whigs (exclusionists)—wanting parliamentary supremacy, Protestant succession, broad toleration, drawing support from Nonconformists and merchants, see Jones, *First Whigs*, passim; and Tim Harris, *Politics Under the Later Stuarts: Party Conflict in a Divided Society, 1660–1715* (London: Longman, 1993), 77–123.
57. On Tories (anti-exclusionists)—defending hereditary succession, royal prerogative, Anglican establishment, drawing support from gentry and clergy, see Harris, *Politics Under the Later Stuarts*, 77–123; and J. C. D. Clark, *English Society, 1660–1832: Religion, Ideology and Politics During the Ancien Regime*, 2nd ed. (Cambridge: Cambridge University Press, 2000), 119–97.
58. On James II's accession (1685) and immediately attending Mass publicly, appointing Catholics to military commands and universities, issuing Declaration of Indulgence (1687, reissued 1688), see John Miller, *James II: A Study in Kingship* (Hove: Wayland, 1978); and W. A. Speck, *Reluctant Revolutionaries: Englishmen and the Revolution of 1688* (Oxford: Oxford University Press, 1988), 76–145.
59. On seven bishops (including Archbishop of Canterbury) petitioning against Declaration, James prosecuting them for seditious libel, jury acquitting to national celebration, see T. B. Howell, ed., *A Complete Collection of State Trials*, vol. 12 (London, 1816), 183–434; and G. V. Bennett, "The Seven Bishops: A Reconsideration," in *Religious Motivation: Biographical and Sociological Problems for the Church Historian*, ed. Derek Baker (Oxford: Blackwell, 1978), 267–87.

60. On birth of James's son (June 1688) making crisis acute—ending prospect of Protestant succession, facing indefinite Catholic rule, see Speck, *Reluctant Revolutionaries*, 146–91; and Tim Harris, *Revolution: The Great Crisis of the British Monarchy, 1685–1720* (London: Allen Lane, 2006), 217–68.
61. On William of Orange landing at Torbay (5 November 1688) with 14,000 troops at invitation of seven prominent Englishmen ("Immortal Seven"), see Tony Claydon, *William III* (London: Longman, 2002), 56–93; and Jonathan I. Israel, ed., *The Anglo-Dutch Moment: Essays on the Glorious Revolution and Its World Impact* (Cambridge: Cambridge University Press, 1991).
62. On William's Declaration justifying invasion—James violated laws, persecuted established church, packed Parliament, threatened popery, see *A Declaration of His Highness William Henry, Prince of Orange, of the Reasons Inducing Him to Appear in Arms* (London, 1688); and Lois G. Schwoerer, *The Declaration of Rights, 1689* (Baltimore: Johns Hopkins University Press, 1981).
63. On James's collapsing support—army officers defecting including John Churchill, navy declaring for William, cities welcoming William, James fleeing to France, Parliament declaring throne "abdicated," see Speck, *Reluctant Revolutionaries*, 192–249; and Steven C. A. Pincus, *1688: The First Modern Revolution* (New Haven: Yale University Press, 2009), 189–305.
64. On the Glorious Revolution remarkably bloodless in England (though not Ireland/Scotland), Bill of Rights (1689) listing James's violations, establishing parliamentary supremacy and crown offered conditionally, see Schwoerer, *Declaration of Rights*; and J. R. Jones, *The Revolution of 1688 in England* (London: Weidenfeld & Nicolson, 1972), 296–337.
65. On Bill of Rights requiring Protestant monarchs taking oaths denying Catholic doctrines, excluding James's descendants, eventually bringing Hanoverian dynasty (1714), see *Bill of Rights* (1 Will. & Mary sess. 2 c. 2, 1689) in *Statutes of the Realm*, vol. 6, 142–45; and Ragnhild Hatton, *George I: Elector and King* (London: Thames and Hudson, 1978), on Hanoverian succession.
66. On limited monarchy—King couldn't suspend laws, levy taxes, maintain standing army, or interfere with elections without Parliament's consent, and Toleration Act (1689), see John Spurr, "The Church of England, Comprehension and the Toleration Act of 1689," *English Historical Review* 104, no. 413 (1989): 927–46; and John Marshall, *John Locke, Toleration and Early Enlightenment Culture* (Cambridge: Cambridge University Press, 2006), 384–449.
67. The Toleration Act of 1689 (*An Act for Exempting Their Majesties' Protestant Subjects Dissenting from the Church of England from the Penalties of Certain Laws*, 1 Will. & Mary c. 18) is in *Statutes of the Realm*, vol. 6, 74–76. On its limited, grudging, pragmatic but revolutionary nature, see Watts, *Dissenters*, 1:363–414; and Spurr, "Church of England, Comprehension and the Toleration Act," 927–46.
68. On the Act's provisions—Protestant dissenters taking oaths, subscribing most Thirty-Nine Articles (excluding church government/ceremonies), registering meeting places—could worship publicly without penalty, see John Coffey, *Persecution and Toleration in Protestant England, 1558–1689* (Harlow: Pearson, 2000), 189–234.
69. On what the Act did NOT do—grant full equality, no office-holding without Anglican communion, no Oxford/Cambridge, didn't extend to Catholics (remaining illegal) or anti-Trinitarians, see Adrian Davies, *The Quakers in English Society, 1655–1725* (Oxford: Clarendon Press, 2000), 236–89; and Colin Haydon, *Anti-Catholicism in Eighteenth-Century England, c. 1714–80: A Political and Social Study* (Manchester: Manchester University Press, 1993).
70. The Act's preamble stating "some ease to scrupulous consciences" might "be an effectual means to unite Their Majesties' Protestant subjects" is quoted from *Statutes of the Realm*, vol. 6, 74. On pragmatic accommodation not principled liberty, see Marshall, *John Locke, Toleration and Early Enlightenment Culture*, 384–449.

71. On why the Act passed in 1689—William III's Dutch Reformed background and need for Nonconformist support, see Claydon, *William III*, 123–78; and Craig Rose, *England in the 1690s: Revolution, Religion and War* (Oxford: Blackwell, 1999), 53–89.
72. On Whig-Nonconformist alliance, exhaustion with thirty years of failed persecution (1660–1689), and Catholic threat making Protestant divisions seem petty, see Coffey, *Persecution and Toleration*, 189–234; and Mark Goldie, "The Theory of Religious Intolerance in Restoration England," in *From Persecution to Toleration: The Glorious Revolution and Religion in England*, ed. Ole Peter Grell, Jonathan I. Israel, and Nicholas Tyacke (Oxford: Clarendon Press, 1991), 331–68.
73. On changing intellectual climate—John Locke's *A Letter Concerning Toleration* (1689) articulating philosophical arguments distinguishing civil and religious spheres, influencing educated opinion, see John Locke, *A Letter Concerning Toleration*, ed. James H. Tully (Indianapolis: Hackett, 1983); and Marshall, *John Locke, Toleration and Early Enlightenment Culture*, 1–152. On economic considerations and Dutch model, see Jonathan I. Israel, *The Dutch Republic: Its Rise, Greatness, and Fall, 1477–1806* (Oxford: Clarendon Press, 1995), 1019–37.
74. On registration requirement serving dual purposes—legalizing worship and enabling surveillance, see Watts, *Dissenters*, 1:415–68; and G. M. Ditchfield, "Ecclesiastical Policy Under Lord North," in *Hanoverian Britain and Empire: Essays in Memory of Philip Lawson*, ed. Stephen Taylor, Richard Connors, and Clyve Jones (Woodbridge: Boydell Press, 1998), 235–51.
75. On registration creating paper trail documenting Nonconformity's extent—thousands of meeting houses registered by 1710, geographic patterns (strongest in London/southeast, cloth-manufacturing regions, weakest in rural agricultural areas), denominational distribution (Presbyterians most numerous initially, declining relative to Independents/Baptists), see Michael R. Watts, *The Dissenters*, vol. 2, *The Expansion of Evangelical Nonconformity* (Oxford: Clarendon Press, 1995), 1–89; and Davies, *Quakers in English Society*, 236–89.
76. On occasional conformity—Nonconformists taking Anglican communion once or twice yearly to qualify for office while attending dissenting meetings regularly, troubling both Anglicans and strict Nonconformists—see G. V. Bennett, *The Tory Crisis in Church and State, 1688–1730: The Career of Francis Atterbury, Bishop of Rochester* (Oxford: Clarendon Press, 1975), 56–89; and Norman Sykes, *From Sheldon to Secker: Aspects of English Church History, 1660–1768* (Cambridge: Cambridge University Press, 1959), 89–134.
77. On the Occasional Conformity Act (1711) penalizing those attending dissenting worship after qualifying by Anglican communion, politically motivated (Tories attacking Whig-Nonconformist alliances), repealed 1719, see Geoffrey Holmes, *British Politics in the Age of Anne*, rev. ed. (London: Hambledon Press, 1987), 78–123; and Bennett, *Tory Crisis*, 112–67.
78. On political exclusion continuing—Test and Corporation Acts until 1828, Nonconformists couldn't hold offices, attend Oxford/Cambridge, formally second-class citizens—see Ursula Henriques, *Religious Toleration in England, 1787–1833* (London: Routledge & Kegan Paul, 1961); and Richard W. Davis, *Dissent in Politics, 1780–1830: The Political Life of William Smith, M.P.* (London: Epworth Press, 1971).
79. On theological tensions remaining—toleration as legal accommodation not theological reconciliation, Anglicans still believing episcopacy divinely ordained, Nonconformists believing it corrupt—see John Walsh, Colin Haydon, and Stephen Taylor, eds., *The Church of England, c. 1689–c. 1833: From Toleration to Tractarianism* (Cambridge: Cambridge University Press, 1993).
80. On the Catholic problem—excluding Catholics creating permanent underclass (2–3% of population), couldn't worship legally, hold office, faced property and education restrictions, Catholic emancipation not until 1829, see Haydon, *Anti-Catholicism in Eighteenth-Century England*; and G. F. A. Best, "The Protestant Constitution and Its

Supporters, 1800–1829," *Transactions of the Royal Historical Society*, 5th ser., 8 (1958): 105–27.

81. On toleration posing challenge to Nonconformist identity—maintaining distinctiveness without persecution to sharpen boundaries, see Watts, *Dissenters*, 2:90–178; and David L. Wykes, "The Contribution of the Dissenting Academy to the Emergence of Rational Dissent," in *Enlightenment and Religion: Rational Dissent in Eighteenth-Century Britain*, ed. Knud Haakonssen (Cambridge: Cambridge University Press, 1996), 99–139.
82. On generational drift, theological cooling, the wealth problem—Nonconformist merchants prospering tempted to conformity and worldliness—see Watts, *Dissenters*, 2:269–362; and Clyde Binfield, *So Down to Prayers: Studies in English Nonconformity, 1780–1920* (London: J. M. Dent, 1977).
83. On English Presbyterianism largely disappearing as distinct denomination by 19th century—many congregations becoming Unitarian, others merging with Congregationalists, still others fading—see Watts, *Dissenters*, 2:363–468; and Raymond V. Holt, *The Unitarian Contribution to Social Progress in England*, 2nd ed. (London: Lindsey Press, 1952).
84. On Presbyterian influences persisting—dissenting academies maintaining high standards, Westminster Confession remaining standard for Reformed churches worldwide, corporate governance model influencing organizations, see J. W. Ashley Smith, *The Birth of Modern Education: The Contribution of the Dissenting Academies, 1660–1800* (London: Independent Press, 1954); and Irene Parker, *Dissenting Academies in England: Their Rise and Progress and Their Place Among the Educational Systems of the Country* (Cambridge: Cambridge University Press, 1914).
85. On Presbyterian hopes failing—national presbyterian church dream died in England, discipline lost coercive power without state enforcement, magistrate wouldn't enforce First Table, uniformity proved impossible, see John Coffey, "Puritanism and Liberty Revisited: The Case for Toleration in the English Revolution," *Historical Journal* 41, no. 4 (1998): 961–85.
86. On Independents winning argument for religious voluntarism—gathered churches prevailing, liberty of conscience becoming consensus, marketplace of ideas, denominationalism—see Edmund S. Morgan, *Visible Saints: The History of a Puritan Idea* (New York: New York University Press, 1963); and William G. McLoughlin, *New England Dissent, 1630–1833: The Baptists and the Separation of Church and State*, 2 vols. (Cambridge, MA: Harvard University Press, 1971).
87. On costs of Independent victory—fragmentation, loss of coherence without creeds/confessions, individualism, social atomization—see Mark A. Noll, *America's God: From Jonathan Edwards to Abraham Lincoln* (Oxford: Oxford University Press, 2002), 3–92; and Nathan O. Hatch, *The Democratization of American Christianity* (New Haven: Yale University Press, 1989).
88. On Church of England remaining established—enduring through 19th–20th century challenges, providing national religious identity, liturgical beauty, via media tradition, global communion—see Owen Chadwick, *The Victorian Church*, 2 vols. (London: Adam & Charles Black, 1966–1970); and Paul Avis, *Anglicanism and the Christian Church: Theological Resources in Historical Perspective*, rev. ed. (London: T&T Clark, 2002).
89. On Anglican expansion creating worldwide communion—third-largest Christian family after Catholicism and Orthodoxy, see Stephen Neill, *Anglicanism*, 4th ed. (London: Mowbray, 1977); and Kevin Ward, *A History of Global Anglicanism* (Cambridge: Cambridge University Press, 2006).
90. On what failed—Great Ejection (1662) driving godly and learned out, establishment breeding complacency, church vulnerable to state's secularization, see John Spurr, *The Restoration Church of England, 1646–1689* (New Haven: Yale University Press, 1991), 387–418; and E. R. Norman, *Church and Society in England, 1770–1970: A Historical Study* (Oxford: Clarendon Press, 1976).

91. On Quaker peace testimony persisting with remarkable consistency—consistent pacifism, alternative service, conflict resolution, speaking truth to power—see Peter Brock, *The Quaker Peace Testimony, 1660 to 1914* (York: Sessions Book Trust, 1990); and Meredith Baldwin Weddle, *Walking in the Way of Peace: Quaker Pacifism in the Seventeenth Century* (Oxford: Oxford University Press, 2001).
92. On Quaker influence on later movements—American Friends Service Committee, Gandhi's satyagraha, King's civil rights activism, non-violent resistance movements—see Hugh Barbour and J. William Frost, *The Quakers* (New York: Greenwood Press, 1988), 201–82; and Margaret Hope Bacon, *The Quiet Rebels: The Story of the Quakers in America* (New York: Basic Books, 1969).
93. On what couldn't scale—peace testimony's costs, small communities required, peculiarity problem, theological drift without creeds—see Richard T. Vann, *The Social Development of English Quakerism, 1655–1755* (Cambridge, MA: Harvard University Press, 1969), 199–245; and Pink Dandelion, *An Introduction to Quakerism* (Cambridge: Cambridge University Press, 2007), 179–234.
94. On forty tumultuous years costing perhaps 200,000 English lives (3–4% of population), dividing families, destroying property, challenging assumptions about authority, see Charles Carlton, *Going to the Wars: The Experience of the British Civil Wars, 1638–1651* (London: Routledge, 1992); and Ian Gentles, *The English Revolution and the Wars in the Three Kingdoms, 1638–1652* (Harlow: Pearson Education, 2007), 431–56.
95. On lessons learned—religious uniformity impossible, persecution couldn't suppress conscience, diversity was fact requiring legal acknowledgment, toleration from exhausted pragmatism, see Coffey, *Persecution and Toleration*, 235–67; and Marshall, *John Locke, Toleration and Early Enlightenment Culture*, 450–672.
96. On sovereignty requiring limits—absolute monarchy and parliamentary absolutism both producing tyranny, constitutional monarchy with parliamentary supremacy but judicial independence and protected liberties more stable, see J. P. Kenyon, *The Stuart Constitution, 1603–1688: Documents and Commentary*, 2nd ed. (Cambridge: Cambridge University Press, 1986); and Jennifer Carter, "The Revolution and the Constitution," in *Britain After the Glorious Revolution, 1689–1714*, ed. Geoffrey Holmes (London: Macmillan, 1969), 39–58.
97. On conscience having claims, violence having limits—military force winning battles but not settling religious questions or creating stable government without consent, see John Morrill, "The Religious Context of the English Civil War," *Transactions of the Royal Historical Society*, 5th ser., 34 (1984): 155–78; and Glenn Burgess, *British Political Thought, 1500–1660: The Politics of the Post-Reformation* (Basingstoke: Palgrave Macmillan, 2009).
98. On lessons only partly learned—establishment role contested, Catholic inclusion delayed 140 years, social hierarchy challenged but not overthrown, franchise restricted to property-holders, see Henriques, *Religious Toleration in England*; and E. P. Thompson, *The Making of the English Working Class* (London: Victor Gollancz, 1963), on later movements for social equality.
99. On gifts to the world—denominational pluralism, constitutional government, religious liberty principle, free press and marketplace of ideas—emerging from failure of uniformity attempts, see Perez Zagorin, *How the Idea of Religious Toleration Came to the West* (Princeton: Princeton University Press, 2003); and John Coffey and Paul C. H. Lim, eds., *The Cambridge Companion to Puritanism* (Cambridge: Cambridge University Press, 2008), 317–45.
100. On questions remaining—balancing liberty and order, maintaining religious commitment in tolerant societies, integrating diverse communities, defining "the people"—see Mark Goldie, "The Unacknowledged Republic: Officeholding in Early Modern England," in *The Politics of the Excluded, c. 1500–1850*, ed. Tim Harris (Basingstoke: Palgrave, 2001), 153–94; and Derek Hirst, "The Concreteness of English Politics, 1640–1642," in *Reactions to the English Civil War, 1642–1649*, ed. John Morrill (London: Macmillan, 1982), 1–23.

BIBLIOGRAPHY

NOTE ON SOURCES

This book draws on 17th-century primary documents, classic historical works, and recent scholarship. Primary sources are organized by type; secondary sources thematically. Modern editions generally modernize spelling and punctuation for readability.

I. PRIMARY SOURCES

A. Collected Works, Journals, and Correspondence

Baillie, Robert. *The Letters and Journals of Robert Baillie.* Edited by David Laing. 3 vols. Edinburgh: Robert Ogle, 1841-1842. Essential for Westminster Assembly and Scottish perspective. Frank assessments of English divines and frustrations of Scottish commissioners.

Baxter, Richard. *The Autobiography of Richard Baxter [Reliquiae Baxterianae].* Edited by N. H. Keeble. Totowa, NJ: Rowman and Littlefield, 1974. Essential for moderate Presbyterianism—ministry at Kidderminster, Army chaplaincy, Restoration negotiations.

Bunyan, John. *Grace Abounding to the Chief of Sinners.* Edited by Roger Sharrock. Oxford: Clarendon Press, 1962. Spiritual autobiography detailing conversion and call to preach. Essential for Independent/Baptist religious experience.

Cromwell, Oliver. *The Writings and Speeches of Oliver Cromwell.* Edited by W. C. Abbott. 4 vols. Cambridge, MA: Harvard University Press, 1937-1947. Standard edition. Essential for Cromwell's religious views, military thinking, and political struggles.

Fox, George. *The Journal of George Fox.* Edited by John L. Nickalls. Cambridge: Cambridge University Press, 1952. Foundational Quaker text. Essential for understanding Quaker origins and Fox's charismatic leadership.

Laud, William. *The Works of William Laud.* Edited by W. Scott and J. Bliss. 7 vols. Oxford: John Henry Parker, 1847-1860. Includes diary, sermons, trial documents. Shows ceremonialism and understanding of episcopacy.

Milton, John. *Complete Prose Works of John Milton.* Edited by Don M. Wolfe et al. 8 vols. New Haven: Yale University Press, 1953-1982.
Includes *Areopagitica* (vol. 2), divorce tracts, political writings. Excellent introductions and annotations.

Nayler, James. *A Collection of Sundry Books, Epistles and Papers.* London, 1716. Controversial Quaker's writings on "Lamb's War" and Quaker practices.

Williams, Roger. *The Bloudy Tenent of Persecution.* London, 1644. Modern edition edited by Richard Groves. Macon, GA: Mercer University Press, 2001. Most radical argument for religious liberty—complete church-state separation, liberty even for Catholics, Jews, Muslims.

B. Contemporary Pamphlets and Polemics (Selected)

Anonymous. *The Agreement of the People* (1647). In *The Leveller Tracts*, edited by

William Haller and Godfrey Davies. New York: Columbia University Press, 1944. Leveller constitutional proposal from Putney Debates.
[Charles I]. *Eikon Basilike.* London, 1649. Modern edition edited by Philip A. Knachel. Ithaca: Cornell University Press, 1966. Purported spiritual autobiography published days after execution. Created cult of "Charles the Martyr."
Clarendon, Edward Hyde, Earl of. *The History of the Rebellion and Civil Wars in England.* Edited by W. Dunn Macray. 6 vols. Oxford: Clarendon Press, 1888. Classic royalist history combining memoir and analysis. Brilliant character sketches.
Edwards, Thomas. *Gangraena.* 3 parts. London, 1646.
Presbyterian catalog of sectarian errors. Polemical but valuable for Presbyterian fears and information about radical groups.
Hobbes, Thomas. *Leviathan.* London, 1651. Modern edition edited by Richard Tuck. Cambridge: Cambridge University Press, 1991.
Philosophical defense of absolute sovereignty. Influenced Anglican uniformity arguments.
Hooker, Richard. *Of the Lawes of Ecclesiastical Politie.* London, 1594-1662. Modern edition edited by W. Speed Hill et al. 7 vols. Cambridge, MA: Harvard University Press, 1977. Foundational Anglican work defending Elizabethan settlement. Shaped Anglican thought for centuries.
Locke, John. *A Letter Concerning Toleration.* 1689. Modern edition edited by Mark Goldie. Indianapolis: Liberty Fund, 2010. Classic philosophical argument for religious toleration. Influenced Toleration Act debates.
Milton, John. *Areopagitica.* London, 1644. Most eloquent defense of free speech in English. Essential for intellectual freedom arguments.
[Westminster Assembly]. *The Confession of Faith.* Edinburgh, 1647. Modern edition with introduction by Jack Rogers. Louisville: Westminster John Knox Press, 1985. Comprehensive Reformed theology statement. Standard for presbyterian churches worldwide.

C. Official Documents and Records

Acts and Ordinances of the Interregnum, *1642-1660.* Edited by C. H. Firth and R. S. Rait. 3 vols. London: HMSO, 1911. Comprehensive legislation collection. Essential reference.
Minutes of the Westminster Assembly. Edited by Alex F. Mitchell and John Struthers. Edinburgh, 1874. Supplement: edited by Chad Van Dixhoorn. 5 vols. Oxford: Oxford University Press, 2012. Van Dixhoorn's edition is now scholarly standard with full transcripts and comprehensive notes.
***Statutes of the Realm.* Vols. 5-6.** London: Record Commission, 1819. Authoritative legal texts including Clarendon Code and Toleration Act.
The Constitutional Documents of the Puritan Revolution. Edited by Samuel Rawson Gardiner. 3rd ed. Oxford: Clarendon Press, 1906. Essential constitutional documents collection with valuable introductions.
The Trial of Charles I. Edited by Roger Lockyer. London: Folio Society,

1959. Trial transcript. Essential for the regicide.
Woodhouse, A. S. P., ed. *Puritanism and Liberty: The Army Debates (1647-9).* Chicago: University of Chicago Press, 1951. Putney Debates transcripts. Essential for Leveller thought and Army political theory.

II. SECONDARY SOURCES

A. General Histories

Carlton, Charles. *Going to the Wars: The British Civil Wars, 1638-1651.* London: Routledge, 1992. Military experience and human cost. Important corrective centering violence and suffering.
Hill, Christopher. *The World Turned Upside Down: Radical Ideas During the English Revolution.* London: Temple Smith, 1972. Influential Marxist interpretation of Levellers, Diggers, Ranters. Engaging and accessible.
Morrill, John. *The Nature of the English Revolution.* London: Longman, 1993. Collection arguing religion's centrality: "The English Civil War was the last of the Wars of Religion."
Russell, Conrad. *The Causes of the English Civil War.* Oxford: Clarendon Press, 1990. Influential revisionist interpretation emphasizing contingency over inevitability.
Russell, Conrad. *The Fall of the British Monarchies, 1637-1642.* Oxford: Clarendon Press, 1991. "Three kingdoms" approach showing how Charles I's multi-realm crisis precipitated war.
Worden, Blair. *The English Civil Wars, 1640-1660.* London: Weidenfeld & Nicolson, 2009. Elegant synthesis combining narrative clarity with analytical depth.

B. Religious Movements

1. Presbyterianism

Paul, Robert S. *The Assembly of the Lord.* Edinburgh: T&T Clark, 1985. Detailed Westminster Assembly study. Essential for ecclesiological debates.
Van Dixhoorn, Chad. *The Minutes and Papers of the Westminster Assembly.* 5 vols. Oxford: Oxford University Press, 2012. Beyond transcripts, introductions provide invaluable context and analysis.

2. Independency

Collinson, Patrick. *The Elizabethan Puritan Movement.* London: Jonathan Cape, 1967. Classic study of Puritanism's development. Essential for pre-Civil War roots.
Nuttall, Geoffrey F. *Visible Saints: The Congregational Way, 1640-1660.* Oxford: Basil Blackwell, 1957. Classic Independent ecclesiology study. Still valuable.
Tolmie, Murray. *The Triumph of the Saints: The Separate Churches of London, 1616-1649.* Cambridge: Cambridge University Press, 1977. Detailed London gathered churches study.

3. Quakerism

Barbour, Hugh, and J. William Frost. *The Quakers.* New York: Greenwood Press, 1988. Comprehensive survey. Excellent starting point.
Braithwaite, William C. *The Beginnings of Quakerism.* 2nd ed., revised by

Henry J. Cadbury. Cambridge: Cambridge University Press, 1955. Classic early Quakerism history. Despite age, remains essential.
Damrosch, Leo. *The Sorrows of the Quaker Jesus: James Nayler and the Puritan Crackdown.* Cambridge, MA: Harvard University Press, 1996. Nayler's life, trial, and significance. Excellent narrative scholarship.
Ingle, H. Larry. *First Among Friends: George Fox and the Creation of Quakerism.* New York: Oxford University Press, 1994. Modern scholarly Fox biography. Demythologizes while respecting achievement.
Moore, Rosemary. *The Light in Their Consciences: Early Quakers in Britain, 1646-1666.* University Park: Pennsylvania State University Press, 2000. Detailed first two decades study. Particularly strong on women's roles and discipline.
Reay, Barry. *The Quakers and the English Revolution.* London: Temple Smith, 1985. Social history examining Quaker participation in revolution.

4. Anglicanism

Green, Ian. *The Re-establishment of the Church of England, 1660-1663.* Oxford: Oxford University Press, 1978. Detailed Restoration settlement institutional history.
Spurr, John. *The Restoration Church of England, 1646-1689.* New Haven: Yale University Press, 1991. Comprehensive study. Standard work on Restoration Anglicanism.
Tyacke, Nicholas. *Anti-Calvinists: The Rise of English Arminianism, c.1590-1640.* Oxford: Clarendon Press, 1987. Influential study arguing Laudian "Arminianism" represented departure from Calvinist consensus.

C. Thematic Studies

1. Political Thought

Burgess, Glenn. *The Politics of the Ancient Constitution.* University Park: Pennsylvania State University Press, 1993. How English understood their constitution pre-Civil War.
Foxley, Rachel. *The Levellers: Radical Political Thought in the English Revolution.* Manchester: Manchester University Press, 2013. Comprehensive Leveller political theory study.
Skinner, Quentin. *Visions of Politics.* Vol. 3. Cambridge: Cambridge University Press, 2002. Includes essay on Hobbes and engagement controversy. Influential on early modern political thought.

2. Religion, Society, and Culture

Collinson, Patrick. *The Religion of Protestants: The Church in English Society, 1559-1625.* Oxford: Clarendon Press, 1982. Magisterial study of Protestant culture shaping social relationships, family, community.
Hughes, Ann. *Gangraena and the Struggle for the English Revolution.* Oxford: Oxford University Press, 2004. Edwards's catalog as source for religious radicalism and Presbyterian fears.
Lake, Peter. *The Boxmaker's Revenge.* Stanford: Stanford University Press, 2001. Microhistory of London parish religious controversy. Brilliant demonstration.

Underdown, David. *Revel, Riot, and Rebellion.* Oxford: Clarendon Press, 1985. Regional culture and economy correlated with Civil War allegiances. Controversial but influential.

3. Military History

Gentles, Ian. *The New Model Army in England, Ireland and Scotland, 1645-1653.* Oxford: Blackwell, 1992. Definitive Army study. Essential for understanding Army's role.

Kenyon, John, and Jane Ohlmeyer, eds. *The Civil Wars: A Military History.* Oxford: Oxford University Press, 1998. Multi-author military history including Ireland and Scotland.

4. Women and Gender

Mack, Phyllis. *Visionary Women: Ecstatic Prophecy in Seventeenth-Century England.* Berkeley: University of California Press, 1992. Women prophets across sects. Religious enthusiasm creating space for women's authority.

5. Print Culture

Peacey, Jason. *Politicians and Pamphleteers: Propaganda During the English Civil Wars.* Aldershot: Ashgate, 2004. Political propaganda production, distribution, consumption.

Peters, Kate. *Print Culture and the Early Quakers.* Cambridge: Cambridge University Press, 2005. How Quakers used printing to spread message and coordinate movement.

Raymond, Joad. *Pamphlets and Pamphleteering in Early Modern Britain.* Cambridge: Cambridge University Press, 2003. Comprehensive pamphlet culture study.

6. Three Kingdoms

Canny, Nicholas. *Making Ireland British, 1580-1650.* Oxford: Oxford University Press, 2001. English colonization of Ireland. Essential for Irish Rebellion background.

Pestana, Carla Gardina. *The English Atlantic in an Age of Revolution, 1640-1661.* Cambridge, MA: Harvard University Press, 2004. How English Revolution affected American colonies. Atlantic perspective.

Woolrych, Austin. *Britain in Revolution, 1625-1660.* Oxford: Oxford University Press, 2002. Comprehensive three-kingdoms narrative. Excellent integrated approach.

D. Biographical Studies

Coward, Barry. *Oliver Cromwell.* London: Longman, 1991. Balanced scholarly biography avoiding hagiography and demonization.

Hill, Christopher. *God's Englishman: Oliver Cromwell.* London: Weidenfeld & Nicolson, 1970. Brilliant Marxist interpretation. Engaging prose despite theoretical framework.

Keeble, N. H. *Richard Baxter: Puritan Man of Letters.* Oxford: Clarendon Press, 1982. Intellectual biography examining voluminous writings. Essential for moderate Presbyterianism.

Marshall, John. *John Locke: Resistance, Religion and Responsibility.* Cambridge:

Cambridge University Press, 1994. Locke's religious thought and political theory connections.
Wedgwood, C. V. *The King's Peace, 1637-1641* and *The King's War, 1641-1647.* London: Collins, 1955, 1958. Classic narratives with Charles I as tragic figure. Elegant prose and command of detail.

E. Reference Works

Oxford Dictionary of National Biography. Oxford: Oxford University Press, 2004. Online edition regularly updated. Comprehensive biographical dictionary. Essential starting point.
Greaves, Richard L., and Robert Zaller, eds. *Biographical Dictionary of British Radicals in the Seventeenth Century.* 3 vols. Brighton: Harvester Press, 1982-1984. Essential reference for Levellers, religious radicals, republicans.

F. Digital Resources

British History Online (www.british-history.ac.uk)
Freely accessible digital library of primary and secondary sources.
Early English Books Online (EEBO) (eebo.chadwyck.com)
Digital images of virtually every book printed in England 1473-1700.
The National Archives, UK (www.nationalarchives.gov.uk)
Official archive. Online catalog and digitized documents.
Quaker Heritage Press, Freely accessible digital library of out of print historical Quaker writings. http://www.qhpress.org/texts/nayler/index.html.

INDEX

D

www.ingramcontent.com/pod-product-compliance
Lightning Source LLC
LaVergne TN
LVHW020703110826
845149LV00012B/2092

* 9 7 9 8 9 9 4 0 4 1 2 0 8 *